D0214863

Democracy, Development and Discontent in South Asia

Democracy, Development and Discontent in South Asia

Edited by

VEENA KUKREJA
MAHENDRA PRASAD SINGH

SAGE Los Angeles • London • New Delhi • Singapore
www.sagepublications.com

First published in 2008 by

SAGE Publications India Pvt Ltd
B1/I-1 Mohan Cooperative Industrial Area
Mathura Road, New Delhi 110 044, India
www.sagepub.in

SAGE Publications Inc
2455 Teller Road
Thousand Oaks, California 91320, USA

SAGE Publications Ltd
1 Oliver's Yard, 55 City Road
London EC1Y 1SP, United Kingdom

SAGE Publications Asia-Pacific Pte Ltd
33 Pekin Street
#02-01 Far East Square
Singapore 048763

Published by Vivek Mehra for SAGE Publications India Pvt Ltd, typeset in 10/12 Book Antiqua by Excellent Laser Typesetters, Delhi and printed at Chaman Enterprises, New Delhi.

Library of Congress Cataloging-in-Publication Data

Democracy, development and discontent in South Asia/edited by Veena Kukreja, Mahendra Prasad Singh.
p.cm.
Includes bibliographical references and index.
1. Democracy—South Asia. 2. South Asia—Politics and government.
I. Kukreja, Veena. II. Singh, Mahrendra Prasad, 1943-

JQ98.A91D46 320.954—dc22 2008 2008009153

ISBN: 978-0-7619-3617-6 (HB) 978-81-7829-781-1 (India-HB)

The SAGE Team: Sugata Ghosh, Koel Mishra, Amrita Saha and Trinankur Banerjee

Contents

Preface

South Asia, and that included for all practical purposes, Afghanistan and Myanmar (if not Persia and Central Asia) until the 18th/19th centuries, joined world history politically via European, mainly British, colonial conquest. Major parts of the region came under direct or indirect colonial control or impact. The modern age came to South Asia with a rush towards the latter part of the 19th and early half of the 20th centuries. The major politico-economic and socio-political forces churning the region in the post-Cold War era are the currents and cross-currents of geopolitical reconfigurations, civic and religious nationalism, globalism, and supranational regional economic integration. Democratization, like economic development, has managed to register an uneven presence and performance in South Asia and its sustained advance cannot be taken for granted even in India and Sri Lanka, the two countries that have continued to adhere to a vigorous electoral democracy and a semblance of constitutional and judicial politics, despite growing internal and external pressures and violence. India has to its credit the rare achievement of working a parliamentary-federal government with entrenched Fundamental Rights of citizens and cultural minorities and welfarist Directive Principles of State Policy under the Constitution of post-World War II vintage, largely uninterrupted, the 42nd Amendment of the Emergency regime (1975–77) notwithstanding, which was undone by the post-Emergency 44th Amendment. This is a unique feat, at least in the Afro-Asian world, with the solitary exception of Japan. Democracy in Sri Lanka is also unbroken, though the post-Independence parliamentary constitution has had to undergo the trauma of national emergencies and a transition to a semi-parliamentary-presidential regime of cohabitation between a directly elected president and a prime minister and his cabinet put in place by a parliamentary majority.

Other countries in the region have a record of limited and intermittent democratic governments, with military-bureaucratic, monarchical, and populist-mobocratic interventions. The process of democratization in the region appears, however, irreversible at the onset of the new millennium in a region with some of the oldest ancient civilizational sites in the Indus, Ganga, and Kaveri valleys, begetting a heritage of composite, multicultural living through the whispering galleries of the past. This history is as colourful as a promising future, only if the present shows the courage and craft of burying the hatchet of semi-feudal feuding, now fraught with nuclear self-destruction.

South Asia today stands at the crossroads of a new era in the making. Straws in the wind suggest that while nationalism may survive in a moderate form the ongoing capitalist globalization, as it did internationalist communism. The emerging new order in the region will be significantly conditioned by global economic forces and geo-political global and macro-regional Eurasian, Australasian, and African international and security reconfigurations. Indo-Pakistan conflict has been the greatest stumbling block that has stood in the way of the region seeking successfully to re-fabricate itself in the world today where every other region, following the spectacular success of the European community, is experimenting with regional integration, economically to begin with, to reap the benefits of the supranational region as a way station to a rational and equitable global order, in a world where the United Nations family of organizations has suffered a partial eclipse, hopefully a temporary and transitional phenomenon.

The chapters in this volume take a fresh look at the imperatives of democracy, development, and discontent in South Asia today. This study consists of 10 chapters. An Introduction by the editors provides an overview of the contemporary South Asian scenario bringing in focus its internal as well as external dimensions.

The opening chapter by M.P. Singh addresses the multicultural identity and democracy in India. India's multicultural national identity and federal democracy are not only historically and contemporaneously constitutive of each other, but are also evolving symbiotically. Indian civic nationalism can be better hermeneutically interpreted through multicultural rather than ethnic national lenses. Political and fiscal parliamentary federal arrangements are particularly appropriate for a country of India's subcontinental cultural diversities and socio-economic and regional disparities. India has found it easier to accommodate linguistic identities than religious communalism, particularly in the colonial context. It is notable that the Indian approach to politics and religion is rather unique. For the state in India is secular, in terms of grant of religious freedoms, but the constitution prompts the state to strive for a common civil code analogous to a common criminal code, and does not expressly put a wall of separation between the state and religion, as in the United States of America (USA) and France. All these factors prepare the ground for a kind of judicialization of politics that would appear also to be in some ways uniquely Indian.

Saleem Qureshi in Chapter 2 provides a retrospective analysis of democracy and army rule in Pakistan situating the politics of that country in its cultural and historical contexts. By the end of his discussion, he finds it too puzzling how to disentangle what goes in the names of civilian rule and martial law. His graphic conclusion is: 'Ultimately, it is up to the Pakistanis themselves to decide whether, in a zoological analogy of the zebra being a white animal with black stripes or a black animal with white stripes, Pakistan is a democracy with military disruptions or a militocracy with democratic interludes.' Qureshi implies that it is difficult to export democracy to Pakistan in the absence of supportive political culture and civil society institutions.

Veena Kukreja, in Chapter 3, discusses the complex interplay of forces of authoritarianism and democracy in Bangladesh. Since its bloody birth, the country has precariously oscillated between unstable democracy and the tightening noose of authoritarian takeover, inherent in uninstitutionalized institutions of government and political parties, as well as the growing trend of Islamic fundamentalism. Unlike Pakistan, feudal legacies in Bangladesh are less formidable, but the latter does not have a still strong feudal landlordism, nor does it have the stranglehold of the armed forces on the state apparatus on account of a greater social mobilization and politicization of the masses, but the country is haunted by the spectre of a failing state if democratic forces are not consolidated.

Chapter 4 by Niraj Kumar takes up the issue of the developmental state in India, mainly in comparison with East Asian developmental states democratic, authoritarian, or mixed. He argues that the Indian developmental state has not received adequate attention in East Asian-centric literature on the theory of developmental state in which the developmental dimension has been given greater importance than the democratic one. If anything, some theorists like Leftwitch, relying heavily on Gunnar Myrdal's characterization of South Asian polities as 'soft states', have made passing comments on India, without a close analysis, as a 'failed developmental state'. This chapter makes a persuasive argument that the two phases of India's strategy of economic development—the first socialistic and the second premised on neo-liberal economic reforms—deserves a serious consideration by theorists of the developmental state, as India has tried to combine the goals of democratic development with economic development. And what is particularly significant is that it has a credible performance in both these domains.

Chapter 5 by Mohammad Nuruzzaman analyses the societal responses to pro-market reforms in Bangladesh. The implementation of pro-market economic reforms in the developing countries, including Bangladesh has rarely been a smooth process. Social responses to reform policies have been rather unfriendly and often violent. This chapter examines popular resistance to pro-market economic reforms in Bangladesh in the decades of the 1980s and the 1990s. It attempts to map out the road to resistance movements, explores the underlying causes that spurred labour resistance to economic reforms, and analyses the success and failures the movements have achieved or recorded both in the organized urban industrial sector and the disorganized rural areas. It arrives at the conclusion that the spate of resistance in the industrial sector in the 1980s and 1990s had the potential to roll back the reform process, but it did not succeed due to workers' disunity, ideological divide between left-wing and right-wing trade unions, lack of organizational network to carry forward the movements, control of pro-globalization big political parties over their respective trade unions, and the dwindling influence of the leftist trade unions in Bangladesh labour politics. Unlike the organized industrial sector, resistance to agricultural reforms in rural Bangladesh is rather dormant. Lack of effective peasant lobbies/organizations, resource constraints to mobilize peasants, centuries-old rural power structure that works against the interests of the poor majority of peasants and political divides between the peasants themselves, cut into the potential of effective peasant resistance to neo-liberal agricultural reforms.

Lawrence Ziring's illuminating chapter (Chapter 6) deals with the issue of ethnicity, tribalism, and politics of frontier policy in

Pakistan. He maintains that the Muslim League was not a welcome expression among the unrecorded majority of Pakistan's population whose loyalties lay elsewhere. Dissatisfaction with the central government was registered in all parts of the country but no less so than among those inhabiting the frontier areas. It is the latter that is the focus of this chapter. The subject of ethnicity and politics in Pakistan, however, is too broad and too complex to be encompassed in a brief article. Attention here is on the Pashtuns, even more so on a portion of the Indo-European linguistic family that inhabits the Pakistani tribal belt, a region almost twice the size of the North West Frontier Province and straddling the Pakistan/Afghanistan border from the Pamirs to the Takht-I-Sulaiman. Here too, the subject is too extensive to incorporate the different Pashtun tribes. The Yusufzais, Afridis, Mohmands, Turis, and others are bypassed for a closer examination of the Wazirs, and especially those Wazirs tribes inhabiting the region known as South Waziristan. South Waziristan is judged a key to Pakistan's integration efforts. It is also the area of principal concern to near and distant observers of the Pakistan scene in this first decade of the 21st century.

In Chapter 7, Veena Kukreja and Mahendra Prasad Singh take a detailed look at ethnic politics in Sri Lanka. The country has been plagued by chronic and possibly one of the most devastating ethnic conflicts in South Asia. Sri Lanka is a multi-ethnic, multi-religious and multilingual country. However, Sri Lankan governments' discrimination against Tamils in five main areas, namely, land, language, education, employment, and power-sharing sowed the seeds of conflict and contributed to turning the Jaffna Tamils into an alienated segment of Sri Lanka society. The only solution to the festering ethnic conflict in the island republic is a federal option that goes beyond the present political arrangement of executive presidency and the government's offer of devolutionary autonomy to the separatists. But constitutional reform is contingent on the peace process aimed at restoration of normalcy. Unless peace returns, the switchover from the present constitution of executive presidency to the desired parliamentary federalism, with a certain degree of asymmetrical status for the Tamil region, would be unthinkable.

Sri Lankan, Napalese, and Bhutanese ethnic and class conflicts differ from the Indo-Pak and Indo-Bangla communal boils in the sense that the latter category of problems are more complicated internally as well externally due to rising tide of Islamic fundamentalism at the regional and global planes. Given the political will of the ruling elites of Sri Lanka, Nepal, and Bhutan, the former category of ethnic strife is more amenable to an early solution.

Chapter 8 by Nalini Kant Jha provides an insightful account of the armed rebellion (Maoist insurgency) in Nepal. He contends that armed overthrow of the Nepalese state has been a long-cherished goal of the communist movement in that country. But since February 1996, they have openly declared 'people's war' against the Nepalese state. They have virtually rendered the state apparatus ineffective and assumed control over rural areas with their own system of governance. As this endemic domestic violence in Nepal has serious security and political implications not only for Nepal, but also for India, which shares a long and open border as well as close socio-cultural linkages with that country, the present chapter examines the origin, evolution, objectives, strategies, magnitude, and support base of Maoist insurgency in Nepal, its implications for security and stability of India, Nepalese and international response to this challenge, and prospects of the end of this rebellion. Jha recommends that the Nepalese state must simultaneously address the long-term causes of the rebellion by initiating radical socio-economic and political transformation programmes directed especially towards removing the grievances of the downtrodden, underprivileged, and excluded people and communities. The state must dare to seize the socio-economic agenda of the Maoists and implement it with all seriousness. This alone can prevent the rebels from cashing in on the support of the people. All the concerned parties must realize that while the goal of a negotiated settlement may be distant and the route tortuous, the journey can be accomplished if the signposts are clear and roadmap adhered to.

In Chapter 9, Awadhesh Coomar Sinha offers a historically, sociologically, and economically well-grounded analysis of ethnic conflict in Bhutan and its regional consequences for the micro-region of north-east India within the South Asian macro-region. The author touches upon the sensitivities of India–Nepal–Bhutan relations with an acute sense of observation and analysis. He also cautions that 'the entire Himalayan region from Kashmir in the west to the north-east Indian states in the east has turned into a zone of conflict. Besides India, the two Himalayan kingdoms are embroiled in the worst type of conflicts not experienced by them in the past.' This obviously is a challenge to the ingenuity of policymakers in India, Nepal, and Bhutan to do everything possible to not let the spectre of more failing states in our neighbourhood haunt us.

In the final chapter, Rajen Harshe takes up the issue of India–Pakistan conflict over Kashmir. In the process of capturing a critical overview of the India–Pakistan conflict over Kashmir, this chapter argues that the causes of this conflict can be traced to the processes of state-formation and nation-building in India and Pakistan that began after the Partition of the subcontinent. Thus, the notions of secular nationalism and two-nation theory were deployed, by India and Pakistan respectively, to integrate Kashmir within their fold. While assessing the viewpoints of the contending parties, the chapter suggests that the resolution of the Kashmir question is dependent on the overall cordiality in India–Pakistan ties. In this context it suggests constructive alternatives to prevent conflicts and ameliorate India–Pakistan relations on the basis of prevailing realities in two ways. Initially it reflects briefly on the possible measures to reconstruct the conflict-ravaged state of Jammu and Kashmir and subsequently it underscores the significance of the hitherto neglected peace-related projects built through trade and development cooperation.

Acknowledgements

Editing this volume has been a pleasure at a time when momentous developments have been taking place in South Asia. The chapters, excepting those by Rajen Harshe, Awadhesh Coomar Sinha and Mohammed Nuruzzaman, were specially commissioned for this volume. The former earlier appeared in the *South Asian Survey*, *Dialogue*, and *Journal of Asian Studies respectively*. Awadhesh Coomar Sinha substantially revised his piece. Our thanks are due to these journals for the permission to reprint. We thank to all our contributors for writing and/or revising their pieces at our request and on the suggestions of an anonymous referee and the SAGE Senior commissioning editor, Ashok R. Chandran. We take this opportunity to thank the Chairman of the board of Directors of SAGE, the late Tejeshwar Singh and Vivek Mehra, who always encouraged us in our work. Sugata Ghosh, Vice-President (Commissioning) picked up the threads of our work at SAGE when Mimi Chaudhary left. We would also like to thank Koel Mishra at SAGE who handled the production of our book. Ameeta Narang of IDSA Library deserves our thanks for helping us with some library resources we needed to explore. Kshitij Kukreja was our trouble-shooter in the use of computer and Nand Lal typed the manuscript with exceptional skill and ease.

List of Abbreviations

AKRSP	Aga Khan Rural Support Programme
AL	Awami League
APHC	All Party Hurriyat Conference
ASA	Association for Social Advancement
BBIN-GQ	Bangladesh-Bhutan-India-Nepal Growth Quadrangle
BCP(MLM)	Bhutanese Communist Party (MLM) Marxist-Leninist-Maoist
BILS	Bangladesh Institute of Labour Studies
BIMSTEC	Bangladesh-India-Myanmar-Sri Lanka Thailand Economic Cooperation
BJMC	Bangladesh Jute Mills Corporation
BKSAL	Bangladesh Krishak Sramik League
BNP	Bangladesh Nationalist Party
BRAC	Bangladesh Rural Advancement Committee
CBOs	community-based organizations
CIA	Central Intelligence Agency
CIS	Commonwealth of Independent States
COAS	Chief of Army Staff
CP	Communist Party
CPB	Communist Party of Bangladesh
CPN-M	Communist Party of Nepal-Maoist
CSOs	civil society organizations
DYTs	District Development Councils
FAO	Food and Agricultural Agency
FATA	Federally Administered Tribal Areas
GDP	Gross Domestic Product
GHP	Gross National Happiness
GNP	Gross National Product
ICT	Information Communication Technology

ILO	International Labour Organization
IMF	International Monetary Fund
IPKF	Indian Peace Keeping Force
ISGA	Interim Self-Governing Authority
ISI	Inter Services Intelligence
ITAK	Ilankai Tamil Arasu Katchi
JAGODAL	Jatiyo Ganotantric Dal
JHU	Jathika Hela Urumaya
JKLF	Jammu and Kashmir Liberation Front
JRB	Jatio Rakhi Bahini
JSD	Jatiyo Samajtantric Dal
JVP	Janatha Vimukhti Peramuna
JVT	joint verification team
LDCs	least developed countries
LDF	Left Democratic Front
LIC	low intensity conflict
LSSP	Lanka Sama Samaja Party
LTTE	Liberation Tigers of Tamil Eelam
MCC	Maoist Coordination Centre
MFN	most favoured nation
MJC	Ministerial Joint Committee
MMA	Muttahida Majlis-i-Amal
NAP	National Awami Party
NAPM	National Alliance for People's Movement
NC	Nepali Congress
NDA	National Democratic Alliance
NSCN	National Socialist Council of Nagaland
PDPA	People's Democratic Party of Afghanistan
PIPFPD	Pakistan–India People's Forum for Peace and Democracy
P-TOMS	Post-Tsunami Operational Management Structure
PWG	People's War Group
RGB	Royal Government of Bhutan
RGN	Royal Government of Nepal
RNA	Royal Nepal Army
SAARC	South Asian Association of Regional Cooperation
SAPTA	South Asian Preferential Trade Area
SAFTA	South Asian Free Trade Area
SEWA	Self-Employment Women's Association
SKOP	Sramik Karmachari Oikaya Parishad

SLFP	Sri Lanka Freedom Party
SOEs	state-owned enterprises
SPA	Seven Party Alliance
SSM	Sarvodaya Shramadana Movement
TC	Tamil Congress
TNA	Tamil National Alliance
TULF	Tamil United Liberation Front
UFD	United Front for Democracy
ULFA	United Liberation Front for Assam
UNDP	United Nations Development Programme
UNHCR	United Nation High Commission for Refugees
UNP	United National Party
UNPO	Unrepresented Nations Peoples' Organization
UNROB	United Nations Relief Organization in Bangladesh
UPFN	United People's Front of Nepal
UPP	United People's Party
USAID	United States Agency for International Development
VDS	Voluntary Departure Scheme

Introduction

Mahendra Prasad Singh
Veena Kukreja

Contemporary South Asia has entered a new threshold of a qualitatively different temper of probable developments both *within* and *among* nations of the region caused and conditioned by domestic (national as well as regional), supra-national, regional, and global factors. South Asia stands at the crossroads of possibilities fraught with alternative scenarios of a great developmental and democratic ascent in the nations of the region, reconciling conflicts at home and the pursuit of complementaries in the cross-currents of powerful forces of federal-national, global, and regional integration in political and economic terms.

The political history of South Asia in the post-World War II era has been a turbulent one. The break-up of Pakistan and the subsequent formation of Bangladesh, are the most conspicuous examples of this turbulence. Nevertheless, over the last 50 years, South Asia has made halting strides toward stability and peace. There has been increased decentralization of political power. These are important steps forward for a region characterized by diversities of ethnicity, religions, castes, classes, and languages. South Asia, home to one-fifth of humanity living in seven developing states, today represents a battlefield due to an imbalanced relationship between state-led institutions and civic forces intent upon establishing an accountable politico-economic order. On the front of political development and socio-economic change, one comes across the dilemmas and dialectics between forces of democracy and authoritarianism, decentralization and centralization of powers, politics of change and politics of status quo-ism, politics of secularism and religious extremism, forces of ethnic groups, and national integration, concentration of economic power into few hands and poverty of the masses. Of course, there are differences of degrees and devices in this South Asian drama of democratic and developmental dialectics. In fact, this makes much of the difference.

Domestic Politics

Political Structures

Currently, South Asia can boast of two long standing democracies—including the world's largest. India and Sri Lanka have been unbroken democracies over the last 50 years. India and Sri Lanka have never had any form of government that was not democratically elected. Both these countries became democratic in the 'second wave' of democratization in the wake of World War II, after the 'first wave' had already consolidated democracies in Western Europe, North America, and the white Commonwealth. The rest of South Asia still waits to join the democratic bandwagon in the 'third wave' (Huntington, 1991).[1] India was a parliamentary-federal democracy with a one-party dominant system under the Indian National Congress in the earlier decades of the post-Independence period and has had a multiparty coalitional dispensation since 1989. Sri Lanka started with a parliamentary system, but subsequently switched over to a constitution combining a parliamentary and presidential form of government. This entails a cohabitation between a directly elected executive presidency and a prime minister at the head of a directly elected multiparty parliament. Conversely, Pakistan had essentially been ruled directly by the military for 28 of its 56 years of existence. Bangladesh has also been ruled by the military for 17 years of its 30 years of independence. Nevertheless, these countries too restored democracy in the last decade. However, Pakistan reverted to military rule in October 1999, 11 years after the restoration of democracy. In Nepal and Bhutan, there are constitutional monarchies with democratic trappings, recurrent bouts of Maoist insurgency in the former, and intermittent democratic protests inviting aristocratic authoritarian repression notwithstanding. However, by the end of 2007 an uneasy coalition between democratic parties and the Maoist movement has sealed the fate of the monarchy and is all set to frame a republican and federal constitution by a constituent assembly to be elected soon. Both are post-traditional or traditional Himalayan kingdoms, diplomatically Indian protectorates.

The existence of elected governments alone is not the sole criterion for judging the extent of political development. Democratization requires institutionalization of the politics of a country. Governance in a democracy is the capacity to rule in accordance with established rules and procedures. Indeed, all South Asian countries have been witness to a growth of institutions of governance that promise to articulate, to varying extents, the demands of the people from the grass roots. These include, for instance, panchayats in India, provincial councils in Sri Lanka, and union councils in Bangladesh. These institutions are representative bodies at the local level that allow people to take an active role in addressing their own concerns. However, the main threat to the efficient working of these institutions is posed by the pervasive inequalities that persist in South Asian societies, manifested through powerful elite groups which often use these institutions to serve their personal and corporate interests. But, the great importance of these fledgling local-level institutions of governance should not be understated. They are critical links between the power structure and the citizen.

Civil Society and Grass-roots Organizations

Another vital element in the maturing of the political process in the region has been civil society organizations (CSOs). These are responsible for numerous innovative initiatives to improve local-level governance. Some of the well known CSOs include the Aga Khan Rural Support Programme (AKRSP) in Pakistan, Bangladesh Rural Advancement Committee (BRAC) in Bangladesh, the Self-Employed Women's Association (SEWA), civil rights groups, ecological movements, and the like in India, and the Sarvodaya Shramadana Movement (SSM) in Sri Lanka. The success of these public interest groups has been due to their ability to organize people at the local level and thereby filling the institutional vacuum that has become apparent over the years. In many ways, for a representative political system to be operational, traditional decision-making institutions at the local level need to be revitalized in terms of more democratic and egalitarian structures. This has been done in India in the shape of the panchayat system. CSO initiatives have been instrumental in helping this transformation come about. The result has been the formation of many supra-village-level groups often called community-based organizations (CBOs) that are able to effectively act as independent bodies advocating the needs and rights of the common people.

The connection between the state, civil society, and the private sector, which underpins effective governance, is weak in the region. However, there are signs that many important coalitions are being firmed up and will continue to be formed. In addition, established civil society initiatives are being strengthened significantly. The fact that there is institutional progress at all levels indicates that an ethic is developing, however slowly, to ensure that democratic process permeates society, not only in the form of federal-level elections, but at the local and provincial levels too. In this regard, other important steps made towards progressive political set-ups in the region include the fact that there have been increasing opportunities for women and under-represented minorities, once again not necessarily through governmental organs per se, but also through CSOs and the private sector.

Indicators of political development are considerably spread across different parts of each country in the region. For example, the panchayat system has been more successful in Karnataka and West Bengal, while relatively weak in other states of India. Similarly, CSOs have been much more successful in mobilizing people and creating local-level institutions in the North West Frontier Province and north and central Punjab than in southern Punjab and interior Sindh in Pakistan. This is because the social, cultural, and economic barriers to such initiatives are much more powerful in the latter areas. These areas are commonly associated with the persistence of the traditional feudal system, characterized by a few large landholdings, estates, and numerous small farmers and landless peasants. In any case, the prospects for continuing progress are good, so long as the successful efforts are acknowledged and continue to be used as benchmarks for other initiatives. The spread of these types of institutions promise real development through a democratic and free political system.

On the other hand, South Asia simultaneously manifests systemic governance crises. As reported in *Human Development in South*

Asia 1999, the region is one of the most poorly governed areas of the world. That report highlights the governance failures in South Asia on several fronts. For instance, the formal institution of governance in the region often bypass the many unfortunate people who suffer from multiple deprivation on account of their income, religion, gender, and ethnicity. The poor have not only been excluded from the benefits of growth, but have also failed to gain political empowerment. Some of the worst consequences of their exclusion are seen in the high rates of crime and violence throughout the region.

Economic Development, Disparities, and Governance

Income disparities in South Asia are amongst the largest in the world. The richest one-fifth of South Asians earn almost 40 per cent of the region's income, while the poorest one-fifth earns less than 10 per cent. All the countries in the region have a dramatic concentration of wealth and power among their richest members. Women in South Asia are the worst off, contending with exclusionary practices embedded in society and polity from the time they are born.

The particular form of economic growth initiated by post-colonial elites in this region is such that the very resource potential which could have been harnessed to overcome poverty is instead being rapidly eroded. The result is that the majority of the people of South Asia remain deprived of basic necessities even after more than five decades of independence. Little industrialization, low agricultural output, low per capita income, very sluggish economic progress, considerable unemployment and underemployment, illiteracy, and high rate of population growth are some of the main characteristics of South Asian countries, which are not conducive for the successful functioning of democracy. In many South Asian countries, democracy is fast becoming a meaningless ritual. Elections are often the only bridge between the state and society. People continually feel excluded from the main political processes through which decisions that directly affect their livelihoods are made.

Crisis of governance is also a crisis of institutionalization because elites who may once have been instrumental in overthrowing a regime perceived by them as illegitimate become anti-institutionalization after having come to play an effective role within the democratic system created by them. Parties which fought for democracy become vulnerable to the new crises precipitated by their leaders' behaviour, paving the way for their decline and, eventually, for the decay of the institutions. The dominance of a narrow band of elite reflects the concentrated nature of political power. The concentration and personalization of state power has coincided with the parallel erosion of institutions of governance. Institutional decay is evident in parliaments that cannot protect peoples interests, in civil services that are heavily politicized, corrupt, and unable to provide basic public services.

Most South Asians also suffer from inefficient and unjust systems of economic management. Governments are large in size, but low in efficiency. Most taxes are regressive, falling far more on the poor and middle classes than on the affluent, because nearly 70 per cent of the region's total tax revenue is obtained by levying indirect taxes. The crushing burden of taxation on the poor is not only enormous, but also increasing. In many countries direct taxes as a proportion of the gross domestic product (GDP) have actually fallen in the last decade, while huge sectors of society—most notably agriculture—remain under-taxed or untaxed.

The informal sector has no access to formal credit, even though businesses with strong political connections manage to get huge loans from public banks without paying them back. This has led to a large stock of non-performing loans.

Even the low levels of revenue that the South Asian governments collect largely fail to materialize into pro-poor expenditures. The bulk of public spending in South Asia goes to providing non-merit subsidies, making up the losses of public corporations and maintaining a large force of civil servants and the military. Total public debt as a percentage of GDP is over 60 per cent in Pakistan, Nepal, Sri Lanka, and India, although most of India's debt is domestic rather than external.

Pervasive corruption in South Asia has led to a shift in government priorities away from crucial services and towards areas that afford greater rent-seeking opportunities. Evidence of corruption in South Asia is widespread: in reduced availability and increased cost of basic social services, in allocation of resources for mega-projects, and in the breakdown of the rule of law. There is a growing perception in many parts of the region that corruption has floated upwards—from petty corruption in the 1950s, to mid-level corruption in the 1960s and 1970s, to corruption at the very highest levels of the state in the 1980s and 1990s.

The employment situation in the region is precarious. Real wages in the manufacturing and agricultural sectors have declined considerably in the period between 1980 and 1995. In Pakistan, in 1990s, with lower output growth and fewer people migrating abroad, the employment situation has worsened significantly. In Bangladesh, which has experienced high levels of urban labour absorption and fairly high levels of growth in the same period, there are still insufficient jobs to counter the number of people joining the labour force. In those situations where jobs have become available in industries such as garments, incomes are far from enough to support families. All of these factors contribute to increasing desperation and deprivation.

In the midst of democratic experiments, politicization of new recruits and groups into the political process had been giving rise to new and differential identities and ever-rising expectations. The callous unresponsiveness of the economic system to the basic needs of the marginalized sections of society makes them desperate and drives them to oppose the system. Sometimes this opposition verges on rebellion. Bereft of participation in their own government, the people have, increasingly, been expressing their discontent with the system by resorting to protest demonstrations or violence in the streets. The governments have also been losing a good deal of their authority to hoodlums, organized criminals, gangsters, and terrorists. Rather than making corrections and accommodations, the governments have been looking for authoritarian measures. Thus, the challenges for democracy in South Asian countries arise out of contradictions of limited resources, but great competition, great poverty, but high aspirations, high politicization, but low accommodation, concentration and centralization of power without accountability and transparency.

Politics of Identities and Interests

South Asia is experiencing a triple explosion of awareness, aspiration, and identities as a result of the shrinking of world, expanding communications networks, and advancing frontiers of technology

(Muni, 2000: 6). The repercussions of this explosion of awareness, aspirations, and identities are positive as well as negative. The positive aspects can be exemplified in terms of people's increasing assertiveness regarding their political and economic rights and empowerment. As a result, 'institutions are being reformed and streamlined to cope with the pressures generated from below. New cultural forms are finding expression to identify with this process of constructive change and transformation' (Muni, 2000).

Muni goes on to observe:

> The explosion of awareness, aspirations and identities in South Asia has also created new and intensified prevailing social tensions which have taken the agitations and protest movements on the one hand and violent conflicts and organized insurgencies on the other along religious, political, and ethnic lines. While agitations and protest movements are a part of political process and have to be addressed by the governments. Within the given framework of political and administrative decisions, the insurgencies and violent conflicts threaten to tear the structure of the state apart. The challenge of coping with these conflicts is indeed complex and without meeting this challenge, the stability and development of the State or the region as a whole cannot be ensured (Muni, 2000: 6).

The phenomenon of ethnicity is an intrinsic component of the social-political realities of the multi-ethnic states of the world. South Asia is no exception to this phenomenon. Today, ethnicization of politics and politicization of ethnicity have become very common. They have destroyed mutual toleration and sharpened ethnic consciousness among various communities. The politicization of ethnic and religious revivalism as also assertion of various ethnic and regional identities is posing serious problems for the security of South Asian states.

Ethno-political tensions and conflicts are present in the states of South Asia because of uneven dynamics of national integration. The post-colonial states of South Asia followed strategies of modernity and economic progress. However, the modernization and development process led to the centralization of development progress. The negative connotation of such centralization was the manifestation of discriminatory attitudes in terms of ethnicities and regions. Discriminatory distribution of rights and privileges together with the arbitrary attitude of power elites led to a feeling of deprivation among minority ethnic groups. The elites largely failed to strengthen the democratic institutions by decentralizing political economic power. Instead, they responded by strengthening and using coercive powers to preserve regime interests against resurgent ethnic groups. The discriminatory practices adopted by the state, the continued neglect by the state or mishandling of the initial demands for linguistic accommodation, regional autonomy, equity in education or in employment avenues have turned the self-conscious ethnic groups into ethnic national movements.

We find in South Asian states a distinct emphasis on particularistic ethnic, linguistic, and religious component of their secular and universalistic goals. The political processes have highlighted the ethnic diversities like the Dzonkha language of the Drukpa culture in Bhutan; Urdu in Pakistan (without any indigenous Urdu-speaking region), and Sinhala Buddhist identity in Sri Lanka. India is a multicultural society with a multiplicity of languages, religions, castes, and tribes. Of 18 languages scheduled in the Constitution, 13 have states of their own in the federal Union. Hindi and English are the official languages of the Union government, while Hindi and other regional languages are so used by various state governments. The national print media is stronger in English, whereas the national electronic media is stronger in Hindi. As a consequence of these divergent developments, the politics of nation-building in each of these countries has got entangled with the majority–minority dilemmas, moderated by multiple ethnic cross-pressures in all larger South Asian countries. These cross-pressures are conducive to democratic nation-building, provided of course that democracy becomes a workable proposition in the first place.

However, the level of politicization of language has not been uniform within and among states. Not all multi-ethnic societies have major ethnic problems and not all ethnic groups are conflict-ridden. Thus, the nature, intensity and extent of linguistic nationalism differs from country to country. Ethnic problem is relatively muted in the plural societies of Bhutan and Nepal in contrast to its stridence in Sri Lanka and Pakistan. To explain this one has to analyse the linkages between the nature of the political system, the economic development processes, the policies followed by the state regarding ethnic demands, and the nature of power structure and the extent to which it accommodates ethnic diversities.

Presently, all South Asian states are under mounting pressure of enormous turbulences unleashed by the process of socio-economic change. The ethnic dimensions of power structure and the policies, strategies as well as tactics adopted by various regimes to cope with various ethnic groups provide the wider setting for an understanding of ethnicity and the process of nation-building. There has been an increasing state penetration into civil society as well as centralization of initiatives and resources in the name of economic development. A centralized political system under these circumstances effectively denied large sections of society participation in decisions that affected their economic, cultural, and social existence. The failure of the state to play its role as a catalyst of transformation in ushering major socio-economic changes has only aggravated the situation. This crisis of governance leading to a decline of legitimacy in most countries of the subcontinent is an important contributory factor in ethnic tension and violence.

All the states of South Asia, perhaps with the exception of the Maldives, are witnessing violent social and political conflicts. In India, Jammu and Kashmir and the northeastern region have been in deep turmoil for a long time. In Andhra Pradesh, The People's War group has been carrying out insurgent attacks, while Veerappan, the sandalwood smuggler, created terror in Tamil Nadu and Karnataka before being killed in a joint police action carried out by the two states. Bihar and Jharkhand have also been in the throes of rural violence, fuelled by radical class-caste organizations and urban criminal violence and kidnapping for ransom. The network of Naxal violence has acquired inter-state spread across Bihar-Jharkhand, Madhya Pradesh, Andhra Pradesh, and 'Maoists' have overwhelmed the state in Nepal.

Ethnic divide or conflicting ethnic militancy in contemporary Pakistan, ranging from autonomy to political segregation, is a manifestation of the ineluctable dilemma of the country: how to weave a national identity out of diverse regional and linguistic loyalties and their political aspirations. Today Pakistan is facing internal turmoil, as all the ethnic groups—the Baluchis, Pathans, and Sindhis—are highly discontented; the Muhajirs (Muslim refugees, migrants from India) feel left out and let down by the Punjabi ruling classes. Unfortunately, the powerful Pakistani ruling elite has remained reluctant to accept the plural composition of society and has reduced this problem to one of law and order, rather than as an issue concerned with governance. The religious elites have also frowned upon ethnic diversity.

The violent situation in Karachi over the past few years has raised a number of issues, including the relationship between the state and ethnic communities, Pakistani nationalism and ethnic nationalisms, the army and bureaucracy and the political leadership. Thus, ethnic militancy or violent ethnic spates in Sindh present the most serious threat to Pakistani state and civil society. This also poses a formidable challenge to the ruling elites of weaving and welding together different and distinct ethnic groups into a nation.

In Sri Lanka, the two-decade-old ethnic conflict between the Liberation Tigers of Tamil Eelam (LTTE) and the state never seems to be anywhere near resolution, periodic efforts for dialogue and negotiations notwithstanding. The roots of insurgency lie deep in the existence of sharp divisions within society owing to regional, ethnic, linguistic, religious, and communal differences along with issues of legitimacy and authority. This ongoing strife in Sri Lanka is a violent separatist movement. The issue is rooted in long-felt economic and cultural grievances of the Sinhalese-Buddhist majority against an aggressive Tamil minority, who fared far too well under the British and have acquired a sound base after independence. While the distribution of economic wealth and employment availability make up much of the reason for grievances on both sides, the role that cultural and religious symbolisms play within Sri Lankan society and within the structures of the state also constitute a sore point in their relations. The violent ethnic conflict, thus, in Sri Lanka assumes significance in the context of what appeared to be a unique malady. Political and social turmoil with a desire to have a decisive mileage in these affairs has caused further distance between the LTTE and the Sinhalese and hampers their rapprochement.

In Nepal, the so-called Maoist insurgency led by the extreme left groups has gained momentum since 1995. The Maoist insurgency is an off-shoot of the socio-economic grievances accumulated over a period of time. The re-introduction of democracy in 1990 raised Nepalese expectations regarding governance. The political instability and frequent change in government gave little time to political parties to concentrate on the issues pertaining to economic development and social uplift. While political survivability of the government remained shaky, the administrative corruption and mismanagement became the hallmark of the government. The Moists capitalized on these grievances and convincingly articulated the aspirations of the people. Moreover, the Maoist established peoples' government in many parts of Nepal. Their ideology of a classless society appealed to the masses in these backward regions. Backed by a strong and committed cadre, the Maoist's perpetuated violence by making government offices defunct in areas under their control. The negotiations with the government failed due to the uncompromising stand taken by the Maoists. Their demands ranged from socio-economic issues, political agenda based on ideology, and foreign policy issues. The Maoist's violent methods to capture power may not have the approval of dominant elites and the international community, but their political and socio-economic agenda have considerable appeal for the poor and the long suppressed Nepalese masses. The king's military methods will not yield easy and desirable results, and for a lasting solution, Nepal's political and social order will have to be drastically transformed so as to accommodate popular aspirations unleashed by the Maoist movement (Muni, 2003).

In Bhutan, the southern Bhutanese of Nepali origin are fighting for their political and economic rights and nearly 1,00,000 of them, pushed out by the royal regime, are languishing as refugees in Nepal.

Most states of South Asia are plural societies with religion, language, and race cutting across national frontiers and influencing intra-regional relations. Thus, domestic ethno-political developments in each of these countries have repercussions on inter-state relations within the region. Cross-border affiliations among ethnic, linguistic, and religious groups make intra-state conflict in one country have its reverberations felt in the neighbouring states, leading to trans-border movement of refugees, political dissidents, and arms.

Ethnic Nationalism and Religious Fundamentalism

Given the geo-political configuration of South Asian states systems and the interlocked nature of the region, there has emerged a certain nexus between domestic and political developments and intra-regional relations. Thus, ethnicity in South Asia has intra-regional implications. Significant ethno-political turmoil and turbulence in one country causes a spill-over effect in its neighbourhood and hence influences inter-state relations within the region.

Internal politico-economic processes combined with transnational ethno-political linkages have led to intra-regional conflicts in South Asia. Thus, ethnic problems in South Asia are influenced by their cross-border linkages making the external factor of the problem as significant as the internal aspect.

Pluralism is the bedrock of the South Asian region, where religion, language, and race transcend national boundaries. Domestic ethno-political developments in each of these countries have significant repercussions in inter-state relations. The intra-state conflict over ethnic linguistic and religious issues often assumes an inter-state character due to cross-border affiliations of ethnic groups. The transformation of intra-state conflict into an inter-state one has been and continues to be a significant factor affecting the nature of international politics. For instance, the problem of tribals in the Chittagong Hill tracts in Bangladesh and of Tamils in Sri Lanka, are closely interlinked with and affect India. Current ethnic conflict in Bhutan between the ruling elite and the Nepalese community is also similar. The change of government policies from inclusive integration to forced assimilation has widened the ethnic strife. The impact of ethnic strife has impacted Bhutan's relations with Nepal and India.

Language acts as an important symbol of group consciousness and solidarity. Ethno-linguistic identities have played a significant role in the socio-political developments in the subcontinent. The use of a dominant language as a vibrant instrument of nation-building is a formidable challenge faced by new states. Language rivalries have assumed salience in the relatively recent period of history. Language cleavages are a basis for blocking social mobility and this is responsible for the disintegration of the political community. Language became the main stimulus for the separation of East Pakistan along with economic, political, and cultural imbalances that existed between the two wings of pre-1971 Pakistan.

In Sri Lanka, language has played a prominent role. The declaration of Sinhala as the sole official language in Sri Lanka in 1956 led to violent riots by the Tamils. The Sri Lankan Tamils felt that their job prospects and educational advancement were threatened by various measures.

A unique feature of South Asia is that linguistic boundaries are by no means congruent with political divisions. Major states of South Asia are multilingual and have an overlapping of languages. For instance, in India, Hindi or Urdu is spoken by a large number of north Indians, while in Pakistan, it is recognized as the official language. Bengali is the official language of Bangladesh and one of the regional languages in India. Tamil, one of the regional languages in India. It is widely spoken in northern Sri Lanka. This has led to the development of language as a factor affecting bilateral relation among states.

The ethnic strife in the Himalayan kingdom of Bhutan has been a very important factor influencing bilateral relations between Bhutan and Nepal. For Bhutan, language has become a vital component in its struggle for survival. The royal government adopted Dzonkha, as the country's language in order to stem the challenge posed to the country's survival by Nepali-speaking southerners. The preferential state policies pursued by the ruling Drukpa elite in Bhutan led to a feeling of alienation among the ethnic Nepalese. The impact of ethnic conflict in Bhutan's relations with Nepal and India was substantial.

The persistent conflict in Sri Lanka between Sinhalese and Tamil had its adverse repercussion on Indo-Sri Lankan relations because large sections of the Tamil population have organic links with Tamils in India.

In sum, ethno-linguistic identity has played an important role in the socio-political developments in the subcontinent. In South Asia, linguistic nationalism has figured prominently in major inter-state relations. However, the nature of ethno-lingual linkages varies within and among states. Thus, the nature, intensity, and extent of linguistic nationalism, as a factor affecting intra-regional relations, differs from country to country.

The South Asian states have so far proved to be a poor match for their detractors. The main reason behind their inability to cope with the conflicts has been the adoption of, basically, a law and order approach towards them. The result has been escalation in violence from both sides and induction of newer and more sophisticated weapons.

As mentioned earlier, most of the violent conflicts today are caused by the divisions that exist in a pluralist society. Hence, the solution must come from power sharing among the various ethnic or other sectarian groups. If some mutual arrangement can be made for power sharing or regional autonomy at the local level, conflict will not get prolonged or result in wastage of human and other resources of the nations. For this a few other conditions must exist. There must be mutual respect for other parties and their genuine demands as part of confidence-building measures. Unless each side views its opponents as honourable and having legitimate demands, relations cannot improve between various groups, which are characterized by widening fears and gaps. In sum, political and constitutional accommodation of the legitimate grievances of the affected people, the agenda of development and good governance has to be implemented seriously and vigorously.

Two concurrent political developments in South Asia over the past three to four decades have facilitated the mobilization of this social discontent and added violence to them. One was the rise of the sectarian state and the other was the expansion of democratic space in South Asia. Nursed by the British colonial political structure, the three major South Asian states, as they came into existence in 1947/1971, were secular in their orientation. Even in the case of Pakistan, which came into existence on the basis of religion, its creator, Muhammad Ali Jinnah, probably did not mean Pakistan to be a theocratic state. In his speech to the inaugural session of the Pakistan Constituent Assembly on 11 August 1947, he presented a clear picture of a secular state. However, his successors reinforced the communal character of the Pakistani state not only along religious lines, but also made it a Punjabi-dominated state. Perhaps it could not have been otherwise; religious communal mobilization of the Pakistan movement was fraught with the lurking danger of Islamic fundamentalism of jihad. Tamil nationalism in Sri Lanka and Hindu nationalism in India are also fraught with religious and linguistic fundamentalism.

In Sri Lanka, in 1956, exclusionary Sinhala identity was unleashed and by 1972, Sri Lanka became a Buddhist-Sinhala state. Nepal proclaimed itself a Hindu state by 1962 and Bangladesh in 1976 became a Muslim/Islamic state. Bhutan and the Maldives were proclaimed theocratic states from the beginning. That left only India, but here also, since the beginning of the 1980s, communal overtones in political processes have been increasing and the demand for a sectarian Hindu *rashtra* has been gathering momentum.

As far as Islamic resurgence in Asia is concerned, Islamic fundamentalism has spread during the last two decades in Pakistan and Afghanistan. Radical Islamic groups of several hues have sprung up in both the countries which are obsessed with a belief that Islamic tenets as propagated by them must prevail. Most radical Islamic organizations justify use of force against these societies and Muslim states which do not follow their interpretation of the Shariat and the Quran. They believe that Muslims who follow the Western secular and cultural norms are, in fact, non-believers and should either conform or be eliminated. The missionary zeal of Islamic fundamentalist movements and their efforts to impose rigid *Wahabi* traditions on the Muslims of the south and central Asian regions has disturbed peace. Being extremely narrow minded and bigoted, fundamentalist groups have generated ethnic, sectarian, and cultural violence in many countries of South Asia.

Pakistan has emerged since the 1980s as the gateway for the organized projection of militant Islam in the region. Strategic considerations and religious fanaticism have enabled Pakistan to exploit the situation of internal conflict in the South Asian region. Islamic militancy is a political and military strategy which seeks to Islamize domestic political arrangements as well as external strategic relations.

Contemporary Pakistan is under dark clouds of religious fundamentalism. It is in the name of Islam that the country has created an image of being the most potent source of religious terrorism, which poses a threat to peace and stability in large parts of the globe, apart from Pakistan itself. The biggest irony of Pakistan's history is that Islam, which was supposedly the *raison d' etre* of Pakistan, was not only being exploited in its state construct of nation-building, but also became the biggest source of most of its internal conflicts in the last decade. The fierce sectarian controversies which rage in Pakistan present a perplexing paradox. During the last two decades, conflicts between different sects have sharpened, that is, between Sunnis and Shias on the one hand, and on the other, among Sunnis themselves. These political conflicts are an expression of a deeper philosophical confusion as to what constitutes an Islamic state.

Pakistan moved towards vigorous Islamization from the mid-1970s, but all such attempts only further accentuated the sectarian conflicts and contradictions in Pakistan. The massive increase of sectarian violence can be seen as the result of the backlash of Pakistan-Afghan collusion in providing training to militants. In the last few years, these conflicts have resulted in unprecedented violence. Sectarian violence was part of a Sunni jihadi culture fuelled by the proliferation of weapons, the mosque schools, and the fallout of the Afghan civil war.

The propping up of militant organizations like the Sipah-e-Sahabe and Tehrik-e-Jafaria have rendered sectarian conflicts violent and bloody. However, Islamic revivalist movements launched by obscurantist religious groups like the Tablighi-Jamaat have further radicalized Pakistani society. In this context, the sectarian divide is cutting deeper and deeper into the social fabric, threatening religious harmony and civil society in Pakistan. Violent sectarianism coupled with a heroin-Kalashnikov culture raises questions about Pakistan's survival as a state.

It is a well-known fact that in the last two decades, 'Pakistan fell prey to the temptation of nurturing militancy in the name of Islam and thought this to be an easy option as a means of promoting its strategic goals in the region, particularly in Afghanistan and India. Pakistan called it "*jihad*" ...obviously the intention was to mobilize and motivate the Pakistani army and irregular armed forces of all kinds in the name of Islam' (Kumar, 2000: 1080). Pakistan first employed this so-called 'Islamic strategy' against the Soviet forces in Afghanistan from 1979 onwards. For Pakistan, the Afghan jihad served well and after the withdrawal of the Soviet forces from Afghanistan in 1989, it started to export to and use the jihad strategy against India.

Pakistan created and nurtured the Taliban and the Al-Qaida for trans-national terrorism to achieve predominance in the Islamic world. The Pakistani establishment apparently felt that by placating the various partners in the Taliban-Al-Qaida it could obtain their help in pursuing its own foreign policy objectives. The most commonly given rationale for this belief by people like General Hamid Gul, General Durani, and General Aslam Beg was that this collective effort succeeded in defeating the Soviet Union when the latter occupied Afghanistan from 1979 to 1989: When a superpower is defeated by this strategy, it will work in other places also. The Pakistani establishment refused to accept that it became possible only due to unrestrained help from the United States (US) and its allies all over the globe.

This misperception continued throughout the 1990s when Pakistan slowly started escalating its operations in India. The end result of it was the Kargil aggression in the summer of 1999. The coming of General Musharraf to power in October 1999 has not helped matters to any significant extent. General Musharraf did nothing to remove this misperception, fearing that any change in his country's Kashmir policy would cost him the very power he was exercising, due to vocal supporters some of these groups had in Pakistan.

There is no lack of evidence to suggest that Pakistan considered Taliban as virtually an extension of its own military apparatus to jointly achieve the objectives of first capturing the whole of Afghanistan in search of 'strategic depth', then Kashmir, and then carry forward the export of jihad into the rest of India, and later beyond South Asia into Central Asia. The success of the Taliban operation in Afghanistan had negative repercussions for India in terms of its spill-over effect in Kashmir. Pakistan considered Taliban-controlled Afghanistan as its 'strategic depth' vis-à-vis India.

It has far more serious implications for the security situation in the post-nuclear South Asia. Pakistan's fanatic groups like the Markazdawa-ul-Irshad, the Harkat-ul-Ansar, Hizbul-Mujahideen, Jamaat-i-Islami, Laskhar-e-Toiba, and Jaish-e-Mohammad are involved in supporting a jihad against India. The expansion of their appeal in the post-nuclear test period only compounds the concerns. The idea of nuclear weapons in the hands of these fanatics is absolutely spine-chilling. Besides India, these jihadi groups are being exported with full backing of resource-rich Muslim countries in conflict zones like Bosnia, Kosovo, Chechnya, Dagestan, the Philippines, and Tajikistan to undertake specific terrorist missions.

Pakistan's peculiar brand of Islam is based on distortion, fundamentalism, misrule, and terrorism. It has done to Pakistan irreparable damage in terms of dismantling of the civil structure of the country and pushing it on the path of self-destruction.

Bangladesh is also trapped in sectarian conflict, between the Islamic fundamentalists and secular forces. Sometimes, the intensity of this conflict becomes extremely severe, such as during the visit of American president, Bill Clinton to Bangladesh in March 2000, when he had to cancel some of his travel plans for security reasons.

The future relationship between militant Islam and internal conflicts depends not only on the strength of militant Islam, but also on the ability of regional and global forces to mobilize secular forces against militant Islamic movements.

'Third Wave' of Democratization

Besides the movement towards the rise of the sectarian state, South Asia has also witnessed restoration of democracy as well as extension of democratic space to varying degrees, particularly since the late 1980s and early 1990s. A third wave of democratization that accompanied the end of the Cold War, was in part, a consequence of American intolerance of authoritative, as distinguished from authoritarian, regimes within the developing world. By the 1990s, almost all the major South Asian states democratized themselves, with the exception of Bhutan and the Maldives. But in these two countries also, pressures for democratization have witnessed an upward movement. Pakistan too has now reverted to military rule, but restoration of full-fledged democracy is at the forefront of the political agenda of its people. In this context, an eminent scholar has aptly remarked:

> The widening of the democratic space has provided impetus to the expression and enhancement of awareness of aspirations, and facilitated mobilization of identities. Besides, in the competitions and struggle for power between democratic forces and the remnants of authoritarian vested interests, extremist tendencies have been exploited. Since the sectarian State has thwarted this democratic space for some minorities and marginalized sections of the people, recourse to violence has been taken by them. The post-Cold War ethos of democratization, human rights and aspirations for economic prosperity have tended to encourage such struggles which will become sharper in the years to come (Muni, 2000: 7).

One of the striking contrasts between the early post-colonial years in South Asian political systems and the 1990s is that in the early 1950s there were only two South Asian democracies, India and Sri Lanka. Pakistan was not a practising democracy; the birth of Bangladesh was still two decades away; and Nepal was a monarchy with few pretensions to democratic practice. India and Sri Lanka have had an unbroken record of democratic government—

warts and all—since independence. Democracy emerged in Pakistan in 1988 after long years of military rule, as was the case in Bangladesh (1990), while Nepal has developed into a constitutional monarchy with a democratic base. The late 1980s, coinciding with the disintegration of the Soviet Union and the collapse of the communist system in central and eastern Europe was the watershed in the spread of democratic systems of government in Pakistan, Bangladesh, and Nepal.

India, in particular, happens to be the rare Afro-Asian country that can boast to its credit not only having established a regular and reasonably free and fair electoral democracy, but also having consolidated the parliamentary-federal constitution adopted in 1950 with liberal democratic charters of Fundamental Rights of Citizens and Directive Principles of State Policy oriented to welfare liberalism. The former has survived the authoritarian Emergency regime (1975–77), and the latter seems to be surviving the neo-liberal economic reforms since 1991 with an accent on marketization and business liberalism. By available indicators, public/state investment in the economy has gone down by nearly one-third, but it is attributable more to privatization of the public sector than a drastic reduction in poverty alleviation programmes. With a relatively 'overdeveloped' service sector of the economy (accounting for 48 per cent of the GDP in 1999) and reasonably developed industrial, manufacturing, and agricultural sectors (accounting for 27, 17 and 28 per cent of the GDP respectively, World Bank, 2000/2001), India has the appearances and pretentions of an industrial society in the making, as distinguished from non-industrial and tribal societies generally prevalent in the region. In Tom Bottomore's (1972: 156–57) characterization, the basic political features of modern industrial societies are:

> (1) the political community as a nation-state, (2) the existence of political movements, parties and pressure groups, (3) the election of the political executive by universal adult suffrage, and (4) the administration of public affairs by a large centralized bureaucracy.

In a land haunted by the pre-Partition 'two-nation theory' of Jinnah, the civic Indian nationalism embodied in the 1950 Constitution has, by and large, prevailed over religious nationalisms. Ethnic separatisms in the northeast and northwest have been more or less contained by now and electoral and federal democratic processes restored after decades of insurgency and terrorism. The so called Hindu 'nationalism' and Sikh 'nationalism' championed by the Hindu right and the Sikh right are part of the electoral-parliamentary-federal processes formally swearing allegiance to the Indian Constitution and are ethnic constituents of a multi-cultural mosaic and a multiparty system. With its roots in India's freedom struggle against colonial rule, the post-Independence 'Congress system' (Kothari, 1970) has transformed into an exasperatingly fragmented multi-partisan configuration with two larger national parties—the Bharatiya Janata Party (BJP) and the Indian National Congress (INC)—rallied around by an assortment of smaller national (all-India) and regional (mostly state) parties. The third such pivot national party—the Janata Party/Dal, since 1977/1988—was hopelessly fragmented along regional and caste (Other Backward Classes, middle-peasant castes) lines by the end of the 1980s. Multiparty coalitions headed by the left-of-centre Janata Dal and the right-of-centre BJP, with an interlude of a Congress minority government, have ruled India since 1989. While instability stared the Janata Dal-led coalition governments in the face, the Congress minority government (1991–96) and BJP led coalition government since 1999 was stable. Power sharing in federal coalition governments and bi-party or multiparty systems in different states have brought about a complex political framework in India, but this has also lent India a remarkable degree of national integration through the federalization of the previously predominantly prime ministerial and parliamentary tenor of politics under Nehru and overly centralized neo-patrimonial prime ministerial regime under Indira Gandhi.

The exclusionary effects of religious and caste riots are appreciably contained by judicial activism, a vigilant press, a statutory National Human Rights Commission and National and State(s) Minority Commissions, civic organizations, and the overstrained—and occasionally negligent and partisan—administration at the lower levels.

Muslim minority/majority politics in federal India and Jammu and Kashmir has entered into a catalytic democratic phase of liberalization today in the wake of free and fair elections in Jammu and Kashmir in 2003. Answering a question on the reasons of the failure of the Indian Muslim political leadership, Ashis Nandy perceptively observed:

> There is no pan-Indian Muslim leadership but there is no pan-Indian Hindu leadership either. There are regional and local leaders and there is nothing wrong with that. Ethnic nationalism and religious nationalism smothers the natural process of displacement of traditional leadership. Middle class Muslim nationalism sabotaged the natural process of electoral democratisation. This natural process of democratisation has not taken place in Pakistan too where electoral process is still dominated by the feudal class.... Please recognise that there are regional non-English speaking leaders we do not know about.... But I do see two potential Muslim leaders of the future—Mehbooba Mufti and Omer Abdullah. In them, I see a new generation of Muslim leaders (*TOI*, 2003).

The top echelons of administration—the All India Services—are a unique federal civil service whose antecedents we trace back to the Maurya *mahamatya/mahamatta* system, the Mughal *mansabdari system*, and the British Indian Civil Service. The post-Independence Indian Administrative Service, Indian Police Service, and Indian Forest Service are federally recruited by the constitutionally autonomous Union Public Service Commission and trained in Union academies of administration and in the field in the states. They are then allocated to respective states cadres. They work mostly in states under the disciplinary control of state governments, and are occasionally loaned on deputation to the Union. They, thus, provide the personnel for the highest administrative positions in both the Union and state governments and are a factor of national unity, regional autonomy, and constitutional politics. Like the party system, the administrative system too has sometimes appeared to be opening up to politics-administration-corruption-crime nexus. Nevertheless, public interest litigation, judicial activism, and the media have spurred on vigilance, investigation, law-enforcement, and prosecution.

The decline of the Parliament and degeneration of electoral and legislative politics is partly compensated by an independent constitutionally autonomous Election Commission of India, a vigorous mass media, old and new mass movements around the issues of production exchange and quality of life, an activist judiciary with expanding power of judicial review predicated on federal division of powers between the Union/state/local orders of government, constitutionally guaranteed individual and group rights, and legally guaranteed corporate and individual contractual rights.

Asymmetrical federalism in Jammu and Kashmir, Nagaland, and Mizoram has offered something akin to a distinctly different pattern of federal linkage with New Delhi that may offer a viable alternative to the Sinhalese–Tamil conflict in Sri Lanka and similar simmering troubles in Pakistan. The major directions of change in India since the 1990s are political federalization and economic liberalization (for example, bureaucratic decontrol, privatization, and globalization). The net effect is the growing autonomy of state governments as well as the private sector of economy and revival of CSOs.

The foundation of a democratic system in Sri Lanka is in similar ways a pioneer in the establishment and maintenance of democracy in South Asia. In India, universal suffrage came after Independence, but it was introduced in Sri Lanka, a crown colony, in 1931, sixteen years before Independence (De Silva, 2000: 47–48). It became the centre of an unusual experiment in preparing a people for independence.

At Independence, one saw the seemingly successful transplanting of British democratic institutions and organizations of civil society in Sri Lanka under the United National Party (UNP), a smooth blending of the democratic experience under the 1931 Constitution, with post-colonial aspirations for the maintenance of democratic forms of government in the mid-1950s. These marked a vitally important phase in the evolution of Sri Lankan democracy. Through the defeat of the UNP, the Sri Lankan polity had demonstrated the strength and resilience of its democratic system by becoming the first state in post-colonial South Asia where the original legatee of the colonial power lost office, peacefully and through the ballot. Thus, by 1956, one of the crucially important stages in the growth to maturity of a democratic system—the peaceful transfer of power from a government formed by one political party to one controlled by its rival or rivals—had been successfully negotiated in Sri Lanka.

For both India and Sri Lanka, the general election of 1977 were of decisive importance: in India, it demonstrated the electorate's rejection of the excesses of the Emergency, through the first ever defeat of the Congress Party at the national level; in Sri Lanka it demonstrated the resilience of the two-party system and a rejection of Mrs Bandaranaike's policies.

In Sri Lanka, where the transfer of power was marked by continuity not upheaval, the democratization processes were affected by these contradictions till the failures in state-building became apparent after the early 1970s that presumably prompted Sri Lanka to switch over from the parliamentary system to the presidential-parliamentary system of cohabitation akin to the Fifth French Republic (later also adopted by post-communist Russia). The high levels of political violence in the island throughout the 1980s and 1990s did not damage the democratic political system to the degree that seemed likely in the late 1980s (De Silva, 1993).

Indeed, the survival and consolidation of democracy in Sri Lanka and India exemplify a refutation of some of the well known and established theories of democratization popular in the West: Alexis de Tocqueville's argument that only a society of equals could sustain democracy; or Seymour Martin Lipset's contention that there has to be a minimum level of economic prosperity and development before one could think of a viable democratic polity.

However, looking at the present situation in Sri Lanka one faces a paradox. On the one hand, Sri Lanka has one of the longest democratic traditions in Asia with reasonably fair elections, high voter turnout, and regular change of government. The long democratic tradition since Independence in 1948 seems to indicate a high degree of legitimacy of the political system. However, the internal conflicts caused a sharp increase in political violence and human rights violations, and questioned the legitimacy of the political system as a whole.

Recently (early winter 2003), in Sri Lanka, President Chandrika Kumaratunga precipitated a dangerous constitutional impasse by striking at the heart of prime minister Ranil Wickremasinghe's popularly elected government. She sacked three key ministers in the UNP government, called out the army, and declared a state of 'short-term' emergency. In keeping with the cloak- and-dagger nature of the unfolding political drama, Kumaratunga's constitutional 'coup' was staged at a time when the prime minister was away on a state visit to the US, ironically to solicit support for the Sinhalese–Tamil peace process. In the recent past, the Lankan president had voiced increasing impatience with the peace negotiations, charging Wickremasinghe with yielding far too much ground to the Tigers. Kumaratunga claimed that her actions were aimed at 'preventing a further deterioration of the security situation' in the island nation. It is ironic that the vast constitutional authority vested in the president of Sri Lanka and utilized by Kumaratunga were created by J.R. Jayawardene, through the introduction of system of political dyarchy—an institutional arrangement, which allows for more than one centre of legitimate constitutional authority, inevitably giving rise to a constitutional deadlock. It was not a surprise move. President Kumaratunga was contemplating such action as she was convinced about the characteristics of the peace process being detrimental to Sri Lanka's vital interests. She had been of this view for at least six months or so. What provoked her decisions were the counter-proposals sent by the LTTE for the interim self-governing authority for the merged north eastern provinces of Sri Lanka and the government's decision to dismantle new LTTE camps in Trincomalee, as factors endangering national security.

Most analysts in Sri Lanka think Kumaratunga's game plan was to divide the ruling United National Front, invite a faction to join her People's Alliance and appoint her advisor Lakshman Kadirgamar as prime minister. But this plan was promptly squashed as 130 members of Parliament pledged their support to Wickremasinghe. Moreover, people's power forced Chandrika to withdraw her emergency declaration. However, the basic prospects in the immediate future seem to be a stalemate in the negotiations.

The restoration of democracy in Pakistan in the last quarter of 1988, after the seemingly unending 11-year long brutal reign of General Zia-ul-Haq, which ended suddenly and unexpectedly with his demise in a mysterious air crash, ushered in a new era of significance in the political history of that country. It is true that democracy was restored in 1988, but the legacy of Zia-ul-Haq's 11-year long autocratic rule was difficult to be deposed. The legacy of Zia-ul-Haq's rule in terms of the 8th Constitutional Amendment had overshadowed the political process throughout the period from 1988 to 1999. The 8th Amendment had been intended by General Zia mainly to provide immunity to the army for its actions during the martial law period and also to arm the military-bureaucratic establishment with an authoritarian veto against an elected government. However, 11 years of democracy (1988–99) were not without roadblocks and pitfalls. It is pertinent to note that the democratic regimes of both Benazir Bhutto and Nawaz Sharif had lived under the shadow of the military. In the 'troika system' of power sharing comprising the president, the prime minister, and the army, the latter reserved the veto power. The restoration of democracy in Pakistan was a semi-restoration of democracy or at best a military-backed regime. A state structure dominated by the non-representative institutions, namely, the military and the bureaucracy, was not inclined to a transformation that readily asserted the ascendancy of elected institutions, and the parliament in particular. However, both Benazir and Sharif, failed to resolve the contradictions between the state structure and political processes in favour of a party-based system by removing a formidable wall of structural obstacles rooted in the very nature of the Pakistani state. The three governments (Benazir Bhutto twice and Nawaz Sharif once) had been casualities of the 8th Amendment. Nawaz Sharif during his second term succeeded in amending Article 52b of the 8th Amendment. But Sharif became a democratic despot, was finally deposed by General Pervez Musharraf in October 1999, and the military took over the reigns of power once again.

The history of independent Bangladesh's functioning under a multiparty competitive system is very brief. The coup of August 1975 marked the beginning of an era of militarized politics which continued until the dethroning of President Ershad by a concerted popular movement in 1990, and the return to parliamentary system with a prime minister as the head of the government. At Bangladesh's first internationally monitored general elections, there was a peaceful transfer of political power to a popularly elected leader, Begum Khaleda Zia, the widow of General Ziaur Rahman. Although the 1991 parliamentary elections signalled the beginning of a new era of democratic politics, the past decade has seen an atmosphere ostensibly favourable to renewed military intervention in Bangladesh, including a deterioration of law and order, widespread political tension, and economic torpor. Nonetheless, the armed forces that previously looked for a pretext to intervene have shown signs of restraint and political maturity. The future of civil–military relations in Bangladesh will depend on how the political forces operate within the system. A respect for democratic values, institutions and practices on the part of politicians will ensure the endurance of an era of demilitarized politics that is now in its embryonic stage.

In Nepal, domestic political compulsions, in combination with fears of being submerged by India, had prompted King Mahendra to introduce the 'partyless' panchayat system under which the king was dominant in all spheres of national life. The panchayat system of one party rule, reaffirmed by a referendum held in 1980, was little more than a legitimizing device for the monarchy and Nepal's traditional landed elite.

Changes in the international system were of vital importance in the revival of Nepal's multiparty system, with the Nepali Congress and the United Front in the forefront. There is no doubt that the democratization of Central Europe in the 1980s had a dramatic impact on the thinking of politicians of Nepal and in the demand and agitation for democratic reforms in the country. At the same time, there was once more the operation of the India factor when Rajiv Gandhi's government imposed crippling economic sanctions on Nepal in retaliation for a Sino-Nepal arms deal. In the late 1980s, the people at large, with politicized students in the lead, revolted against the prevailing party-less panchayat system. The successful Conference of Nepali Congress in January 1990 provided irrefutable evidence of the strength of opposition forces. In Nepal, after a strong pro-democracy movement, King Birendra on 9 April 1990, announced the return of democracy to the kingdom after a gap of 30 years. What clearly influenced him to change his obdurate stand was the kind of popular support the pro-democracy movement had attracted. The new order produced by the 1990 movement was transformatory in nature despite the continued acceptance of the constitutional role of the king. For the first time, a broad coalition was forged between the movement and the king, producing a constitution with certain key elements of democratic governance: sovereignty of the people, a multiparty system, constitutional monarchy, and inalienable freedoms of the people (Baral and Rose, 1997: 208). In May 1991, Nepal elected its first democratic parliament through multiparty elections.

During the last 12 years, Nepal's exercise of democracy are replete with crises resulting from a new experimentation in creation of a civil society. The country witnessed both crises of legitimacy and the mechanism of conflict management. The endemic crises of legitimacy and conflict in Nepal are the by-product of failures of leaders and parties, either in the government or out of it. Lack of confidence, vision, and direction of change seems to be producing political crises, raising the issue of credibility of the system as a whole despite many positive developments that have taken place since 1990.

The 1 June 2001 massacre in the palace spelled a bad omen for the monarchy (Baral, 2002: 198 –203). The Nepalese demonstrated an extraordinary resilience in coping with the palace massacre and the problem of succession to the throne. Public demand was for making the monarchy more transparent and democratic.

However, last year Nepal witnessed ongoing civil war, escalated violence, deterioration in the human rights' situation, and declaration of emergency (13 November 2002). The decline of democratic institutions and political parties facilitated the resurrection of royal power (Kramer, 2003: 208–14). The two royal steps, namely, dismissal of the caretaker prime minister, Sher Bahadur Deuba, and nomination of a nine-member 'clean' cabinet with Lokendra Bahadur Chand, a well known monarchist, as prime minister, are a setback to the survival of democracy and constitutional rule (Kramer, 2003: 213). Nepal's crisis seems to worsen as one finds a triangular power struggle going on among the Maoist rebels, political parties, and the monarchy/army combination. This has raised worries about the future of democracy in Nepal.

In sum, democracy as civilian control of the state and use of regular election and other democratic procedures to select governmental leaders seems to be acquiring deep roots in South Asian countries. It seems that people have come to believe that a regime, to be legitimate, must enjoy the confidence and consent of people, which defines the contents of popular sovereignty. Therefore, future prospects of South Asian countries seems to be the growing awareness among the people for consolidation of democracy both as governmental structure as well as means for socio-economic development and transformation.

External Dimension

South Asia as a geopolitical region has always been a troubled one with its internal political instabilities and intra-regional conflicts. As a distinct entity, it has two important characteristics that influence the interaction between the states of the region. First, it is essentially Indo-centric, with India occupying a central place, both geographically and in terms of socio-cultural continuities and economic infrastructure. Second, there is an asymmetrical and hierarchical power structure with India being the dominant power in the region in terms of size, population, resource base, potential for economic development, military strength, and viability of constitutional, political, and administrative structures. These two characteristics, in conjunction, make India the big brother in South Asia with all its negative connotations.

The Indo-centric nature of the region, along with India sharing borders with all South Asian countries and none of the others linked together by common frontiers have led to a spill-over effect of serious ethnic upheavals in the subcontinent on India and vice versa, the interaction pattern being between India and each of the rest. This is very much evident in India's relations with all her neighbouring countries. Ethnicity is one of the major factors affecting the foreign policies of these countries.

India–Pakistan relations have been full of conflicts and tensions ever since 1947. Their relations during the last 56 years have been nurtured on the infrastructure of historical mistrust and the superstructure of the unresolved territorial dispute on Kashmir. They have fought three full-scale wars and a limited war in Kargil in the summer of 1999. The intervals between the wars have also been full of alarms and tensions. With the overt nuclearization of India and Pakistan in 1998, the situation has worsened. Since then, any conflict between the two neighbours has the potential of escalating into a nuclear war in the subcontinent.

India–Pakistan relations have a decisive bearing on the strategic equations in South Asia. Pakistan has the wherewithal of a middle power, but a great incongruity exists between its external facade of a regional achiever with nuclear weapons and attainment of 'strategic depth' in Afghanistan (before the fall of the Taliban in Afghanistan), and fundamental internal contradictions. The armed forces in Pakistan for five- and-a-half decades manifested a near pathological determination to keep South Asia in turmoil, doing little to curb religious extremism and breeding terrorism within its borders, while spiting any efforts towards peace.

Export of terrorism provides an outlet for Pakistan's domestic frustrations (such as lack of a national ethos and identity), helps mobilize masses and gains support of Islamic parties and their loyalists in the Pakistan Army and the Inter-Services Intelligence (ISI). According to one observer, 'It has been averred that centrality of the annexation of entire Kashmir is part of Pakistan's national security policy and grand strategy. The new rail line that will connect Karachi and Central Asia must pass through India-held Kashmir to be engineeringly and economically effective' (Kak, 2000; also see Bodansky: 1998).

Political and strategic circumstances have cast Pakistan as the anti-status quo power with relatively greater temptation to alter the prevalent South Asian equilibrium. Pakistan's proxy war since 1980s and its unstinted efforts are targeted to weaken India's internal cohesion and territorial unity through what has been termed as 'death by a thousand cuts'. Pakistan has been determinedly exporting, promoting, and supporting cross-border terrorism into Kashmir (and even elsewhere in India) by proclaiming that jihadis are not terrorists (as India calls them), but are 'freedom fighters'.

The relations between India and Pakistan have entered a new phase in the post-11 September 2001 world. General Musharraf joined the world coalition against terrorism reluctantly under pressure and threat from Washington. After the terrorist attack on the Indian Parliament on 13 December 2001, General Musharraf came under pressure from the US and had agreed publicly in his 12 January speech to wage war domestically and renounce terrorism in Jammu and Kashmir. However, the actions Pakistan has taken against various terrorist outfits so far are superficial. Pakistan continues to support cross-border terrorism politically, diplomatically, morally, and financially. Musharraf talks of Kashmir as being part of every Pakistani's blood. The US alliance 'Operation Enduring Freedom' in Afghanistan has made little dent in curbing cross-border terrorism in Jammu and Kashmir. In India, those who expected that Pakistan, the source of cross-border terrorism, would be a prime target of the US war against terror have been disappointed. The fact is that cross-border terrorism is continuing and perhaps increasing. Instead of Pakistan proving its commitment to dismantle the terror infrastructure within its territory, there is daily news about more and more young men being recruited in their training camps, indicating otherwise.

Relations between India and the other five South Asian Association of Regional Cooperation (SAARC) countries—Bangladesh, Nepal, Bhutan, Sri Lanka, and the Maldives—are fairly normal. Apart from the fact that there are a few disputes or problems between India and the rest, none of them is so obsessed as Pakistan about India's size and strength. Like many other nations in other continents, they treat it normal for states to be of different sizes/strengths, and not to bother about the situation.

On the other hand, unlike Pakistan, these other states consider the positive aspects of India's size/strength for mutual benefit.

Indeed, two of them, Sri Lanka and the Maldives, have taken advantage of India's military strength to request India's intervention (Sri Lanka twice) for preventing destabilization of their government, with no other state (even from outside the subcontinent) objecting to Indian intervention.

A relatively recent and extremely significant component of the geo-strategic reality of South Asia is the emergence of a lethal cocktail of religious extremism/fundamentalism, small arms proliferation—financed by narcotics trafficking—and cross-border terrorism, which are playing havoc with pluralistic societies like India. Central Asian states Uzbekistan and Tajikstan, and Russia and China are also targeted.

> There is clearly a transition from politically oriented terrorism to one that is more religiously or ideologically motivated, with the attention shifting from West Asia to South Asia. The change of locus coincided with the West-supported resistance to the erstwhile Soviet Union in the Afghanistan-Pakistan area which became the epicentre of the international terrorist earthquake. Pakistani establishment, and the extremist religious terrorist organizations it supports, employ *Sunni Wahabi* militant Islam as an ideological camouflage to mount destabilising *jihadi* terrorist actions in the neighbourhood (Kak, 2000).

There are over 7 million AK-47s on the loose in South Asia and if all types of guns are included the number could quadruple. As to narcotics, the International Narcotics Control Board has estimated that anything up to $ 150 billion now finds its way to the drug mafia in Pakistan. A substantial part of this is used for the purchase of weapons and financing of ISI operations in India and elsewhere (Kak, 2000: 9–10).

The 1990s in South Asia had witnessed an increased levels of terrorist violence which were largely a fallout of Cold War politics. In the wake of Soviet military intervention in Afghanistan in 1979, in order to wage a proxy war via Pakistan, the US propagated Pakistan as a 'frontline state', which led to high levels of infusion of light weapons to the region. Media reports regularly underline the destruction brought about by small arms in Afghanistan, Pakistan, India, Bosnia, etc., as these weapons of terror diffuse quietly, but with an increasing rate, into the hands of non-state actors. Consequently, there is a rise in armed conflicts and violence in the states posing a threat to the security of the suffering states. Afghanistan has been the greatest victim as well as leading source of the small weapon in the world. It is also the epicentre of the weapons diffusion process in South Asia. The region with its fragile ethnic and social structure presents an interesting paradox where proliferation of small arms and spread of internal conflicts with cross-border implication go hand in hand. In the South Asian region, over 2,60,000 troops are engaged in fighting insurgent groups, armed with small arms and light weapons, while within Pakistan, the government faces a dangerous mix of internal proliferation and ethnic/sectarian violence that has been described as the 'Kalashnikov culture' (Cooper, 1996).

It is worth noting that:

> ...while the Soviets and the Americans, subsequently withdrew from Afghanistan, they had left what today may be considered the supporting structures for terrorism in South Asia, Central Asia and in other regions as well. These developments along with the liberalization/globalization process, which almost coincide, have also led to an increasing nexus between drug trafficking, terrorists and organized crime (Behera, 1991).

Further, the strategic objectives of countries like Pakistan that want to destabilize India and wrest Kashmir by force have been promoting cross-border terrorism. Mujahidins trained earlier in Afghanistan and now in Pakistan are fanning across the region leading to an increase in violence and terrorism. Kashmir has borne the brunt of this fundamentalist drive.

The intertwining relationship of light weapons and the narcotics trade has set off a fundamentalist drive into Kashmir, Tajakistan, Chechnya, Bosnia, Xinjiang, and elsewhere. A close scrutiny of the evolution of militancy in Jammu and Kashmir and Punjab indicates that it had covert/overt linkages with narcotics smuggling (Kartha, 1995). The drug syndicates are providing them financial assistance and offer small arms to raise the level of activities of these movements. Export and promotion of illicit narcotics and terrorists suit Pakistan's foreign policy aspiration in this region. According to one study, the amount Pakistan spends on sponsoring terrorism in India is nearly the same as it generates from illicit narcotics trade, that is, approximately US$ 2 billion (Haq, 1991: 17).

It is an established fact the Pakistan government in collaboration with the ISI uses drug money and arms to fund terrorism in India.

Pakistan also seeks to create ethnic divisions in the social fabric of the country by exploiting the religious sentiments and economic backwardness of Muslims in the bordering states of Jammu and Kashmir, Punjab, Rajasthan, Assam, Nagaland, Manipur, and other states. Besides, the ISI of Pakistan is proliferating firearms in Mumbai, Bihar, Uttar Pradesh and the northeastern states of India. It has been admitted that it has the potential and adequate fire power to destabilise India (Kartha, 1991).

The picture that has emerged since the mid-1990s is very alarming. Increasing evidence suggests that terrorism in Jammu and Kashmir is transfiguring into an all-India, pan-Islamic campaign. The Mumbai and Coimbatore bomb blasts along with a few other events here and there travelled a complicated web of inter-relationship between terrorists groups in Jammu and Kashmir and underworld and Islamic fundamentalist organizations.

As evident, the threats from terrorism have transcended the territorial boundaries of South Asian states. The phenomenon of globalization, porous borders, free-flowing information, enhanced communication, and increasing trend of migration has facilitated the grounds for cross-border linkages between terrorist groups engaged in fighting insurgent groups. Thus, 'terrorism in South Asia has not only been given a regional character by pan-Islamic fundamentalism but also by the increasing nexus between various terrorist groups in South Asia. Despite differing ideologies and objective goals, groups of various hues have established linkages with each other, creating at times opportunistic alliances. Such alliances help in seeking training, weapons procurement, sharing intelligence and in some cases drug trafficking which is a means of raising much needed resource for the terrorist groups' (Behera, 1991: 15–16). There are creditable reports that Kashmiri terrorists have haa and still have contacts with Khalistani terrorists. The Hizb-ul-Mujahidin had contacts with the Khalistan commando force. Kashmir terrorists have also established links with the ULFA. Initially, ULFA was trained by the Hizb-e-Islami of Gulbuddin Hekmatyar. The ULFA was also trained by the National Socialist Council of Nagaland (NSCN) and subsequently established links with the LTTE as well. The LTTE is believed to have given or sold weapons to the People's War Group (PWG). The Tamil National Liberation Army and the Tamil National Retrieval Troops have been trained by the LTTE and may have possible links with the forest brigand Veerappan, who was killed in a police encounter a few years back. The Maoist guerrillas in Nepal are believed to be getting weapons and training from Naxalite groups in India. There are reports of ISI connections with the LTTE, the LTTE's linkages with the PGW, Bodos, and ULFA in India. The Bodos and ULFA have also established bases within Bhutan. In India's northeast, there are reports of arms and money flowing to Bodo, ULFA, and Naga insurgents through private channels from China through Myanmar. What this points to is that there is a fairly well coordinated networking between various terrorist groups in South Asia. And accessing weapons from the international black market or from like-minded sympathetic groups is not difficult. It needs the right contacts with groups, who control transit points in the gun-running business.

Much more formidable in this increasing networking is the growing nexus between Islamic fundamentalists and the criminal fringe elements in various countries of South Asia. These include the underworld dons of Mumbai, smugglers of Nepal, and the drug mafia in Pakistan. This is a trend that was evident since the liberalization of the economy in India since 1991. Its impact was felt in the Mumbai bomb blasts of March 1993. Organized crime provides an important support base for terrorism by its involvement in arms trafficking, drug trafficking, smuggling, money laundering, kidnappings, extortions, and counterfeiting currency. Some terrorist groups themselves are involved in some of these activities, if not all. The LTTE's ability to raise funds and procure weapons from the international arms black-market is well known (Behera, 1991).

New technologies have transformed the nature, conduct, and reach of terrorist groups. Already terrorist groups in South Asia have started using them. Terrorist groups in Kashmir and the LTTE have been able to access dual technology like GPS, sophisticated communication systems, and computers to enhance their capabilities. The Harkat-ul-Mujahidin and the Lashkar-e-Toiba are known to have an enviable communication system, a publicity cell, and the ability to raise funds through the internet. The LTTE has waged cyber-warfare against Sri Lankan diplomatic missions abroad (Behera, 1991).

While it has to be acknowledged that geopolitical reasons, the globalization process, and advances in technology have given an added impetus to terrorist groups in South Asia, the most significant impetus to terrorism in South Asia has been provided by the strategic objectives of neighbouring countries. Pakistan had been waging a non-conventional covert war against India as a 'low cost option' since 1984, initially in Punjab, then in Kashmir since 1989, and later in other parts of India too. Here one finds a linkage between Pakistan's attainment of nuclear capability in 1987 and its support for cross-border terrorism in Kashmir. Reassured by the inability of India to retaliate by conventional war, it has intensified the level of terrorist violence in Jammu and Kashmir. Pakistan's intelligence agency, the ISI, has evolved an elaborate infrastructure for recruitment, training, and support from the profits of drug trafficking for the terrorists that it infiltrates into Kashmir. This is increasingly being recognized by the international community as well.

The terrorist attacks on the World Trade Centre and the Pentagon in the US on 11 September 2001 resulted in a shift in all geo-political dynamics—international, regional, and local. The extraordinary situation in which it was placed forced the US to co-opt Pakistan—the fountainhead of terrorist activities—into its 'crusade' against global terrorism.

Ironical as it may sound, the prime suspect of the terrorist attack, Osama bin Laden, the most wanted man in the world and the perceived symbol of evil, received his first lessons in the art of clandestine operation and subterfuge from the Central Intelligence Agency (CIA). Bin Laden, the legendary US ally of the 1980s, became a dreaded terrorist of the 1990s and the most privileged guest of the Taliban. The two converted Afghanistan into what a US State Department Report on the 'Patterns of Global Terrorism' called the new epicentre of international terrorism.

Pakistan created and nurtured the Taliban to acquire the much wanted 'strategic depth' vis-à-vis India and Iran. The US was interested in the Taliban as a possible operational asset against Iran and as the facilitator of oil and gas pipelines from Turkmenistan to Pakistan through Afghanistan.

Pakistan as an ally of the US in the war against terrorism was playing a double game—helping the US offensive while trying to ensure that their old Taliban allies have a prominent role in post-war government. General Musharraf had opposed US support to the Northern Alliance. The ISI was playing a double game of pretending to help the US yet allowing the flow of weapons into Afghanistan. In the post-Taliban scenario, General Musharraf has announced his project of restructuring Pakistani society under immense US pressure. However, in reality, one finds that the evidence of close ties Islamabad has had with the Taliban, Bin Laden, and the Al-Qaida, and these three had with terrorist militias like the Lashkar-e-Toiba , JeM, and Harkat-ul-Mujahidin directly and through Pakistan's ISI, destroyed its credibility with the US and other Western countries. Recent developments reveal that Pakistan is replicating its 'bleed thy neighbour' policy in Afghanistan. Egged on by Islamist clerics and ably aided by Pakistan, the Taliban is making inroads in the country. Their return poses a threat to the entire region.

South Asia is the poorest region of the world with approximately 40 per cent of its population continuing to live below the poverty line defined as a per capita income of US$ 1 per day. World Bank Reports on world development indicate that half of South Asia's adult population cannot read or write; public spending on education and health is the lowest in the developing world; girls' enrolment in schools continues to remain significantly low; population growth has put immense and alarming pressures on the environment; some countries have the world's highest deforestation rates; and that South Asian cities are among the most crowded and polluted in the world. This, indeed, is a dismal and bleak picture in the new millennium.

On the economic front, South Asia, composed of poor nations, is confronted with a desperate and continued struggle against widespread pervasive poverty, hunger, illiteracy, malnourishment, industrial and technological underdevelopment, rapidly growing population, and the disastrous impact of environmental degradation. Yet, South Asia offers a glimmer of hope and optimism in spite of daunting and overawing problems. South Asia is regarded as one of the rapidly growing regions of the world with considerable untapped potential. There have been significant achievements in reducing absolute poverty, eradicating endemic diseases, and in feeding the teeming millions who inhabit South Asia. Literacy rates and life expectancy have gone up significantly and money is now being spent in core social sectors. South Asia is well endowed both in human and natural resources and the people are hard working, innovative, and resilient.

While the efforts made by the governments of South Asia to tackle the problems mentioned here are noteworthy and have met with some degree of success, there is no escape from the reality that efforts by individual governments need to be buttressed and supplemented through bilateral and regional cooperation which is indispensable if the process of socio-economic development is to be hastened (Ram, 2002: 23).

In the context of today's world, when cooperation among regional countries is most crucial, South Asia has given regional cooperation within the framework of SAARC at best a low-key position. Even though SAARC has now been in existence for close to 18 years, its member countries have not been able to optimize the benefits of regional cooperation and cooperative efforts. Even as the rest of the world is moving inexorably towards dismantling barriers of suspicion and tension and towards cooperation, South Asian countries, unfortunately, continue to remain messed up in political conflicts and disharmony. The preoccupation of the ruling elites of South Asian countries with outdated conflicts hangs around their necks as so many dead albatrosses. It reflects the tragedy of their inadequate efforts at nation-building. Similarly, Indo-Pakistani animus, experiences of cross-national ethno-political spill-overs across Indo-Sri Lankan and Indo-Nepalese frontiers destabilizes regional peace and retards regional cooperation. In today's changed world situation, it is imperative for South Asia to strive for peace, harmony, progress, and stability. The inevitability and pace of globalization and technological advances leave South Asia no choice other than to evolve cooperative relations if the new challenges have to be met and opportunities fully exploited.

In South Asia, the time has come to let economics dominate politics in the relations among nations. In the context of economic relations, the early implementation of the South Asian Preferential Trade Area (SAPTA) and South Asian Free Trade Area (SAFTA) assumes significance. This is precisely the kind of cooperative effort which is likely to benefit all and have a direct impact on the people to whom the benefits of these arrangements are likely to accrue. Success of such regional cooperative arrangements will, in turn, generate confidence in SAARC and help dispel doubts and reservations.

Economic cooperation in the region is also moving forward along sub-regional interaction as in Bangladesh-Bhutan-India-Nepal

Growth Quadrangle (BBIN-GQ) and Bangladesh-India-Myanmar-Sri Lanka Thailand Economic Cooperation (BIMSTEC). The latter is perceived as the vital land bridge between SAARC and ASEAN. Engagement of strategically important Myanmar as an integral component of the recharged 'look east' policy, construction of the Tamu (Manipur)–Kalemyu (Myanmar) road as part of the highway traversing the Asian landmass, and the announcement of the Ganga–Mekong initiative have an immense regional geo-economic import. Deeper economic linkages with the Central Asian states are an equally important strategic imperative. Cooperation in security along the arc from Central Asia through South Asia onto Southeast Asia and East Asia holds great promise, despite the current geo-political and techno-economic constraints on transportation corridors and pipelines.

Unless SAARC shows demonstrable progress in ameliorating the quality of life of the people of South Asia through meaningful regional cooperation, it would not be able to become an effective instrument of social and economic development of the region. It is imperative for South Asian states to take stock of the cost of conflicts and tensions and of missed opportunities and embark upon an irrevocable course of cooperation and peace and understanding which alone will benefit all the countries of the region. There is need to mend various fault lines, reconcile past differences with future inter-dependence, confront the challenges to progressive and liberal values from terrorism and religious extremism, and cope with social strains caused by unequal development.

South Asia cannot progress without ensuring peace and stability in the region. This is also in the wider interests of the world community as a whole. It is the world's most populous region, with nuclear capabilities. It has the potential of emerging as one of the world's biggest markets for international products, services, and investment. It cannot, therefore, be allowed to remain a festering sore of insurgencies and ethnic conflicts. The forthcoming SAARC summit in Islamabad should be utilized predominantly to promote regional economic integration. It should not degenerate into a comical Indo-Pakistani soap opera. If the European Union is projected as lessons learnt by warring Europeans, it should also be brought into sharp focus in South Asian societies.

Problems arising from a number of other sources—poverty, ethnic conflict, challenge of national disintegration, inter-state conflicts, low-intensity conflict, cross-border terrorism, fear of nuclear war and divergent security perceptions, and the like—demand more immediate attention. In the present conflict-ridden scenario, it is imperative to think of ways and means of initiating and promoting confidence-building measures that can clear the way for regional cooperation and peace. To yield better results, these efforts among states must be supplemented by people-to-people cooperation and the building of civil society initiatives and institutions. The contradictions among forces of nationalism, regionalism, and globalism must be reconciled and complementarities among them enhanced.

Note

1. For idea of 'waves', see S.P. Huntington, *The Third Wave: Democratization in the Late Twentieth Century* (1991).

References

Baral, Lok Raj and Leo E. Rose (1997). 'Democratization and the Crisis of Governance in Nepal', in Subrata K. Mitra and Dietmar Rothermund (eds), *Legitimacy and Conflict in South Asia*, pp. 208. New Delhi: Manohar.

Baral, Lok Raj (2002). 'Nepal in 2001: The Strained Monarchy', *Asian Survey*, 62(1): 198–203.

Behera, Ajay Darshan (1991). 'Looming Danger of Terrorism in South Asia', *World Focus*, 14 March.

Bodansky, Yossef (1998). 'Pakistan, Kashmir and Trans-Asian Axis', *Indian Defence Review*, October–December, pp. 66–80.

Bottomore, T.B. (1972). *Sociology*. New York: Vintage Books.

Cooper, Kenneth J. (1996). 'A Kalashnikov Culture', *Washington Post*, 14 March.

De Silva, K.M. (ed.) (1993). *Sri Lanka: The Problems of Governance*. New Delhi: Konark.

———— (2000). 'Working of Democracy in South Asia', in V.A. Pai Panandikar (ed.), *Problems of Governance in South Asia*, pp. 47–48. New Delhi: Konark.

Haq, Iqramul (1991). *Pakistan: From Hash to Heroin*. Lahore: Anoor Publishers.

Human Development Report in South Asia, 1999 (Karachi: Mahabub Ul Haq, Human Development Centre, 1999), pp. 12–13

Huntington, S.P. (1991). *The Third Wave: Democratization in the Late Twentieth Century*. Norman and London: University of Oklahoma Press.

Kak, Kapil (2000). 'Geo-Strategic Realities of South Asia', *World Focus*, 25052: 9.

Kartha, Tara (1995). 'Southern Asia: Narcotics and Weapon Linkages', in Jasjit Singh (ed.), *Light Weapons and International Security*. New Delhi: Pugwash Society and IDSA.

Kartha, Tara (1999). *Tools of Terror: Light Weapons and India's Security*. New Delhi: Knowledge World IDSA.
Kothari, Rajni (1970). *Politics in India*. New Delhi: Orient Longman.
Kramer, Karl-Heinz (2003). 'Nepal in 2002: Emergency and Resurrection of Royal Power', *Asian Survey*, 63(1): 208–14.
Kumar, Satish (2000). 'Militant Islam: The Nemesis of Pakistan', *Aakrosh*, 3(6) (January 2000), reproduced in *Strategic Digest*, 30(8): 1080.
Muni, S.D. (2000). 'South Asia: The Challenge of the Millennium', *World Focus*, 250–251–252 (October–November–December): 6, 7 and 15.
———— (2003). *Maoist Insurgency in Nepal: The Challenges and the Response*. New Delhi: Rupa and Co.
———— (2006). 'South Asia: The Challenge of the Millennium', *World Focus*, 250–52: 6.
Ram, A.N. (2002). 'SAARC-Missed Opportunities', in *World Focus*, 250–52: 23.
The Times of India (New Delhi), 29 November 2003, Interview with Ashis Nandy.
World Bank (2001). *World Development Report 2000/2001: Attacking Poverty*. New York: Oxford University Press.

1

Multicultural Identity and Democracy in India

Mahendra Prasad Singh

My purpose in this chapter is to discuss the nature of the twin-born phenomenon of nationalism and democracy in India. Both are axial values of Indian modernity. Despite partaking in the universal phenomenon of nationalism, its Indian version has some distinctively national and mixed (Western) genealogies. Despite its horrendous undemocratic potentialities, Indian nationalism is, in my understanding, by and large, a democratic phenomenon. My argument is that civic Indian nationalism and federal democratic constitutionalism are not only historically constitutive of each other, but also mutually sustaining in their contemporary complex dynamics. Indian civic nationalism, in my understanding, is predicated on the all-inclusive imagined Indian national community, accommodating multicultural cleavages cohabiting within the territorial boundaries of the Republic of India.

Evolutionary Trajectory

Indian nationalism is agglomerative in its inclusionary cultural foundations (Kurve as quoted in Kothari, 1970). This composite cultural formation is an evolutionary by product of the structures of Indian subcontinental geography and history. The natural physical boundaries of this landmass surrounded by the Himalayas and the oceans served as a territorial template for a kind of socio-cultural formation marked by an overarching unity in diversity that made possible shared destinies of an admixtures of races and linguistic and religious communities, both indigenous and migrants, and also aggressors from the Mediteranean, Central Asia, Mongolia, Persia, Arabia, and Europe. All major world religions and indigenous animistic faiths and four major and minor linguistic families—Indo-European, Dravidian, Tibeto-Burman, and local tribal tongues—are present even in the divided India. The nature of this subcontinental culture causes the suffix Indo- to such cultural constructions as Indo-Islamic sects and Indo-European linguistic family to which Sanskrit belongs (Ahmad, 1999: Part 2; Katzner, 2002: Part I and III).

Given this cultural crucible, it is hardly surprising that the ruling elites in South Asia were animated by ambitions of subcontinental state power, especially during the periods of the states founded by the Mauryas around the 3rd and 2nd centuries BCE, the Mughals in the 16th and 17th centuries CE, and the British in the mid-18th to mid-20th centuries. Larger regional kingdoms like those founded by the Guptas, Harshvardhan, sultans of Delhi, Vijayanagara rayas, Marathas, etc., were also propelled, if less successfully, by similar designs of subcontinental political power (Singh, 1994, 1995).

Given also the wide scatter of religious, Bhakti, and Sufi shrines throughout the subcontinent, the mass culture was also pretty subcontinental in scope. Both Bhakti and Sufi saints belonged to heterodox Hindu and Islamic systems of socio-religious thoughts and practice respectively. Bhakti and Sufi saints, for example, wrote and preached in the prevalent language of the people rather than in Sanskrit or Persian. They also tended to reject caste and religious differences in the society of their respective regions of the subcontinent. The linguistic connectivity was facilitated in the subcontinent by Sanskrit, Pali/Prakrit, Persian, and Hindi/Urdu (Dinkar, 1962).

With the advent of British rule, English, like Sanskrit and Persian in the past, became the language of the all-India elite. Urdu/Hindi, what Mahatma Gandhi called Hindustani and advocated for adoption as the lingua franca of the emergent Indian nation, started its uphill task to transform its early existence as the language of the mass public sphere—army, market, media, and popular communication. The Constituent Assembly of India adopted Hindi in *Devnagari* script and English as the official languages of the Union of India. Fifteen years thence, Hindi was to become the sole official language, but this switchover was stalled by protests interspersed with violence, especially in Tamil Nadu, in 1965. Under the improvised Nehru formula, English was allowed to continue indefinitely until Hindi was consensually accepted as the sole official language of the Union. By the three-language formula, the states agreed to promote English, Hindi, and the regional language of the state concerned. With patchy implementation the status quo seems to be continuing indefinitely (Nair, 2002).[1]

Besides the foregoing aggregative notion of Indian nationalism, there is the related constructivist or emergent view of it, whereby it is more than a mere sum total of its parts. To quote Amartya Sen (2005: 356):

> The inclusionary view of Indian identity, which we have inherited and which I have tried to defend, is not only not parasitic on, or partial to, a Hindu identity, it can hardly be a federation of the different religious communities in India: Hindu, Muslim, Sikh, Christian, Jain, Parsee and others. Indian identity need not be mediated through other group identities in a federal way. Indeed, India is not, in this view, sensibly seen even as a federal combination of different communities.

Sen here also slips from the plane of rhetoric to the plane of philosophy of 'being' and 'becoming'. He seems to reject the idea of the absolute other and step on the idea of inclusionary difference where difference could be the third space between the same and the other.[2]

Sen's point is well made and would appear to have empirical validity as well as theoretical fruitfulness both as an instrument of interpreting the rational in Indian history and of reconstructing India's 'Tryst with Destiny'. This is particularly pertinent and topical at a time when the rise of identity politics worldwide after the universalist ideological ambience of the post-World War II and Cold War years has drawn attention from 'economic harms' to 'cultural harms'. This has brought forward the phenomenon of 'the widespread decoupling of cultural politics from social politics, of the politics of difference from the politics of equality'; and it casts upon us the task 'to devise an expanded conception of justice that can accommodate both defensible claims for social equality and defensible claims for the recognition of difference'.[3]

Amartya Sen rejects the notion that Indian identity must always have a presumptuous dominant strand or a self-same static identity. In an interesting review of Sen's book, Ramachandra Guha discerns at least four multiple elements in Sen's own identity on display in this work:

> First, there is the *Bengali cosmopolitan,* the product of an intellectual culture that while deeply rooted in its language and region, has yet had the longest and most sustained exposure to the winds—not all noxious—blowing in from the west. Second, there is the *Indian liberal,* his consciousness shaped by the transition from colonialism to nationhood, the firm upholder of the freedom and integrity of an independent India, yet one who refuses to reduce the nation or nationhood to a single cultural or religious essence. Third, there is the *left-wing democrat*, who deplores inequalities of all kinds—but of class and gender especially—yet believes that in shaping a more just word 'what is really needed is a more vigorous practice of democracy, rather than an absence of it'. Fourth, there is the *broad minded economist*, who knows his theory, yet insists in locating economic actors and institutions in their social and historical context.[4]

Nationalism in India first emerged along with democratic aspirations in British India in the 19th century among the English-educated new professional middle classes. A feeling of precursive Indian nationalism was sparked in the rebellion of the sepoys of the East India Company, some dispossessed Indian ruling elites, and jagirdars/zamindars in 1857 against the British. But it was a spontaneous and ill-organized moribund kick of the old feudal order about to be subdued again, and slowly but surely to be transformed partly by the takeover of India by the British Crown and more fully by the post-colonial Indian state. It was only a step ahead, towards emerging Indian nationhood, following the rise of the Marathas, Sikhs, Jats, Afghans, etc., against the tottering Mughal state in the 18th century, that could neither herald the departure from feudalism nor the birth of democratic nationalism. It may also be conceded that what Canadians call First Nations—a term for their aboriginal tribes—has existed in India right from the earliest recorded history. But nationalism as an ideology is a modern phenomenon in India. It was a product of the emergence of print capitalism in British India. Far from being a discovery,

Indian nationalism is an imagined and invented political community by the English-educated new middle classes and the classes of bourgeoisie and politically mobilized peasants and workers. Niharranjan Ray perceptively observes:

> Since India had never experienced what is called a mercantile economy in the Western sense of the term, and since in a colonial situation she was not destined to experience an industrial social economy, she had no other means to evolve a national *bourgeoisie*, again in the western sense of the term, except by bringing into being a professional, city-oriented and English-educated middle class which alone could be the harbinger of the modern ideology of nationalism (Ray, 1973: 2).

A characterization of nationalism as ethnic/cultural or civic in terms of dichotomous categories would be superficial and erroneous in the Indian context. The phenomenon of nationalism in India is more complex and needs to be understood on its own ground and in its own terms. It lacks the passion of tribal primordialism and ethnic fundamentalism of the nationalism of either the religious or linguistic type. It is existentially and discursively rational, and to an extent passive, yet very real. There are reasons for these patterns. Hinduism is not a religion in the same sense as Christianity, Judaism, and Islam. The term Hindustan, from which India is linguistically derived, etymologically originated from *Sindhu* or Indus. It is a geographical rather than an ethnic term and was originally used by foreigners for the people living around and beyond the river. The territorial name Sindh also originates from the river's name. To say this is not to say that external attribution and internal identification have not produced a Hindu religious identity today. Nor is it to say that there is no attempt at revivalism and fundamentalization of Hindu identity on the part of the *Sangh Parivar*.[5] However, the 'oceanic circles' consciousness of Hinduism has been inherently accommodative, and Hindu communalism is, at least in large parts, reactive and it suffers from the complex of 'minority syndrome' despite its apparent demographic majority.

Indian nationalism as an ideology is generally supposed to be a product of the 19th-century India, and Indian parliamentary federation and constitutionalism are products of the 20th century. To be sure, terms like *rashtra*, *sabhas*, *samitis*, *ganasanghas*, etc., can be traced back to the Vedas and *Suttas*, the Ramayana and the Mahabharata, yet it makes social science conceptual and theoretical sense to agree with Lord Meghnad Desai when he observes 'I don't believe that democracy is rooted in Indian culture or any culture for that matter. It is a modern phenomenon that we learnt under the foreign rule.... Democracy is not merely formal procedures of parliamentary behaviour and the practice of election. But it has to be that at least before it can be anything else.'[6]

The Indian nation was born in democracy, or, more accurately, in the desire for participation in British colonial administration that graduated to the desire for democracy and national freedom. The Indian nation was first born in the regions—Bengal, Bombay, and Madras coastal areas in British India—and gradually enveloped the hinterland that critically and creatively responded to and appropriated—and were appropriated by—what came to be known as Indian nationalism. The nation, to be sure, was not writing on a *tabula rasa*. There was a sense of multi-regional and multicultural shared civilizational destiny produced by the subcontinental geographical template and *long duree* historical experience. These two conditioning factors had produced sovereignty cults of *chakravarti* kingship, Kautilya's *dharmanyaya* of the state (distinct from various shastric *nyayas*), Ashoka's *dhamma*, Mughal *sulah-i-kul*, Maratha *ajnapatra*, British *paramountcy*, which eventually culminated in the Indian nation-state constructed in the Indian Constitution of 1950.[7]

Even though the contemporary Indian nation-state is a modern phenomenon, its cultural and structural roots go back far into the past and have had a more or less subcontinental spatial spread. Its antecedent composite cultural catalytic formation is suggestively sketched out by the Hindi poet Ramdhari Singh Dinkar as a product of four 'cultural revolutions' and acculturative tendencies: (*a*) Aryan-Dravidian (Mongoloid) racial aggregations and admixtures and Indo-European/Dravidian/(Tibeto-Burman) linguistic agglomerations and transitions; (*b*) Vedic or Brahmanical foundational worldview and Jain, Buddhist, Bhakti, Sikh, Sufi, and a variety of neo-Hindu reform movements; (*c*) Hindu–Muslim encounter, coexistence, and osmosis; and (*d*) Indo-European contact and British colonial conquest of India. The vast panoramic overview of Dinkar's historiography of India's composite culture verges on a kind of Darwinist evolutionism. The idea of India of Dinkar's imagination is reminiscent of the American 'melting pot' model of assimilative nationalism. However, the Indian national culture appears to be nearer to the 'vertical mosaic' model of Canadian multicultural nationalism. For focusing on the areas of overlap and transitions on the margins, Dinkar glosses over the internal zones of primordial groups that are keen to preserve their distinct identities while they share in the common cultural matrix. In this context, Gurpreet Mahajan (2002) suggests a useful distinction between pluralism and multiculturalism: the former is 'simultaneous presence of many cultures and communities within the same social space', 'while the latter' is concerned with the issue of 'equality', asking 'whether the different communities, living peacefully together, coexist as equals in the public arena'.

Like pluralities of communities existing in the same social and geographical space, Indian history is also marked by the simultaneous presence of pluralities of states in the same territorial space through much of the time. But in all periods one among many of the regional states had greater pretension of being a higher species state, either in terms of good or a great state—Rama's Ayodhya and Yudhistir's Indraprastha in the epics Ramayana and Mahabharata, Mauryan Magadha in the post-Vedic period, Chandragupta's and Samudragupta's Magadha and Harsha's Thaneshwar in the post-Gupta period, the Delhi Sultanate, Vijayanagara, and Mughal states in pre-Mughal and Mughal India, and the British Raj in the colonial period.

The role of the ideal state of contemporary India and its assets could, in the words of India's leading scholar administrator, B.P. Singh (2000), be summarily described as follows:

> First, there is the ancient past that we have inherited, both in respect of social forms and structures and the general heritage of arts, sciences, technology and education. The second is our recent past and the emerging pattern of the future wherein we have made enormous progress both in socio-economic and in political fields. And the third is our administration which has provided the necessary infrastructure and is the implementation machinery for bringing about economic growth with social justice.

In modern India, nationalism (Benedict Andreson's 'imagined community'),[8] the *nation* and the independent new *state* appeared on the horizon together. There was no lag between the national community and the projected state. Both remained in the making in British India and were born together in 1947. Probably the first Indian nationalist organization, a precursor of the Indian National Congress, the *locus classicus* of Indian nationalism, was the Indian Association established on 26 July 1876 in Calcutta, earlier mooted as the Bengal Association. Surendranath Banerjea, among the leading founders, later reminisced that the provincial nomenclature was ruled out:

> ...for the idea that was working in our minds was that the Association was to be the centre of an all–India movement. For even then the concept of a united India, derived from the inspiration of Mazzini, or, at any rate, of bringing all India upon the same platform, had taken firm possession of the minds of Indian leaders in Bengal (Banerjea, 1925, reprinted 1963: 38).

The first proto-nationalist campaign was launched when an important meeting was held on 24 March 1877 in Calcutta which appointed Banerjea a special delegate to visit different provinces of British India to canvass an association and civil service reforms facilitating entry of Indians in administration. The same year and the following, Banerjea travelled by the newly constructed railways and other modes of transport through upper India from Calcutta to Lahore and to western and southern India through Bombay to Madras (ibid.: 37–51). The Indian proto-nationalist idea and action took firmer structural roots with the founding session of the Indian National Congress chaired by Alan Octavian Hume in December 1885. This nationalist idea graduated through Moderate and Extremist phases and can be said to have acquired mass nationalist-oriented overtones by the time of the Swadeshi movement in Bengal in the first decade of the 20th century and a fuller articulation of Swaraj, in the sense of political liberation from British colonial rule, by the second and third decades of the 20th century coinciding with the Gandhi–Nehru era in the history of the Indian National Congress.

Despite the colonial context of the rise of nationalism in India, I find Partha Chatterjee's argument of it largely, if not entirely, being a 'derivative discourse' and lacking in free will a bit Orientalist and parochial. Chatterjee distances himself both from the Andersonian idea of nationalism as a universal phenomenon as well as from any argument of distinctively uniquely Indian flavour to its brand of nationalism, excepting probably some elements in

Gandhi.[9] I would take up cudgels with Chatterjee, both on the assumptions of certain elements of uniqueness of cultures and on the philosophical objection to empirical foreclosure of future possibilities—historical and evolutionary.

Staying, for the time being, within the four walls of Indian history, I find the 19th century conceptualization of the Indian national community a great and grand innovation. In the past, ethnic identities/nationalities existed apart from the state and had only two common foci: the ruler (*raja*) and the territory (*janapada/rashtra*). The rulers often changed and so did the territories in the sense of expanding or shrinking. Indian nationalism would appear to be a relatively new cultural and ideological construct that fused the new national consciousness, territory, and state into one ('We, the people of India, having solemnly resolved to constitute India into a sovereign, socialist, secular, democratic republic...').[10]

It was thus that the Indian nation-state was born in 1947. The birth of this entity was the product of the legal transfer of power from the British Parliament to the Constituent Assembly of India elected in 1946 by provincial legislatures, which were themselves elected in 1936 on the basis of nearly 25 per cent of franchise premised on educational and property qualifications under the Government of India Act, 1935.

In typical Western, particularly European, understanding, the nation precedes the state and attains a fuller realization in the state. In modern Indian history, the state preceded the nation, which in some ways is still in the making. That is why any observer who is inclined to make a declaration that Indian nationalism has turned the corner on its unity and integrity must look over one's shoulders in agonizing reappraisal. In a way of saying, it seems to be India's destiny, not only in this area, but many other areas, to be perennially on the threshold of arrival: about to reach there, but not quite there.

The blueprint of the foregoing idea of Indian nationalism, which may well be called primarily the civic-territorial one,[11] was forged during the anti-colonial freedom struggle fought on the nationalist platform put together by the Indian National Congress, which, before becoming the ruling party in independent India, was a confluence of a variety of ideological tendencies, factions, and organizations. The only organizations that remained largely irreconcilably outside its pale of influence and aggregation were the

Muslim League and the Justice Party/Dravida Kazhagam. Despite this relative failure, the Congress always had a big Muslim and Tamilian non-Brahman following.

The most fully grown statement of the ideology of Indian nationhood is, of course, the Constitution drafted and adopted, after a nationwide debate in provincial legislatures, premiers' conferences, press, and the intelligentsia, by the Constituent Assembly of India (December 1946–November 1949). The most significant pre-1950 programmatic and ideological charter was the Karachi Resolution of the Indian National Congress (1931) that clearly presaged the 1950 constitutional charters of Fundamental Rights and Directive Principles of State Policy that envision a liberal democratic and welfare state. Similarly, the penultimate pre-Independence blueprint of dominion federalism on the pattern of the white Commonwealth under the British Crown was presented in the Motilal Nehru Committee Report (1928). The federal-provincial division of governmental powers and responsibilities outlined in this document bear striking resemblance to the pattern finally settled in the 1950 constitution, going beyond the feeble federal scheme under the Government of India Act, 1935.[12]

Contemporary Dimension

In the context of the relationship between nationalism and constitutional democracy (or constitutionalism, in short) in India—broadly used as a label term for an elected government limited by the rule of law and institutional checks and balances, and wedded to socio-economic transformation by legislation—the most difficult horn of the dilemma that it has been India's fate to be confronted with relates to the relationship between state and religion. The discussion that follows here is limited to the secular dimension of Indian constitutionalism and its symbiotic relationship with Indian nationalism.

It is important to keep in mind that the Indian approach to the problem of the relationship between politics and religion appears to be unique. That may be the reason why the framers of the Constitution avoided using the word 'secular'. For the state in India is neither *de jure* secular, as is the case in the United States of America (USA) and in France, nor is it *de facto* secular as is the case in the

United Kingdom. Following the War of Independence in America and the Revolution in France, a wall of separation was put up between the state and religion. The Anglican Church of England is the state church of the United Kingdom, yet the British state is non-discriminatory to all its subjects for all practical purposes. What has come to be known as secularism (*panthnirpekshata*) in India is characterized by constitutionally mandated equal respect for all religions on the part of the state (*sarvodharma samabhava*), individual freedom of religion, cultural, and educational rights for religious minorities, and prohibition on taxation for religious purposes. Yet, the state is not constitutionally barred from legislating on religious reforms, management of religious shrines and their estates and property. In fact, the Directive Principles of State Policy expect the state in India to strive for a common civil code for all Indians irrespective of religious affiliations.[13]

The threat to secular public policies of the Indian state and minority rights of citizens surfaced in a big way by the 1990s when the Hindu right Bharatiya Janata Party (BJP) gradually gathered electoral momentum in the wake of the party's emotive Somnath to Ayodhya *rathayatra* that triggered the so-called Ayodhya movement, agitating for the construction of a Ramamandir in Ayodhya at the site of the Babri Masjid there, alleged to have been built by Mir Baqui, a Babar general, after destroying the temple on Ram's supposed birthplace. The mosque was demolished by a frenzied Hindu mob in the presence of some top BJP leaders on 6 December 1992. At the time a BJP government happened to be in power in Uttar Pradesh (UP) and a Congress minority government headed by P.V. Narasimha Rao was in power in the centre. New Delhi dismissed the BJP governments in UP, Madhya Pradesh, Rajasthan, and Himachal Pradesh on the plea that the constitutional machinery in UP had broken down and BJP governments in the rest of the Hindi belt also needed to go in the interest of effective implementation of the ban on some Hindu (and Muslim) communal organizations clamped in the trail of the demolition of the disputed structure in Ayodhya.

Since then BJP governments have come and gone in several states in northern and western India, including the BJP-led National Democratic Alliance (NDA) government headed by Atal Behari Vajpayee (1998–2004) in New Delhi. Several policies of these governments have been often decried as motivated by *'Hinduization'* of the Indian state. The secular character of the state, however, has not suffered a complete collapse. This may be explained by the fact that democracy and constitutionalism are no longer a mere top-dressing on Indian soil; they have taken deep, though not unshakable, roots. It is notable that even the Hindu right BJP does not formally question secularism as such. Instead, it has attacked what it calls 'pseudo-secularism' or 'minority-ism' of the Congress and some other parties, now mainly from the left-wing. This may presumably be so due to the fact that the party did not come to power on its own anywhere, except in UP earlier and Gujarat later, until before the general elections in the summer of 2004. It is also notable that its stint in government in these two states was marked by the demolition of the Babri Mosque in Ayodhya City in the district of Faizabad in 1992 in UP and a communal bloodbath in 2002, reminiscent of the comprehensive rioting around the time of India's Partition, in Gujarat. In the elections held immediately after these catastrophic events, the BJP lost in UP, including in the city of Ayodhya itself, and won a triple back-to-back majority in Gujarat. Ironically, UP is economically backward and Gujarat, economically dynamic! Interestingly, the former happens to be the home-state of Nehru, the architect of the Indian state, and Gujarat, is the home-state of Gandhi, the father of the Indian nation.

BJP governments in other states and in New Delhi before 2004 have ruled at the helm of coalition governments in partnership with some secular and communal parties, both regional and national. Secular partners of these governments have generally acted as restraints on the Hindutva agenda of the BJP. For example, when the NDA agreed to work under BJP's leadership in the coalition governments in New Delhi between 1998 and 2004, before being replaced by the Congress-led United Progressive Alliance government in 2004, the Hindu right party acquiesced to dropping the issues of constructing a Ram Temple at the site of the demolished mosque, legislating a common civil code for all Indians irrespective of religious differences, and amending the constitution to drop the special status article relating to the state of Jammu and Kashmir. The agenda of the 'Hinduization' of education by the BJP Union human resource development minister, Murali Manohar Joshi, was also sought to be resisted by the non-BJP-ruled states in inter-governmental federal forums. Conversely, non-BJP partners in the NDA ruling in New Delhi sought to dampen, to the extent possible, the aggressive Hindutva agenda of BJP state governments by pulling the strings of federal levers of power against the latter. The real threat to civic nationalism and secular state in the country can come only in the event of a complete collapse of civil society as a result of corruption/criminality/terrorism/recurrent rioting, and a capture of state power by Hindu and other communal parties in New Delhi and India's major states. By present reckoning, this would appear to be largely unlikely. This is because the Indian National Congress is back at the helm of parliamentary federal coalitional power with the support of the left following the May 2004 Lok Sabha elections. The Congress and the left rode back to power in the 2004 Lok Sabha polls in a critical and realigning election in which minorities, rural, and Scheduled Caste/ Tribe voters generally voted against the Hindu right party and its allies in the NDA (Singh and Saxena, 2005: 52–79). Additionally, the five BJP state governments in saddle in Gujarat, Rajasthan, Madhya Pradesh, Chhattisgarh, and Jharkhand not only fought the 2005 general elections on a developmental agenda (*bijli, sadak, pani* [electricity, roads and water]), but also appear circumspect in avoiding stirring patently communal issues. The BJP national president, L.K. Advani, during a visit to Pakistan during the summer of 2005 made appreciative allusions to Jinnah's 11 August 1947 speech in the Constituent Assembly of that country conjuring up a rainbow coalition of religious and ethnic minorities (obliquely directed at apprehended Punjabi domination in the newly created state) and described him as an essentially a secular leader who apparently used a communal strategy as a tactic to win a separate homeland for Muslims after British withdrawal from India.[14]

It augurs well for the continued existence of India's 'Sovereign Socialist Secular Democratic Republic' that opposition to these constitutional values is not condensed enough to precipitate their imminent fall. India's strategic interests and classes and communities have developed vital stakes in the continued governance and management of institutions of the state, market, and civil society against internal breakdowns and external subversive and terrorist threats. India's determined pursuit of political democracy and socio-economic development simultaneously, rather than one at the cost of the other, by and large, has paid off. The international community in the post-Cold War scenario, especially after 9/11 and 7/7, has also become somewhat more conducive to India's 'Tryst with Destiny' as a democratic developmental state and multicultural society, earlier with socialistic pretensions and since 1990s with neo-liberal economic reforms in a more globalizing world.

In addition, in my view, democracy is a necessary, if not sufficient, condition for the survival of Indian nationalism. Additionally, it is also important that the nature of this democracy remains *more* parliamentary and *more* federal than it has mostly been in the past, especially in the 1970s. A collective cabinet system in a parliamentary federal framework is functionally more suitable than a presidential federal executive in the American mode here. This is so, I think, both to ward off authoritarian potential of elite and mass political cultures of India, and to ensure collegial representation to the wide and complex social and regional diversities in legislative and executive organs of the pluralist and federalist Indian political system. Significantly, there was a time when the plea for national integration was made from the centre and was less effective, at times even counterproductive. Today, in the era of greater pluralization and federalization of Indian politics, especially since the 1990s, the banner of national unity and integrity is being carried jointly by national and regional parties ruling in states and in federal coalition governments in New Delhi. India, federalizing and regionalizing within and globalizing and regionalizing externally, is adjusting to a brave new world. In the opening decade of the 21st century, India stands on the threshold of immense possibilities and challenges, a continued 'Tryst with Destiny' of glory and burden which Jawaharlal Nehru invoked at the midnight hour in the Constituent Assembly of India on 15 August 1947.[15]

Nevertheless, one of the ironies of nationalism and democracy in the age of capitalist globalization is that in the inevitable contradictions of the forces of nationalism, regionalism, and globalism, democracy must fight with its back to the wall against ascendant capitalism, and, especially in the context of South Asia, against globalism. The twin factors of the legacy of the Indo-Pak conflict and the relatively more developed Indian economy being surrounded by more backward economies in the region, coupled with geopolitical global and regional security complications—together account for the fact that South Asia today is more globalized than regionally integrated in economic and security terms. For these reasons, nation-states in South Asia, at least India, Pakistan, and Sri Lanka, present the spectacle of being 'national security states' to come to terms with external as well as internal challenges to their existence. Thus, the impact of globalization in terms of reducing the sovereign pretensions of the nation-states and increasing the importance of provincial and local governments, often dubbed in a compound term as 'glocalization' (globalization + localization), is somewhat muted in South Asia.

Notes

1. Rukmini Bhaya Nair remarks that 'a linguistic subject [in India] must translate herself into different registers under the aegis of the three language formula—a "core" self-symbolized by her mother tongue, a "national" self represented by Hindi or some other link language by English or another "library" language'. It is time that such an idealistic arrangement is made more representative in democratic, for in real life, the educational situation is both gravely unjust and terribly complicated. 'Even so, it would be hard to deny the availability of rich linguistic opportunities for the representation of self in everyday life. On this translation is not an arcane academic specialty for her but a "sociological compulsion".' See the Introduction to her edited work *Translation, Text and Theory: The Paradigm of India* (New Delhi: Sage Publications, 2002), pp. 17–18.
2. My comment on Sen's formulation here is indebted to the insight gleaned from Scott Lass and Mike Featherstone, 'Recognition and Difference: Politics, Identity, Multiculture' in their edited volume of the same title (2002: 8).
3. See Nancy Fraser, 'Recognition without Ethics?' in Scott Lass and Mike Featherstone (2002: 21–22).
4. Ramachandra Guha (2005: 4420)

   A somewhat disembodied-statist sans nationalist-idea of India as contrasted with that of Pakistan, may be sampled in Sunil Khilnani (1997). In a similar Nehruvian vein, Tarun Tejpal writes: 'The idea of India was based not on religion, not on commerce, not on race, not on language. It was set on the plane of a deeply shared culture and history, and built by the brick and mortar of the great ideas of modernity-equality, liberty, justice.' Tarun Tejpal (2006: 3).
5. A common name for a slew of Hindu-oriented political and cultural organizations like the Rashtriya Swayamsevak Sangh, Bharatiya Janata Party, and the Vishva Hindu Parishad.
6. See 'The Art of the Essayist' Anuj Kumar in conversation with Lord Meghnad Desai', *The Hindu, Metroplus*, Delhi, 24 September 2005: 1.
7. On *Chakravartin* and Kautilya's *dharmanyaya* of the state, and Ashoka's *dhamma*, see Romila Thapar (1997) new revised edition with Afterword, Bibliography, and Index; on Mughal *sulah-i-kul* see Douglas Strewsand (1989), on Maratha *ajnapatra*, see Andrew Wink (1956), on the paramountacy of the British Crown, see Barbara Ramusack (2004).

8. Benedict Anderson's theory of rise of nationalism in Europe is of interest here from the perspective of comparative history: 'At bottom, it is likely that the esotericization of Latin, the Reformation, and the haphazard development of administrative vernaculars are significant, in the present context, primarily is a negative sense—in their contributions to the dethronement of Latin.... What in a positive sense, made the new communities imaginable was a half-fortuitous, but explosive, interaction between a system of production and productive relation [capitalism], a technology of communications [print], and the fatality of human linguistic diversity.' See Anderson (1991: 42–43).
9. Partha Chatterjee, *Nationalist Thought and the Colonial World: A Derivative Discourse?* (Chatterjee, 1986) The question mark in the title of this book dissolves in his *The Nation and its Fragments: Colonial and Postcolonial Histories* (Chatterjee, 1995: see especially p. 5).
10. Preamble to the Constitution of India.
11. On 'ethnic' and 'civic' nationalisms, see Anthony D. Smith (2001: 39–42).
12. All Parties Conference, Bombay, 1928, President Dr M.A. Ansari, published by General Secretary, All India Congress Committee, Allahabad, 1928. Signed by the Chairman Shri Motilal Nehru, Allahabad, 10 August 1928.
13. A common criminal code was already first codified by the British Indian state in the mid-19th century.
14. 'We should begin to work in that spirit and in course of time all these angularities of the majority community—the Hindu Community and the Muslim Community—because even as regards Muslims, you have Pathans, Punjabies, Shias, Sunnis and so on, among the Hindus you have Brahmins, Vishavanites, Khatris, also Bengalis, Madrasis and so on will vanish... you are free, you are free to go to your temples. You are free to go to your mosques or any other place of worship in this State of Pakistan. You may belong to any religion or caste or creed—that has nothing to do with the business of the State.' Quoted from Kalim Bahadur's chapter in Pandav Nayak (ed.), *Pakistan: Society and Politics* (1984: 32).
15. Honourable Pandit Jawaharlal Nehru (UP: general seat) speaking on the motion regarding pledge by members at the midnight hour on 14 August 1947. *Constituent Assembly Debates*, Book No. 1 (1999: 3–5).

References

Ahmad, Aziz (1999). *Studies in Islamic Culture in the Indian Environment*. New Delhi: Oxford University Press.

Anderson, Benedict (1991). *Imagined Communities: Reflections on the Origin and Spread of Nationalism*. London & New York: Verso.

Bahadur, Kalim (1984). 'Problems in the Evolution of a Constitutional Framework for Pakistan', in Pandav Nayak (ed.), *Pakistan: Society and Politics*. New Delhi: South Asian Publishers.

Banerjea, Surendranath (1925). *A Nation in Making: Being the Reminiscences of Fifty Years of Public Life*. Bombay: Oxford University Press, Reset and reprinted in 1963.

Chatterjee, Partha (1986). *Nationalist Thought and the Colonial World: A Derivative Discourse?* London: Zed Books for the United Nations University.

———— (1995). *The Nation and its Fragments: Colonial and Postcolonial Histories*. New Delhi: Oxford University Press.

Constituent Assembly Debates (1999). Book No. 1. New Delhi: Lok Sabha Secretariat, 3rd reprint.

Dev, Arjun, Indira Dev and Supta Das Gupta (eds) (1996). *Human Rights: A Source Book*. New Delhi: National Council of Education Research & Training.

Dinkar, Ramdhari Singh (1962). *Sanskriti Ke Char Adhyaya*, 2nd edn, (Foreword by Jawaharlal Nehru). Patna: Udayachal.

Fraser, Nancy (2002). 'Recognition without Ethics?', in Scott Lass and Mike Featherstone (eds), *Recognition & Difference: Politics, Identity, Multiculture*. London: Sage Publications.

Guha, Ramachandra (2005). 'Reviews: Arguments with Sen: Arguments about India', *Economic and Political Weekly*, 40 (41), 8–14 October 2005: 4420.

Katzner, Kenneth (2002). *The Languages of the World*, 3rd edn, London and New York: Routledge.

Khilnani, Sunil (1997). *The Idea of India*. New York: Farrar Straus Giroux.

Kothari, Rajni (1970). *Politics in India*. Boston: Little, Brown & Co.

Kumar, Anju (2005). '"The Art of the Essayist" Anuj Kumar in conversation with Lord Meghnad Desai', *The Hindu, Metroplus*, Delhi, 24 September 2005: 1.

Mahajan, Gurpreet (2002). *The Multicultural Path: Issues of Diversity and Discrimination in Democracy*. New Delhi: Sage Publications.

Nair, Rukmini Bhaya (2002). *Translation, Text and Theory: The Paradigm of India*. New Delhi: Sage Publications.

Preamble to the Constitution of India.

Ramusack, Barbara (2004). *The Indian Princes and Their States*. Cambridge: Cambridge University Press.

Ray, Niharranjan (1973). *Nationalism in India*. Aligarh: Aligarh Muslim University.

Sen, Amartya (2005). *The Argumentative Indian: Writings on Indian History, Culture and Identity*. London: Allen Lane/Penguin Group.

Singh, B.P. (2000). *India's Culture: The State, the Arts and Beyond*. New Delhi: Oxford University Press.

Singh, M.P. (1995). 'Indian State: Historical Context and Change', *The Indian Historical Review*, 21(1–2), July 1994 and January 1995.

Singh, M.P. and Rekha Saxena (2005). 'Lok Sabha Elections 2004: Change with Continuity', *Think India's Quarterly*, 8(1), January–March 2005: 52–79.

Smith, Anthony D. (2001). *Nationalism: Theory, Ideology, History*. Cambridge: Polity Press.

Strewsand, Douglas (1989). *The Formation of the Mughal Empire*. New Delhi: Oxford University Press.

Tejpal, Tarun (2006). 'Pakistan and the Idea of India', *Tehelka: The People's Paper*, 3(31), 12 August 2006: 3.

Thapar, Romila (1997). *Asoka and the Decline of the Mauryas*. New Delhi: Oxford University Press.

Wink, Andrew (1956). *Land and Sovereignty in India: Agrarian Society and Politics under the Eighteenth Century Maratha Swarajya*. Cambridge: Cambridge University Press in association with Orient Longman.

2

Restoration of Democracy in Pakistan: A Critical Analysis of Political Culture and Historical Legacy

Saleem Qureshi

Would Pakistan's form of government be of any academic and political interest if it were a Central Asian state or a state tucked away somewhere in the middle of Africa? It is doubtful. Pakistan has been a frontline state in Afghanistan's wars; first as a conduit for American help to the mujahidin against the Soviets and now against the Taliban and Al Qaeda in support of the United States (US). In both conflicts, Pakistan was on the side of America, whose scholars have variously called Pakistan a 'failed' state, a 'soft' state, and even a 'rogue' state.

Pakistan is an established nuclear power and a rival of India, and occasionally an enemy of India. Whose finger is on Pakistan's nuclear trigger and how safe is its nuclear arsenal are matters of significant importance and great concern to its neighbours as well as global powers, hence the concern with Pakistan's form of government. There is an assumption, particularly in the US, that democracies do not go to war, and as such, if Pakistan were to become a democracy it would also become immune to attractions of war. Therefore, democracy for Pakistan remains a major concern for Pakistan's 'well-wishers'.

Or, is this special concern triggered by Pakistan being a Muslim country and possessing nuclear weapons, Pakistan could share either expertise or components with other Muslim countries, even with Muslim groups regarded as terrorist by the Americans? Would there be a difference between a democratic or dictatorial government in Pakistan as far as the safety of its nuclear materials is concerned? Do the personnel of democratic governments possess or are endowed with very different social and moral values as compared to the personnel of dictatorial governments? After all, the personnel of both governments come from the same society, and are socialized in the same societal norms and values. Can dictatorship survive in a country if it does not have any support within society? A dictatorship without support in society would need brute force to keep it in power. As such it would be a society under military occupation and the government would be a military government. Such a government is only temporary and can last only as long as the force is there, because those in authority are not accepted as legitimate rulers. Can, therefore, a society imbued with social and moral values that support dictatorship suddenly turn around and embrace democracy? These are all interesting issues for students of government and democracy. Pakistan is indeed a fascinating laboratory, having had both dictatorship and democracy, elected parliaments and military coups as well as a nuclear arsenal.

Pakistan has the distinction of being almost unique in that it was the first state in modern times whose establishment/creation was directly related to the religion of Islam. Religion, as the foundation of Pakistan, automatically implies the existence of a wide and powerful constituency with the ability to demand and secure a prominent, even determining, role in the politics of the country. In the case of Pakistan it was not only that Islam was the major religion of the people, which it was, and therefore its conceptual precepts would be the guiding principles of its government, but what was more readily understood and aspired to was the connection between Pakistan and the glorious empires and civilizations of the past that Muslims had built. In this way, Pakistan was to be the contemporary manifestation of the glory that once belonged to Muslims. And this glory could be recreated without having to seek the approval of non-Muslims. The idea of Islam, thus, was very much an inspiration and a vision to enthuse Muslims in the struggle for Pakistan, which it had done. Now that Pakistan had been achieved what was going to be the role of Islam and how in concrete terms could it be accommodated in the political processes of the 20th century? Would Pakistan experiment with Islamic politics or with political Islam? Would Pakistan have Islamic democracy or would it be democratic Islam holding sway over Pakistan? No clear answer to any of these questions was presented and there were as many answers as people interested in expressing themselves.

We may have had some indications or answers to a number of questions regarding the *raison d'etre* of Pakistan had there been any debate on the issues relating to why a separate state was needed for Muslims when they had lived among Hindus for centuries, at times in political units where government power had rested in Hindu hands. Notwithstanding the arguments advanced in support of the nationalism of Muslims, the only clear example that is available is that of Islamic internationalism and that was the Khilafat movement during and after World War I. Nothing of this magnitude materialized in support of the demand for Pakistan. Perhaps, there would have been no Pakistan had the Congress leadership shown either patience and waited for Jinnah to die or modified their vision of an India with a strong central government since the Cabinet Mission Plan of 1946 offered just that and Jinnah had accepted it and had the Working Committee of the Muslim League endorse it. Pakistan happened neither in response to the yearnings of a nation waiting for a state nor a state being occupied by claimants from history. Pakistan was an accident that came about because Congress leadership failed to take into account the fact that the power of deciding rested with the British, who were not inclined to abandon a minority that had stood with them in World War II, as against the Congress opposition. Not that this interpretation of history should be taken as authoritative, but it should be seen as being plausible in view of the evidence. This author does not take the view that Pakistan was inevitable, rather the author's view is that the creation of Pakistan should be seen in the context of circumstances and the political developments and exchanges that took place in a tripartite setting.

Since what this chapter is discussing is the 'Restoration of Democracy' (Chadda, 2000; Stern, 2001) it would imply that at some time in the past, democracy did function in Pakistan, but then it was lost or replaced by a different, undemocratic form of government. As such, democracy would neither be a new nor an unfamiliar form, just as the form of government that replaced democracy, that is, dictatorship. These alternations between democracy and dictatorship would suggest that support for neither is strong enough to withstand contrary pressures. Military governments have been cheered when they have overthrown civilian governments as have been civilian governments that followed the ouster of military governments. One obvious but rather surface explanation could be that the breakdown of civilian governments resulted from their being overwhelmed by the multiplicity of demands being placed on them, and because they had not existed long enough to have endeared themselves to the masses and had not become entrenched in the social and political ethos of society. Nonetheless, what remains undeniable is the survival of the yearning for democracy as can be witnessed from expressions of opposition to dictators, demands for democracy, and the eventual ouster of dictators. It could thus be argued that societal supports for democracy do exist but they are yet not strong enough to prevent the 'saviour on horseback' or the 'righteous ruler' from seizing control of government. What this writer will argue is that Pakistan has a dual political culture (Qureshi, 1991), if not multiple, that it contains both democratic and authoritarian tendencies, and neither is strong enough to overwhelm the other on a permanent basis. As can be seen, even military rulers who tried to camouflage their seizure of power under grandiose claims still felt compelled to give a façade of democracy to their dictatorships. And it has to be acknowledged as a tribute to the democratic component in Pakistan's political culture that the dictators failed to fool the public and were eventually removed under popular pressure.

Democracy—Is it a Bottom–Up or a Top–Down Process? The Role of Leadership

Since we are discussing the restoration of democracy we are looking at the future, and any prediction to be meaningful must draw upon the past, for it is known and it provides us more reliable clues to the value system of the society, rather than a completely theoretical speculation that ignores the past. History is, thus, a more reliable ally of political forecasters than anything else. The Muslim past, the history of Islamic empires, and what aspect of it is remembered very fondly, is what people would like to see replicated in contemporary times. Looking back it becomes clear that the greatness of Muslims was achieved by societies that were well run by individuals of sterling character, who were dedicated to the Quranic ideals and were very cognizant that their actions were judged by God. This may not have been true in every individual case but this was the historic ideal. In this ideal the greatest emphasis was placed on the quality of leadership and in early Islamic history one finds a string of heroes, great individuals of character beyond reproach. There was almost no emphasis on institutions or institutional development. All the focus was on individuals, individual leadership, leadership which was not a gift of people but it came from above—from God to Caliph, from Caliph to commanders. As the Quran (Surah 4, Verse 59) says:

> Obey Allah, and obey the messenger, and those of you who are in authority.

And, further:

> O Allah! Owner of Sovereignty! Thou givest sovereignty unto whom Thou wilt, and Thou withdrawest sovereignty from whom Thou wilt (Quran, Surah 3, Verse 26).

In traditional and conservative societies like Pakistan, leadership represents the concrete manifestation of power and as such is more identifiable than theoretical concepts such as a division of powers. The great leaders of the past carry a force of legitimacy of their own. In most societies, whether democratic or otherwise, the precedent of past greats is eulogized and all manner of leaders have mined history for suitable and useful parallels. In short, it is leadership that is at the root of power relationships and power structures.

In England, in 1642, when Sir Robert Walpole lost the support of the majority in the House of Commons, he submitted his resignation as the leader of the government, though at that time neither was there any rule nor any convention requiring resignation. On the contrary, Walpole by resigning introduced a principle that the leader of the government, that is, the prime minister, must at all times command the support of the majority in the legislature. Now it is an established fact of parliamentary democracy that either the legislature supports the government or creates an alternative government. This cardinal principle of democracy owes its creation to the leadership of Sir Robert Walpole.

On Independence in India, in a parallel convention-setting landmark action, the leader of the Indian National Congress, Jawaharlal Nehru, chose to locate the real power of the government in the legislature, the body representing the people by electing to hold the position of prime minister. Nehru could have assigned himself almost any position of his preference within certain limits, but he took a decision that identified the basic principle of parliamentary democracy with the legislature, with 'people's representatives'. His stewardship of Indian politics and his leadership in government for 17 years helped entrench the democratic principle. After Nehru it would have been difficult for his successors to alter the principle of parliamentary supremacy, though his own daughter, Indira Gandhi, a dozen years later tried to subvert the constitution, but by this time the institutional supports of democracy were strong enough to withstand this onslaught.

Political culture is a subjective phenomenon and reflects people's perceptions and values about politics and personalities. The most popular politicians in the history of Pakistan have been civilian leaders. Jinnah obviously has been the most loved one. He always talked of democracy and tried to work through civilian institutions. It is another matter that Jinnah's understanding of how democracy works reflected his apprenticeship in the British Indian Legislative Council and not the Westminster type, which Jinnah neither experienced nor understood. Bhutto, on the other hand, a more modern and better educated politician than Jinnah, talked a great deal after he was turned out of the Ayub government. However, once in power, he fell back on the *'Vadera'* (Sindhi landlord) model that he was familiar with. So while both of these highly popular politicians talked of democracy, neither provided a personal leadership model in the service of democracy, contrary to what Nehru was able to do for India. And, one could perhaps argue, that both Jinnah and Bhutto had strong unitarian and authoritarian tendencies in their personalities. While Nehru was content to accept the number two position (protocol wise), that position was also the position of real power tempered by the supervision/control of an assembly. Jinnah, of course, could not accept to hold the number two spot. The ceremonial position of Governor General that he chose to hold, he made the real centre of power. And it was from this position that the third head of state, Ghulam Muhammad, was able to sabotage the spirit of the constitution by invoking the letter of the law. Bhutto also tried to hold the number one spot in the beginning of his tenure, but he was told that if he wanted to act as the effective executive he would have to step down from the office of president and become the prime minister. Bhutto was not Jinnah, and did not have the kind of public adulation that Jinnah enjoyed and so Bhutto had to exchange presidency for prime ministership. All these manoeuvrings would not have been necessary if the political culture of Pakistan were simply militaristic or what may be termed Islamic. These manoeuvrings were necessary because of the pulls of two tendencies—the Anglo-Indian/democratic and the Islamic/authoritarian tendencies—in opposite directions. That the democratic tendency has not completely overwhelmed the authoritarian does not mean that it does not exist.

Jinnah was a man of exceptional legal and political talent and possessed a sterling character and most probably it was his character, straight and honest, that endeared him to his followers who came to repose total and unreserved confidence in him. Jinnah was neither a philosopher nor a visionary as much as revisionist historians of Pakistan might want him to be. He was a pragmatic politician, an expert at the political chess-game. It has perhaps suited both India and Pakistan to assign the blame/credit to Jinnah for the Partition of India. To India he became a rank communalist and the same trait made him an ardent Muslim nationalist to Pakistanis. But actually Jinnah was neither. By taste, temperament, and lifestyle, Jinnah was a secular person. Since Muslims had chosen him as their leader, it was his responsibility to secure the best political deal for his clients. Up to the last minute Jinnah was willing to accept a united India on the basis of the Cabinet Mission Plan of 1946, but the India this would have created would have prevented the realization of the vision that the Congress leadership had, that is, a strong centre, not a weak centre and hence, the Congress agreement to Partition. Thus Pakistan came as a sudden shock to Jinnah, not as a godsend, and that is why there were no plans or blueprints for anything in a future Pakistan. Jinnah had to improvise as he went along. There were no plans for governmental structures and no really competent personnel to man government offices. There was Jinnah and a few faithful lieutenants around him. Therefore, it is very likely that Jinnah felt he had to keep the reins of government and the ruling party in his own hands. The criticism that Jinnah loved power and concentrated it in his own hands sounds somewhat suspect, for Jinnah was at the apex of adulation and no political office was going to add to the glory he already possessed. However, be that as it may, Jinnah chose to become Governor General as well as Speaker of the Constituent Assembly, along with holding the ministerial portfolio of Kashmir Affairs, while also being the president of the All Pakistan Muslim League. Various rationalizations have been offered by his followers for this concentration of office. However, what is obvious is that Jinnah concentrated executive, legislative, and political, as well as ceremonial and effective political positions all in his own hands. While Pakistan was supposedly a parliamentary democracy, Jinnah, as Governor General, presided over cabinet meetings reducing the prime minister to the level of just another minister. Not only that, Jinnah would consult bureaucratic heads of departments over the heads of their political masters, that is, the ministers. None of this could in any way be justified by reference to any kind of democracy. Why did Jinnah do this? Why did he concentrate all these offices in his own person? Was he not intelligent enough or knowledgeable to realize that his own political actions were likely to promote dictatorship, not democracy? Not assigning any unworthy motives to Jinnah one could still argue that this concentration was not something that Jinnah wanted to do, rather this was the pattern of governmental operation that he was familiar with and in it he saw no weakness.

Jinnah's political conduct was not so much a departure as it was an affirmation of the tradition of government that the British had introduced, developed, and refined in India. The form of government was modern and it had democratic elements. It pretended to provide representation to people, while limiting it only to a handful. It had functioned quite well for almost three quarters of a century and was the first taste of democracy, or, to put it another way, the first modern democratic political experience for Indians.

The pattern of government in British India in a way provided, what can be called a sort of tutelage for Indians by the British, as to how to work a government that may eventually become democratic. In colonial India the Governor General who constituted the sole executive also presided over the legislature and dealt directly with the bureaucratic heads of departments called secretaries. Jinnah's political apprenticeship had been spent in this government, or in this kind of a set-up that gave the impression of providing representation to people, whereas in reality it was tightly controlled by the chief executive. This was quite different from the actual set-up at Westminster and its workings. Jinnah, in spite of spending his summers mainly in England, it seems, did not spend any time in learning about how the 'Mother of Parliaments' worked, or how a democratic government was instituted. In addition to all this, Jinnah was handicapped by an absence of higher education. Since he did not quite complete high school studies, Jinnah never engaged in university education and, therefore, was not exposed to the writings of thinkers such as Locke and Rosseau, Hume and Mill and their like. Thus, having neither actual experience of government nor of the theory through learning, Jinnah could not be expected to institute what he was not aware of. From all that is known, Jinnah did not read much beyond daily newspapers, he hardly wrote anything other than his letters that reveal almost nothing. His speeches were political and entirely related to the issues of the day; they were not discourses on political philosophy. And, therefore, if all the factors around Partition and the beginnings of Pakistan are taken into account, Jinnah did what he could and what he considered the best; but the best that he instituted was not good enough for the prospects of democracy in Pakistan's future. Those who followed were not persons of Jinnah's stature; they did not have his character or his selfless devotion to the cause of the Pakistani people. Grabbing power, personal glory, and amassing fortunes was what motivated his successors, and these are not political traits that contribute to, strengthen or facilitate democracy. Military rulers as well as civilians vied for glorified titles, like General Ayub Khan became Field Marshal and Zulfikar Ali Bhutto had himself called *Qaid-e-Awam* (leader of the masses). Not that these were lesser people. Jinnah's first lieutenant and Pakistan's first prime minister, Liaquat Ali-Khan, was called *Qaid-e-Millat* (leader of the community) and Jinnah's successor as Governor General, Khwaja Nazimuddin, was called *Nazim-e-Millat* (manager or guide of the community). This officiocracy and attachment to titles is not a sign of democratic commitment. And, these were the founders or early leaders during the formative phase of Pakistan and not only was their influence going to be lasting; they were also shaping the institutions and values of a nascent country (Khan, 1998).

While Jinnah's statements are replete with assertions affirming democracy, there is no evidence to show that he took steps to launch it or act or behave in a manner that would be conducive to, or contribute to, the creation of conditions supportive of democracy. The most that can be said is that he may have thought that his words would inspire his followers to work for democracy, while unfortunately his own actions were more reminiscent of colonial administration. Perhaps, and it could well have been possible that at the moment he was preoccupied with making Pakistan a going concern while waiting to institute democratic reforms later, once Pakistan was solidly established. Regardless of these speculations this, however, remains a fact that the foundation of Pakistan was not laid on democratic essentials and Jinnah did not live long enough to institute any structural changes.

There are other factors that also need to be taken into consideration. Democracy was not a home-grown concept, despite Jinnah's repeated assertions that Muslims learnt democracy 1400 years ago. Traditional Muslim education and normal primary and secondary education in India did not contain curricula dealing with democracy.

It was this British tutelage, the introduction of institutions, rule of law, a system of elections (however restricted) political freedoms (again, quite limited) that introduced ideas of modern government and the gradual extension of powers to elected Indian political class. Though small, the educated and particularly western-educated Indian professional class—practically all national liberation leaders, whether Hindu or Muslim came from this class—became the torch bearers of freedom and democracy. It was from among this class that freedom fighters and nationalist political leaders emerged, who used the democratic rhetoric learned through western education to argue the case of Indian freedom and also the case of Muslims for a separate state of their own, on the grounds of democratic self-determination. While not very deep in Indian history and also imbibed by the rather small western educated class, this British legacy constitutes the essence of modern, democratic approach to politics and should truly be called the Indo-British legacy as a component in Pakistan's dual political culture.

Another important factor that merits consideration is that the impact of the British introduced constitutional development impacted directly on what became India and only marginally on what became Pakistan. The British started the process in the 19th century starting with municipal governments, which were expanded to provinces in the Act of 1909, further expanded in a diarchy 1919 and again a sort of expanded diarchy introduced through the Act of 1935, though its federal provisions remained to be implemented. Among the areas in Pakistan which benefited from this progression were the provinces of Bengal and Punjab, which were partitioned and were subjected to massive inter-religious massacres and also lost the most politically active segments of the society. Pakistan, thus, started its life without the real benefit of this tutelage and, perhaps, only a memory.

The Structure of Muslim Society

Historically, the three pillars of Muslim societies have been the feudals, the clergy and the praetorians (Qureshi, 1981). Of the three the praetorians have been the most important and also most powerful. From its very beginning the Islamic polity was organized more or less as an army hierarchy. The Caliph was *amir-al mumineen*, or commander of the faithful, who appointed battlefield commanders. Since the conquests came before the civil administration was organized, the initial government offices were arranged on army lines: there were no offices other than military offices. That tradition continued up to the Mughal times in India where officers of state were ranked according to the numbers they commanded. The military tradition is thus very deeply embedded in Muslim political culture and Muslim psyche and its acceptance is practically readymade in Muslim culture. Also, the upper echelons of the military generally came from the feudal class which also produced the higher scholars and the clergy. In a way there was a value symbiosis between these three since they can be called the three faces of basically the same social unit. They have worked well together, each reinforcing the other two. It was the introduction of modern European style education that brought western concepts into traditional societies, as well as opened the conceptual world of Europe to the newly educated classes. The quest for democracy was part of this education and the newly educated classes were the most ardent advocates of enfranchisement. These advocates of democracy constituted the professional middle class, the backbone of modernization including democratic politics. This was also the class which Macaulay had called British in taste and orientation but Indian in fact. It was this class from which came the members of the Indian Civil Service (ICS) the steel framework for Indian administration and working close to the British the members of this class also made a difference in government. It was also from this class that professionals—lawyers, doctors, teachers, etc.—came and provided leadership for the independence movement, democracy and enfranchisement. Muslims did not take to modern education readily and therefore their numbers in both the ICS and the professional class remained rather small. At the time of Pakistan's birth there were few Muslims in the ICS to provide trained and professional cadres of civil servants. Also, there were not enough professionals in the political arena to sustain the form of government which could have grown into a strong and stable democracy. This modern education deficit has continued in Pakistan to this day. This educational vacuum has been filled in by *madrassas*, schools attached to mosques that provide not education, but indoctrination in a grossly narrow range of religious subjects, fostering an ideology that is built on denial of reason and tolerance. So, what Pakistan has produced in large numbers are the Taliban (Rashid, 2001) of Afghanistan as well as their political cousins in the Pakistan of today. Had any thought been given to the connection between modern, professional education and support for democracy, perhaps different political developments may have taken place in Pakistan. Unfortunately the situation as it obtains today does not infuse much confidence. Investment in education has been meager, rural education and female education have not been attended to and the rate of literacy, instead of going up, has declined. Thus one of the major supports of contemporary democracy has been allowed to weaken.

Righteous Ruler to the Rescue: But Needs Cover of Democracy

Even more than the Indo-British model the political values of Muslims can be traced back not only to the few Quranic verses, but also to the long Muslim history which can be described as the primary political legacy of Muslims. The rhetoric and the slogans of the Islamists, of course, talk about an 'Islamic order', 'Islamic state', 'Islamic political system', 'Muhammad's system', though it is never clear what such a political order would be in terms of structure, location of responsibilities, process of coordination, etc., beyond the generalities and platitudes of pious rulers guided by God's message who rule justly. Even in these platitudes what emerges is that there must be a ruler, and the important qualification that is sought is his personal piety, his rule being based on God's message and that he rules justly. There is no concern about where such a ruler comes from and who examines or determines his qualifications and who judges whether he fulfils the requisite requirements.

Were it possible to deduce clear answers regarding Islam, either from the scriptures or from history, today's Muslims could attempt to replicate the past. The scriptures are not very helpful because contradictory interpretations can be, and have been obtained. History is also not very helpful because the entire history of Islam is one of empires, ruled by absolute rulers. The ruler could be removed by being blinded, killed or banished, but there is no provision of change of a ruler as a result of public desire. Neither is there any historical precedent of sharing of power in Muslim history. The examples of the Abbasid Caliph with the Memluk Sultans of Egypt in the 13th century and that of the Turkish Sultan between 1922 and 1924 show that the Caliphs in both cases could not adjust to purely ceremonial roles. However, the example of the Buwayhid sultans and the Abbasid caliphs in the 11th century shows an arrangement under which effective and ceremonial offices were held separately without constant fighting between them. Though it worked for a time, yet the arrangement was never institutionalized or formalized, and in reality it depended on one holder's power becoming weak while at the same time another holder's power becoming strong. Also, the literature of the time did not focus on this development as having some positive consequences. The lament of the writers was about the loss of power of the Caliph and an admonition to people to obey whoever held the power. Unfortunately for Islam, in Pakistan, the Islamist activists have not used these developments to construct something which would be practical in contemporary times. Instead, they have chosen to go back to the Medina Caliphate and advocate its replication.

Both the Pakistani Abul Ala Maudoodi and the Egyptian Syed Qutb have written extensively about the desirability of Islamizing polities and replicating Muhammad's Medina in the 20th century. But they are entirely theoretical, idealistic and nostalgic, not realistic or practical. The only Islamist who succeeded in establishing an Islamic political system was Ayatullah Khomeini of Iran. Though quite innovative in form, Khomeini's *Villayat-e-faqih* essentially went back to the Islamic legacy in which the ultimate and final decision-making authority is vested in one person, in this case a *faqih,* jurist. This jurist is a pious person, who rules justly and is guided by God's message and is responsible only to God. Thus the substance of the Islamic legacy is rule by a righteous ruler bound only by the *Sharia,* which is the closest thing to what can be called Islamic law. Since the righteous ruler does not acquire his office as a result of people's choice, there is no popular control or restraint that can be exercised on his actions and decisions. Islamist jurists of the past have emphasized the paramount necessity of order and the maintenance of the unity of Muslims. This has been accepted in Islamic circles as the 'doctrine of necessity', meaning that whosoever has power has to be accepted as the legitimate ruler because there is no practical way of getting rid of him short of rebellion which leads to chaos and chaos is what historically Islamic jurists have always abhorred.

This long history which has been idolized in Islamic lore has left a very deep legacy in Muslim psychology. That legacy says that greatness can be achieved only with a strong leader, that strong leaders should be accepted as a gift from God and the Muslim army is people's army and people's protector. It will not be an exaggeration to say that historically stable Muslim polities have been sustained by strong armies, either ruling directly or supporting a ruler who might not be a military dictator.

Politics in Pakistan: Democracy and Dictatorship

Between 1947 and 1958 when the army sent politicians packing, prime ministers came and went—seven in all—while the legislature stayed unchanged. In the dismissal of prime ministers, the legislature rarely upheld the principle of parliamentary supremacy, for it invariably supported the Governor General who did the dismissing of prime ministers. The Governor General, not the Prime Minister, became the effective chief executive. The legislature went to the farcical extent of supporting the dismissal of Prime Minister Khwaja Nazimuddin by Governor General Ghulam Mohammad in 1952, when just a short while back, it had placed confidence in the prime minister by voting the budget presented by his government. There was, so to say, some democratic strength left when the Speaker of the Assembly, Maulvi Tameezuddin Khan, brought a suit against the Governor General for wrongful dismissal. Politics in Pakistan, thereafter, became even more murky and the existing political institutions and politicians allowed the deterioration of institutions and processes as well as public alienation from politicians who came to be seen as 'scalawags' and 'scoundrels', in the words of Governor General Iskander Mirza. In 1958, graffiti and posters appeared which beseeched Iskander Mirza to hand over the government to the army. Mirza obliged by staging a coup in October 1958, thus inaugurating the first military government in Pakistan. Mirza appointed General Ayub Khan, Commander-in-Chief of the army as Chief Martial Law Administrator, but was soon himself dismissed by Ayub. General Ayub Khan thus became the first military ruler of Pakistan. His rule lasted from 1958 to 1968, when he transferred power to another general, Yahya Khan.

Ayub's rule was generally benign; he introduced economic reforms which improved the economy of Pakistan considerably. However, what is important from our perspective is how Ayub viewed politics in Pakistan and how did he proceed in that respect.

Ayub acknowledged that he could not rule for long as a military dictator by paying homage to democratic norms. He encouraged the organization of a political party which invited him to join it as its leader. He gave Pakistan a constitution, established legislatures and held elections for these legislatures as well as for President—in the famous election of 1965 for President Ayub was opposed by Miss Fatima Jinnah, sister of Muhammed Ali Jinnah, who came within a whisker of defeating Ayub. Of course, Ayub's political endeavours were directed toward acquiring democratic legitimacy, not in running a democracy. Consequently, power always remained either in Ayub's hands or in the hands of his surrogates. And eventually the Pakistani public got fed up and rose up against his dictatorship. There were demonstrations by trade unions, student organizations, Islamic parties, etc., suggesting a cross section of public that was expressing its opposition to authoritarian government. From our perspective what is important is that the popular protest led to Ayub giving up power to another general, Yahya Khan,[1] who could restore order only by committing his government to hold general, free and fair elections. He prohibited members of his government from running in those elections, meaning that real transfer of power was in the offing and the victors in the elections were going to be those whom the voters were going to vote for. In the end, though, it did not happen that way, the country fractured between competing power interests of two parties, each one of which secured a majority in its own wing. The eastern wing separated and became the independent state of Bangladesh, while West Pakistan became Pakistan and, therefore, from here on the examination of the prospects of democracy will focus on this part of Pakistan (Qureshi: 1984).

Zulfikar Ali Bhutto, the leader of the socialist-oriented Pakistan People's Party became president. Because Bhutto was unwilling to loosen his grip on power, he was, in a way, forced to discard the presidential form of government and replace it with the parliamentary form. So if Bhutto was going to exercise effective executive power he had to do it as prime minister in a parliamentary democracy, which would subject the prime minister to legislative supervision and accountability. While not much credit is given to the relevance of opposition forces in Pakistan even when confronting those exercising the power of the state, however, they have always been there and have forced the autocratic rulers to bend and acknowledge institutional proprieties. This lends credence to the argument that while occasionally set aside, the commitment to democracy was always there and asserted itself whenever it could. At a cursory glance Pakistan seems to be bumbling from one political set up to another and not finding its moorings, but a closer examination will indicate that at the bottom of all kinds of political shenanigans is the urge for freedom of political choice and the fact that regard for institutional propriety was always strong and sought to assert itself whenever there was an opening. Thus, after almost a decade of rule by the two generals—and all of it was not totally authoritarian rule or rule under martial law—when the opening occurred, democratic impulses reasserted themselves.

Bhutto as a democratically elected leader through open and competitive election and a person of secular tastes and tendencies was expected to usher in the era of real democracy. During the electoral campaign he had talked a lot about democracy and eulogized democracy in many speeches (Bhutto, 1971), however, in his political behaviour he was a Sind grandee or *Vadera*. His imperious and arrogant style alienated a lot of his support base so that when General Zia-ul-Haq ousted Bhutto in a coup in 1977 there were practically no demonstrators in the street in support of a popularly elected leader. Still Zia was apprehensive that if he held elections Bhutto could again play his charm and get elected. Therefore, Zia could not afford to hold elections. He could not use democracy to legitimize his coup having just overthrown a democratically elected prime minister, therefore he had to resort to some other legitimizing device. Zia identified Islamization as his legitimizer; additionally, by introducing Islamic reforms, Zia could utilize the Sharia rules (Qureshi, 1980) of evidence to secure a guilty verdict against Bhutto in a contrived murder trial. This would remove Bhutto from threatening Zia even from behind the bars and save Zia from the charge of wantonly killing an elected prime minister. Also, to show that he was really committed to Islam, Zia appointed some Jama'at-i-Islami ministers and adopted a religious posture in the public presentation of his persona (Nasr, 1995). While the Islamists lionized Zia, it was clear that he was merely exploiting Islam for Pakistan was overwhelmingly Muslim anyway. Islam was being put to the service of a soldier who had violated his oath of office by staging the coup and further brought Islam into disrepute by using it to kill his political rival. In spite of anointing himself in Islam, Zia could not suppress the democratic stirrings and had to make concessions in the democratic direction. He felt compelled to usher in parliamentary government, hold elections to largely toothless legislatures, elected legislatures nonetheless, appoint a prime minister and extend the same system to the provinces. Zia's actions do give credence to the fact that Islam alone—even in Islamic Pakistan—was not sufficient to legitimize autocracy and additional layers of democratic legitimacy were needed.

Zia's Islamization did nothing to improve the ethics of society, it only put a premium on demonstrative public behaviour and personal piety. At the same time his Islamization had a retarding effect on almost every other aspect especially political and economic development. Zia's regime was in a way saved by the Soviet invasion of Afghanistan which made Pakistan the main conduit of anti-Soviet help—arms, funds, personnel—and spared Zia from making further democratic concessions. The policies of Zia's regime can also be assigned fundamental responsibility for the creation of the Taliban phenomenon, which a decade later would rule Afghanistan and become the main impediment to Pakistan's progress, creating an environment of political chaos, instability, and violence.

After Bhutto's execution, his family fled into exile and agitated for the restoration of democracy from abroad. Bhutto's daughter, Benazir, had taken upon herself the mission of her father and taken over the reins of his Pakistan People's Party. On Benazir's return to Pakistan in 1986, the rapturous reception that was given to her, now the leader of opposition to Zia's regime, would have unnerved even General Zia-ul-Huq. Her procession from the airport to her residence took about six hours and almost 100,000 people welcomed her.

General Zia's regime ended with his death in a plane crash in 1988. As with Ayub so with Zia, the political set up established to keep its sponsor in power came to an end when the sponsor lost control. After Zia's death as after Ayub's removal, the political system reverted to democratic form, political parties alternated, prime ministers came and went. Benazir Bhutto of Pakistan People's Party was elected twice in elections as was her rival Nawaz Sharif of the Muslim League. However, both Bhutto and Sharif were dismissed from office by the president for corruption who called for fresh elections each time. The process came to an end in 1999 when Prime Minister Nawaz Sharif tried to get rid of the army chief, General Musharraf, who was returning from a conference in Colombo. The prime minister ordered the plane to leave Pakistan's airspace, however, the pilot decided to land in Pakistan anyway because the plane was running out of fuel. That was when the army decided to act and deposed the prime minister. Here is a clear case of democratic political leaders, that is, Bhutto and Sharif, making a mess of democratic polities, treating the country, its resources and the political process as their personal property. Benazir Bhutto's husband was also given a ministerial position in her government and came to be called Mr Ten Per cent for the ten per cent cut he demanded in every government contract awarded. So, it is obvious that the military came back once again. Unfortunately for Pakistan both of these civilian, democratic political leaders and their performance in office came to be seen as venal and treacherous. This did nothing to enhance democracy; if anything, it made the military look like the face of virtue in contrast. General Musharraf came to power at a time of great global distress and internal regional and ethnic stress. However, even he had to resort to a reversion to a democratic parliamentary system, as skewed as it may appear to democratic purists. To this author it seems that in the stress that Pakistan is currently going through, perhaps, what is more important is deft handling of national and international conflicts rather than full compliance with the wishes of Pakistan's 'well-wishers' and of the demands of Pakistan's democrats. This means that the restoration of full democracy in Pakistan has to wait for a more propitious future.

Contemporary Parallels: Lessons for Democracy

The two Muslim majority states where Islamic identification has been very deep and strong, and where a religious structure did exist, and where democracy has been on trial, are Turkey and Iran. In terms of the religious potential to affect/subvert/control politics, these two countries offer useful lessons for the prospects for democracy in Pakistan.

Ottoman Turkey has historically defined itself by Islam to the extent that the state gave itself no name (Ottoman is the European version of Osman whose descendents established the empire) except that it was the empire of Islam, ruled by the *padshah* of Islam who was advised by the Sheikh ul Islam. Kemal Ataturk terminated the link with Islam, banished the last Caliph in 1924, and launched the secular republic of Turkey (Macfie, 1944) He did this under the authority of martial law and guided the republic and provided critical leadership for 14 years thereafter. And yet the republic faced traumatic jolts after the political system was opened to multiparty competition. The Democrats who came to power after the election of 1950 pandered to the Islamic constituency and were overthrown in a military coup in 1960. The second attempt at building a multiparty democracy came to a halt as a result of a coup in 1970. Once again the military intervened in politics with a coup in 1981; and in 1999 what could be called a soft coup took place, when the military actually did not take over government, but simply forced out the Islamist prime minister, Necmetin Erbakan, of the Refah Party (Kees and Kruijt, 2002). However, the 2003 electoral victory of the Justice and Development Party led by Recep Tayyip Erdogan (Heper, 2003), the Islamist prime minister, seems to have inaugurated the era of the accommodation of political Islam within the secular democracy of Turkey. Perhaps it may be difficult to make a definitive statement that democracy in Turkey is established solidly now and the possibility of another military coup need not be feared, however, current indicators do seem to point in this direction.

What Turkey's example shows is that the road to democracy is a long and slow one. There are likely to be glitches and failures on the way; conservative forces, particularly religious forces, would struggle to bend the political processes toward their desired objectives. To focus on every one of these glitches and stumbles as failure of democracy is to take a rather short-sighted view of what it takes to achieve democratic progress. After eight decades of apprenticeship, Turkey now seems to have succeeded in integrating democracy, Islam, and secularism. There may yet be more stumbles on the way to democratic stability, but it can now be said with some confidence that the march toward democratic stability is irreversible in Turkey.

The example of the Islamic Republic of Iran (Milani, 1994) does not offer an easy and ready-made parallel. However, if one were to focus on the structures and functioning of government it can be seen that popular representation in the *Majles* (parliament), is a fundamental feature of the Islamic Republic and elections to the *Majles* have been held regularly. Normally functioning government institutions exist and continue to function. Of course, the Islamic Republic is not the French Republic and does not pretend to be a copy of a western model. The authority of the Supreme Leader, the *Faqih*, is unchallenged and the rule of law does not exist for public protection. What is interesting from the perspective of democracy is that the Islamic Republic, while rejecting western models, still pays homage to the democratic principle. And what should be an eye opener is that the Islamic principle in the Islamic Republic is under challenge, not only by the non-clerics but even by the younger clerics who want the political system to become imbued with the rule of law, civil society, and true democracy (Horowitz and

Scharabel, 2004). And this change, what *The Economist* (July 17–23, 1999) called the 'second revolution', has started even before the Islamic revolution is three decades old.

To write the obituary of democracy too early is to project a very short-term and pessimistic outlook. True, the march of democracy has been bumpy, there have been glitches, pitfalls, and short falls, yet the examples of Turkey and Iran do indicate that democracy is not on life support. Over time it has been gaining strength and the converts to its cause are increasing. The examples of Turkey and Iran are pertinent for determining the prospects of democracy in Pakistan. Islamists have generally tended to view politics in their societies through the prism of the 7th century Medina and have considered all other forms if not outright illegitimate then at least not acceptable. The developments in Turkey and Iran show that over time Islamic perspectives can become mellow enough so as to be able to accommodate themselves to the forces that seek the rule of law, minority rights and civil society. Turkey has made much more solid progress in that regard; Iran's conservative interpretation of Islam is being challenged by more pragmatic and liberal interpretations of Islam. In Pakistan, the boost that Islamism got as a result of the Soviet invasion of Afghanistan and the growth of the *madrassa*-indoctrinated Taliban is being reversed by the decision of the government of General Musharraf, as it has become a participant in the war against the Taliban in Afghanistan, with the inevitable consequence of the Musharraf government going after the Islamists in Pakistan. This struggle against the Islamists in Pakistan opens the political space for secularists and makes the Musharraf government receptive to secularists. Democracy to be real and successful has to be anchored in secularism, in that politics has to be viewed as a human endeavour, flexible enough to be susceptible to and respond to changes in human conditions and human society. And yet where the society is Islamic, a role must be found for Islam in that Islamists should find space in the political process for themselves, and it has to be done so that neither secularism nor Islam stifles the other. As it appears in the case of Turkey, this balance between the two has started to take shape and, as it seems to this writer, the same process is at work in Pakistan. Each non-democratic attempt to capture power strengthens the forces of democracy and justifications of grabbing power in the name of Islam are not accepted as sufficient any more. Thus, democracy, even weak or flawed, remains the preferred form. Having reverted to democracy so many times in the past, it should not be unrealistic to conclude that the roots of democracy in Pakistan, though not robust as yet, are certainly getting stronger and an enduring democratic future cannot be ruled out.

Focusing exclusively on the formal structures of democracy ignores the importance of societal supports that sustain and keep those structures in place. Identification of democracy primarily with elections is also flawed, because, as is well known, communist dictatorships held regular elections and those elections had no meaning. It is, therefore, necessary to identify the core of democracy in order to assess the prospects of democracy. The essential feature of democracy is the limitation of authority and its balancing with liberty. Authority does not voluntarily agree to its own limitation; limitation has to be imposed, which can only be done if an equal or balancing authority or power exists outside the government. Successful democracy, as such, needs pockets of power in society that are independent of government, and command more or less equal weight. In the case of Pakistan the struggle for Partition necessitated that the Muslim minority in India stand united and speak with one voice. The Muslim League, under Jinnah's leadership, insisted that it, and it alone, should be considered the sole spokesman of Muslim India (Jalal, 1985). After repeatedly refusing to accept that assertion, eventually the Congress felt compelled to negotiate with the Muslim League on League's terms. In the quest for this status the League's attitude toward other Muslim organizations was either to co-opt or to absorb them or to destroy them. Political pluralism was not tolerated and not practised by the Muslim League in British India and, therefore, when Pakistan finally emerged there were no legitimate, independent foci of power to temper and moderate the government. Before secular and democratic parties could develop, the political space was pre-empted by religious parties until the emergence of Pakistan People's Party. Traditionally opposition to the Muslim League by any Muslim group or party before Partition was seen as treason and as old habits die slowly, the emergence of popularly supported but nationally dedicated organizations in Pakistan has been slow. On top of all this the sledge hammer of branding as non-Islamic or hostile to Islam by Islamists has been used generously. Also in the initial period after the birth of Pakistan it was more important to make it going rather than democratizing it. Now that the birth travails of Pakistan are in the past and political pluralism is a fact of politics, the march of democracy can be expected to be firm and hopefully unstoppable.

The *Times of India* expressed a very sober thought on the prospects and priority of democracy in Pakistan:

> Our single-minded preoccupation with the problems and prospects of democracy in Pakistan runs the risk of missing the woods for the trees. The fact is, democracy in a purely formal sense, is far less central to the current and future health of many Third World polities, including Pakistan, than many assume. In common with many post-colonial societies, what Pakistan requires before all else, is a strong framework of public and statutory institutions that is committed to upholding basic liberal values and freedoms. Contrary to what the proponents of democracy believe, these fundamental rights—commonly subsumed under the somewhat old-fashioned concept of rule of law—are neither synonymous with democracy nor necessarily guaranteed by it. Focus on the institutionalization of core values. Democracy can wait.

The editorial does catch the spirit of democracy, except that the rule of law is possible only under an institutionalized system where those who are charged with upholding the law are autonomous and independent of those who can threaten or inflict pain. The march of democracy assumes the development and strengthening of institutions, and the rule of law can only be upheld if the institution doing this upholding is strong and really independent. In Pakistan institutional development has been slow as the components that will eventually sustain a stable political system have more often been at war with each other, instead of working in a synchronized fashion. Institutional development and primacy of the rule of law took centuries in England and decades in France. It has taken decades in Turkey and in the case of Pakistan it may take longer. However, it seems reasonable to assert that the march of democracy in Pakistan too has become irreversible.

Analysis and Prognosis

The issue in Pakistan's case is not so much of restoring democracy as it is of strengthening of forces that are the essential supports for democracy (Jilani, 1998). As we have discussed, democracy was never extinguished by pure dictatorship and even dictators felt compelled to seek support of democratic forms. An analysis of what has happened could indicate the strengths and weaknesses of societal supports for democracy.

Pakistan's history can be divided into six periods including the current one. The founder's period that ended with the first military coup lasted from 1947–58; the Ayub-Yahya period, 1958–70; the Zulfikar Ali Bhutto period, 1970–77; the Zia-ul-Huq period, 1977–88; Benazir Bhutto–Nawaz Sharif period, 1988–99; the current Musharraf era, 1999 onwards. Of these the three periods, that is, the founder's, Bhutto, and Bhutto–Sharif were periods of civilian rule and can be called periods of democracy. The other three were rule by the military with a democratic façade.

The founder's period was by and large liberal and secular, so have been all the others except the Zia period. Thus, liberal secular politics has held sway for all the time except the decade of Zia's rule. Though relatively short, Zia's period deliberately ushered in a period advocating a religious ideology and the imposition of narrow dogmatism in public life. Murderous Islam took shape during this period and the negative, destructive forces unleashed during this period have been difficult to control. Though General Zia also resorted to covering his dictatorship under the guise of democracy, this period can be counted as a net loss in respect of secularism, liberalism, and democracy.

General Ayub's period was essentially modernizing and secularizing as is the current period under General Musharraf. Both Ayub and Musharraf, held more or less free elections and have had to contend with Islamist legislators. Before Ayub held elections he had brought in the Family Laws Ordinance in 1959, which attempted to restrict polygamy without abolishing it. The elected legislators in the new legislature proclaimed themselves to be dead set against this ordinance and attempted to vote it out of existence, to some extent out of genuine commitment to their religious beliefs and to some extent to show their clout against the military ruler. Women protested and demonstrated against this attempt of the legislators, but the day for women was saved by the 'dictator' who firmly refused to oblige the legislators. The Islamists considered Ayub to be too liberal and secular and their opposition to him, which in part eventually led to Ayub's ouster, was fundamental. During the entire Ayub period, the Islamist parties and the most fundamentalist of those, the Jama'at-i-Islami, remained at loggerheads with the government.

General Musharraf also had to contend with the elected members of the legislatures. In two provincial legislatures, the North West Frontier Province and Baluchistan, the Islamists are the majority and so those provinces have Islamist governments, whereas in the Federal Parliament Islamists form the official opposition. Religious and sectarian violence is an everyday occurrence and in spite of all his efforts General Musharraf has not been able to find a way either to control the Islamists or to reconcile them to his government.

It appears evident that during periods of the general's rule, Islamist political activity tends to accelerate and they are able to secure electoral support. Since General's Ayub and Musharraf did not project Islam as the *raison d'etre* of their politics, Islamist activity was more vigorous and focused in opposition. Since General Zia projected Islam, the Islamists cooperated with him, gave support and provided legitimacy to his government, though they could not sustain Islamist succession to General Zia. Also, the Islamist opposition to Ayub and Musharraf and support to Zia indicates that the Islamists are not so much anti-dictators as they are anti-secular and anti-liberal because they were quite happy with Zia's dictatorship which was far more restrictive than either Ayub's or Musharraf's. The Islamists have been and continue to be a political force, but they do not seem to have the kind of widespread and majority support that can enable them to control the government through elections. Besides, they do not claim authority so much as representatives of people as they claim it in the name of God. Any democratic political system in Pakistan will have to take the Islamist forces into account.

The Bhutto period, 1970–77 and the Bhutto–Sharif period, 1988–99, have been periods of civilian and electoral political domination with secular-liberal overtones.

The Benazir Bhutto–Nawaz Sharif period, 1988–99 was perhaps the highest point of Pakistani democracy as well as the lowest point of democratic leadership. Free elections were held, Bhutto and Sharif alternated as prime ministers, each occupying the office twice. However, nothing of any significance was accomplished by either leader, except that both were seen looting the state and were dismissed on charges of corruption. Corruption cases are still pending against both.

In Pakistan, in terms of legacy and history there are two powerful forces that have the capacity to intervene and make a difference to the prospects of democracy. They are the Islamists and the military.

Can the Islamists win a majority and form an Islamist government? Theoretically they could because they have won seats in the federal parliament; won majorities in the Frontier Province and in Baluchistan. However, realistically it does not seem possible at the national level because the fundamentalist Islamists have a very narrow base of support as can be seen in the number of seats they have won federally. Also, a distinction must be made between fundamentalist Islamists and eclectic Muslims who comprise the overwhelming majority and do not normally support the fundamentalist kind of parties. The best example of the kind of party that could garner their support would be a Muslim League, as in the pre-Musharraf period was Nawaz Sharif's Muslim League. The various Muslim Leagues through the history of Pakistan have been Muslim parties of the eclectic variety. Historically, while Muslims have been keen on their religion, in politics they seem to have preferred eclectic and secular leaders. A case in point was the All India Muslim League, an eclectic Muslim party under Jinnah's leadership. At the height of political controversy regarding Partition, while most of the reputed Islamic *ulema*, including Maudoodi opposed Partition, the overwhelming majority of Muslims voted for the Muslim League disregarding the advice of the learned and famous *ulema*. And that approach to religion and politics does not seem to have really changed. So, yes, theoretically the Islamists could win a national election, but in reality that possibility has to be considered remote. Eclectic Muslims are not likely to be easily radicalized.

The Taliban debacle and the bloody mayhem that the Islamists in Pakistan have perpetrated have on the one side stigmatized the extreme Islamism and on the other fractured the Islamists in Pakistan. It does not seem that Islamists could mount a concerted attack either through the ballot or through the bullet. Consequently, the Islamists threat to the eclectic character of the Pakistanis and to democracy can be discounted. Not that they will cease to exist or to operate but that the Islamists, most likely, are going to be confined to the fringes.

On the basis of history and the experience of the past, it could be argued that the most potent threat to democracy could come from the military. However, as we have seen, the main reason for military intervention in the past were: a weak public opinion, an incompetent and fractured civilian leadership and public frustration with the political process which made the public receptive to any political change. The fact that in 1969 it was the public that chased the generals out in spite of their pretence to operate under a democratic system says something about what the public would now be willing to accept. Zia-ul-Huq fared a little better for using Islam, and had he not been killed in the air crash he would have had to change his politics for opposition to his regime was building up. Nonetheless, in spite of every thing, Pakistan finds itself again, a third time, ruled by a general. However, a major difference this time is that the military take over was not initiated by the military, but in a bizarre twist it was the elected Prime Minister Nawaz Sharif who brought this situation on himself by his own action.

Steps reflecting progress in the democratic direction have been taken, and though small, those steps move Pakistan on the path of democracy. However, the military and its positive image should make any optimistic outcome to be forecast with a certain amount of reservation. And, the reason is that the military has a large constituency in Pakistan for what is Pakistan today has been historically the recruiting ground for the British Army. The army established its headquarters in Rawalpindi. And the continuing conflict with India over Kashmir has kept the army in somewhat the same kind of esteem as the army enjoyed in Turkey, that is, defenders of national honour and freedom. Organizationally, the army is the most effective, efficient, and hierarchic. It can be put to action in a minimum amount of time and be on to the task promptly. It also has monopoly of weapons of destruction. It is easy to identify an external enemy and mobilize the country behind the army. However, it may not be that easy to focus on a domestic enemy, especially after three army takeovers. This brings in focus the Turkish model for Pakistan, that is, the military takeover of the government cannot be ruled out, nor can it be asserted that it lurks in the future too. Public opinion in Pakistan seems to have progressed somewhat and there seems some evidence of this from the haste with which Musharraf had to establish a democratic framework, hold elections, and appoint a prime minister.

The prospects for democracy depend upon the commitment of the political class to sustain democracy, even when out of power, and on the officers of the army realizing that periodic military interventions weaken Pakistan internally and internationally. Military rule on a long-tem basis cannot be the answer and for democracy to be stable and enduring it has to be real democracy and not a fake replica. Ultimately, it is up to the Pakistanis themselves to decide whether, in a zoological analogy of the zebra being a white animal with black stripes or a black animal with white stripes, is Pakistan a democracy with military disruptions or a militocracy with democratic interludes.

Note

1. Yahya Khan was dubbed Tweedle Khan by *The Economist*.

References

Bhutto, Z.A. (1971). *Politics of the People, Marching Towards Democracy*. Rawalpindi: Pakistan Publications.

Chadda, Maya (2000). *Building Democracy in South Asia, India, Nepal; Pakistan*. Boulder: Lynne Rienner Publishers.

Heper, Martin and S. Tokas (2003). 'Islam, Modernity and Democracy in Contemporary Turkey: The Case of Recep Tayyip Erdogan', *Muslim World*, April, 93(2), 157–85.

Horowitz, Shale and Albrecht Scharabel (eds) (2004). *Human Rights and Societies in Transition*. New York: United Nations University Press.

Islam, Nasir (2001). 'Democracy and Governance in Pakistan's Fragmented Society', *International Journal of Public Administration*, 24(12): 1335–55.

Jalal, Ayesha (1985). *The Sole Spokesman*. Cambridge: Cambridge University Press.

Jilani, Hina (1998). *Human Rights and Democratic Development in Pakistan*. Lahore: Human Rights Commission of Pakistan.

Khan, Roedal (1998). *Pakistan—A Dream Gone Sour*, Oxford: Oxford University Press.

Koonings, Kees and Dirk Kruijt (eds) (2002). *Political Armies: The Military and Nation Building in the Age of Democracy*. London: Zed Books.

Macfie, A.L. (1994). *Ataturk*. New York: Longman.

Milani, Mohsen M. (1994). *The Making of Iran's Islamic Revolution*. Boulder: Westview.

Nasr, S.V.R. (1995). 'Democracy and Islamic Revivalism', *Political Science Quarterly*, 10(2): 261–85.

Quran. Surah 3, Verse 26.

Quran. Surah 4, Verse 59.

Qureshi, Saleem (1980). 'Islam and Development: The Zia Regime in Pakistan', in Kenneth P. Jameson and Charles K. Wilber (eds), *Religious Values and Development*. Oxford: Pergamon Press. Reprinted from World Development, Vol. VIII, Nos 7–8 (1980), pp. 563–75.

———— (1981). 'Military in the Polity of Islam: Religion as a Basis of Civil-Military Interaction', *International Political Science Review*, 2(3): 271–82.

———— (1984). 'Critical Elections and the Destruction of Pakistan', in M.M. Khan and J.P. Thorp (eds), *Bangladesh: Society, Politics & Bureaucracy*. Dhaka: The City Press.

———— (1991). 'Political Culture of Pakistan, The Mass Dimension', in Manuel J. Pelaez (ed.), *Papers in Jurisprudence, Political Thought and Comparative Politics*. Zaragosa, Spain: Grafitas Comita.

Rashid, Ahmed (2001). *Taliban, Islam, Oil and the New Great Game in Central Asia*. London: I.B. Tauris Publication.

Stern, Robert (2001). *Democracy and Dictatorship in South Asia*. New Delhi: India Research Press.

The Economist, 17–23 July 1999.

The Times of India, as quoted in *The International Herald Tribune*, Paris, 8 July 2004.

3

Democracy and Authoritarianism in Bangladesh

Veena Kukreja

Bangladesh, despite three-and-a-half decades of independence, continues to be plagued by political instability, popular unrest, and economic uncertainty. Contemporary Bangladesh is at the crossroads and in the midst of a host of internal crises, which could potentially undermine the country's stability. Rising political violence and religious militancy, coupled with the government's vindictive attitude and the main opposition party's intransigence, weak institution-building, absence of political accountability, worsening law and order situation leading to the induction of the military in civic duties have created an unstable environment that is likely to inflict further damage to Bangladesh's fragile democracy.

Bangladesh's political evolution suggests that for most of its history, the country has oscillated between unstable democracy (1972–75 and 1991 onwards) and benign authoritarianism (1975–1990 except for four months of Abdus Sattar's civilian rule). In 1971, when Bangladesh came into being, it held the promise of becoming a stable democracy. However, the promise was soon belied and the country became a victim of military intervention in 1975. During his three years and eight months of rule, Sheikh Mujibur Rahman (Mujib), popularly known as 'the father of the nation', soon turned authoritarian. In such a situation, the absence of another civilian countervailing force to the discredited civilian regime facilitated the army's role of the guardian, which was already alienated and antagonized by Mujib. It was under such circumstances that Bangladesh entered (on 15 August 1975) the era of *coups d'etat* and eventually witnessed military rule under General Ziaur Rahman and General H.M. Ershad respectively until 1990. The militarization of Bangladesh as a result of its failure to sustain democratic institutions and shunting back to military rule is one of the most tragic developments in South Asia/Third World in the last quarter of the 20th century. It is particularly so because the very emergence of the country as an independent nation was a result of a movement, extending over 25 years—with unparalleled success—for the establishment of democracy in military-ruled Pakistan.

Democratic Experience under Mujibur Rahman (1972–75)

Bangladesh became independent in 1971 and Sheikh Mujibur Rahman assumed power in January 1972. Following Independence, Bangladesh, like many other developing countries, confronted the formidable task of nation-building—the problem of simultaneously building an input and an output sector—both a stable state apparatus and a political community (Jahan, 1972).

Level of Political Institutionalization and the Role of Political Parties and Leaders towards Institution-Building

Bangladesh at the time of its liberation, appeared to have set out on the right course, and circumstances seemed to be favouring a healthy demarcation of civil–military role in the country. As in India, at the time of its independence, parties and politicians in the newly formed Bangladesh were more influential than the civil–military bureaucracy. The Awami League (AL) was riding the crest of popular esteem, and its political programme was a success. Purged of the Pakistani element, the civil–military bureaucracy was numerically depleted, was faction-ridden, and was in no position to challenge the authority of party rule (Jahan, 1980: 64–66). But the pre-liberation consensus was quickly eroded. A sharp polarization between the centrist AL and the radical left occurred in the first year of liberation when the group professing Maoist ways took up arms. Neither a truly national consensual leadership nor effective political institutions emerged after 1971. This not only accounts for Mujib's arbitrary attitude in the tradition of a patriarch, but his eventual decline as well. He was not able to develop a strong political organization mainly due to his style of personality politics. The AL was an umbrella party containing within its fold different interests and philosophies. The coalitions within the party of different interests were unstable and institutionalization was poor. Political factionalism was rampant.

Although the national liberation movement was carried out in the name of the AL,[1] it did mobilize the support of various groups behind the cause of Bengali nationalism within a very short time. But that was not as much the result of a grass-roots organization like the Congress in India as it was the result of a charismatic leader, Mujib, who with a precise sense of political timing and hypnotic hold over the masses manipulated nationalistic symbols (Khan, 1972: 306–11; Franda, 1982: 10). To borrow Duverger's classification of political parties, AL, like the Pakistan People's Party in Pakistan, was in a category that was a mix between a 'branch' type party and a party of notables (Duverger, 1954: 63–79).

From the beginning, Mujib gave priority to the need of party-building. In the light of his past experience he emphasized two factors, namely, strengthening of the youth fronts and the use of patronage. The AL used its students and labour fronts—Student League and Jatiyo League—for recruiting support for the party. To counter the increasing popularity of the Jatiyo Samajtantric Dal (JSD) among the youth, in November 1972 the AL started a new Youth Front called The Awami Jubo League headed by Mujib's nephew Sheikh Fazlul Huq Moni. He took recourse to patronage—the old style of party-building. Being the party in power, AL had access to a lot of patronage.[2] However, contrary to the viewpoints represented by some social scientists, such as Joseph LaPalombara and Myron Weiner (1966: 439), and J.S. Nye (1967: 412–17), the politics of patronage in Bangladesh had a dysfunctional impact on the strengthening of political parties and other civilian institutions. The creation of, as a prominent Bangladeshi scholar contends, 'a parasitic affluent class, divorced from production and squandering easy money on conspicuous consumption only aggravated the economic problems while the political damage to the regime was irreparable' (Maniruzzaman, 1980: 161). Additionally, the AL's greatest asset—its *Bangapita* (father of the nation) and *Bangabandhu* (friend of Bengal) imbued with his own apparent popularity and new-found international image, advanced his own vague ideology package called the four pillars of Mujibism (the *Mujibvad*): nationalism, secularism, socialism and democracy.[3]

The AL like the Indian National Congress had grown into a platform or umbrella rather than a cohesive or monolithic organization, containing within it a wide range of political interests and ideas. There were factional schisms among old AL leaders (that is, between Tajuddin Ahmed and Syed Nazrul Islam) as well as among the more youthful party leaders (that is, between Sheikh Fazlul Huq Moni and Tofael Ahmed). These schisms went down to the district and sub-divisional levels of the party (Maniruzzaman, 1982: 134–35).

Factionalism too, beleaguered the administration. In 1972, there was bitter infighting between the 'Mujib-nagar' and 'non-Mujib-nagar' administrators (Jahan, 1980: 83–84), in 1973 a third category of schism was added, those who returned from Pakistan.

Functioning of Democracy

In spite of the trappings of a parliamentary democracy, the three years and eight months of Mujib government were essentially a period of his personal rule. Initially, his 'personal popularity counterbalanced the decline in the reputation of his party' (Rahman, 1978: 27). But in the long run, institutional poverty and excessive reliance upon charisma and patrimonialism coupled with the lack of consensus on the norms of political conduct led to the negation of democracy. The pre-Independence consensus on parliamentary democracy soon vanished; also a sharp polarization between the centralist AL and the radical left[4] quickly occurred in 1974. The latter believed that the salvation of the poverty-stricken masses could only be accomplished through a social revolution on the Chinese Maoist model (Maniruzzaman, 1982: 170). While the Sheikh was able to arouse the masses for national revolution, he proved unsuccessful in the more challenging task of running the problem-ridden new state.

Moreover, Mujib's zamindari (landlord) political style, like Bhutto's in Pakistan, of dealing with opposition as well as with dissidents in his own party led him towards authoritarian rule (Akter Banu, 1981: 18–19). When issues, such as restoration of abandoned properties to their rightful owners and violation of fundamental rights by the government tended to divide the majority, Mujib and his advisors disciplined the dissenting members of their party by reminding them that the Constituent Assembly was constituted for the purpose of constitution-making, and, therefore, it must not be considered as a sovereign deliberating body in the spirit of parliamentary democracy! In due course, a chain of actions, a printing and press ordinance, a three month ban on strikes, the prohibition of public gatherings, and the declaration of a state of emergency under which civil rights were suspended, and finally the establishment of a single-party system in 1975, all undermined the spirit of liberal democracy.

Legacies of Pakistani politics continued in Mujib's dealing with opposition. The political culture of confrontation and intolerance, which Mujib symbolized, was not an unusual phenomenon of the united erstwhile Pakistan. As the economy continued to flounder and criticism about the inefficiency and corruption of his party members mounted, Mujib started becoming more intolerant of the opposition.[5]

Simultaneously, with the eclipse of the AL as a political force, a series of revolutionary forces grew in strength, who were not content with mere liberation. The year 1974 witnessed a sharp polarization of policies with the AL and its pro-Moscow and rightist supporters, on the one hand, and the several open and underground communist parties, on the other.[6] Although, the left parties were highly fragmented and characterized by ideological and personal incompatibilities of their leaders, all agreed that Bangladesh's revolution was presently unfinished and believed that the AL represented only the first part of a two-stage revolution.[7]

To silence the opposition, Mujib's government became more and more oppressive and assumed dictatorial powers by violating democratic norms and practices. He also relied more on extra-constitutional means to maintain his power, and, in the process, only hastened the disintegration of civilian rule.

Legitimacy Crisis

Politics in Bangladesh was degenerating during this period (1972–75). All political parties were beset by factional crisis or marked by inter-party and intra-party division, mutual jealousies of political leaders, and adoption of unfair means to gain political power. This led to the erosion of legitimacy. In this naked struggle for power between various groups using their own methods, party process was reduced to a plethora of groups organized along patron–client lines. In other words, one might call it, in the context of Bangladesh, gang politics or *dada-dal* relationship[8] in which leaders compete for power in a constant shift of alliances, splitting off from one actually in power or another in the opposition.

The prevalence and intensity of gang politics (at the national and local levels) brought certain strong elements into the political system, such as undue favours and pushes, which as a normal rule beget mass-scale corruption.

In this atmosphere of rampant corruption, strikes, violence and general lawlessness, Bangladesh turned rapidly into a praetorian polity. Not only was corruption widespread among the top AL members, but the Sheikh's family also came under fire for alleged misuse of power. This gradually tarnished the image of the unquestioned hero of Bangladesh (popularly known as the father of the nation), who was reduced to the principal villain of the piece. Legitimacy became more fragile and the crises worsened due to the deteriorating law and order situation and increased violence.[9]

The Level of Military Institutionalization

It is interesting to note that the armed forces of Bangladesh constitute less than 0.09 per cent of the country's population, but they play a primary role in the power structure of the country. Bangladesh's army, like Burma's, could be characterized, borrowing, Janowitz's typology, as an 'army of national liberation' (Janowitz, 1964: 13), which played a heroic role in the struggle for independence. In countries where the army played an active part in the freedom movement it had a tendency to maintain a sustained interest in the political development which normally went beyond its purely military role. It felt that its contribution to and sacrifice for the achievement of independence was much greater than that of the civilian politicians. As a result, the military leaders believed that they had as much right to shape the political destiny of their countries as the civilian leaders.

Cohesiveness and Representativeness

Unlike Pakistan, the Bangladesh army, in spite of its small size, was highly non-cohesive, factionalized, and plagued with ideological conflicts. The Bangladesh Army was raised mainly out of 3,000–4,000 trained personnel of the East Bengal Regiment who had deserted the Pakistani Army and a large number of young freedom fighters, some of whom had guerrilla private armies. To these were added, immediately after Independence, the repatriated army personnel from Pakistan and new recruits to form the Bangladesh Army.[10]

Political Orientations

The repatriates retained much of the conservative outlook that characterized the armed forces in Pakistan. However, the bulk of the freedom fighters became highly politicized.

These freedom fighting *jawans*, held two distinct views with regard to the future institutional framework of the defence forces in Bangladesh. One group favoured retention of the conventional army. The other group advocated the transformation of Bangladesh armed forces into a kind of 'productive army' on the pattern of the Chinese People's Army (Lifschultz, 1979: 85–88).

Military's Corporate Interest

Bangladesh, here, furnishes an apt illustration of Finer's concept of corporate self-interest in terms of the overriding motives for military intervention.

Despite the conflicting political orientations, the Bangladesh armed forces shared consensus at least in one respect—they were dissatisfied with the AL government for several reasons. The creation of the Jatio Rakhi Bahini (JRB), a 20,000-men strong, well trained and equipped parallel para-militia, which had unquestioned loyalty to Mujib rather than to the nation at large, irked the regular armed forces (Jahan, 1980: 8–14).[11] The army felt neglected and it regarded the JRB with suspicion. Besides the numerical strength of the JRB,[12] which was regarded by many as an 'alternative army',[13] what antagonized the regular army was the indiscriminate use of the JRB under the legal cover of the collaboration order. Furthermore, the corporate interests of the armed forces were seriously jeopardized by Mujib's preferential treatment towards the development of the parallel militia compared to the meagre facilities provided to the regular army (Siddiqui, 1986: 6–7).

Military Expenditure

The fact that the military usurped power in Bangladesh in spite of the military's low level of defence expenditure indicates that the relationship between the level of defence spending and military intervention is imperfect. High level of military expenditure is neither a sufficient nor necessary condition for military rule. The yearly budget, only a meager 16 per cent of total expenditure, was gradually reduced in the successive annual budgets. In the 1973–74 Budget, only a meagre 16 per cent of total expenditure was allowed for defence.[14] In the 1974–75 Budget, it came down to 15 per cent, and in the 1975–76 Budget, the estimated expenditure on defence forces was less than 13 per cent. Most of the modest allocation was spent on buying arms and ammunition for the JRB and on special barracks for the JRB personnel at a time when the army had to be content with 'mostly a collection of obsolete weapons', whereas the JRB was receiving the lion's share of new equipment (*The Guardian*, 16 August 1975).

Grievances

The training institutions were destroyed in the 1971 war, and in some cases, cantonments were razed to the ground, but the AL government did not take any speedy and effective measures for the reconstruction of these institutions and the defence forces remained poorly equipped.[15] Second, the rank and file of the armed forces had been living on much the same level as the civilian population—in virtual poverty, in overcrowded barracks and so on. In 1976, they put forward a series of demands—improved pay, better health facilities, that all future officers be drawn from the ranks (Boswood, 1977). In 1977, too, a series of demands were made. But only some of the demands were conceded.

The discontent of repatriated officers over loss of seniority to freedom fighting officers and of the army over the supposedly favoured treatment accorded to the JRB was compounded by the fact that they were not paid their salary for the 18 months they had spent in Pakistan before being repatriated to Bangladesh.

The army also felt frustrated and deeply humiliated when, in 1974, after being used in civil operations such as recovery of arms and smuggled goods, and anti-corruption drives, it was hastily called off when smuggled goods were discovered in the houses of Mujib's close associates and party stalwarts.[16]

Additionally, all the groups in the defence services shared a common anti-Indian orientation for several reasons. Most members of the armed forces who fought during the liberation war had the feeling that the Indian Army just walked in when the job was nearly finished, and thus robbed them of the glory of liberating Bangladesh. They were also bitter about the fact that the Indian Army took away all the sophisticated weapons left by the Pakistanis as the 'prized booty'. Finally, the rumours that Mujib's second son, Sheikh Jamal, who was inducted into the army, would soon have a senior position in the army, further alienated the army (Franda, 1975: 3). Many senior officers also became apprehensive about Mujib's efforts to bring the army completely under the control of the one-party government. The army, navy, air force, and the security force were each to be represented by one senior officer in the central committee of the party (Khan, 1984: 136).

Aid to Civil Authorities

Despite their grievances against the AL regime, the armed forces practically remained immobilized because of the schism and cleavages that affected them during the early years. When they were asked by Mujib to move to the aid of the civil authorities and when, in fact, they conducted a number of successful operations recovering illegal arms and combing 'extremists' and anti-social elements, in checking smuggling (*Bangladesh Observer*, 10 July 1974), hoarding, and profiteering, they not only regained their confidence, sense of unity and cohesion, but also perceived that their services were indispensable.

As the internal threat mounted, their increasingly growing role in checking smuggling, black-marketing in border belts, and in maintaining law and order, made them not only sensitive to power, but also made them aware of the basic weaknesses of the regime, particularly of the corrupt practices of the top-ranking leaders of the regime.[17]

Socio-Economic Dynamics

A survey of the socio-economic scene in Bangladesh suggests that Bangladesh manifested a fairly high level of social mobilization. In this context, a well known Bangladeshi scholar cogently argues that Bangladesh represents a polity in which, paradoxically, one would expect a low rate of citizen participation in the political system, but in which, in fact, one finds a tradition of mass movement often associated with electoral campaign, which acts as a 'counterweight' that 'politicizes people and tends to higher participation' (Jahan, 1980: 169–70).

Level of Economic Development

At the time of liberation, Bangladesh was one of the poorest countries in the world and it inherited an under-developed economy which was basically colonial and semi-feudal as also extremely primitive and backward.[18]

After liberation, the AL regime was confronted with the threefold challenge of providing immediate relief to the returning refugees, reconstructing the economic infrastructure back to the 1969–70 level, and planning for a socialist economy in Bangladesh. It is noteworthy, given the bourgeois nature of the AL leadership, even the six-point programme of the AL, which ultimately led to the break-up of Pakistan, was basically an elite programme, designed to benefit the upper classes of East Pakistan, that is, the rising business and industrial classes, rich professionals, and urban-centred groups (Ahamed, 1985: 70–95).

After liberation, Mujib was aware of the objective realities and the popular mood. He declared 'one thing is clear to me: to give our people a fair deal Bangladesh would have to find its way to socialist reconstruction' (Ali, 1973: 105). However, within the AL leadership there were conflicting views regarding the kind of socialism to be introduced in Bangladesh. One faction, headed by the finance minister, Tajuddin Ahmed, was in favour of a socialist economy. This group was pro-Indian and pro-Soviet and against accepting any aid from 'imperialist nations', especially the United States (US). Another major faction was led by Khondaker Mushtaque Ahmed (minister of foreign trade and commerce), who was pro-American and in favour of a mixed economy as well as foreign aid (Maniruzzaman, 1982: 134).

In the first two years after liberation, Mujib could avert economic crisis in the country mainly with the help of the massive relief operations carried on by the United Nations Relief Organization in Bangladesh (UNROB) and other international agencies.[19]

During the years 1972–75, agricultural production suffered a serious setback. The decline in production was far more dramatic in the industrial sector. Not surprisingly, the gross domestic product (GDP) in 1974–75 was still short of the 1969–70 level. Thus, there was a 'negative growth rate'[20] in per capita income. This is what Mujib's development strategy produced—'progress with poverty' (Islam, 1984: 8).

Through the nationalization of big industries, banks, and insurance companies, the government gained control over 86 per cent of the total industrial assets and 87 per cent of the foreign trade of Bangladesh. The government mostly appointed party men, who had very little managerial ability, to manage the newly nationalized industries. They had direct access to, and control over, considerable financial resources, and, thus, plenty of opportunities for personal gain through the misuse of power and money. Another important arena for corruption was smuggling of jute and rice to India (Reddaway and Rahman, 1975), which reached 'alarming proportions, thus draining agricultural products out of the country

(Lifschultz, 1974: 348), and accounted for more than 85 per cent of the country's foreign exchange.

The pre-Independence pledges regarding land reforms and land distribution were not honoured. A ceiling of 100 *bighas* (33 acres) was imposed and land revenue on small holdings (8 acres) was abolished. But there was no land reform and the Planning Commission's suggestion regarding the reduction of land-ownership ceiling to 8 acres was rejected (Islam, 1977: 100). Furthermore, despite the high profits of the surplus farmers, proposals for taxation of this sector of the rural population were similarly rejected, as was the suggestion for the elimination of agricultural subsidies, which benefited primarily this group of farmers (Islam, 1977: 13).

In this context, Kirsten Westergaard aptly remarks, 'as with its industrial policy, the agricultural policy of the AL government very much reflected the pattern of intermediate regimes with its neglect of an agrarian revolution and heavy reliance on agricultural subsidies (Westergaard, 1985: 75–76). However, corruption characterized the rural cooperatives, which aimed at distributing fertilizer, pesticides, tube wells, and credit at subsidized rates, but 'the dominant groups which had access to state power dominated them and used them for their own interests' (Islam, 1984:13). Apart from the cooperatives, agricultural inputs distributed by state-appointed dealers and distributors also manifested considerable misallocation and corruption.

From the beginning of 1974, the economic situation in the country became critical (Khan, 1974). While the economy was virtually in a stage of collapse, the situation was aggravated by the 'worst' floods in history—in July and August 1974.[21] The famine conditions resulted in deaths due to starvation[22] and disease which necessitated huge import of food grains.

While much of the petty bourgeoisie benefited from the development strategy of the state, the bourgeoisie and the working class emerged as forces fundamentally inimical to the regime. The bourgeoisie found itself deprived of economic and political power (Lifschultz, 1974: 51), whereas the workers, landless labourers, and marginal peasants saw a sharp decline in their real wages and deterioration in their living standards (Chowdhury, 1976: 346).

It is noteworthy in case of Bangladesh that the rising expectations of the Bengalis only served to intensify the crisis and their leaders failed to fulfil them. The masses expected a better life after the Pakistani exploitation ended. Instead, the increasing economic deterioration of life manifested itself in extensive frustration of the masses in the wake of high social mobilization, which became the pivot of Mujib's decline.

The survey of the socio-economic scene in Bangladesh suggests that Bangladesh manifested a fairly high level of social mobilization. But Mujib's development strategy aggravated the economic crisis, which compounded the political problems of the country. There was continued low production, excessive money supply, deficit financing, and decline in foreign exchange resources. All this led to severe inflationary pressures and price-rocketing. On the other hand, the real wages of the workers and peasants declined substantially. Thus, there was neither growth nor redistribution during the period from 1972 to 1975. The workers did not see any change between Ayub's system of 'private capitalism' and Mujib's 'state capitalism'. Even as the bourgeoisie and workers were antagonistic to the regime, the AL faced an internal crisis. Many of the petty bourgeois elements who received no benefits because of a lack of access to decision-makers also became critics of the regime.

The interaction between various variables and civil–military boundaries suggests that Bangladesh (during 1972–75) conformed precisely to Huntington's description of 'praetorian polity', which is characterized by a 'low level of institutionalization and high levels of participation' (Huntington, 1968: 80–85) in which social forces using their own method act directly in the political sphere.

If one follows institutionalization 'as the process by which organization and procedures acquire values and stability' (Huntington, 1968: 1–24), then any measure of the process in Bangladesh exemplifies that the country's civil and military establishments did reflect a comparatively high degree of 'autonomy' and 'complexity'—two of Huntington's criteria of institutionalization. They might, however, score lower on measures of 'adaptability' and 'coherence'—Huntington's other two criteria—since both might be seen to have features of rigidity and to have displayed disunity at critical points during the first decade of Bangladesh's political evolution.

On the other hand, the political parties during 1972–75 had been marked by low institutional development. The opposition in Bangladesh consisted of a large number of splinter parties, ranging the gamut from the right to the left. The AL was the party of independence and maintained organized cadres. Yet, it could not provide the necessary stability and national cohesion for keeping the democratic system intact, and neither could it facilitate the articulation of pressing demands within society. The party system in Bangladesh failed to develop into a mediation organ between the needs, problems, and wishes of the electorate and the purposes, limitations, and problems at the level of national government. The parties became instruments of power play for their leaders. All parties beset by factionalism and jockeying for power lacked the will for party-building on a truly national basis.

Two to three years after the birth of Bangladesh, the situation deteriorated at a rate faster than in Pakistan during 1947–58. With the erosion of values and interpersonal trust in society, an air of anarchy reigned supreme. Society expected the use of state power towards economic emancipation by means of shared sufferings in the short run and of shared prosperity in the long run. But the AL equated the state to the ruling party and used state power for self-aggrandizement. The inevitable consequences were disparity, discontent, and the attendant socio-political tensions. At the root of the economic crisis in Bangladesh was the Mujib government's political approach to economic management. The party channel became the key channel of control of the direction of economy, which resulted in inefficiency, widespread corruption, and immoral practices of party cadres and relatives. The problem was compounded by the subsequent schism and factionalism within the AL, in the army and bureaucracy, and the growth of armed opposition to the regime. Furthermore, the 'privatization' of the government, the arbitrary definition and use of the law, rotation of elites between prison and cabinet with political reshufflings, the government's purposeful indifference to pro-government criminals, the ruling elites' connivance on political grounds with the misdeeds of the law-breakers, the government's arbitrary use of state power to gag and annihilate the opposition, and rampant violence, all eroded the legitimacy of the government.

Thus, being pressed by the exigencies of the situation such as the growing economic crisis, the increasingly violent role of the radicals and reactionary parties, deteriorating law and order situation, and above all, the ineffectiveness of the AL due to its intraparty factional strife, Mujib took recourse to some authoritarian measures for consolidating his power. With the proclamation of emergency (on 28 December 1974) and by switching to a one-party system (25 January 1975), Mujib finally gave up the façade of parliamentary democracy and resorted to the device of one-party dictatorship (by the newly formed Bangladesh Krishak Sramik League or BKSAL) and totalitarian control (Ahmed, 1984). In such a situation, the absence of another civilian countervailing force to the discredited civilian regime, the army, notwithstanding its imperfect organization and inner factionalism, appeared to be the only organ for focusing frustrated aspirations lacking a coherent ideology. It was under such circumstances that Bangladesh entered (on 15 August 1975) the era of *coup d'etat*.

Militarization of Bangladesh

In 1975, after four years of its birth, Bangladesh was once again at the starting point. In 1975, Bangladesh witnessed a chain of *coups d'etat*—the 'constitutional coup' of Sheikh Mujibur Rahman on 25 January, the bloody coup of the junior officers on 15 August in which the Sheikh was assassinated and Khondaker Mushtaq Ahmed was brought to power, the coup of Khaled Musharraf on 3 November in which Mushtaq was toppled from power, and, finally, the army mutiny or 'Sepoy Revolution'[23] of 7 November in which Musharraf was killed and General Ziaur Rahman (also known as Zia) emerged as the *de facto* leader of the military regime. Sheikh Mujib's brutal downfall,[24] violent counter-coups and uprisings in the military made many political observers and analysts sceptical about the viability and stability of Bangladesh.

The striking feature of the Bangladesh coup of 1975 was that it was bloody, whereas all the Pakistani coups had been peaceful. Essentially, the long term causes of the coups, both in Pakistan and Bangladesh, were similar, namely, poor institutionalization, lack of political consensus, and an excessive reliance upon the charisma of individuals to weld political structures. To gain personal power both Bhutto and Mujib used analogous styles of politics and depended upon resentful armed forces to crush political dissent. Both aborted any civilian alternative to their personal rule.

The coups in these two countries have to be seen essentially in terms of the failure of the civilian countervailing forces. It can be plausibly argued that the military intervenes not because of its strong organization, but owing to the shortcomings and weaknesses of those whom it overthrows. Hence, the causes for intervention are to be found in the political and socio-economic environment rather than in military institutions themselves. Given the absence of orderly political processes in Pakistan and Bangladesh, the armed forces were easily able to proclaim themselves as the sole defenders of national sovereignty. Unfortunately, in such polities, it becomes inevitable to draw upon the institutional viability of the armed forces to circumvent the functional problems of democratic government.

Military Regimes of Zia and Ershad: Strategies and Tactics of Survival and Legitimization

Capturing power may not be problematic for the functionaries of the armed forces; the consolidation of their authority is infinitely more difficult. Only by converting power into authority and legitimacy can they ensure their sustenance and survival.

In the first flush of their tenure, South Asian military regimes sought to project themselves as some kind of missionary, progressive, neutral, and patriotic guardians of the nation. But military solutions to social problems can be counter-productive, and the military is inexperienced in handling social problems. Therefore, like their counterparts elsewhere, South Asian military rulers have sought 'creative relationships with civilian political groups' (Kukreja, 1991: 77). This arrangement also brings about a cosmetic 'civilianization' to what is essentially a military administration. Through a combination of common sense and opportunism, four strategies for the survival and legitimization of South Asian military regimes are evolved. They are, collusion with the bureaucracy, elimination of political opponents, populist policies, and constitutional legitimization and democratization. The present study analyses the extent and reasons for the success or failure of these strategies in fortifying the regimes of Ayub Khan, Yahya Khan, Zia-ul-Haq, Musharraf, Ziaur Rahman, and Ershad. While studying their strategies one is made aware of how strikingly similar they were, except for the tactical differences demanded by the exigencies of the situation.

Civil–Military Partnership

As has been emphasized by Henry Bienen, the term 'military regime' is a misnomer, for all military regimes have large civilian components. This happens because the military lacks the administrative skills and it wants to give a degree of civilian touch to the regime (Bienen, 1978: 205–25; Bienen and Fitton, 1978: 27–57).

As far as the case of Bangladesh is concerned, under Ziaur Rahman, military bureaucracy evolved an alliance with the civil bureaucracy in order to consolidate power at both the national and local levels. Much of the prestige of those civil servants who seemed to have lost the *esprit de corps* during the Mujib era was restored. By 1980, civil servants dominated most of the high-level decision-making posts. This is why the regime of Zia has been described by some observers as the revival of civil–military bureaucracy complex—a prototype of Ayub's regime in Pakistan during 1958–69 (Kukreja, 1991: 155–57).

Ershad's government drew a close parallel with that of Zia-ul-Haq's regime in Pakistan as it was essentially a military provenance. The military officers exercised enormous power and influence over civil administration and in the decision-making arena. This pattern of military–civil service coalition, in fact, provided 'cohesion without consensus' as they resisted civilian demands for political participation by relying on the control apparatus of the state (Kukreja, 1991).

Elimination of Opposition

Another short-term strategy of survival, perpetuation, and consolidation followed by Ayub, Zia-ul-Haq, Ziaur Rahman, and Ershad consisted of elimination of politics at the initial stage and the deliberate policy of dividing and isolating the supporters and the opposition at a later stage. Zia undertook a planned purge of the war heroes from the positions of strength within armed forces (Manirazzaman, 1988: 221; Lifschutz, 1979: 47–63). At the same time; Zia had ensured that there was no challenge to his power and supremacy in the army by removing his potential rivals from the centres of power and placing trusted officers in their places. After securing his position in the armed forces, Ziaur Rahman mounted a concerted drive against the civilian groups.

In this context, Ziaur Rahman used the carrot and stick strategy. The stick was mostly for the uncompromising opponents of the regime—the AL and the JSD. The leaders and workers of both these parties were arrested and thrown in jail. The promised parliamentary election and the resultant power-sharing offer was the carrot meant for other political parties. Apart from intimidating the AL, a policy of coercing all other dissenters was also let loose in Bangladesh.

Both Ziaur Rahman and Ershad went on a witch-hunt and a concerted drive against those civilian groups, which they had once overthrown. Even Ziaur Rahman, despite his occasional and tactical praise for Sheikh Mujib, did not hide his antagonism to the 'Awami-Baksalites'; reviving Mujib's memory was for him only a means to consolidate his position.

Following the divide and rule policy, he secretly assured some JSD leaders of economic and political opportunities if they remained quiet. Ziaur Rahman not only tried to split the AL, but also sought to thwart any such alliance which might emerge to oppose him from time to time, including that of parties which had supported the 1975 coup. General Ershad, on the other hand, wanted to consolidate his position within the army, the regime's only support base or primary constituency. After the 1981 coup, Bangladesh witnessed the hanging and sacking of a large number of freedom fighters in the army (Kabir, 1985: 185).

Ershad faced stiff opposition from a large number of political parties and factional groups, students, lawyers, and workers. Although the military was in no mood to make concession to the political parties demanding a share in state power, it was forced to offer a national 'dialogue' with the opposition (Rahman, 1984: 240–41).

Populist Policies

Populist policies, unlike popular politics usually prove to be short-sighted, insincere, and are designed essentially to buy mass support.

They, therefore, hamper development as well as an equitable and just social order in the long run. Ziaur Rahman's development strategy reveals, more or less, a similar picture. Ziaur Rahman tried to establish legitimacy on the basis of 'Bangladeshi nationalism' and a reassertion of the Islamic identity of Bangladesh. The nationalist ideology also produced a concomitant 'development ideology' (Franda, 1981: 357–80; Maniruzzaman, 1980: 193), which emphasized self-reliance and self-sufficiency of the economy.[25] However, a cursory overview of the economic policies reveals a combination of radical rhetoric and conservative implementation, particularly coupled with burgeoning growth of an 'enclave economy' which eventually produced insurmountable dilemmas for Zia, in both urban and rural areas (Ahmed, 1978: 1168–80).

As far as the use of Islamization as a legitimization strategy is concerned, Ziaur Rahman reasserted the Islamic identity of Bangladesh through a constitutional amendment. The amendment deleted 'secularism as one of the fundamental principles of the state ideology', substituting it by 'absolute trust and faith in Almighty Allah'.[26] Ziaur Rahman had manipulated symbols intelligently to recruit the support of the Islamists. Under Zia, Bangladesh became an influential member of the Organization of Islamic Conference (OIL) and strengthened the country's position as a Muslim nation (Kukreja, 1991: 163).

The Ershad government further sought to exploit the medium of Islam. He exhorted his countrymen that Bangladesh would not survive unless it went out to set up Islamic rule and administration. He declared Islam as the country's only way for emancipation. He declared Bangladesh an Islamic state after winning the March 1988 parliamentary elections. The establishment of the 'Zakat Fund', an organization of 'aid Islam' mission, and the declaration of Friday as a holiday were indicative of the regime's interest in the Islamization process reminiscent of Zia-ul-Haq's regime in Pakistan (Kukreja, 1991: 165).

Following the legacy to his Pakistani counterpart, the Islamic orientation of Lt. General Ershad shared many similarities with the irrevocable 'Islamization of Pakistan' by Zia-ul-Haq. Although Islamization had bolstered Ershad's image on the international scene, but at the national level, the rapid pace of Islamization was resented by progressive forces as these Bengali Muslims remained keenly aware of their distinct Bengali cultural identity.

Legitimization through Civilianization and Democratization

Given the truism that in all modern political systems ruling groups must respond to the rising appetite for political participation in some way, be it authentic or populist, the military rulers in Pakistan and Bangladesh felt the need for the civilianization and democratization of their military regimes. In fact, comparison of the two Zias and Ershad with Ayub is too obvious to escape notice.

The pattern of leadership under the military–bureaucratic regime can hardly provide the best basis of organizing mass support, either for economic development or political institution-building. Military rulers being acutely aware of the necessity of a self-sustaining political process start very cautiously and gradually thrash out their political civilianization programme, partly in response to the developments within the armed forces and partly in consonance with the degree of political base that they could establish. A study by this author reveals that the military rulers' systematic and carefully orchestrated 'civilianization' and 'democratization' process, broadly speaking, involves three steps: (*a*) aggregation of regime support involving co-option of the important sections of the political groups, on the one hand, and expansion of participation at the rural level on the other; (*b*) constitutional legitimization through referendums, presidential and parliamentary elections, which gives the regime an image of winning a popular mandate to rule; and (*c*) institutionalization of a political party which helps the regime to mobilize political support (Kukreja, 1991).

To create his own support base, Zia began to cultivate those who had suffered deprivation and humiliation under the previous regime. In a manner akin to Ayub Khan, he sought to marshal rural elite support and votes through the introduction of *gram sarkar* and village defence force in each village (Franda, 1981: 4; Kamaluddin, 1980: 26–71). The local councillors could be mobilized for this and manipulated through 'development' and 'nation-building' activities.

Significantly, Ziaur Rahman, like Ayub before him and Zia-ul-Haq later (who held local council elections), followed the safe strategy of establishing a local base before holding presidential or parliamentary elections. Although not successful in the Union *parishad* elections, Ziaur Rahman successfully wooed the local bodies through subsidized inputs in land, gave incentives and patronage to local landlords, and operated in much the same way as Ayub had done through the rural work programmes (Zaman, 1984: 200–01).

General Ershad followed in the footsteps of Ziaur Rahman. His election schedule aimed to start with *upa-zila* (local bodies or sub-district)[27] election to be followed by presidential and then parliamentary elections. The envisaged sequence indicated Ershad's desire to use the *upa-zila* officers in getting himself elected president, akin to Ziaur Rahman's Union *parishad* elections held in 1977.

Referendum

The referendum is an important technique of bolstering legitimacy and was adopted by Ayub, Ziaur Rahman, Zia-ul-Haq, and Ershad. Interestingly, all of them first proposed a presidential system, then secured their personal authority through referendum, and finally held presidential (in Ziaur Rahman's and Ershad's case parliamentary) elections after the referendum.

Ayub held a referendum on 15 February 1960, after the Basic Democracies Order of October 1959, in a ballot paper simply marked 'yes' or 'no' through the device of a white versus a black box. Each ballot was numbered and registered against a specific voter so that the government could identify defaulters. Without a choice of candidates, Ayub declared himself the first 'elected' president of Pakistan. Ziaur Rahman did exactly the same, except that he first became president in April 1977 on the basis of presidential proclamation of August 1975, and subsequently held the referendum in May 1977, in which he once again secured, without a rival, an overwhelming majority—98.97 per cent, of the votes. Both held the referendum about two years after assuming power. Taking a leaf from the experience of their predecessors, Zia-ul-Haq and Ershad also followed the same device to gain legitimacy (Kukreja, 1991: 171–72).

Elections and Party-Building

In most military regimes, more often than not, elections and party-building have been used as legitimizing device. Ayub, Ziaur Rahman, Zia-ul-Haq, and Ershad understood the utility of election as a way of gaining legitimacy. Holding a referendum without a political party is possible, but to fight an election requires the instrument of a party; non-party elections, however, do occur (as in case of Zia-ul-Haq's regime). The imperative of political perpetuation supported by a mass base makes military rulers turn towards party-building, and they get embroiled in it, denying the myth of their 'non-political' outlook. In the process they legitimize their own power base by either taking over the existing political party or floating a new party through money, job, as well as other forms of patronage (Khan and Zafarullah, 1960: 66).

Ziaur Rahman followed a similar logic. He evolved his own party, gradually splitting the opposition. Ultimately, he formed his own BNP with himself as president for five years by uniting the Jatiyo Ganotantric Dal (JAGODAL), and National Awami Party (NAP), United People's Party (UPP), Muslim League and parties of the minorities. It was this party which emerged victorious in the parliamentary elections of February 1979.

Ershad also went to float a political party, namely, the Jatiya Dal (National Party) for the purpose of winning parliamentary elections. However, these government parties, whether the Pakistan Muslim League (PML) in Pakistan, BNP or Jatiya Dal in Bangladesh, had no grass-roots base. They were not homogeneous; there was no inner party democracy; and basically they indicated the military rulers' authoritarian bent of mind and their continuing quest for a civilian face. It can be said that all government parties, PML, BNP and Jatiya Dal, were born in power, grew with power, and continued in power until they were ousted by another military officer. These parties were formed by the generals in power and are not a result of any popular movement outside the office. Therefore, they commanded only a neophyte's open support in view of their state patronage instead of mass support, which is derived on the basis of programmes and ideology.

Presidential elections were the culmination of the expansion of political participation in our case studies of Ayub, Ziaur Rahman, Zia-ul-Haq, and Ershad. Ziaur Rahman in Bangladesh introduced electoral politics soon after the referendum, just like Ayub. In June 1978, a presidential election was held in which he secured 76.63 per cent of the popular vote. To seal his survival, Zia went a step further and held parliamentary elections in February 1979. About 50.94 per cent voters cast their vote and Zia's BNP secured 207 out of 300 seats. Victory was secured through 400 defections from the JSD to Zia's BNP (Haque, 1980: 221–22; Jahan, 1980: 214). Ershad followed his footsteps in Bangladesh in holding parliamentary elections, presidential election, and lifting the martial law. Ershad and his Jatiya Dal indulged in massive rigging and irregularities in presidential as well as parliamentary elections. These elections were then described as 'historic events' by the military rulers. But such measures are expedient as they aim at providing a civic gloss to what is essentially a military rule.

Following his Pakistan counterpart, General Ayub, Ziaur Rahman exhibited considerable political acumen in successfully consolidating his hold through presidential elections and a populist policy of rural economic development. The emulation, by Zia-ul-Haq and Ershad, coupled with manipulation of Islam as a demonstrably successful strategy is therefore entirely understandable. But, in the ultimate analysis, Ayub was overthrown, Ziaur Rahman was assassinated, and Zia was killed in a mysterious air crash, for their authority had no moorings in genuine popular sanction. Ershad despite his massive victories in the referendum and farcical elections in Bangladesh was confronted with the tremendous political unrest and movements conducted by opposition alliances and ultimately he had to resign. The military regime has to face a crisis of legitimacy sooner or later (Haider, 1999: 57–80; Kukreja, 1989: 836).

Restoration of Democracy in Bangladesh: 1991 Onwards

Following a mass upsurge that overthrew the military regime of General Ershad in 1990, a democratically elected government was ushered in (Hakim, 1998: 283–90). Bangladesh has witnessed three relatively peaceful free and fair elections, in 1991, 1996, and 2001, all undertaken under caretaker governments. The polity, however, is overshadowed by weak institution-building coupled with personalized politics, legitimacy crisis, and deteriorating law and order situation leading to induction of the military in civil duties, rising tide of Islamic fundamentalism, weakening of social cohesion and lack of responsible opposition.

Weak Political Institutionalization

Even three-and-a-half decades after its creation, Bangladesh has not been able to establish or build strong institutions that would safeguard and guarantee the essence of democracy. The lack of an institutional mechanism to restrict and curb authoritarian tendencies, as well as to establish independence of various institutions, has led to the problems of governance. The absence of checks and balances lead to the lack of accountability of the political leadership. The opposition often disregards the parliament and has treated the institutions as merely a forum for and by the ruling coalition. If protest actions outside the Jatiya Sangsad weakens the parliament, absence of a clear division of responsibilities among various branches of the state has led to the concentration of power in hands of the executive (Dutta, 2003: 234).

The transition to democracy in Bangladesh is not full-fledged, it lacks consolidation. The holding of regular, periodic, free and fair elections to the parliament is a positive development from the pre-1991 era when 'controlled' elections were used as 'legitimization' strategy for the military regimes of General Ziaur Rahman and General Ershad respectively. Even though three national elections have been held since 1990 (1991, 1996, and 2001), the democratic process remains fragile. Opportunistic alliances, immaturity of leadership, unwillingness to accept the people's verdict, and lack of responsible opposition make the polity unstable and insecure.

Since 1991 when the first multiparty elections were held, two parties (The AL and the BNP), two personalities (Sheikh Hasina, Khaleda Zia), and two families (those of Mujibur Rahman and Ziaur Rahman) have dominated Bangladeshi politics. The two dominant parties—the BNP and AL—had alternated in power, with the BNP winning in 1991, the AL in 1996, and a BNP-led coalition again in 2001. According to an astute scholar:

> [W]hile the dominance of two dominant parties generally tends to create a stable political system, in Bangladesh the close contestation has created a deadlock. Neither party is willing to accept electoral defeat and serve as a 'loyal opposition' in parliament. As a result, parliament has never functioned properly. Each election has been followed by prolonged boycott of parliament by the opposition. The government in power has also indulged in acts of

> suppression and harassment of political opposition. Both parties have nurtured thugs and criminal elements to intimidate the opposition. Both have attempted to control government and non-government institutions by appointing partisan supporters to head key institutions. Media and civil society groups have long identified these problems plaguing Bangladesh's fragile democratic political system, but parties have ignored their criticisms (Jahan, 2003: 223).

Since the opposition is constantly at logger-heads with the government, democratic culture cannot grow in this environment. Neither of the main political parties accepts the legitimacy of its rival, even when elected. When the BNP has been in power, it has sought to disgrace the AL, while the AL has always seen itself as the true heir of independence, a party with a mass base, unlike the cantonment-created BNP. For the last decade, whichever party has been out of power has harassed the government, calling it a killer, corrupt, oppressive, terrorist, anti-poor, and backing up its accusations with an indiscriminate use of *hartal*s, political strikes, which shut down the country. *Hartal*s are modelled on the popular protests in India against the fading powers of the Raj. The symbolism is important, since it represents a total rejection of the other party. The opposition participates to a constitutional minimum in parliament and stages frequent walk-outs. The party in government uses the law against its opponents, charging them with corruption, misappropriation of state resources, implication in criminal activities of all kinds including treason and murder.

Longstanding animosity between the BNP and the main opposition, the AL, has intensified. The two parties blame each other for patronizing criminal elements, engaging in undemocratic behaviour, and hatching plots to annihilate the other and destroy the country. Parliament remains mostly non-functional, as the AL repeatedly walks out or boycotts sessions, alleging government restrictions on their participation in parliamentary debates. Partisanship continues to affect the functioning of the civil bureaucracy and civil society organizations. The destructive confrontation between the government and the political opposition has continued. The administration has become even more embroiled in partisan conflict. An alarming rise in violence and crimes, often committed by people with close ties to political parties, has increased citizen disenchantment with political processes.

According to a well known scholar:

> Civil society organizations and the media depicted this confrontational politics as destructive, urging the two main parties to engage in dialogue to reach a consensus on issues of national interest and on basic principles of democratic competition, but failed to elicit any positive response. However, civil society organizations and the media did succeed in bringing some transparency to the state of politics and administration. Through investigative journalism, newspapers highlighted the problems facing the country. Their reports exposed the deteriorating law and order situation, corruption, the criminalization of politics, and inefficiencies in administration. Transparency International ranked Bangladesh number one in corruption worldwide, for the third year in a row (Jahan, 2004: 57).

Despite regular and periodic elections, Bangladesh continues to be confronted with a crisis of legitimacy. Lack of public trust and confidence in the elected government has institutionalized the arrangement of caretaker administration as an integral component of Bangladeshi election politics. One Bangladeshi scholar, Mohammod A. Hakim, has maintained that this could be an ideal model for other Third World countries. The mechanism/arrangement, however underlines the deep-seated distrust among the political parties and lack of popular confidence in the ability of an elected government to conduct non-partisan elections (Hakim, 2003: 47–65). Each parliamentary election has been followed by allegations of rigging, intimidation, and other forms of malpractices by the party losing the polls.

During Khaleda Zia's first government, the AL organized 173 days of *hartal*s and the BNP retaliated with 85 days of total stoppage of public activities when Hasina was in power (Shehabuddin, 1999: 151).

The parties in power have also displayed lack of maturity and political acumen. Unable to overcome past antagonisms, they tend to treat the opposition as an opponent rather than a legitimate player in a democracy. Indeed, Hasina's refusal to give adequate coverage to the opposition in the state-controlled media led to a BNP-sponsored *hartal*. Similarly, immediately after assuming office, Khaleda filed a series of corruption cases against members of the former Hasina government, banned a number of AL leaders from leaving the country, and incarcerated a host of second rung leaders.

The prolonged trading of charges between Khaleda and Hasina has reached a new and dangerous level. In a measure reminiscent of personal vendetta of the pre-independence period, Khaleda began a process of revisionist historiography in Bangladesh. Efforts are being made to systematically erase Mujibur Rahman's role in the liberation of Bangladesh.

Rising Tide of Islamic Fundamentalism in Bangladesh

In recent years, Bangladesh has experienced an alarming rise in Islamic fundamentalism and is fast becoming a hotbed of Islamic terrorism. The fear that Bangladesh is hurtling towards the black hole of religious extremism is a very real one. The current BNP/ Jamaat-e-Islami regime has been fanning the fires of radical Islamism. Now, the tactic support of state authorities has given them a carte blanche to operate with brazenness. Terrorist acts are part of a systematic attempt to destroy Bangladesh's secular and democratic political parties, as well as its vibrant intellectual and cultural life, and to convert the country into a hard line Islamic one. It would be no exaggeration to say that Bangladesh is another Afghanistan in the making (Karlekar, 2005).

Since the restoration of democracy in Bangladesh in 1990, the country is witnessing the rising tide of Islamic fundamentalism. Various government measures provided tacit support to this process, attributed to the presence of the Jamaat-I-Islami (a right-wing Islamist party), in the ruling coalition. Thus, by the time of the first free and fair multiparty elections that were held in 1991, the Islamization process and religion-based politics were firmly in place and most political parties, including the secularly-inclined AL, were reconciled to the Islamic indoctrination of Bangladesh. During the election campaign, although military rule was the prime concern, parties found it judicious and politically rewarding to champion Islamic issues. This trend continued since then and has led to the rehabilitation of the Jamaat in Bangladesh politics.

As a result, the secular-oriented AL and the right-wing BNP were not averse to enlisting the support of the Jamaat and the party has emerged as a major player in coalition building.

In some form or another, the Jamaat has played a significant role in the formation of all the three governments since 1991. The alliance with the Jamaat largely enabled the BNP to secure an absolute majority in 1991 and 2001. The growing Islamic fervour in Bangladesh and growth of the Jamaat manifested themselves in far reaching changes that are taking place in the country. Despite its avowed commitment to secularism, the AL has adopted a number of overtly religious positions to win over mainstream voters. During the 2001 Jatiya Sangsad elections, its manifesto promised not to enact any legislation contrary to the Quran and pledged to establish a Shariat bench in the Supreme Court. The Jamaat, which fought the election as an ally of the BNP, sought to regulate and institutionalize, 'mosque-based education'. Other parties have also adopted an overtly religious position in their manifestoes.

The BNP is following the policies of Ziaur Rahman's military regime, which is pro-Islam, and almost anti-India. As facts reveal, a moderate democratic and secular nationalist government of Mujibur Rahman was replaced by the authoritarian forces in August 1975 and his policies of anti-imperialism, anti-colonialism, non-alignment, and close friendship with India at the regional level underwent change under the military regimes of General Ziaur-Rahman and General Ershad respectively.

On the other hand, the AL, though it re-emerged as a major influence in Bangladeshi politics (Mujibur Rahman's daughter Sheikh Hasina won the 1996 elections), has still not re-acquired its pre-eminent position in the interplay of political forces in the country, and has failed to reinstate the ethos and ideology of the liberation movement. Also, the socio-economic dynamics of both the society and power structure of Bangladesh have changed profoundly compared to the period between the mid-1950s and 1975. 'The characteristics of this change, as one perceives them, are: the ethos and ideology of the movement for autonomy and the liberation struggle are no longer relevant to Bangladesh politics, second, there is a re-emergence of Islam as a factor which is considered necessary to consolidate Bangladesh's separate national identity' (Bhardwaj, 2003: 204–05). The increasing influence of the Jamaat and other religious groups confirms this assessment. This was clearly reflected in the October 2001 General Elections.

Growing Islamic Militancy

Religious intolerance and militancy has increased dramatically. Various government measures provided tactic support to the Islamists. In January 2004, ceding to the demands of Islamist partner of the coalition, the Islami Oikya Jote (Islamic United Front [IOJ]), the government banned the publications of the Ahmadiyyas, a Muslim sect. The IOJ, in collusion with other small Islamist groups, desecrated and demolished Ahmadiyya mosques in various parts of the country.

In rural western and north-western Bangladesh, a gang of Islamist militants, headed by a man calling himself 'Bangla Bhai' (Bengali brother), unleashed a reign of terror beginning in April 2003.

Bangladesh is now in the eye of a new storm—Islamic extremism and terrorism. For years Dhaka congratulated itself and was feted as a model Muslim country that had rejected extremism and stayed on a secular, democratic path. But looking through post 9/11 lens, there seem to be demonic winds of terror swirling over the Padma, Jamuna, and Meghna rivers that were muses for Rabindranath Tagore and Kazi Nazrul Islam.

Contemporary Bangladesh is emerging as a hub of and haven for Islamic fanatics of various shades. Bangladesh's image has already been tarnished, on the one hand, by the violent activities of indigenous and foreign jihadis, and the present BNP-Jamaat-e-Islami governments' unwillingness to destroy the poison tree of Islamic fundamentalism, on the other. It could be a new born in the nursery of fanatics who pose a far greater danger to Bangladeshi civil society and polity than the army did during the military regimes of Gen. ~al Ziaur Rahman or General H.M. Ershad, who jack-booted their way to power.

The Jamaat-e-Islami and IOJ, which share power with BNP under the leadership of Prime Minister Khaleda Zia, masquerade as 'Islamic moderates'. Wolves in sheep-skins, they have successfully guided the present regime to a pro-Pakistan, pro-Islamist position.

In a sense, the process of Bangladesh's Islamization in the mould of Osama-bin Laden's world view began during the military rule of General Ziaur Rahman who was subsequently assassinated. He used Saudi funds to set up *madrasas* and mosques. This policy was later followed and more vigorously so, by General H.M. Ershad.

By the time parliamentary democracy was restored in Bangladesh in 1991, tens of thousands of *madrasas*, now universally recognized as jihad factories, fuelled by Saudi Wahabi 'charity' and Pakistani Wahabi-Deobandi funds, had mushroomed all over Bangladesh. Over the years, men who studied in these *madrasas* have come to occupy offices in government, civil administration, police, and the armed forces of that country. The poison of fanaticism/religious extremism has simultaneously seeped into every branch of Bangladesh's government.

The Harkat-ul-Jehad-I-Islami-Bangladesh (HUJIB) an appendage of Al-Qaida based in Bangladesh is one of the most sinister terrorist organizations (Ali, 2004: 1143). It was established by Al-Qaida[28] and the Islamic International Front to train *Akaran* Muslims from Mynanmar in jihadi activities. It was also charged with the responsibility of imparting jihadi knowledge to the Muslims from Indonesia, Thailand, Cambodia, and Brunei—to set the South-east ablaze, so to say.[29] HUJIB, whose members call themselves the 'Bangladeshi Taliban' is believed to have a network of arms trafficking and cadre of 16,000-strong heavily armed activists run by a Chittagong-based man called Shaukat Usmani. This organization aspires to abolish parliamentary democracy in Bangladesh and bring in Shariat rule. It seeks to establish an Islamic order in Bangladesh similar to the Taliban's erstwhile one in Afghanistan by, among other things, waging war against liberal intellectuals. It wants Bangladesh's Bangla culture and ethos to be supplanted by Wahabism imported from Saudi Arabia, which is rabidly anti-India.

Simultaneously, and also greatly facilitated by the ascendance of Islamists, Bangladesh has become the camping ground of jihadis of various shades of green—from those flying Osama bin Laden's banner to those on the ISI's payroll. In sum, patronage of cross-border terrorism, and an increasingly violent trend towards Islamic fundamentalism within, is a deadly combination. It has turned Pakistan into a rogue state, Bangladesh is very close to becoming one (Karlekar, 2003: 6).

There is no dearth of evidence about the nexus between members of the ruling coalition in Bangladesh such as the Jamaat-e-Islami and the Jamaat-ul-Mujahidin Bangladesh (JMB).

The JMB actively supports moves to establish Islamic emirates in Muslim majority districts of Myanmar and in southern Thailand. It also has links with extremist Islamic groups in Malaysia and Indonesia. It has close links with pro-Taliban and pro-Al-Qaida outfits in Pakistan. Maulana Rahman has claimed that the Jagrata Muslim Janata Bangladesh (JMJB) has over 10,000 full-time cadres and around a 1,000,000 part-time activists.

There are reports that Bangla Bhai enjoys the support of influential BNP cabinet ministers like Aminul Haq and Fazlur Rahman Patal from the Rajshahi District. The JMB is also known to enjoy a measure of sympathy and support from sections of the police and military intelligence set-up.

The governments' response to JMB and JMJB terrorism has been extremely suspect. Despite the mounting evidence of their activities, until fairly recently, the state agencies continuously denied the very existence of these entities.

The most troubling aspect of Harkat-ul-Jehad-I-Islami's (HUJI) rise in Bangladesh is its connections with religious groups. The group has camps in the inaccessible, hilly terrains of Cox Bazzar and Banderban and along the no man's land adjacent to the Bangladesh–Burma border. The group enjoys the support and patronage of about 30 *madrasas* in Chittagong. These camps are used for recruitment and weapons training. American journalist Alex Perry alleges, '...southern Bangladesh has become a haven for hundreds of Jihadis in the land. They find natural allies in Muslim guerrillas from India hiding across the border, and in Muslim Rohingyas, tens of thousands of whom fled the ethnic and religious suppression of the Burmese military junta in the late 1970 and 80s' (Perry, 2002). All these terrorist activities have converted Mujib's dream into a nightmare.

If the Al-Quada is allowed to entrench itself in Bangladesh, it would have successfully established a semi-arc of terrorist networks stretching from Dhaka to Jakarta, with a sizeable presence along some of the most important stretches of international waters, including the Bay of Bengal, Indian Ocean, South China Sea, and the Pacific Ocean.

The axis of terror, closer home is deepening its base in Bangladesh, with the proliferation of training camps, which turn out a lethal cocktail of anti-India jihadis and insurgents. Indian intelligence agencies have put together irrefutable information about the existence of 190 camps not only concentrated along the India–Bangladesh border, but also in districts like Sylhet, Mymensingh, and Khagrachhari. In addition to being trained in jungle warfare and ambushes, these terrorists are also using women and children as shields.

Dhaka threatens to become India's biggest security nightmare. Terrorist groups such as the Al-Qaida and LeT are using Bangladesh as a safe haven for the export of terrorism. Out of the nearly 200 terrorist camps that exist in Bangladesh, ULFA runs 33 camps, the National Front of Tripura runs 21 camps, and the National Democratic Front of Bodoland has 19 camps. In this context, India is upset with Dhaka's insensitivity.

Bangladesh's Civil Society under Seige

The re-emergence of Islamic identity has torn the social cohesion and intensified the communal divide in Bangladesh. If the Bengali cultural identity excluded the non-Bengali Chakmas, the Islamic identity excluded the Chakmas as well as Hindus and Buddhists. Since its early days, Bangladesh has followed a policy detrimental to the minorities, most visible in the case of the Chakmas.

Predominance of the Islamic identity and the corresponding dilution of secularism and Bengali cultural identity have worked against the tradition of religious tolerance and accommodation. In this context a Bangladesh scholar aptly remarks:

> Although technically speaking, there is nothing to prevent minorities to participate in mainstream politics in Bangladesh and hence being in their own kinship structures into play, the fore-grounding of a majoritarianism inscribing Bengali as a state language and Islam as a state religion automatically marginalises religious and ethnic minorities from attaining a central role in determining class hegemony (Guhathakurta, 2002).

The political landscape underscores the plight of the minorities. The number of minority members of Parliament (MPs) in the Jatiya Sangsad, for example, diminished from 14 in 1996 to four in 2001.

Islamic extremism coupled with weakening social cohesion and growing domestic violence has emerged as a major challenge to the ruling party of the country. Bangladeshi society has been poisoned, too. Fanatic Islamists have successfully ruined 'Barsha Baran', the Bengali new year's day celebration for three years in a row with the help of bombs and guns. They have forced an 'Islamic dress code' on women, who have been forced to give up wearing the traditional Bengali saree. Urdu words and Arabic phrases are being increasingly introduced in common parlance and people are actively discouraged not to observe 'Ekusha February' to commemorate the movement against West Pakistan's attempt to impose Urdu on Bengali-speaking East Pakistan.

Contemporary Bangladesh's secular civil society is under siege. Recent years have witnessed a spate of death threats being issued by Islamic fundamentalists on secular and liberal intellectuals of Bangladesh. On 27 January 2005, a grenade attack on an AL rally in Habibganj District killed four people, including a former finance minister. In sum, rising Islamic fundamentalism fuelled by Pakistan's ISI and Saudi-funded Deobandi madrassas have deeply divided political class with vicious political antagonism.

> The coordinated series of 459 bomb blast explosions within a single move rocked 63 of Bangladesh's 64 districts on August 17, 2005, which was little more than the visible tip of the menacing iceberg that threatens this luckless country. All societies that foster terrorism have eventually themselves fallen prey to this scourge. Bangladesh cannot be an exception, though the country's political leadership has sought to cover up the realities of state complicity with flat denials of state support to extremism and terror, even as they have sought to mark the steady spiral towards Islamist extremism, lawlessness and disorder (Gill, 2005: 8).

The Jamaat-ul Mujahidin, a terrorist group that pledges allegiance to the Taliban in Afghanistan, distributed leaflets claiming responsibility for the blasts and demanding the introduction of 'Allah's Law', in Bangladesh claiming to speak for 'The Soldiers of Allah'. The leaflets also demanded that President Bush and Prime Minister Tony Blair 'leave Muslim countries' (Parthasarathy, 2005: 2).

The blasts have been blamed on the Jamaat-ul Mujahidin Bangladesh, an armed faction closely linked to the Jamaat-e-Islami, a partner in the ruling coalition and to the notorious JMJB and its brutish 'commander', Siddiqur Islam alias Bangla Bhai (in fact, the 'link' with the JMJB is more than just that—the two organizations are virtually inseparable and Bangla Bhai also heads the military operation of the JMB).

Begum Khaleda Zia today faces the same predicament that General Musharraf does in Pakistan. How does a ruler who co-opts and cooperates with fundamentalist organizations prevent these organizations from resorting to violence and provoking hatred against powers like the US and UK and thereafter pursuing their own extremist and often sectarian political agenda at home? (Parthasarathy, 2005).

The BNP government responded to the August bomb blasts by banning the JMB and the JMJB and arrested some 300 of their activists. Not surprisingly, Bangla Bhai escaped arrest. However, the ban is widely acknowledged to have had little impact. Some arrests were, of course, made but most of the arrested leaders were shortly released. Even in cases where cadres were arrested in connection with acts of terrorism, after 'encounters', or in connection with the manufacture and storage of explosives, Islamist militants from these groups have been routinely released.

It appears that the ruling coalition continues to believe that it can 'manage' and orchestrate Islamist extremism and terrorism to serve its own partisan, political, and economic objectives—and this, indeed, may well be the source and motive for the current spate of countrywide bombings. In this belief, Bangladeshi politicians are not alone. The leadership in Pakistan has long travelled this path, but is now discovering that the chickens, eventually, come home to roost. It appears that every society has to go though its own learning process—a process, in this case of terrorism, that is most destructive of the human soul, of the spirit of man, and of society (Gill, 2005).

Economic Development

As far as economic development is concerned, a wide range of international institutions and foreign governments have contributed directly to the deception, speaking in glowing terms of Bangladesh's arguable 'successes' in development, in health sector reform, in population control, and in non-governmental sector operations, all of which have been projected as examples for other developing countries to follow. The truth of the comprehensive political mischief and administrated mismanagement in Bangladesh has systematically been brushed under the carpet (Gill, 2005).

This truth is now becoming increasingly difficult to conceal, even in the most prejudiced circles despite the state's relentless policy of suppression of the national press and of denials of access to the international media. It is significant in this context that an independent study carried out by Foreign Policy and the Fund for Peace which drew up a listing of 60 of the world's failed and failing states on the basis of 12 specific 'indicators of instability', placed Bangladesh at the 17th position, among the 20 'critical states' that are most at risk (Gill, 2005).

Embarking in 1987 on the Washington Consensus (WC)[30] reform programme, Bangladesh has been pursuing the path enthusiastically since the early 1990s, subscribing to the whole package of reforms as it evolved over the years. The country successfully achieved and, more or less, maintained macro-economic stability since the early 1990s. But that success could not be translated into faster economic growth, much less into accelerated poverty reduction. Moreover, the glaring socio-economic disparity has been accentuated further and environmental degradation has continued unabated.

According to a Bangladeshi economist:

> The basic problem with the ruling paradigm is that it is a divider of society. It enables the power elite (economic, political, bureaucratic, military, and professional) to acquire more wealth as well as market, political and social power. The poorer segments of society are expected to be either protected by safety net programmes or to benefit from 'trickle-down' effects of economic growth. Trickle-down effects are of little avail, as had been the case in the pre-reform period. In reality, the poorer segments of the population remain deprived and excluded (Ahmad, 2004: 125).

The alternative approach suggested by a Bangladeshi economist, aimed at consolidating and building on the impressive achievements in several respects and breaking out of the trap characterized by low rate of development, persisting widespread poverty, and sharp social division has necessarily to be based on prevailing ground realities. The key ground realities to be addressed include widespread poverty; glaring and increasing socio-economic disparity, social, political, economic exclusion, pervasive corruption and criminalization of politics and economics, centralized and poor governance, virtually non-existent local government, high rate of illiteracy and low quality of education among people at large, low productivity, unemployment, and unabated degradation of environment. These realities are either in contradiction to the letter or spirit or both of the ruling neo-paradigm or are so much subordinate to the paradigm's dominant thrust or the interests of the dominant groups that they are talked about, but, by and large, ignored in practice.

In the proposed approach, 'market is important but balanced roles of market and state are called for. Reforms are essential, but the present reform agenda must be recast based on the prevailing realities on the ground as indicated above and guided by the dynamics of a paradigm shift to sustainable development and participatory democracy' (Ahmad, 2004).

The concept of sustainable development, 'places the human being rather than capital, as is the case in the currently ruling paradigm, at the centre of policies, and programmes are undertaken to reduce socio-economic disparity and promote participation of people at large in all processes—social, political, economic, environmental—of social transformation.... Participatory democracy ensures equitable, active participation of people at large in the social transformation processes. To that end, it calls for the institutionalization of democracy at all levels of society, including through appropriate devolution of political power to each level and promotion of vertically and horizontally coordinated dynamic social capital (policies, institutions, norms, values, ethics linkages) throughout society (Ahmad, 2004: 126).

Conclusion

Hostility between the ruling coalition and the main opposition party, a spiralling trend of violence, the government's utter disregard for the rule of law, the diminishing importance of parliament, the opposition's predilection for street agitation, and growing religious militancy have all delivered serious blows to democracy in Bangladesh. More than a decade after the nation embarked on its second journey toward establishing a peaceful democratic society, the recent developments have raised concerns, at home and abroad, about the future of democracy in Bangladesh. Some have even questioned whether Bangladesh should already be considered a failed state (Ali, 2005: 112).

Preoccupied with personal animosities and rivalries, the government of the day is unable to address basic issues such as protection of the lives and properties of ordinary citizens. The introduction of special courts, tough legislations, and military assistance could partly remedy the situation. The consolidation of democracy along with checks and balances, greater accommodation, and tolerance of political differences, are essential if Bangladesh is to avoid a return of military rule.

Notes

1. For an authoritative and comprehensive analysis of the role of the AL in Bangladesh liberation consult Md. Abdul Wadud Bhuiyan (1982).
2. For details of the politics of patronage under the Mujib government consult Talukdar Maniruzzaman (1980: 158–62, 1982: 146–47).
3. For an understanding of the Mujibbad, see Khandakarkar Mohammad Elias, Mujibbad.
4. There were several radical revolutionary parties in Bangladesh—the Jatiyo Samajtrantic Dal (National Socialist Party), Purbo Bangla Sarbohara Dal-Marxbadi-Leninbadi (Communist Party-Marxist-Leninist of East Bengal), Purbo Bangla Communist Party—Marxist-Leninist. Of these parties, the Jatiyo Samajtrantic Dal (JSD) worked as the front organization of an underground party, the Bangladesh Communist League, and the other parties worked solely as underground parties. These revolutionary parties maintained that the 1971 Bangladesh revolution war had not finished.
5. Mujib started his political career with the party organization. As the secretary of the party from 1963 to 1965, Mujib, on a number of occasions, showed his intolerance towards the opposition parties. The most notable incident was in 1957 when he used rough tactics to block the establishment of the Leftist National Awami Party.
6. In spite of the power struggle that was going on between different groups, the leftist parties found common grounds in their criticism of the League's policies. They accused the AL government of collusion with New Delhi and Moscow to suppress the opposition, particularly those members who were advocating a neutral foreign policy for the country.
7. For an exclusive analysis of the leadership, organization, tactical, and doctrinal issues of the various revolutionary parties in Bangladesh, consult, Maniruzzaman, *Group Interests and Political Changes: Studies of Pakistan and Bangladesh*, pp. 142–69. See also Shapan Ghaani (1972: 20–21).
8. Bangladesh politics was and is highly gang-studded. For details of the influential role played by the gangs as a social force in Bangladeshi national politics see, Mofakhkhar Rahman (1978: 36–43). For a theoretical and comparative

perspective on what is called here 'gang politics' or *dada-dal*, see Giovanni Sartori (1979: 244–323).

9. For details of data regarding political violence, see M. Anisuzzaman (1978: 25–35). Also see Maniruzzaman, *Group Interests and Political Changes: Studies of Pakistan and Bangladesh*, p. 147; and *Bangladesh Observer* (Dhaka), 7 July 1973 and 29 December 1974, the statement of the state minister for information and broadcasting in parliament on 28 January 1974, reported in *Banglar Bani* (Dhaka), 29 January 1974; and the *Ittefaq* (Dhaka), 1 December 1973.
10. For details of divisions along ideological lines in the army and rivalries among the officers refer to Sinha (1979: 33).
11. See Jahan (1980: 84) and Sinha (1979: 8–14).
12. There were 26,500 men in the armed forces and in the parallel militia there were 29,000 men. The government was more interested in developing the latter. It was planned that this militia would be increased annually so that by the end of 1980 its total strength would be about 1,30,000. It was also planned that one regiment of the JRB would be placed under the command of each district governor. See Ahmed (1980: 161) and Maniruzzaman, *Group Interests and Political Changes: Studies of Pakistan and Bangladesh*, p. 172.
13. *The Guardian* (London), 23 August 1975. Also see Zillur R. Khan (1976: 115, 1981: 544).
14. See Government of People's Republic of Bangladesh (1973), Ministry of Finance, *Budget Estimates*, 1974–75.
15. Mujib never wanted a strong army; he made it clear on a number of occasions. For details see M. Rashiduzzaman (1977: 800).
16. Mujib further alienated the officers of the armed forces by demoting and sacking several army officers on the prompting of some AL leaders who had personal scores to settle with the officers concerned. See Maniruzzaman, *Group Interests and Political Changes: Studies of Pakistan and Bangladesh*, pp. 132–33. Also see Amit Roy, 'Fall of an Idol', *The Sun*, 21 August 1975.
17. In the military operation in April 1975 against the smugglers, hoarders, and black-marketers, a large number of AL workers were arrested, but they were released later at the influence of the close associates of Mujib. See Ahamed (1986: 24, 27–28).
18. See Government of People's Republic of Bangladesh, Planning Commission, *The Annual Plan*, 1972–73 (Dhaka), p. 1.
19. During the first two years after liberation Bangladesh received a total of US$ 1,377 million as grants and credits from different sources. See *Bangladesh Observer*, 26 March 1974.
20. In order to meet the minimal standard of living Bangladesh needed to generate a rate of growth in GDP at least 5–6 per cent per year (Islam, 1974: 9). Also see, *Bangladesh Observer*, 12 July 1975.
21. According to one source, the flood caused damage to more than 1 million tons of food grain and Taka 150 million worth of jute and jute goods (*Bangladesh Observer*, 8 August 1974).
22. For details of starvation deaths in Bangladesh see Lifschult (1974a, 1974b). The minister of food and relief told the Jatiya Sangad (parliament) on 22 November 1974 that 27,500 persons had died of starvation, though unofficial sources placed the death toll at 100,000 (*Bangladesh Observer*, 23 November 1974).

23. The term 'Sepoy Revolution' has been used by Maniruzzaman, See his *Group Interests and Political Changes: Studies of Pakistan and Bangladesh*, 177.
24. About 46 members of the Mujib family were estimated to have been killed during the putsch. See, 'New Disunity in Bangladesh', *The Guardian*, 23 August 1975.
25. See Government of Bangladesh, Planning Commission (1980).
26. For the full text of the Proclamation (Amendment) Order 1977, see *Bangladesh Observer*, 23 April 1977; see also *The Constitution of the People's Republic of Bangladesh*, as amended up to 28 February 1979.
27. For details of the restoration of political process see Kirit Bhaumik (1984) and Peter J. Bertocci (1966).
28. The 23 February 1998, 'Declaration of Jihad against Jews and Crusader' by Osama-bin-Laden was also signed by Fazlul Rahman, the head of HUJI in Bangladesh. Since then HUJI has emerged as the linchpin of Al-Qaida operations in Bangladesh and has been commented upon by various neutral and international observers. Refer Rohan Gunaratna (2002: 219–20). See also, Bertil Linter (2002: 11); Alex Perry (2002).
29. The Al-Qaida as fountain head of global terrorism has been on the move since 11 September 2001, searching for new areas to establish more secure bases. Bangladesh is one country which fits neatly into the Al-Qaida's preferred options. It is an impoverished nation, politically enfeebled, economically backward, and with ports which have been active hubs for transnational crime, including weapon running. But more significant is the traditional presence of extremist religious groups jostling for political space left vacant by frequent bouts of political instability and military interventions. Mrs Zia came to power with the backing of the hardcore Islamist Jamaat-e-Islami and IOJ. The timing of her victory coincided with the beginning of the US-led global war against terrorism. Most anti-terrorism experts hold that in the aftermath of the coalition forces attack, Al-Qaida elements fleeing Afghanistan established several modules inside Bangladesh. Sources say the Dhaka establishment either looked the other way or colluded to make this possible.
30. The WC was developed by the World Bank and the IMF with support from US and other developed countries in the 1970s to promote neo-liberal free market dispensation through privatization, deregulation and globalization. To that end, stabilization and structural adjustment programmes were designed, which were required to be implemented by all the developing foreign-aid seeking countries. Economic growth was once again targeted as the quintessential developmental goal, with poverty reduction and improved income distribution relegated to the background.

References

Ahamed, Emajuddin (1978). 'Development Strategy in Bangladesh: Probable Political Consequences', *Asian Survey*, 18(11) (November 1978): 1168–80.

———— (1980). *Bureaucratic Elite in Segmented Economic Growth: Bangladesh and Pakistan*. Dhaka: University Press.

Ahamed, Emajuddin (1985). 'The Six Point Programme: Its Class Basis', in Emajuddin Ahamed, *Bureaucratic Elites in Pakistan and Bangladesh: Their Development Strategy*, pp. 70–95. New Delhi: Young Asia Publication.

——— (1986). 'The August 1975 Coup d'etat', in S.R. Chakravarty and Virendra Narain (eds), *Bangladesh: Domestic Politics*, Vol. II. New Delhi: South Asian Publisher.

Ahmed, Moudud (1983). *Bangladesh: Constitutional Quest for Autonomy*. Dhaka: Dhaka University Press.

Ahmad, Qazi Kholiquazzaman (2004). 'Bangladesh: An Alternative Paradigm', *South Asian Journal*, April–June: 125.

Akter Banu, U.A.B. Razia (1981). 'The Fall of Sheikh Mujib Regime—An Analysis', *The Indian Political Science Review*, 15(1) (January 1981): 18–19.

Ali, Riaz (2005). 'Bangladesh in 2004: The Politics of Vengeance and the Erosion of Democracy', *Asian Survey*, 65(1) (January–February 2005): 1143.

Ali, S.M. (1973). *After the Dark Night: Problems of Sheikh Mujibur Rahman*. New Delhi: Thomson Press.

Anisuzzaman, M. (1978). 'Violence and Social Change in Bangladesh', *South Asian Studies*, 3(1) (January–July 1978): 25–35.

Bangladesh Observer, 10 July 1974.

Baxter, Craig (1984). *Bangladesh: A New Nation in an Old Setting*. Boulder: Westview Press.

Bertocci, Peter J. (1966). 'Bangladesh in 1985: Resolute Against the Storm', *Asian Survey*, XXVI(2) (February 1966).

Bhardwaj, Sanjay (2003). 'Bangladesh Foreign Policy vis-à-vis India', *Strategic Analysis*, 27(2) (April–June 2003): 275.

Bhaumik, Kirit (1984). 'General Ershad Consolidates His Hold', *PTI Features*, 4(29A) (12 January 1984, Special Issue): PF-A 664.

Bhuiyan, Md. Abdul Wadud (1982). *Emergence of Bangladesh and the Role of Awami League*. New Delhi: Vikas.

Bienen, Henry (1978). 'Military Rule and Political Process: Nigerian Example', *Comparative Politics*, 10(2) (January): 205–25.

Bienen, Henry and Martin Fitton (1978). 'Soldiers, Politicians and Civil Servants', in Keith Panter-Brick (ed.), *Soldiers and Oil: The Political Transformation of Nigeria*, pp. 27–57. London: Frank Cass.

Boswood, Bryan (1977). 'How Long Before the Next Coup?', *The Australian* (Canberra), 10 October 1977.

Chowdhury, Nuimuddin (1976). 'Real Wages in Nationalised Sector in Bangladesh', *Political Economy*, 2(1): 346.

Datta, Sreeradha (2003). 'Bangladesh's Political Evolution: Growing Uncertainties,' *Strategic Analysis*, 27(2) (April–June 2003): 234.

Dixit, J.N. (2001). 'Indo-Bangladesh Relations: Need for Better Handling', in J.N. Dixit (ed.), *India's Foreign Policy and its Neighbours*, pp. 204–05. New Delhi: Gyan Publishing House.

Duverger, Maurice (1954). *Political Parties: Their Organization and Activity in the Modern State*. New York: John Wiley and Sons.

Franda, Marcus F. (1975). 'The Bangladesh Coup', *American Universities Field Staff Reports*, 19(15): 3.

——— (1979). 'Ziaur Rahman's Bangladesh: Political Realignments', Part I, *American Universities Field Staff Reports* (Asian Series), 25 (1979): 5.

Franda, Marcus F. (1981). 'Bangladeshi Nationalism and Ziaur Rahman's Presidency', Part II, *American Universities Field Staff Reports*, 7 (1981): 4.

———— (1982). *Bangladesh: The First Decade*. New Delhi: South Asian Publishers.

Ghaani, Shapan (1972). 'Leftist Vignettes in a Half Revolutionary', *Far Eastern Economic Review*, 75(10) (4 March 1972): 20–21.

Gill, K.P.S. (2005). 'Bangla Chickens Home to Roost', *The Pioneer*, New Delhi, 20 August 2005, p. 8.

Government of People's Republic of Bangladesh, Ministry of Finance (1973). *Budget Estimates, 1974–75*. Dhaka: Government of Bangladesh.

Government of People's Republic of Bangladesh, Planning Commission (1974). *The Annual Plan, 1972–73*. Dhaka: Government of Bangladesh.

———— (1980). *The Second Five Year Plan, 1980–85*. Dhaka: Government of Bangladesh.

Guhathakurta, Meghna (2002). 'Assault on Minorities in Bangladesh: An Analysis', available at http://www.meghbarta. net/2002/January/minor.html//minor.

Gunaratna, Rohan (2002). *Inside Al-Qaida: Global Network of Terror*.New Delhi: Roli Books.

Haider, Zaglul (1999). 'Role of Military in Politics of Bangladesh: Mujib, Zia and Ershad Regimes (1972–90)', *Journal of South Asian and Middle Eastern Studies*, 22(3) (Spring 1999): 57–80.

Hakim, Muhammad A. (1998). 'Bangladesh: The Beginning of End of Militarized Politics?', *Contemporary South Asia*, 7(3) (1998): 283–90.

———— (2003). 'Parliamentary Election in Bangladesh Under Neutral Caretaker Governments: A Lesson for Massive Rigging Prone Countries?', *Asian Thought and Society*, 25(73) (January–April 2003): 47–65.

Haque, Azizul (1980). 'Bangladesh in 1979: Cry for a Sovereign Parliament', *Asian Survey*, 20(2) (February 1980): 221–22.

Huntington, S.P. (1968). *Political Order in Changing Societies*. New Heaven: Yale University Press.

Islam, Nurul (1974). 'The State and the Prospects of the Bangladesh Economy', in E.A.G. Robinson and Keith Griffin (eds), *The Economic Development of Bangladesh Within a Socialist Framework*, p. 9.London: Macmillan.

———— (1977). *Development Planning in Bangladesh: A Study of Political Economy*. London: C. Hurst and Co.

Islam, Serajul (1984). 'Bangladesh: Impact of Development Strategy During Mujib Era', *Regional Studies*, 11(3) (Summer 1984): 8–20.

Jahan, Rounaq (1972). *Pakistan: Failure in National Integration*. New York: Columbia Press.

———— (1980). *Bangladesh Politics: Problems and Issues*. Dhaka: University Press Ltd.

———— (2003). 'Bangladesh in 2002: Imperiled Democracy', *Asian Survey*, 43(1) (January–February 2003): 223.

———— (2004). 'Bangladesh in 2003: Vibrant Democracy or Destructive Politics?', *Asian Survey*, 44(1) (January–February 2004): 57.

Janowitz, Morris (1964). *The Military in the Political Development of New Nations: An Essay in Comparative Analysis*. Chicago: The University of Chicago Press.

Kabir, Bhuian Md. Manoar (1985). 'Bangladesh Politics in 1981–84: Military Rule and the Process of Civilianization', *Social Studies*, 8(1) (June 1985): 185.

Kamaluddin, S. (1980). 'Bangladesh: A Spadeful of Revolution', *Far Eastern Economic Review*, 18 January 1980: 26–71.

Karlekar, Hiranmay (2003). 'Bangladesh: A Rogue State?', *The Pioneer*, New Delhi, 5 September 2003, p. 6.

——— (2005). *Bangladesh: The Next Afghanistan?*, New Delhi: Sage.

Khan, Azizur Rahman (1974). 'Bangladesh Economic Policies Since Independence', *South Asian Review*, 8(1) (October 1974): 20.

Khan, Mohammad Mohabbat and Habib Mohammad Zafarullah (eds) (1960). *Politics and Bureaucracy in New Nation: Bangladesh*. Dhaka: Centre for Administrative Studies.

Khan, Zillur R. (1972). 'March Movement of Bangladesh: Bengali Struggle for Political Power', *Indian Journal of Political Science*, 33(3) (July–September 1972): 306–11.

——— (1976). 'Leadership, Parties and Politics in Bangladesh', *The Western Political Quarterly*, 29(1) (March 1976): 115.

——— (1981). 'Politicization of the Bangladesh Military: A Response to Perceived Shortcomings of Civilian Government', *Asian Survey*, 21(5) (May 1981): 544.

——— (1984). *Martial Law to Martial Law: Leadership Crisis in Bangladesh*. Dhaka: The University Press.

Khandakarkar, Mohammad Elias (1972). *Mujibbad*. Dhaka: National Publication.

Kukreja, Veena (1989). 'Military Regimes of Zia and Ershad: Strategies and Tactics of Survival and Legitimization', *Strategic Analysis*, 12(8) (November 1989): 836.

——— (1991). *Civil–Military Relations in South Asia*. London: Sage.

LaPalombara, Joseph and Myron Weiner (eds) (1966). *Political Parties and Political Development*. Princeton: Princeton University Press.

Lifschultz, Lawrence (1974a). 'Reaping a Harvest of Misery', *Economic and Political Weekly*, 25 October 1974.

——— (1974b). 'Bangladesh: A State of Siege', *Far Eastern Economic Review*, 85(33) (30 August 1974): 348.

——— (1979). *Bangladesh: The Unfinished Revolution*. London: Zed Books.

Linter, Bertil (2002). 'Is Religious Extremism on the Rise in Bangladesh', *Jane's Intelligence Review*, 14(5) (May 2002): 11.

Maniruzzaman (1982), *Group Interests and Political Changes: Studies of Pakistan and Bangladesh*. New Delhi: South Asian Publishers, pp. 132–33.

Maniruzzaman, Talukder (1980). *The Bangladesh Revolution and its Aftermath*. Dhaka: Bangladesh Books International Ltd.

——— (1988). *The Bangladesh Revolution and its Aftermath*. Dhaka: Bangladesh Books International Ltd.

Nye, J.S. (1967). 'Corruption and Political Development: A Cost–Benefit Analysis', *American Political Science Review*, 61(2) (June 1967): 417–27.

Parthasarathy, G. (2005). 'Troubled Neighbours: Bomb Blasts in Bangladesh', *The Sunday Pioneer*, 21 August 2005, p. 2.

Perry, Alex (2002). 'Deadly Cargo', *Time*, 15 October 2002.

Rahman, Ataur (1984). 'Bangladesh in 1983: A Turning Point for the Military', *Asian Survey*, 26(2) (February 1984): 240–41.

Rahman, Matiur (1978). *Bangladesh Today: An Indictment and a Lament*. London: News and Media Books.

Rahman, Mofakhkhar (1978). 'Gang Politics in Bangladesh', *South Asian Studies*, 13(1) (January–July 1978): 36–43.

Rashiduzzaman, M. (1977), 'Changing Political Patterns in Bangladesh: Internal Constraints and External Fears', *Asian Survey*, 18(9) (September 1977): 800.

Reddaway, W.B. and Md. Mizanur Rahman (1975). 'The Scale of Smuggling Out of Bangladesh', *Research Report Series No.* 2. Dhaka: Bangladesh Institute of Development Studies.

Sartori, Giovanni (1976). *Parties and Party Systems: A Framework for Analysis*. Cambridge: Cambridge University Press.

Shehabuddin, Elora (1999). 'Bangladesh in 1998', *Asian Survey*, 39(1) (January–February 1999): 151.

Siddiqi, A.R. (1986). 'Bangladesh—The Military Factor', *Defence Journal*, 12(4) (April 1986): 6–7.

Sinha, P.B. (1979). 'Armed Forces of Bangladesh', *Occasional Paper No. 1*. New Delhi: IDSA.

Talukdar, Maniruzzaman (1982). *Group Interests and Political Changes: Studies of Pakistan and Bangladesh*. New Delhi: South Asian Publishers.

Westergaard, Kirsten (1985). *State and Rural Society in Bangladesh: A Study in Relationship*. Scandinavian Institute of Asian Studies Monograph Series No. 49. London: Curzen Press.

Zaman, M.Q. (1984). 'Ziaur Rahman: Leadership Styles and Mobilization Policies', *Indian Political Science Review*, 18(2) (July 1984): 200–01.

4

India: A Failed Democratic Developmental State?

Niraj Kumar

Observers of developmental studies have called India a democratic developmental state, which has adopted a different strategy of overall development as compared to the East Asian developmental states. After an evaluation of the different phases of Indian development, this chapter attempts to find the answer to the question: Why has India been regarded partly successful as a democracy and largely a failure as a developmental state. After a comparative study of developmental states of East Asia and India, it tries to look into the future prospects of India's success as a democratic developmental state.

The Indian Model of a Democratic Developmental State

Although the term developmental state, with an accent on the Japanese economic miracle, has been coined in the context of East Asian states, it has often been used in the Indian context as well. The Indian case also becomes very interesting because it is a democratic country, and it will be interesting to see whether democracy and development can go together. Japan today is a good illustration that democracy and development can, in fact, go hand in hand, but then historically the early phases of Japanese economic development were triggered by an authoritarian, nationalist, modernizing elite. Except Japan, most of the successful developmental states from East Asian countries recently have had authoritarian political rule. The Indian developmental state has all the institutions that are essential for late industrializing countries. The most important ingredient of the developmental state, the willingness of the leadership, was always there in the case of India. This was reflected even in the pre-Independence era. Three documents have been taken here to highlight the willingness of the leadership, as well as the people of India, for democracy and development. These documents are the Karachi Resolution of the Indian National Congress, 1931, the Constitution of Independent India (1950), and the Second Five-Year Plan (1956–61). (The reason behind taking the Second Five-Year Plan into consideration is that the First Five-Year Plan was adopted in haste and was not even properly chalked out.)

In the pre-Independence era, the major thrust of the Karachi Resolution was to establish the ideals of *swaraj*, which meant political as well as economic freedom. The Karachi Resolution says:

> This Congress is of the opinion that to enable the masses to appreciate what 'Swaraj', as conceived by the Congress, will mean to them, it is desirable to state the position of the Congress in a manner easily understood by them. In order to end the exploitation of the masses, political freedom must include real economic freedom of the starving millions. The Congress, therefore, declares that any constitution which may be agreed to on its behalf should provide, or enable the government to provide Swaraj… (Dev, 1996: 1).

It implied that all the fundamental rights and economic rights, which are important for democratic development, should be provided to the people.

In Independent India, the Constitution became the most important document, which sought to establish a proper fit between the goals of democracy and development. Therefore, one can substantiate this argument that the Indian democratic developmental state sought to start a simultaneous pursuit of democracy and development. The Preamble to the Indian Constitution, starts with the resolve to constitute India into a 'Sovereign, Socialist, Secular, Democratic Republic' and wants to secure to all the citizens 'Justice, social, economic and political; Liberty of thought, expression, belief, faith and worship; Equality of status and of opportunity;

and to promote among them all; Fraternity assuring the dignity of the individual and the unity and integrity of the Nation…' (Constitution of India: i). What it attempts to establish is that India wanted to strengthen its democracy. Fundamental Rights in the Constitution have the goals of establishing political freedom and social justice. The dimensions of economic and social security found place in the Directives Principles of State Policy. Sample the relevant Directives: 'The State shall, in particular, direct its policy towards securing—(*a*) that the citizens, men and women equally, have the right to adequate means of livelihood; (*b*) that the ownership and control of the material means of the community are so distributed as best to subserve the common good; (*c*) that the operation of the economic system does not result in the concentration of wealth and means of production to the common detriment;….' 'Right to work, to education and to public assistance in certain cases'(Article 41). 'Provision for just and humane conditions of work and maternity relief'(Article 42), 'Living wages for workers'(Article 43), 'Participation of workers in management of industries'(Article 44), 'Provision for free and compulsory education for children'(Article 45) (Constitution of India: 13–14).

Coming to the actual working of the Constitution, the role of the government becomes very important. In the stewardship of the leaders like Jawaharlal Nehru, India chalked out its first blueprint of development. It came in the form of five-year plans. Since the First Five-Year Plan (1951–56) had a long-range perspective of doubling per capita income in 27 years; the short-term goals were rather modest because there were other problems to take care of. Most of the targets fixed in the First Five-Year Plan had been achieved. Thus, there was not much to do in this plan period.

In fact, the Second Five-Year Plan was perhaps the most significant because of its basic objective to establish 'a socialistic pattern of society'. The planners realized the necessity to take the responsibility of realizing the goals set in the plans. State intervention was evident in the initial phases of development in case of India. India did embark on a statist model and, accordingly, it took up the initiative with regard to industrialization. It did start with a growth-centric interventionist model with planning, which is evident in the five-year plans that followed immediately.

With democracy in the initial decades more or less assured, the Indian model of the developmental state created a revolution of rising expectations that were to be later overtaken by spiralling frustration in the post-Nehru decades. The architects of the Nehru–Mahalanobis model had laid emphasis on the role of the state. They prioritized the areas where there was immediate need for development. A two-sector model—public and private—was adopted. The public sector came under the supervision of the government. Most of the strategic units came under this sector. Nehru fortuitously did not have to face the dilemma of choosing between development and democracy. During the time of Indira Gandhi, this dilemma had to be faced rather dramatically. She adopted populist measures of ad hoc welfare to retain her pre-eminent position in the elections. This populist politics and aroused mass expectations were enormously whetted by the anti-authoritarian/corruption JP (named after socialist turned Gandhian Jayaprakash Narayan) movement and the first non-Congress Janata Party government in New Delhi. In the wake of these events a limited package of neo-liberal economic policy made its entry into the Indian economic regime in the 1980s. However, statism was not really on the retreat in any significant way. The economic indicators started showing an upward movement and the growth rate also went up in this period. However, this was because of heavy borrowings. It was not real development, but deceptive development. An era of economic liberalization really started in 1991 in the midst of a severe balance of payment crisis that confronted the Congress minority government headed by P.V. Narasimha Rao and his finance minister, Manmohan Singh.

In the light of the experience of Indian development, one can easily understand why India can be called a democratic developmental state. Bagchi (2004: 38–39) talking about Indian developmental state tried to define a decentralized developmental state as:

> In terms of its moral content, it will combine both negative and positive freedom, and organizationally it will guarantee both procedural and substantive democracy. People will be free to change governments through free and fair elections; at the same time, they will have reasonable prospect of earning a living through gainful employment.

The idea of the democratic developmental state can be attributed to those Third World countries where the goals of development was considered, but not at the cost of civil and political rights like in India where there was a simultaneous pursuit of democracy and development, which we have already seen in our earlier discussion of the Indian National Congress's Karachi Resolution of 1931, the Constitution of Independent India, and the Second Five-Year Plan.

Now it is time to define the terms democracy, development, and democratic developmental state to understand in what perspective this discussion will move. The term democracy is defined in terms of institutional procedures to guarantee basic civil and political rights and allow political competition between political forces, usually organized through parties. Development here reflects the fact that the tidal wave of democratization over the past decade or more has brought liberal democratic institutions to numerous countries which, to varying degrees, have still to make a decisive economic transition of the kind experienced by their industrialized predecessors, and their newly industrialized erstwhile counterparts, notably in East and Southeast Asia. For these societies, development includes a process of economic change involving the construction of more complex and productive economies capable of generating a higher material standard of living. This requires extensive involvement—both direct and regulatory—on the part of the state. It is also widely recognized that economic growth should be complemented to the extent feasible by the pursuit of certain social objectives: the alleviation of absolute and relative poverty; the correction of glaring inequalities of social conditions (between genders, classes, regions, and ethnic groups); provision for personal safety and security; and the tackling of looming threats such as environmental degradation. These are predominantly societal or public goods that require the decisive involvement of states. Overall, to the extent that democratic polities are instrumental in organizing socio-economic progress along these lines, they can be described as developmentally successful; to a considerable extent, their success depends on the existence and efficacy of a democratic developmental state.

Assessment or Evaluation of the Indian Model: Whether it has Succeeded or Failed?

It is well known that Independent India started as a dominant party democracy under Nehru and that it pursued the goal of establishing a 'socialistic pattern of society' and national economic self-reliance through democratic planning within a federal political set-up. By the late 1960s, the Indian model of socialism yielded at least partly to the Indira Gandhi brand of personalized and populist mass politics that made a serious dent in the Nehru–Mahalanobis model of economic development. These changes ultimately culminated in a multiparty coalition politics, first briefly in the major states of north India between 1967 and 1971, and in states like West Bengal and Kerala, and finally in New Delhi since 1989, as well as in several states with coalition governments. I now proceed to examine the economic performance of the Indian developmental state in three major phases: (*a*) Indian socialism, (*b*) Indian populism with an authoritarian tinge in the 1970s, and (*c*) The neo-liberal economic reforms 'by stealth' during the 1980s and the accelerated pace of these reforms since 1991.

The Phase of Indian Socialism

In an attempt to fulfil the aspirations of the Indian state to industrialize India and develop it faster, initially, emphasis was laid on the public sector. The state's character was more developmental then than now. However, India had shown some sign of a developmental state, but it was never a command economy. When the Nehru–Mahalanobis model initiated the five-year plans, planning and state intervention were dominant themes on the economic and political scene since the inception of the First Five-Year Plan in the early 1950s. The first three five-year plans (covering the period 1956–66) should be treated separately from the subsequent ones. There was continuity in the formulation and implementation of the first three plans due to Nehru's personal commitment, and the overwhelming support commanded by the Congress Party. India also enjoyed political stability at the Centre. It was because of the leaders of the Indian National Congress, such as Nehru, Patel, Pant, Azad, Rajendra Prasad, and others. Since they had fought for Independence, people had natural regard and support for them.

The First Five-Year Plan (1951–56) had a long-term perspective of doubling the per capita income in 27 years. The short-term goals were rather modest because there were other problems which had to be urgently attended to, for instance, those arising out of war and

Partition. The estimated national income in 1950–51 (at 1952–53 prices) was Rs 9,110 crore. The target was to raise it to Rs 10,000 crore by 1955–56. This implied no more than an annual rate of growth of 2.13 per cent, and it was achieved. Another attempt was to raise the rate of investment in the economy. It was estimated to be 4.9 per cent of the national income in 1950–51. The target was to raise it to 7 per cent at the end of the plan period. This too was achieved. Significantly, all this was achieved without a price rise; in fact, there was a small decline in prices. Thus, the First Five-Year Plan prepared the ground for more ambitions planning in the future.

The Second Five-Year Plan was perhaps the most significant because its basic objective was to establish a socialistic pattern of society. Essentially, this meant that the basic criterion for determining the lines of advance was not to be private profit, but social gain, and the pattern of development and the structure of socio-economic relations needed to be so planned that they resulted not only in appreciable increases in national income and employment, but also in greater equality of income and wealth. The benefit of economic development needed to accrue more and more to the relatively less privileged classes of society. It is not surprising that given these objectives, the planners felt that the market as a resource allocation mechanism could not be relied upon, and that the state had to take up many responsibilities as the principal agency acting on behalf of the community as whole. The public sector had to expand rapidly. It had not only to initiate development which the private sector was unwilling or unable to undertake, it had also to play a dominant role in shaping the entire pattern of investments in the economy, whether it made the investment directly or whether these were made by the private sector. This version of a socialist economy provided the foundation for economic policies underlying state intervention in the economic life of Indian citizen. The intervention included state ownership and monopoly in parts of both the real and monetary sectors, and a complex system of controls and licenses regulating activities in the private sector (Majumdar, 1997: 28).

The Second (1956–61) and Third (1961–66) Five-Year Plans aimed at a growth rate of 5 per cent per annum, but they did not achieve the target, which hovered around an average of 3.5 per cent. Although it was below the target, it was not quite so low. Keeping in view the two wars (Indo–China War in 1962 and Indo–Pakistan

War in 1965), which India fought in this period, the growth was well acceptable, if not very impressive. As viewed by Rudra Sil (2000: 323–24):

> Nehru's development strategy was clearly influenced by the global context in which it was conceived. His development goals, not unlike the goals of leaders in other post-colonial countries, were influenced by the level of wealth and technology evident in the west. And his strategy for achieving those goals was simultaneously influenced by the efficiency evident in Western capitalism and by the dramatic achievement engineered by socialist planners in the U.S.S.R. in the 1930s–40s. Nehru's overarching faith in scientific rationalism and his commitment to a 'third way' paved the ground for his mixed strategy of economic development, combining the best of two modern economic systems.

But even in this era, India did not really have an economy which most of the successful developmental states had in their early phases of development. The nature of planning was somehow adapted to India's federal democratic state. Although the centre was strong, because of the federal character of the Indian state and lack of social infrastructure, the role of developmental state could not come into its own.

The Phase of Indian Populism

There was a break in the planning process during 1966–69, which was a period of plan holiday. Regular planning was substituted by three somewhat ad hoc annual plans (1966–69). Planning was then resumed in 1969 with even more ambitious targets in the Fourth Five-Year Plan covering the period 1969–74. The discontinuity and other distortions in the five-year plans due to the external shocks (rise in international oil prices, the strain caused by the birth of Bangladesh), and bad harvests had set the stage for major crises in 1973–75. Meanwhile, there was a significant change in the political scene and a decline in the sense of optimism with which the first two plans had been greeted. The Fifth Five-Year Plan was not completed because of the change of the party in power in 1977. The average rate of growth in gross domestic product (GDP) for the period of 1966–77 was 3.58 per cent.

India's development performance during the first phase of Indira Gandhi's reign was adversely affected by at least two features of the politics of this period. These were (*a*) increasing electoral pressures emanating from the political arrival of the peasantry, particularly the middle castes of peasant cultivators, as a result of the 'ruralizing elections' that crossed critical threshold by the Fourth General Elections in 1967; and (*b*) the gathering momentum of a massive mass movement organized, first in Gujarat by Morarji Desai, and later in Bihar, with wider geographical spread across the major northern and western states started by students and the non-Congress opposition, that drafted the socialist-turned-Gandhian, Jayaprakash Narayan, from virtual political retirement to offer overarching leadership to these movements. They were subsequently joined by some trade unions and the Hindu and Sikh right-wing forces. Prime Minister Indira Gandhi managed to checkmate and appropriate the newly emergent peasantry through populist electoral mobilization by the Congress Party, remodeled in her own image. But the containment of the pressures from mass movements and a sizeable section of unionized railway men, who staged a nation-wide strike in1974 led by George Fernandes, proved to be a more difficult proposition. The new strategy of electoral mobilization was attempted by Indira Gandhi by assuming a more progressive, pro-poor, ideological posture by splitting her own party in 1969 and forcing the right-wing old guard 'Syndicate' faction out. They formed a separate party called the Congress O (Organization) that emerged as the first officially recognized opposition party in the Lok Sabha by virtue of its size. In a swift move, Mrs Gandhi nationalized 14 major private commercial banks, abolished the privy purses of former princely rulers, and proceeded to have a snap mid-term poll in 1971 on the catchy slogan of *'Garibee hatao'*, which she won hands down. But this spectacular electoral success was not without concomitant costs. Her adventure was to make a direct personal appeal to the masses, bypassing the intermediate structures of the Congress Party and federal autonomy of state governments. Populist politics, if somewhat undemocratic, was progressive in a way, but it overturned the rationalist calculations of economic planning. Scarce resources were diverted on partisan and personal preferences to electorally profitable, but economically unproductive expenditures and channels. That was the beginning of the diversion of huge amounts of revenue to subsidies and loans on economically irrational and unfeasible banking security considerations.

The populist measures helped the Congress Party win massive majorities in Parliament and in the state legislatures in 1971–72. But these successes were soon overtaken by protest movements of an almost nationwide nature and the worst trade union strike by railway men, fuelled by the revolution of rising expectations of the masses and the classes, which overloaded the limited capabilities of the state to meet them. Beginning in 1973–74, these agitations virtually put the government under a siege that finally led to the imposition of Emergency by the Indira Gandhi's government in 1975. The wages of this contested over-centralization of power in a prime-ministerial regime, obliterating, for all practical purposes, the federal features of the political system, were enormous. The net upshot of all these intra-elite controversies and mass political conflicts was a serious detrimental effect on the developmental as well as democratic dimensions of the Indian state.

The post-Emergency 1977 elections ushered in a new phase in Indian politics. This phase started with the first non-Congress government in New Delhi formed by the Janata Party, which restored the democratic features of the Constitution by enacting the 44th Constitutional Amendment, dismantling the authoritarian features earlier introduced by the 42nd Amendment passed by the Emergency regime. The Janata Party government's premature fall in 1979 resulted in the restoration of the Congress Party to power in 1980, led first by Indira Gandhi (1980–84) and subsequently by Rajiv Gandhi (1984–89), which in turn was followed by the Janata Party-led National Front government (1989–91), the Congress minority government (1991–97), Janata Party-led National Front government (1996–98), Bharatiya Janata Party (BJP)-led National Democratic Alliance (NDA) government (1998–99 and 1999–2004), and Congress-led United Progressive Alliance (UPA) (May 2004 to date).

We are clubbing these periods together because all these governments either initiated or accelerated neo-liberal economic reforms and pursued these policies with varying pace, despite their divergent positions and policies on cultural issues, for example, secularism versus 'cultural nationalism', which is a euphemism for Hindu communalism. The Congress-led UPA has stood by the secularist credentials, though its left allies from outside have continued to complain about its neo-liberal capitalist proclivities or reforms and constantly put it under pressure to promote economic nationalism to countervail globalism. The policies of successive governments will be discussed a little later. When we analyze the economic indicators of these periods, we find a consistent average growth of 5 per cent despite the changes in the political scenario and a brief period of the Emergency. Agriculture did not do well, but industry and services grew much faster in the post-liberalization period (See Table 4.1).

Table 4.1
Economic Indicators

Indicator	*1980s*	*1992–93 to 1996–97*	*1997–98 to 2001–02*	*2002–03*
GDP Growth (% of year)	5.6	6.7	5.5	4.4
Agriculture	3.4	4.7	1.8	–3.1
Industry	7.0	7.6	4.5	6.1
Services	6.9	7.5	8.1	7.1

Source: World Bank (2003: ii).

The Phase of Neo-Liberal Economic Reforms

The Seventh Five-Year Plan covered the period 1985–90. The year 1990–91 was a very crucial one. The climatic crisis resulted in near bankruptcy in early 1991. Some of the forces that triggered the crises were beyond the control of Indian planners. The 1980s witnessed the turning point in many of the socialist economies that had strong links with India. The Congress Party under Rajiv Gandhi had lost momentum, and the political system at the centre faced serious tensions due to lack of a mature leadership. The economic and political scenario was very grim. Inflation was 12 per cent a year and rising. The food prices were also rising. The current account deficit was about US$ 10 billion. All the economic indicators were showing warning signals. This was the background in 1991 when the minority Congress government under the leadership of P.V. Narsimha Rao took charge. Dr Manmohan Singh, a distinguished economist, was made the finance minister. He started an era of neo-liberal economic policies marked by radical departures from the past policies (Majumdar, 1997: 30). This was a turning point in Indian economic history. The process of economic liberalization started. The market forces were given a relatively free hand in steering the economy of the country, and this vital change in the scenario created an opening for a major reorientation in the strategy of economic development. It significantly started the process of gradual transformation of the Indian state from its role as a bureaucratic state to a regulatory state. While the state sector of the economy was not entirely dismantled, there was a comprehensive policy to accelerate the process of bureaucratic deregulation, privatization, and globalization. In this shift in the policy paradigm there appeared a new possibility of a renegotiated partnership between the state playing a reduced regulatory role and as a facilitator of economic development in partnership with the market. In service-delivery and socio-economic change, the voluntary sector or non-governmental organizations in civil society were also invited to play an important role.

Now it has been more than a decade since the structural reforms for economic liberalization were initiated in the Indian economy. The reforms made in this period produced unprecedented economic growth. Before the reforms in 1991, the rate of economic growth remained constant at around 3 per cent. But by the mid-1990s both GDP growth and agricultural growth exceeded 7.5 per cent annually, industrial growth also remained high. Social indicators like literacy and longevity also improved (Ray, 2002: 323–24).

Even though the high rate of growth has reduced inequality, it has led to an increase in the number of poor people and also in the widening of regional disparity. Ironically, even after liberalization and a higher growth rate, there was hardly any reduction in poverty between 1991 and 1997. Compared to this period, poverty was declining in the pre-liberalization period.

Aswini K. Ray (2002: 45) has opined, referring to the India's National Sample Survey (NSS) data that the rate of economic growth in the pre-reform (1991) period was around 3 per cent. After liberalization in the mid-1990s, the GDP growth exceeded 7.5 per cent annually. Further, he observes:

> Paradoxically, the rate of growth, distributed inequitably, has led to an increase in the member of poor people, and also to the widening of the regional disparity of the colonial era. The comparative figures of this period before and after the reforms are more revealing in this context. At the height of the era of controlled economy, rationing, price controls and nationalization of the 1970s and 1980s,

poverty actually declined 2 per cent annually. By contrast, there was hardly any reduction in poverty between 1991 and 1997. A survey in 1997 shows that every third person—34.4 per cent of the population—lived in condition of absolute poverty, the same as in 1990. It also showed that the decline in poverty was marked in the period 1994/95–1997, despite the high GDP growth rate (Kabra, 2003; Tremblay, 2003).

Why has India Partly Succeeded as a Democracy and Largely Failed as a Developmental State?

In India since Independence, as already argued, the planners have tried to strike a balance between democracy and development. This is evident through various documents even in the pre-Independence era. After Independence, the leaders were willing to develop India faster and catch up with the developed countries. But they wanted to combine the goals of democracy and development both. Nehru as the leader of the nation had to take into consideration the aspirations of the common people. He was inspired by the tremendous success of the Soviet socialist state-led planned economic development. Inspired by Soviet success, Nehru opted for state planning, albeit in a democratic framework, with a major role of the state in development. The public sector was given preference over the private sector. But the type of conjunction of factors required was never present in the Indian economy. The nexus that was required between the political leaders and the bureaucracy was missing. The political executive and the permanent executive (bureaucrats) both need to work together, otherwise policies cannot be implemented efficiently. The steering agencies that coordinated between planning and executing the policies made by the planners in case of most of the successful developmental states were missing in India. For example, the most powerful agency was the ministry of international trade and industry (MITI) in the case of Japan (Johnson, 1982), and the ministry of trade and industry in the case of South Korea (Wade, 1990). So, the result was that we registered some development, but as far as the economic indicators were concerned, it was not even satisfactory.

Coming to the post-liberalization period, we have registered a higher growth rate in certain economic indicators, but the vital part of the economic indicators still show very little improvement. Problems like population growth, poverty, illiteracy, and unemployment still persist in India.

The Indian strategy of economic development, as discussed earlier, has passed through an early, middle, and more recent phases: (*a*) the Nehru–Mahalanobis model, or the phase of Indian statism; (*b*) the populist democracy phases of the 1970s and 1980s; and (*c*) the phase of neo-liberal economic reforms. Both the capitalist and socialist world inspired the first phase of Indian development under the leadership of Nehru. He chalked out a middle path of mixed economy. The central planning system of the Soviet type, which gave rapid industrialization to the Soviet Union, inspired him. Considering the fact that India is a federal democratic country, even though there was central planning in India, the commanding role of the state was missing in this phase of development. So, this period neither brought rapid economic development and industrialization nor did it bring about equity in society. India registered a moderate growth in this period. Poverty also decreased marginally in this phase of statism.

The second phase of Indian development can be described as the phase of Indian populism, since the elections were fought and won by Indira Gandhi's catchy slogan *'Garibee hatao'*. The objective was made clear in this phase by the state that it wanted to bring equity in the society. This period saw authoritarian governance for the first time in India when in 1975 the Indira Gandhi government declared Emergency. This came to an end in 1977 after two years of repressive governance. Despite the declared objective of alleviation of poverty in India, poverty existed. At the apex level, planning was done, but the Centre was unable to implement those policies at the grass-roots level since there was no coordination between the political executives and the administrative executives.

In both these phases of the history of development, the willingness for development was there, but the apparatus used was not correct. The major component of development was missing. Land reforms were never successfully implemented in any of these periods and that is a major requirement for a successful developmental state.

From the mid-1980s, the process of economic liberalization started in India under internal and external pressures. When the Congress-led minority government under the leadership of P.V. Narshimha Rao came to power at the centre in 1991, the process of liberalization got momentum. Structural adjustment programmes were implemented. The rupee was devalued and privatization of government companies started. From the Rao government onwards, all succeeding governments followed suit. The problems India faced at the time of Independence still persist. The objective to make India a developed country is a distant dream.

Now the question arises: Why has India partly succeeded as democracy and largely failed as a developmental state? First, we will try to seek the answer of 'Why has India been called a failed developmental state'? The answer is very complex. It will be inappropriate to compare India with East Asia since the countries of East Asia are geographically very small in comparison to India, which is a very large country with an ever-increasing large population. Heavy foreign aid kept flowing to these countries, whereas foreign aid to the Indian economy was neither substantial nor continuous. We will compare India with these countries to show how some factors helped them to develop, but at the same time, hampered growth in India. Colonial rule, for example, in the case of South Korea was brutal, but modernizing. In India colonial rule was not that modernizing and ruined industrial growth. Korea, on the other hand, was heavily industrialized by the Japanese colonial masters and when the Japanese left Korea, the Koreans had nothing to do but run the industries, which directly came under state control. Most of these newly industrializing countries have a Confucian culture, a homogenous society, which in itself is modernizing and progressive, whereas in India, caste and class disparities make the situation worse.

The policies of land reforms were very important for any developing country since the major chunk of the population was dependent on agriculture. In India, the British as well as the Indian ruling elite never fully implemented the policies of land reforms. Agriculture in India was the largest employment-providing sector in the post-Independence period and it still continues to have the status of a major sector, next to the service sector. Even after the Green Revolution, the effect of it cannot be seen throughout India. Several parts of the country still depend on conventional methods of cultivation and harvesting.

Illiteracy is a major problem in India. A large number of the population lives below the poverty line in India, which is not the case with other successful developmental states of Asia. Even the percentage of population growth is very high in India as compared to these developmental states.

The basic problem with India is that the willingness was always there, but the policies were not implemented properly. The kind of cooperative nexus among the political executives, bureaucrats, and the business class, which was available in most of the successful developmental states throughout the developmental years, was missing in India. And even now India does not have this kind of nexus. Vivek Chibber (2004) in his article, 'Reviving the Developmental State? The Myth of the National Bourgeoisie', has attributed the failure of the Indian developmental state to the non-compliance of the local capitalists with the state planners, apart from the failure of the planners and union and state bureaucracies. In India, the private sector was energized by the government, but never yielded spectacular results as did the East Asian economies. On the other hand, in most of the successful developmental states, governments preferred targeted industries to promote and provided all the support to these industries and expected good results. If a particular firm did not produce results, it was punished and their assets were confiscated and given to the profit making business houses. So being authoritarian states for most of these years, the successful developmental states were relatively autonomous from the socio-economic forces.

The governments took advantage of the cheap labour in East Asian developmental states and motivated the labour force by giving them the assurance of a better life. The state generated a national feeling among the working class for the need to work hard in the interest of the state, even if it got low wages. The state paid back, it provided better education, provided social security, and improved public health. This kind of initiative was never taken in India.

> Growth in the Indian economy, which has steadily accelerated since 1979, needs to be bolstered to 7–8 per cent per year by an appropriate mix of policies. Higher growth is essential for the rapid elimination of poverty. While India has an impressive 23-year record of growth averaging 5.7 per cent per year, the potential for even better performance is large. Many countries in East Asia have sustained higher economic growth over periods longer than 23 years. With

> the magic of compounding even small differences in the annual growth rate, make over decades, a magnified difference in outcomes. For example, in 1963 South Korea had initial conditions that were in many respects much worse than India. Yet average annual growth of 7.96 per cent over 33 years transformed South Korea into a developed country (Economic Survey, 2003–04: 13).

This can be seen from the data in Table 4.2:

Table 4.2
East Asian Growth Rates: (1961–96)

Country	*GDP Growth*
Hong Kong	7.97
Indonesia	6.39
Korea	7.96
Malaysia	7.22
Singapore	8.74
Thailand	7.71

Note: Compound rate of growth of GDP at 1995 US Dollar.
Source: Economic Survey, (2003–04: 13).

The neo-liberal policy shift in India since 1991 emphasized the goal of economic development by encouraging market forces much more than in the past under the statist model of development. Business liberalism was promoted at the cost of political liberalism that accelerated the process of greater integration of the Indian economy with global capitalism. Without formally admitting it, equity and democratic rights were made secondary to the objective of economic growth. Yet, the performance of the Indian economy even in this period has never been as impressive as any of the East Asian developmental states.

This may be for a number of reasons. First, the onset of a multi-party system at the federal level in India since the 1989 Lok Sabha election has brought in its trail mostly unstable coalitions and/or minority governments led by either the Indian National Congress, the Janata Dal and later the Bharatiya Janata Party and subsequently the Congress Party again. Ironically, the neo-liberal policy package was more comprehensively introduced by the minority Congress government of Rao. This is ironic because the Congress was the architect of the statist model of development in the past. Electoral reverses soon made the party lukewarm to reforms, although economic compulsions stood in the way of full reversal of the course of economic reforms. The United Front governments that followed were led by Janata Dal, a left of centre party like the Congress, and included communists (Communist Party of India and Communist Party of India-Marxist), either in the cabinet or in its parliamentary support bloc. They were even more reluctant reformers, but were restrained by the failing statist model not to change the course of economic reforms, only to slow the pace. The right-wing BJP-led NDA government turned out to be a more enthusiastic votary of neo-liberal economic reforms and more receptive to foreign direct investment (FDI) and multinational companies, even though it originally came chanting the mantra of *swadeshi* (economic nationalism). It also turned out to be at least as stable as the Congress minority government (in the sense of completing their five-year mandate), as compared to the extremely unstable Janata-led National United Front governments. Yet, all these governments were hampered in the sustained promotion of market-oriented economic development. The United Front was dogged by governmental instability and frequent snap elections. And the Congress minority government, as well as the NDA, was hounded out of office in quinquennial elections that followed their first term in office. Their defeats were largely attributed to the disaffection of weaker and rural sections of the population.

Second, in addition to governmental instability, social conflicts, and political violence in Indian society has continued to rise in large parts of the country. Communal riots, caste and class conflicts, inter-party clashes as well as political corruption have increased in recent decades in alarming proportions. These factors have also proved to be a serious impediment to economic development. Most observers apprehend that this trend is likely to become more critical as a result of inequalities and economic and regional disparities inherent in neo-liberal economic policies and globalization. During the NDA regime the presentation of the annual budget to the parliament was the occasion to repeat the resolve of the government to introduce labour law reforms that would be business-friendly and congenial to economic growth. However, no such reforms were actually introduced, presumably due to different political pressures and pulls from various coalitional partners, as also from the powerful trade union movement in the organized sector. Strikes and bandhs called during the NDA regime were joined in not only by the trade unions affiliated with opposition parties, but the largest segment of the labour movement affiliated with the

BJP, also joined them. This did not, however, prevent the government from taking recourse to policies that informally encouraged casualization of the employees and workers by offering casual and contract jobs at rates lower than current rates in the job market, not only in the unorganized sector, but also in the organized sector. Moreover, the annual resolve to reduce fiscal deficit also remained an empty promise as the government found it unable to downsize its own personnel and expenditure.

Privatization was flaunted as the open sesame to the Eldorado of economic growth; the NDA government resorted to more comprehensive privatization of the economy than any government preceding it. However, the approach to privatization was neither systematic nor prognostic. The United Front government had adopted a more systematic as well as pragmatic approach to privatization by appointing a disinvestment commission of experts whose recommendations guided the privatization process of the government. The NDA disbanded this commission and created a ministry of disinvestment. After the initial steps towards privatization, the public sector units were exposed to competition, which had a positive effect on their performance. This improved performance of the public sector was not taken into consideration and the NDA government, on political considerations, to placate the favoured large and medium sized private business houses, ideologically privatized even profit making state undertakings. So far as FDI was concerned, foreign multinational capital moved into India gingerly and preferred mostly to enter into joint ventures with Indian business houses rather than to open up new frontiers of investment and enterprise. For the foregoing reasons, the performance of India as a developmental state continued to be less remarkable than the other successful developmental states of East Asia.

The 2004 Lok Sabha elections have brought to power the Congress-led United Progressive Alliance (UPA) in the wake of the debacle of the previous NDA régime, commonly attributed to adverse effects of its economic policies. In addition to it other regional allies in the cabinet, the Communist parties supported the UPA from the parliamentary floor with their best electoral performance ever in Indian elections. The economic document of the Congress Party presented during the election campaign, offered a fine-tuned version of the 1991 economic reforms policy of the Rao–Manmohan Singh economic team of the Congress government of that time, in combination with the goals of economic growth with equity, abolition of illiteracy, hunger, and unemployment. It set the target of GDP growth to 8 to 10 per cent in the next five years. After the polls Sonia Gandhi was elected as the leader of the UPA by virtue of being the leader of the Congress parliamentary party. However, in a dramatic turn of events she abdicated her imminent accession to the office of the prime minister of India and instead nominated Manmohan Singh to the office of prime minister, which the allies promptly endorsed. The UPA formulated a common minimum programme (CMP) comprising six basic principles for governance: (*a*) promotion of social harmony, (*b*) at least a 7–8 per cent annual economic growth, (*c*) welfare and well-being of farmers, farm sector and workers, specially those in the unorganized sector, (*d*) improvement in the lot of women and their empowerment, (*e*) equality of opportunity for Scheduled Castles, Scheduled Tribes, Other Backward Classes (OBCs) and religious minorities, and (*f*) releasing 'creative energies of our entrepreneurs, businessmen, scientists, engineers and all other professionals and productive forces of society' (CMP of the UPA, 2004: 2–3).

It is apt to raise the question whether the UPA regime will be able to achieve a sustained rate of economic growth comparable to the East Asian developmental state. Given the fact that the government has completed only two years, it is premature to answer this question. One thing is very clear, however, that it is still far from its promises made in the election manifesto.

The UPA government has shown positive signs by maintaining a good average of annual growth rate of around 7–8 per cent. But the problem is that the growth in agriculture, on which more than 60 per cent of India's population still depends as their main source of livelihood, has been negligible, at less than 2.5 per cent. The growth in industry is also not very impressive, but the robust growth of services has somehow compensated the average GDP growth per year. So, one can easily visualize that the eradication of poverty is not possible in the near future.

Unfavourable investment climate restricts private investors in India's private sector. Even foreign investment is very low in comparison to China. The main cause of this poor investment is infrastructure constraints. Scarcity of power, unfriendly investment climate, bureaucratic hurdles and so on, are the other hindrances towards investment, which has to be taken care of by the government.

The UPA government claims that it has been able to achieve a GDP growth rate of 6.9 per cent in 2004–05 and reduce inflation. It has also passed a bill on National Rural Employment Guarantee. This act is meant to provide at least 100 days of work to all the work force. The UPA government is trying to improve the well-being of farmers and workers in the unorganized sector. The National Commission for Farmers was set up by the UPA government under the chairmanship of agricultural scientist M.S. Swaminathan. But after an interim report by the body, the government has decided to discontinue this exercise. But the government presumably intends to take at least the interim report seriously.

The UPA government has so far neglected the promises made in the common minimum programme of raising expenditure on education to 6 per cent of GDP from 4.26 per cent, and on health to 2–3 per cent of GDP from the present 0.8 per cent. The government has also passed a bill on reservation for Other Backward Classes (OBCs) in central educational institutions. This has brought a new debate on further extension of reservation policies adopted by the government. There were certain protest movements from both anti-reservationists and pro-reservationists. The government is still working out a scheme of feasibility for implementing the new reservation policy in a phased manner without reducing the general seats. In the meantime the Supreme Court has stayed the programme for further judicial consideration.

A Right to Information Act has also been passed to make democratic governance in the country more transparent and accountable. The performance of the UPA government is not spectacular, but taking into consideration the compulsions of coalition politics, it cannot be called meagre. Social tensions have increased in the aftermath of the bomb blasts in Mumbai and Malegaon in the autumn of 2006. The government has failed to ensure internal security and social harmony, yet the people of India have definitely shown patience by being calm even after these bomb blasts.

Future Prospects of India's Success as a Democratic Developmental State

All that can be said with some degree of certainty is that India will continue to move on with a reasonable degree of success, seeking to reconcile both democracy and development. If the internal Emergency of 1975–77 as well as the fiscal crisis of the early 1990s, which precipitated neo-liberal economic reforms, suggests anything, it is the following: India can ill-afford to sacrifice either democracy for economic development or economic development for democracy. Both these objectives must be pursued in combination to ward off intense political upheavals and extreme economic deprivation and starvation. Neither spectacularly successful as a developmental state nor spectacularly successful as a democratic state, even if India muddles through into the new millennium, it may someday become an economic and political power to reckon with. Since its birth in 1947, it has been India's fate to be on the threshold of arrival, but never quite there. Given proper leadership and a vigilant citizenry, that awaited arrival is well within the realm of practical politics. The moment of real arrival is still to come.

References

Bagchi, Amiya Kumar (2004). *The Developmental State in History and in the Twentieth Century*. New Delhi: Regency Publications.

Chibber, Vivek (2004). 'Reviving the Developmental State? The Myth of the National Bourgeoisie', Paper posted at the Scholarship Repository, University of California, available at http://repositories.cdlib.org/uclasoc/trcsa/20, 2004.

Common Minimum Programme 2004 of The United Progressive Alliance. New Delhi, 2004, pp. 2–3.

Dev, Arjun (1996). 'Karachi Resolution of the Indian National Congress of 1931' in *Human Rights: A Source Book*. New Delhi: National Council of Educational Research and Training.

Economic Survey 2003–04. New Delhi, Government of India, Ministry of Finance, p. 13.

Johnson, Chalmers (1982). *MITI and the Japanese Miracle: The Growth of Industrial Policy, 1925–1975*. California: Stanford University Press.

Kabra, K.N. (2003). 'The Political Economy of Federalism in India: Elements of an Emerging Approach', in B.D. Dua and M.P. Singh (eds), *Indian Federalism in the New Millennium*. New Delhi: Manohar Publications, pp. 302–17.

Majumdar, M. (1997). *The East Asian Miracle and India*. Calcutta: The Asiatic Society.

Ray, Aswini Kumar (2002). 'Globalization and Democratic Governance: The Indian Governance', in Catarina Kinnvall and Krishna Johnson (eds), *Globalization and Democratization in Asia: The Construction of Identity*, pp. 323–24. London: Routledge.

Sil, Rudra (2000). 'India', in Jeffery Kopstein and Mark Lietiback (eds), *Comparative Politics: Interests, Identities and Institutions in a Changing Global Order*, pp. 323–24. New York: Cambridge University Press.

Tremblay, Reeta C. (2003). 'Globalization and Indian Federalism', in B.D. Dua and M.P. Singh (eds), *Indian Federalism in the New Millennium*. New Delhi: Manohar Publications, pp. 335–50.

Wade, Robert (1990). *Governing the Market: Economic Theory and The Role of Government in East Asian Industrialization*. New Jersey: Princeton University Press.

World Bank, India (2003). *Sustaining Reform, Reducing Poverty*. New Delhi: Oxford University Press.

5

Societal Responses to Economic Reforms in Bangladesh: The Workers' and Peasants' Movements in the 1980s and 1990s*

Mohammed Nuruzzaman

Introduction

Political protest movements and demonstrations against pro-market reforms in Bangladesh were widespread in the decades of the 1980s and 1990s. The urban industrial workers and rural peasants were in the forefront of political resistance to economic reforms. At times, the protest movements assumed such a critical dimension that these dominated the overall political life of the country. Referring to the volatile political environment in Dhaka, the capital city of Bangladesh, Clare Hamphrey, while conducting a USAID (United States Agency for International Development) commissioned study on privatization in Bangladesh, wrote in 1992: 'Strikes are automatically called whenever a public enterprise is even rumoured as a potential candidate of privatization. Several union-sponsored Disinvestment Resistance Committees sprang up over the proposed privatization of Rupali Bank in early 1987. Small demonstrations are almost a daily occurrence in the central commercial district of Dhaka. Citywide and countrywide strikes are in vogue' (Hamphrey, 1992: 83).

This chapter extensively analyses the political reactions and the pattern of popular resistance to pro-market economic reforms in

* Reprinted with permission from *Journal of Asian and African Studies*, 41(4): 2006.

Bangladesh in the decades of the 1980s and 1990s. It attempts to map out the road to resistance movements, the underlying causes that spurred labour resistance to reforms, and the successes, if any, and failures the movements have achieved or recorded, both in the organized urban sector and the disorganized rural areas.

The Road to Resistance Movements

Societal responses in the developing world to pro-market reforms have rarely been friendly; the reactions are often sharp and violent. The experiences of reforms accompanied by political flare-ups in Bangladesh and other South Asian countries strongly validate this point. There are two specific factors leading to this particular development. In the first place, reforms are imposed by the ruling elites; they are not negotiated outcomes between different social groups and concerned governments. The governments that implement economic reforms rarely think it necessary to engage the societal groups in dialogue over reform policies and, thus, strike out a balanced approach. Particularly, the groups that are affected most are often bypassed in the name of promoting competitive market structures and efficiency in the allocation of national resources (Haggard and Webb, 1994). This is particularly true of Bangladesh where reform policies were initiated and largely implemented by undemocratic and authoritarian military regimes from the mid-1970s to the end of the 1980s. There was no dialogue between the regimes and different societal groups, or even media discussions on the course of reforms and possible consequences. The situation did not improve much even under the democratic governments in the 1990s. The lack of a democratic culture eventually led to a face-off over reform policies between affected groups, on the one hand, and the government and the business-industrial community, on the other.

The second important factor was the indifference to, or unwillingness, of government leaders to make redistributive interventions in the implementation process of economic reforms. This was largely due to the class character of the ruling parties; the development model in operation might also be held responsible for it. The neo-liberal development model is biased towards and obsessed with the idea of the so-called 'perfect market', which does not exist in the real world, but takes a blind position regarding distributional justice. This model is not concerned about poverty or growing economic disparities, but favours growth at any social cost. The industrial and agricultural wage labourers and other vulnerable social groups are completely left out, as their social security issues rarely figure in the neo-liberal project.

Of late, the World Bank and the International Monetary Fund (IMF) are emphasizing the necessity for introducing comprehensive social safety nets to mitigate the adverse impacts of reforms, but, particularly in Bangladesh, the poor and vulnerable groups are not the major beneficiaries of social safety measures. Funded by different United Nations (UN) agencies, including the Food and Agricultural Agency (FAO), the United Nations Development Programme (UNDP), and USAID, the social safety net programmes like 'food for work' and 'vulnerable group development and road maintenance programme' covered only one-fifth of the extremely poor in Bangladesh until the early 1990s. About 25 per cent of the social safety measures directly benefited the non-poor (Farid, 1993: 190–91). This state of economic and social conditions directly and indirectly pushed the working class, the rural and urban poor, and other vulnerable groups to voice their concerns and resist pro-market reforms that put their survival at risk. However, a brief note on the divergent positions of various societal groups on economic reforms is necessary to understand the complex dynamics of resistance to market-oriented reforms in Bangladesh.

Different Social Groups and their Positions on Economic Reforms

Economic reforms, particularly deregulation and privatization of state-owned enterprises (SOEs), enjoy the least social support in Bangladesh. Almost all social classes and groups, excluding the business and industrial class, are expressly opposed to privatization and decry the capitalist model of development. This may be largely because of the long history of exploitation under the British and Pakistani capitalist classes, and is rooted in egalitarian social values many Bangladeshis cherish and would like to see flourish in their society. Contrary to the pro-market mood currently prevailing throughout the world, there is an anti-market national sentiment in Bangladesh. The majority of Bangladeshis prefer an economic system wedded to social justice and economic equality of citizens. According to a survey conducted at the end of the 1980s, the idea of an Islamic economic system, which emphasizes Islamic values in the conduct of business and upholds distributional justice, enjoys overwhelming support among the middle class households (approximately 50 per cent of the respondents), the working class (66 per cent), and government employees (23 per cent). Support for a socialist economy comes up next to the Islamic economic system while preference for a capitalist system has a marginal support of 5–7 per cent in all three groups (Siddiqui, 1990).

The opposition to pro-market economic reforms largely stems from the social outlook and the degree of opposition varies among different social groups. The left-leaning academics see reforms as a way of creating a new exploitative class with the blessings of the bilateral and multilateral donors and institutions. They view reforms as an unfolding process where the state actively supports the rich to get richer and leaves the poor to become poorer. As its consequence, the whole society is being polarized along two clearly drawn out lines—the 'haves' and the 'have-nots'. They cite the widening gaps in income and wealth distribution between the top and bottom strata of Bangladeshi society to defend their contention.[1] The leftist contempt for market-oriented development programmes, in fact, relates to historical experiences of exploitation by the trading and industrial classes during the British and Pakistan periods. After Independence in 1971, the leftist social forces favoured the implementation of a socialist development programme. The business and industrial class was characterized as a 'class of surplus extractors, social failures and opportunists' (Rehman and Ahmad, 1980). This leftist outlook still considerably dominates the academic domain in Bangladesh.

The bureaucrats, though a privileged social group, also oppose the dismantling of the regulatory system to liberalize the economy. They, however, oppose economic reforms not because of humanitarian concerns or egalitarian social values, but simply because of the fear of losing control over decision-making processes and other extractive benefits associated with their official status. The bureaucrats of the subcontinent—India, Pakistan, and Bangladesh—enjoy high social status and are more accustomed to exercising control over the economy and society. This mind-set is a direct result of the long period of bureaucratic management of economic development in all three countries. It is no surprise that the initial opposition to economic reforms came from the bureaucrats who were less prepared to relinquish control over their traditional domains of foreign exchange allocation, import trade, investment, and marketing decision-making (Muhith, 1993: 257–58). A section of Bangladeshi bureaucrats, when Shafiul Azam was the minister of commerce and industries under General H.M. Ershad during the early 1980s, was in favour of implementing reforms in the industrial sector, but after the minister quit the government on health grounds in mid-1984, the opposing bureaucrats gained the upper hand and slowed down the pace of industrial reforms.

The positions of political parties on economic reforms are sharply divided along ideological lines. The two dominant political parties of the country—the Bangladesh Nationalist Party (BNP) and the Awami League (AL)—favour the reform agenda wholeheartedly. The BNP, in particular, has a historical alliance with the business and industrial community since the time it was floated by late President Ziaur Rahman in the late 1970s. The chief patrons of BNP were the traders and industrialists who substantially dominated the various central committees of the party and were elected as members of the national parliament. The same trend was visible again when the BNP came to power for a second term in 1991 under the leadership of Begum Khaleda Zia. Business dominance became a reality in BNP and the government chose to implement reform policies that suited the interests of the business and industrial class.

Similarly, the AL, originally a petty bourgeois party, tilted towards the traders and industrialists by amending its party manifesto in the early 1990s. Still, party leaders continued to speak as if they represented the working class and other popular classes. At one stage in the 1980s, when the movement against the military dictator General H.M. Ershad was at its peak, Sheikh Hasina, the president of the AL, threatened to re-nationalize all privatized industries, but that was more a political ploy to win the support of the working class. In fact, Hasina's AL was no less ready than the BNP to undertake the economic restructuring measures to engineer rapid economic growth. A senior trade union leader confided to this author that in 1994 Sheikh Hasina sent a confidential note to the IMF, the World Bank, and other bilateral donors, promising quick implementation of the privatization process in Bangladesh. That note dispelled the suspicion of the donors about the AL's socialist overtones and the party had the blessings of the donor community to win the 1996 elections to the national parliament.[2]

The leftist political parties, because of their ideological convictions or anti-capitalist stance, strongly oppose the pro-market reforms. The leftist leaders, as a whole, see the current globalization wave as a new phase of imperialist expansion, a process of recolonization of the developing world. Globalization, according to them, promotes the interests of core capitalist countries, both economically and politically, and makes the rest of the world further dependent on them. They see it as a mechanism to shift the increasing crises from the centre to the periphery. The ostensible result of globalization, they contend, has been the growth of a parasitic plundering class in the developing world, including Bangladesh. This class neither gets technology nor much expected investments from the capitalists in the centre, but simply misappropriates state resources in the name of capital accumulation to boost industrial production. The net results are huge losses for the poor and the working class.[3] The leftist reactions to economic reforms had widespread repercussions in the industrial sector and the trade unions affiliated with the leftist parties were in the forefront of the opposition to reform policies. But much progress could not be made due to factors this chapter elaborates on next.

Exceptional enthusiasm for reforms has come from only one class, the businessmen and the industrialists. This class initially believed that economic reforms would bring new technologies and more investment would create new markets for their finished products. That original belief actually failed to see the light of the day, and a section of big industrialists are now frustrated since their products are losing markets in the face of a massive inflow of finished foreign products. Some of them have already parted with industrial production and turned into the risk-free business of commission agents for foreign companies and enterprises.[4] Despite the massive implementation of reforms, foreign investors, instead of investing in the industrial sector, which they perceive as risky, preferred to invest with the Grameen Bank (rural bank), BRAC (Bangladesh Rural Advancement Committee), and other non-governmental credit organizations, where returns from investment are usually high. Yet, the majority of the businessmen and industrialists continued to support reform policies that were in some ways congenial to their interests. Minor business and small-scale industries were severely affected by pro-market reforms and they have vehemently opposed further reforms in the economy, but to no avail.

The enthusiasm of business and industrial elites for economic reforms in Bangladesh stands in sharp contrast to that of the Indian bourgeoisie. The established Indian businesses and industrialists were more suspicious of and hesitant to accept reform policies initiated by the late Indian Prime Minister Rajiv Gandhi in the mid-1980s. The big Indian industrialists accept imported capital and technology, but want trade barriers in place to prevent the entry of foreign finished goods that may shrink the domestic markets of one billion people for their own products. They are more eager to preserve the protective measures extended by the state during the import-substitution industrialization phase. Joint ventures are welcome, but not the multinationals, who might challenge the local industrialists and destabilize the balance of industrial power (Dutt, 1997). One wonders why the less developed Bangladeshi bourgeoisie were more eager to step on the road to comprehensive economic reforms.

The contrast between the Bangladeshi and Indian established business houses may be due to the historical pattern of development of the bourgeois classes in these two countries. Whereas the Indian bourgeoisie emerged as a well developed class by 1947, the year India won independence from British colonial rule, the Bangladeshi bourgeoisie is a development only of the 1960s, and is less exposed to varied industrial experiences. The late President Ayub Khan picked up a section of Bengali Muslim traders to create a social support base for his undemocratic rule in the then East Pakistan. They received every measure of state patronage like easy access to public loans and underwriting facilities to develop themselves as a bourgeois class (Alavi, 1972). But in the process they developed a mind-set to make easy money by depending on state support. Decamping with loan money (the total amount of loan default currently stands at Taka 250 billion [US$ 4.8 billion]),[5] and plundering the resources of privatized mills and factories are obvious manifestations of this historical pattern of development. Since economic reforms, particularly privatization and deregulation programmes, promised an opportunity for easy wealth and powers, a substantial section of the Bangladeshi bourgeoisie was quick to capitalize on it.

THE INDUSTRIAL WORKERS AND RESISTANCE TO ECONOMIC REFORMS

Industrial labour in Bangladesh is often portrayed as volatile and violent and less disposed to structural economic changes. Labour resistance, indeed, increased in the 1980s when massive structural changes were taking place in the industrial sector. The resistance was largely the consequence of the fear of job loss and uncertainty associated with privatization of public sector mills and factories. This made the working class turn a deaf ear to the promise of more jobs and increased income under a vibrant private sector economy. The fear was not baseless, since historically industrial labour had been mistreated and exploited in Bangladesh. The lack of social security for the working class was another factor that prompted industrial workers to block the road to reforms.

The Historical Background

Historically speaking, the current industrial work force is the second or third generation of industrial workers in Bangladesh. When India was partitioned in 1947, the then East Pakistan had no noteworthy industrial units, not even a single jute mill, although it was the largest supplier of raw jute in the world market. A good number of large-scale jute, sugar, and cotton textile industries were established in the 1950s and 1960s by Karachi-based industrial entrepreneurs. A few Bengali entrepreneurs entered the field subsequently. The Pakistani state actively aided the entrepreneurs by extending direct support and patronage, while suppressing the workers through the enactment of various anti-labour laws. The Essential Services Maintenance Act, promulgated in 1952, prohibited trade unions and declared work stoppage or absence from work a punishable offence. The law equally applied to both industries and services essential to the community of people. It was only in

1969 that the government allowed the industrial workers to form trade unions at the plant level. The Industrial Relations Ordinance of 1969 recognized workers' rights to create and join associations of their own choice, elect collective bargaining agents and determine the procedures to resolve labour disputes, including the right to strike and lockouts (ILO, 1991).

The general anti-labour position of the Pakistani ruling elites was partly due to the Muslim League's lack of connections with any labour front during its movement for an independent Pakistan and partly due to the lack of firm ideological convictions. Persuaded by American advisors, the Pakistani rulers adopted a development strategy that recognized 'functional inequality' in the development process where concerns for the working class surfaced less (Candland, 2003).

Needless to say, the anti-labour position of the Pakistani state encouraged the industrial elites to resist the demands of the working class for job security, wages commensurate with living costs, and other social security provisions. Especially in the then East Pakistan, where the majority of industrialists were West Pakistanis and anti-West Pakistani sentiments were running high, Bengali workers gradually became militant and started to protest the anti-labour attitudes and policies of the industrialists and the government. The obvious outcomes were prolonged strikes, lockouts, and pitched battles between workers and security forces (Ahmed, 1978).

After Independence, the AL government attempted to control labour militancy through constitutional as well as economic measures. The workers had played a prominent role in the 1971 War of Independence and the political leaders were apparently sensitive to the legitimate demands of the working class. The Bangladesh Constitution of 1972 declared the building of 'an exploitation-free society and emancipation of the toiling masses from all forms of exploitation' as a basic objective of the state, and the First Five-Year Plan (1973–78) was drawn setting forth that objective in broader socio-economic and political contexts (Islam, 1977). At the same time, the government adopted a carrot-and-stick policy to curb trade union activities. Presidential Order No. 55, promulgated in May 1972, banned all strikes and lockouts in nationalized industries. Similarly, the labour policy of the government, announced in September the same year, attempted to restrict labour rights to strike and collective bargaining in the public sector mills and factories (Islam, 1983). The AL, therefore, dealt with labour in two ways—simultaneous recognition and repression.

The AL government, however, tried to compensate the withdrawal of the rights to strike and collective bargaining by satisfactory wage rates. The Industrial Workers' Wages Commission, constituted in 1972, recommended that all workers in the public sector industries be put under a uniform wage structure and that workers should receive additional fringe benefits. The government legislated the 'State-owned Manufacturing Industries Workers' (Terms and Conditions of Service) Act in 1973 to implement the recommendations of the Wages Commission. A second wage commission was constituted in April 1977 after the overthrow of the AL government in August 1975 to revise the uniform wage structure. The new government emphasized wage rates 'commensurate with the modalities of piece rate versus working time'.[6] A series of wage commissions have subsequently been established in the 1980s and 1990s to revise wage structures as demanded by the industrial workers.

Workers' Social Security

The social security provisions for the working class are almost non-existent in Bangladesh and whatever security exists is the bare minimum, compared to other countries in the South Asian region. The state of Bangladesh still clings to a few social security laws legislated by the colonial British Government in the 1930s and 1940s and the Pakistani government in the 1960s. The British Government passed the Trade Union Act in 1926 granting workers the rights to unionize at the plant level, introduced the Workers Compensation Act in 1932 and issued the Maternity Benefits Act in 1939. The Compensation Act, amended in 1957 and 1980, provided workers in the organized sector package benefits including injury at work, sickness, death, and survivors' benefits, and disability pensions. The Maternity Benefits Act was meant for the female workers who were eligible for leave with full pay for six post-natal months (Anderson et al., 1991).

During the united Pakistan period the ruling elites did not undertake any special social security measures for the workers, but enacted a few laws that sought to improve the working environment and procedures of work in the mills and factories. The government passed the Factories Act, 1965, Employment of Labour (Standing Orders) Act, 1965, the Shops and Establishment Act, 1965, Road Transport Workers' Ordinance, 1961, and Water Transport (Regulation of Employment) Act, 1965.[7]

The Employment of Labour (Standing Orders) Act, 1965, was rather repressive as it provided the procedures under which workers could be dismissed or removed from service by the employers. The termination procedures could be interpreted in different ways, but the employers were in an advantageous position to use the procedures against the employees. The Factories Act, 1965, on the other hand, dealt with accident prevention and safety measures for the workers. It provided for adequate lighting and ventilation in the working environment and attempted to ensure welfare measures such as leave with wages, rest, and recreation. The Employees Social Insurance Ordinance, 1962, that provided benefits for sickness, work injury, and death was implemented in West Pakistan while East Pakistan remained out of its purview. The Companies Profits (Workers' Participation) Act, enforced in 1968, was implemented on an all-Pakistan basis, but it applied to firms or factories with 100 or more workers. Workers in such factories with a capital of Taka 2 million were eligible to receive 2.5 per cent of the profits made by the factories (Anderson et al., 1991).

The social security provisions for workers in independent Bangladesh remain as poor as they were during the Pakistan days. The government of late President Ziaur Rahman amended the Workers' Compensation Act of 1932 for the first time in 1980 to match the worker's compensation with the economic needs of the time. In 1985, the military administration of General H.M. Ershad amended the 1968 Companies Profits (Workers' Participation) Act and raised the rate of profit sharing to 5 per cent. This is rather insignificant when one takes India's commendable progress in the workers social security front (Anderson et al., 1991).

The International Labour Organization (ILO) issued the guidelines for minimum social security of workers in the developing countries in 1952. India enacted the Employees State Insurance Act in 1948, four years before the ILO came up with the guidelines. The Act provided for compulsory insurance in the areas of health, maternity, and accident benefits. In a quick succession, India also enacted the Coal Mines Provident Fund and Bonus Scheme Act in 1948 and the Employees Provident Fund Act in 1952. Legislation relating to workers' provident fund exists in Bangladesh, but glaring negligence is visible in the health, sickness, and accident-related benefits areas. The National Labour Law Commission, constituted in July 1992, in its June 1994 report to the government recommended death benefits for workers' survivors and the creation of private sector retirement funds, but progress achieved on these recommendations are not known.[8]

In addition to the negligible social security measures currently existing in Bangladesh, the workers are often denied the basic rights to collective bargaining. The two military regimes of General Ziaur Rahman and General H.M. Ershad severely curbed trade union rights and restricted workers' rights to strike and lockouts. The workers in Bangladesh have a long tradition of democratic struggle for their rights since the Pakistan days, and the imposition of martial laws that banned trade union movements in independent Bangladesh from time to time highly agitated the workers. This was the objective situation prevailing in the country when the military government of General H.M. Ershad declared the 1982 New Industrial Policy that chalked out an elaborate plan to privatize public sector industries. But industrial workers, fearing massive job losses, and seeing an insignificant social security system and lack of alternative opportunities for employment, were suspicious of the privatization plan. The opposition the workers subsequently put up to privatization turned from street demonstrations to violent activities, including lockouts, disruptions in production, and detention of management (Hamphrey, 1992).

At this stage, it is necessary to briefly highlight the dominant characteristic features of the trade union movement in Bangladesh. The basic attributes of labour can be said to determine its movement against privatization, the emerging trends in the movements and the extent of success or failure the movements record in the course of development. To begin with, industrial labour in Bangladesh is characterized by an ever-growing organizational multiplicity. By the late 1990s, there were some 700 trade union federations representing diverse ideological positions and pursuits (a federation of trade unions has at least two trade unions affiliated to it) (Rahman and Bakth, 1997). The industrial sector of Bangladesh may be small and less diversified, but the mushroom growth of trade union federations indicates that a significant portion of workers prefer to get involved in unions and associations. Out of 5.6 million workers in the manufacturing and non-manufacturing industrial units, 1.6 million workers in the manufacturing sector alone are members of different trade unions (World Bank, 1994).

Second, the workers are highly politicized. Almost all trade union federations are affiliated with political parties. The biggest trade union federations happen to be the labour fronts of the three biggest political parties of the country—the BNP, the AL, and the Jatiya Party (National Party). The labour fronts of these three big political parties represent some 64 per cent of the workers in the industrial sector (Rahman and Bakth, 1997). In some cases, some labour leaders also happen to be political leaders at the district or national levels. The top leadership of the political parties appoints labour leaders either from within the working class or from the rank and file of the parties with which the trade unions are affiliated. In either case, the appointed labour leaders remain loyal to the parent political parties.

Third, the labour movement is dominated by the pro-nationalist labour fronts of the three big political parties. In the years before and following Independence in 1971, industrial labourers were affiliated with the radical left political parties—the National Awami Party, Jatiya Samajtantrik Dal (National Socialist Party), the Bangladesh Communist Party, the Bangladesh Workers Party, and so on. The radical left unity, however, gradually broke down due to differences between communist leaders over the long persisting Sino-Soviet ideological rift and the tactics to be followed in the national context. The fragmentation of the left political parties and radical trade unions frustrated the general workers who later turned to the nationalist trade unions that had the blessings of the ruling party of the day. The rising trend in membership of pro-nationalist trade unions overshadowed the radical trade unions and forced them to take a back seat in labour politics.

According to the US Department of Commerce statistics, in the mid-1990s, the pro-BNP Bangladesh Jatiyatabadi Sramik Dal (Bangladesh Nationalist Workers' Party) had a membership of 160,000–225,000 workers, the pro-National Party Jatiya Sramik Party (National Workers' Party) had 100,000 members, and the Jatiya Sramik League (National Workers' League), a pro-AL trade union, had a membership of 58,000 workers.[9] The Trade Union

Centre, an affiliate of the Communist Party of Bangladesh and the largest of the radical trade unions, had only 25,000 workers as its members. The influence of the radical trade unions diminished with the decreasing trend in their membership.

Despite multiplicity and diverse origins, the trade unions' opposition to the privatization programme was at par. Attempts were made to face the programme from a common platform. Workers were forced to unite and launch a collective movement when their initial fear of job loss and retrenchment came out true in the wake of the earlier rounds of privatization. The provision that new owners of privatized mills and factories would not retrench workers for at least one year was not honoured. Many experienced workers were dismissed and they did not receive the accumulated gratuity money either. The new owners also failed to pay the workers the provident fund money accumulated prior to the divestiture (World Bank, 1994). Frustration of workers was widespread and the possibility of further loss and a bleak future forced them to lay the foundation for a national-level organization to halt privatization efforts.

Emergence of the Sramik Karmachari Oikya Parishad

The workers' opposition to the privatization programme took concrete shape in 1983 when they formed the Sramik Karmachari Oikya Parishad (SKOP—United Front of Workers and Employees). As a united labour platform of almost all trade union federations which were mostly affiliated to different political parties, the SKOP valiantly fought for the rights of the workers and was initially successful in extracting benefits like wage increase and generous bonuses for the workers and employees. Throughout the 1980s, it was most vocal against the privatization programme. In 1984, the SKOP articulated a five-point demand that called for an immediate halt to the privatization programme and demanded renationalization of the hitherto privatized mills and companies. The demands were revised in 1988, but remained highly antithetical to the policy of privatization (World Bank, 1994). In the early 1990s, the tone changed somewhat as it adopted new issues for collective bargaining. The introduction of a national minimum wage, equally applicable to workers both in the public and private sectors, and a proactive role in policies that affect employment and industrial relations were new issues that dominated the SKOP's agenda. The SKOP leaders demanded that trade unions be consulted on all issues relating to privatization and contraction of employment (Rahman, 1994).

There was a shift in the SKOP's position from outright opposition in the 1980s to gradual acceptance of privatization in the 1990s. Although the SKOP leaders publicly opposed privatization, in reality, they adopted a pragmatic position on retrenchment of workers and public sector industrial units that were making consistent loss. They identified managerial inefficiency and wrong investment decisions as the causes of consistent losses by the public sector industries (this in effect justified privatization) and demanded that the government should address the problems of the industrial sector properly. The SKOP leaders were not opposed to trade liberalization, but wanted protective measures to be taken to save local industries from the onslaught of less expensive and highly competitive foreign products (Rahman, 1994).

The shifting positions of the SKOP on issues of privatization and trade liberalization gradually made it less militant against and more responsive to negotiations with the government. During 1991–93, a series of negotiations took place between the SKOP and the government, which resulted in the signing of five major agreements. The agreements were marked by some non-material achievements like the formation of the National Wage and Productivity Commission in 1992 and the National Labour Laws Reform Commission in the same year (Rahman, 1994).

In terms of material benefits for the workers, the success of the SKOP was not very significant. Its demand for a national minimum wage, involving both private and public sector workers, was rejected by the government as well as the private sector entrepreneurs. It was, however, able to record some achievements on sectoral minimum wages. In 1992, the SKOP demanded Taka 1,000 as minimum wage for public sector industrial workers and mounted nationwide transport blockades, demonstrations, and general strikes to realize the demand. The government, in response, constituted the National Wage Commission in 1992 and directed it to come up with recommendations for a public sector minimum wage. An influential member of the Wage Commission disclosed to this author that the Commission, considering the rising living costs in the country, recommended Taka 1,850 plus benefits as the minimum monthly wage for a public sector worker, but the government arbitrarily fixed it at Taka 950.[10] Workers' reactions to the new fixation were sharp and they accepted it grudgingly at best. This minimum wage did not apply to private sector industrial workers.

The responsibility of fixing a minimum wage for private sector workers and employees was left to the Minimum Wages Board, the counterpart of the National Wages and Productivity Commission. Originally formed in 1961, this Board consists of representatives from the government, labour, and management. The SKOP demanded that the Minimum Wages Board recommend a minimum wage for private sector workers sooner rather than later. It may be mentioned that the private sector entrepreneurs label the SKOP as an extra-legal body and oppose minimum wage fixation on the ground that upward revision of wages depends on overall productivity and the margin of profitability. Unless productivity goes high, minimum wage fixation will remain a difficult issue (Rahman, 1994). The issues involved were complex and negotiations went on continuously. It took almost seven years for the government to wind up the negotiations and in July 2001 the Ministry of Labour and Employment declared Taka 1,200 as the minimum monthly wage for a private sector worker. The SKOP leaders, in the mean time, intensified their campaign for a minimum national wage. The efforts culminated in the signing of two agreements, between the SKOP and the government in January 1998 and July 1999, that pledge-bound the government to declare and codify a national minimum wage for workers and employees in the public and private sectors as a whole. This objective, however, still remains unrealized.

The government, on the other hand, came up with carefully designed policies that largely circumscribed the effectiveness of the SKOP as a national association of workers and employees. The voluntary departure scheme (VDS), announced by the government in the late 1980s, offered attractive financial benefits for workers who were ready to accept voluntary retirement. Under VDS, a public sector worker with 30 years service was entitled to receive a gratuity equal to five years pay. The worker would also receive other benefits payable under service rules. The response of workers to VDS was highly positive. According to a World Bank estimate, a large number of workers, some 9,000, of the Bangladesh Jute Mills

Corporation (BJMC) preferred to go into voluntary retirement by the end of 1993 (World Bank, 1994). In addition to VDS, the government also promised to train the retired workers to help develop marketable skills that would help them to get new employment. The Jute Retraining Scheme, set up by the government in the early 1990s, is helping affected workers of BJMC. But such a retraining initiative was not extended to workers in other industries like cotton textile mills (Kashem, 2000).

Has the SKOP Failed?

SKOP, as the national platform of workers and employees, has a record of both success and failure. It has played an instrumental role to press hard for minimum wages for workers consistent with the rising living costs in the urban areas. But apart from the realization of minimum wages for the public and private sector workers, its performance on the resistance to privatization is poor and often frustrating. The private sector has largely taken over the public sector that once comprised more than 90 per cent of industries, banks, and insurance companies under government control. There are grievances that the SKOP's role against the privatization move was passive and sometimes mysterious. The important question is—why did the SKOP fail to mount a formidable challenge to privatization efforts of the government? This question merits special importance since labour unity in neighbouring India was successful in withstanding the pressures of privatization.[11] The reasons for the SKOP's failure to build up an effective resistance are explored in the following pages.

It may be mentioned that SKOP emerged in a political environment dominated by anti-autocratic movements against the military regime of General H.M. Ershad. By pursuing parallel programmes, it followed the lead of parent political parties to oust the military dictator, thereby compromising its independent programmes to fight exclusively for the rights of the working class and employees. There was hardly any difference between the SKOP as a labour organization and the SKOP as a political front. When the Ershad regime was toppled in December 1990, the SKOP was not able to field candidates for the 1991 elections to the national parliament. Its unity loosened and the leaders were busy working for their parent political parties. The result was the near complete absence of labour leaders in the national parliament who could speak for the protection and promotion of workers' rights and interests. Unlike India, where labour has a special representation in the Lok Sobha (lower house of the Indian parliament), the trade union leaders in Bangladesh were always sidelined by the politicians. Whereas labour occupies around 10 per cent of the seats in the Lok Sobha and political parties take pains to draft trade union leaders as possible candidates for parliamentary elections (Mathur, 1993), there is no such parallel development in Bangladesh. It may be mentioned that V.V. Giri, the late President of India, was once a trade union leader.

The linkage between trade union federations and political parties effectively ate into the vitality of the SKOP as a collective form of opposition to privatization. The direct impact of the linkage was that whenever major political parties differed on political issues, the trade unions affiliated with them followed suit. Trade union leaders were appointees of the top political leadership and they could not take a stand against their own political party. Positions along political party lines seriously divided the SKOP in the decades of the 1980s and the 1990s. As its consequence, occasional frictions, conflicts, and clashes flared up between rival trade unions that damaged labour unity and undermined the possibility of a united anti-privatization movement.

There is always a contradiction between a political party and its labour front. While the political party supports globalization and structural reforms, its labour front opposes it. This contradiction, however, did not surface because of the control of the political parties over their respective trade unions. The SKOP includes the labour fronts of the BNP and the AL—the two parties that have consecutively formed governments in the 1990s. The dominance of the ruling party's labour front has always been a major factor in the trade union movement. It discouraged the development of a strong organizational network to steer ahead the movement against economic reforms. A prominent leftist leader, in an interview with this author, pointed out that it was impossible to build up resistance to pro-market reforms while working with the ruling party's labour front.[12]

The lack of dedicated leaders and strong commitments to the cause of the workers was another factor that greatly derailed the

SKOP from its original objective of resisting pro-market reforms. A few leftist political and trade union leaders particularly allege that many trade union leaders, particularly from the Jatiyatabadi Sramik Dal and the Sramik League, pay only lip service to the labour movement and do not support it seriously. They are often bought over by the government and bribed from time to time to keep labour agitation under control. The Bangladesh Institute of Labour Studies (BILS), established in 1995, is construed to have played an invisible role to bribe trade union leaders, although BILS's declared objective is to promote unity and consolidate the strength of the trade union movement.[13]

Last but not least, there were no initiatives to create a broad-based social coalition to fight pro-market reforms from a united platform of the workers and other civil society groups. 'A social coalition', according to an influential labour leader, 'may be treated as a platform for social revolution. We are not ready for that stage'.[14] Because of divergent interests, other social groups either avoided alignment with the working class or did not think it appropriate to roll back the reform process. Another respected leftist politician pointed out that the print and electronic media were quite indifferent to the cause of the working class and showed little sympathy for the anti-globalization movement. The SKOP had to play the role of a lone ranger.[15]

The Left Democratic Front and Resistance to Reform Policies

The leftist political and trade union leaders played a crucial role to form SKOP, but they were not happy with the performance of this national-level labour organization. Frustration with the SKOP led them to unite the leftist forces and initiate a unified movement to safeguard workers' interests. The polarization of leftist forces resulted in the creation of the Left Democratic Front (LDF) in 1994. An alliance of 11 left-wing political parties, the LDF criticized the bourgeois social structure as the prime cause of the economic backwardness of the country and argued that the World Bank–IMF political and economic dictation promotes misery of the popular masses. The LDF, in particular, identified the rush to a free market economy as the cause of the deepening crisis in the national economy and vowed to resist economic reforms that fill up the coffers of the plundering rich class.[16]

It is difficult to say to what extent the proclaimed objectives of the LDF have been achieved, but one thing is abundantly clear—the promised stiff resistance to pro-market reforms did not take place. There are both organizational weaknesses and ideological differences that instead of promoting unity, bred disunity and disharmony between the leftist forces. The obvious results are fragmentation, weakness, and incapacity to mobilize the working class along broad-based social objectives. Since its creation in 1994, the LDF leaders are still unable to design the organizational structure of the alliance and give it a grass-roots dimension. The constituent members of the LDF prefer to draw and carry out programmes on individual party lines. No minimum consensus exists on how to proceed to develop grass-roots consciousness and unity among the workers and peasants to wage the battle for social transformation.[17]

Simmering ideological differences also exist on strategic and tactical lines. Some leftist parties, particularly the Communist Party of Bangladesh (CPB), took the position that social change is possible only when communists are able to capture state power and they support electoral participation in the bourgeois political process to achieve that end, while others find this position a deviation from communist convictions. The Jatiya Gano Front (National People's Front) and like-minded parties, on the other hand, think it more appropriate to prepare the workers and peasants for a social revolution as a way to capture state power. It does not make sense, the chief coordinator of Jatiya Gano Front opines, to capture state power while keeping the social structure in its current form. Such ideological differences obstructed efforts by the LDF to become a unified political movement of the leftist forces and make it an alternative political platform. At one stage, there was some discussion about a united labour front of the left-wing parties. The CPB, the Bangladesh Workers' Party, and the Bangladesh Samajtantrik Dal (Bangladesh Socialist Party) (Khalequzzaman) expressed keen interest in the idea, but due to intra-party dissension about a SKOP-like leftist labour front the idea died out subsequently.[18]

Apart from organizational weaknesses and ideological disarray, leftist leaders in general lack such political agenda that articulates their social concerns and a well thought-out action plan. They currently share such concerns as human rights, women's empowerment, and democracy, which are the traditional domains of the centrist political parties, gender activists, and the non-governmental organizations (NGOs). But actions on all these concerns rarely translate into the development of an alternative political agenda.[19] The leftist politicians are no longer maintaining a leftist position solely dedicated to the cause of the working class. There may be some programmes but no well conceived plan to implement the programmes. Much explanation of the fragmented nature of resistance and disarticulated attempts of the leftist parties to resist pro-market reforms in Bangladesh can be found here.

The Peasantry and Resistance to Economic Reforms

Unlike the organized industrial sector, resistance to market oriented reforms in the rural sector remains mostly dormant. The mass of peasants are dissatisfied with and angered by the way the government has implemented sweeping agricultural reforms. They are most affected by the withdrawal of subsidies on agricultural inputs and irrigation equipment, but their looming dissatisfaction has rarely turned violent in the decades of the 1980s and 1990s. The apparent reasons for the absence of organized resistance to agricultural reforms are cited as the weakness of the peasantry as a pressure group or lack of an effective farmer lobby, the geographical dispersion of farmers across the country and associated difficulties to organize them, diverse ideological orientations, and a poor resource base (Abdullah and Shahabuddin, 1997). These reasons might have contributed to making the peasants less effective, but this in no way implies that rural resistance to reform policies does not exist. There is resistance, but not as violent and organized as in the urban industrial sector.

Occasionally, the poor peasants have openly protested the consequences of agricultural reforms, but the protest movements were suppressed brutally. The progressive rise in fertilizer prices since 1991 and the marketing of adulterated agricultural inputs (mainly fertilizer and pesticides) made the peasants come out on the streets and protest. In 1995, police opened fire on a peaceful peasants demonstration in Mymensing District, in the eastern part of Bangladesh, which resulted in the death of 18 peasants. The opposition political parties reacted sharply to the killings, but did not mobilize a strong peasant movement across the country to protect the interest of the peasant community. The poor peasantry, as an unorganized group, found themselves all alone on the road and failed to steer towards a national movement to make their voice heard.

Peasants' protest movements against pro-market agricultural reforms are not confined to Bangladesh alone; they are found elsewhere, both in the developing as well as the developed world. The Brazilian peasantry's protest against globalization was met with the massacre of 19 poor landless peasants in April 1996. These led to the creation of the 'Via Campesina'—an international movement of peasants and small farmers' organizations. Peasants and small farmers are equally vocal against pro-market agricultural policies in the developed world as well. In the Netherlands, for example, where some 4,000 small farms disappear every year, the farmers are joining efforts to bring about changes in the current agricultural model.[20]

Perhaps India remains the best example where peasants and small farmers' movements against globalization have achieved some degree of success. The grass-root action groups in India—small and marginalized farmers and other depressed social groups—formed the National Alliance for People's Movement (NAPM) to campaign against reform policies. NAPM's struggle for three objectives—to stop further social and economic marginalization, degradation of labour, and environmental destruction—was largely successful, as it was able to force the state governments and the multinational corporations to temporarily halt a few mega-projects, including the Narmada River Project designed by the World Bank (Pasha, 1999: 243).

There are no comparable grass-root movements against globalization in Bangladesh. There exist no mega-projects either, that could provide a fertile ground for a mass movement. The Bangladeshi rural people are affected, but they are not mobilizing support to halt the reform process. Except for a few sporadic protest movements by the landless people, the absence of mass-oriented movements against agricultural reforms at the national level can be attributed to two sets of reasons—the dynamics of rural social and economic structure and the situational deficiencies—factors that obstruct unity among the rural people and leave them in a state of disarray.

Dynamics of Rural Social and Economic Structure

Historically, rural Bangladesh has been a vast sea of poor people. About 85 per cent of the total population of Bangladesh lives in the rural areas and directly or indirectly depends on agriculture for its livelihood. According to the Labour Force Survey of 1995–96, the total number of rural households stands at 13.82 million. A vast number of the households, about 63.2 per cent, are agricultural labour households. The most staggering problem, especially after Independence, has been a continuous rise in the percentage of landless people. In 1960, there were 2.10 million landless households in rural Bangladesh, but by 1983–84 that figure had increased to 3.77 million. The 1983–84 Agricultural Census estimated that 48.88 per cent of people were functionally landless (having less than 0.50 acre of land). Thereafter, in the next 15 years, the percentage of functionally landless people reached an alarming stage and increased by 2.42 per cent per annum between 1983–84 and 1995–96. The landless and marginal farmers (having up to one acre of land) together constituted 72 per cent of the rural population in 1996. In 1984, this group together constituted some 63 per cent (Saha, 2001: 74–75). The rising trend in the percentage share of the functionally landless and marginal farmers indicates a process of creeping, but destructive, marginalization taking place in rural Bangladesh.

At the other end of the spectrum are the rich and surplus farmers. This group controls the major portion of agricultural land and acts as the guardian of the people. According to the 1983–84 Agricultural Census, some 24.72 per cent of households owned 42.67 per cent of the total agricultural land in Bangladesh. And, a small percentage of people (4.94 per cent) having 7.5 acres of land, or more, controlled 25.64 per cent of agricultural land. The percentage of big landowners is observed to have declined by the mid-1990s. By 1996, the figure of landowning people at the upper end decreased from 4.94 per cent to 2.53 per cent and the control over land ownership came down from 25.64 per cent to 17.48 per cent. The rich and surplus farmers' group (having control over 2.50–7.50 acres of land), as a whole, constitutes 17.61 per cent of rural households and controls 39.41 per cent of land (Saha, 2001: 76).

The rich and surplus farmers establish their control over rural life through a variety of methods. They may refuse to sign lease contracts with the sharecroppers, who, according to the 1996 Agricultural Census, cultivate some 62 per cent of agricultural lands (Saha, 2001: 80), or scrap the already existing contracts. They may also express unwillingness to extend loans to the marginal farmers who defy their commands and have no access to institutional sources of agricultural credit. They may also frighten the functionally landless or marginal farmers with the threat of eviction. During the 'Permanent Settlement' period (1793–1950) the zamindar class earned notoriety for applying such methods against their *raiyots* (cultivators), but their departure from the scene in 1951 did not put an end to this infamous process. The zamindars were simply replaced by the rich and surplus farmers.

Control over land and the landless and marginal farmers brings the rich and surplus farmers the advantage of being at the apex of the rural power structure. A series of studies conducted in the 1960s, 1970s, and 1980s[21] found that the rich dominated the union council (village-level administrative unit) elections and other development committees. The presence of the vast majority of the landless, the marginal, and small farmers is rarely noticeable on the union council boards or numerous cooperatives and rural development committees. The interests of the rich and surplus farmers, as a logical consequence, are protected more than that of the poor and small farmers. The economic and political powers, originating from land ownership and wealth, thus, enable the rich to maintain control over rural life and quell any challenge to their social position.

The rich and surplus farmers are also a part of the national power structure. They are structurally aligned with the bureaucracy and the political elites. The major political parties, in order to expand their organizational base, usually pick up the wealthy people in the rural areas who can contribute money and supply manpower, particularly during the election period. Administrative elites also have a tendency to favour the rural rich. A significant portion of Bangladeshi bureaucrats have a rural background and they are the sons and daughters of rich and surplus farmers. The poor and marginal farmers usually lack the resources to support their childrens' education at the college or university level, which could make them competent for government jobs.

The relationship of the dominant and the dominated in rural Bangladesh, which Erik J. Jansen characterizes as a 'patron–client relationship'(Jansen, 1991: 49), is, however, changing gradually. Two particular factors that have led to the erosion of the patron–client relationship in the 1980s and 1990s to some extent, may be mentioned here. The first factor is massive intervention by NGOs in the rural areas. The incapacity of the government to deliver the benefits of development to the rural poor and reduce poverty gave the NGOs a unique opportunity to devise and implement development programmes in rural Bangladesh. In 1999, there were some 20,000 registered NGOs, local and foreign, operating in different rural areas. NGOs primarily extend micro-credit to the rural poor, who do not have the collateral to obtain loans from institutional sources. Other activities of NGOs include skill training, education, health, family planning, and sanitation services (The World Bank, 1999: 43). Atiur Rahman and Abu N.M. Wahid, in a study on the impact of Grameen Bank activities, carried out in 1992, found that the availability of finance to the sharecroppers and wage labourers greatly affected the power and influence of the landed elites. The Grameen Bank members, as organized groups, engaged in substantial off-farm income-generating activities, were less dependent on their traditional patrons and were less ready to follow the dictates of their masters during election times (Rahman, 1992).

The other factor that curtailed the power of the rural rich is rural infrastructural development. Massive development of roads and communication systems in the 1990s has made it possible to connect almost all villages with district and *upazilla* (sub-district) towns and commercial centres. Now a poor man can earn enough money by driving a passenger van or using a pushcart to move goods from one place to another.

However, in a country where scores of millions live in poverty, the operations of the Grameen Bank and other development NGOs or infrastructural development can not totally eliminate the centuries old pattern of influence and dominance of the rich all of a sudden. Out of 13.82 million rural households, micro-credit programmes of the four biggest NGOs in Bangladesh—Grameen Bank, BRAC, Proshika, and the ASA (Association for Social

Advancement)—covered only 5.77 million by 1996 (World Bank, 1999). This indicates that the rural power structure is still biased in favour of the rich who, with a certain degree of control, shape the basic patterns of rural social and economic order.

The landless are the only class that has defied the existing power structures to establish rights on *khasland* (land under no private ownership but legally belonging to the state). Reclaimed from riverbeds, *khasland* is mainly found in the southern part of Bangladesh. The Bangladesh Krishok (farmers) Federation, established in 1976, was waging a long struggle to distribute the *khasland* to the landless. A section of the rural rich and wealthy people was using the *khasland* under illegal occupation. The Krishok Federation launched a strong movement in 1980 and occupied four *char*s (small chunk of land surrounded by waters) in Patuakhali District, but was forced by the police to leave the *char*s. The continuous movement of the landless people, however, forced the government in 1987 to introduce laws favouring the distribution of *khasland* and *char*s among the landless people (Doli, 2000).

The movement for *khasland* distribution intensified in the early 1990s. Ten thousand male and female peasants participated in a hunger strike in July 1991. Having failed to draw the attention of the government, 30,000 peasants waged a heroic struggle against the local big land owners and illegal occupants and occupied four *char*s of 22 acres of *khasland* in Patuakhali District on 1 January 1992. The unity of the landless eventually forced the government to recognize their rights and give them a lease for one year. In the years following the Patuakhali success, a total of 22 *char*s in the southern part of Bangladesh with an estimated 60,000 acres of *khasland* have been occupied and distributed among more than 100,000 landless people (Doli, 2000).

Situational Deficiencies

The success story of the landless in southern Bangladesh was not replicated by the poor, landless and marginal farmers in other parts of the country. The apparent non-availability of *char*s and *khasland* and the absence of Krishok Federation-like associations explain this point. But it is difficult to understand why the small and marginal farmers, while being affected by the privatization of agricultural inputs and equipment, failed to mobilize and organize protest movements as an expression of their rejection of agricultural reform policies. The present author gathered information about reforms from members of the peasantry in different areas of south-central and north-western Bangladesh in February and March 2002 and discovered a host of factors that effectively discouraged the peasantry from organizing resistance movements. These factors are discussed next.

Absence of Peasants Associations and Organizations

Rural Bangladesh is characterized by a lack of organizations and leadership which can unite the peasants and articulate their grievances against wholesale reforms in agriculture. The peasants, as poor people, do not have the necessary funds to mobilize mass movements either. The big political parties have peasant fronts, but few, if any, leaders of the peasant fronts come from the peasant class or live in rural areas. The so-called peasant leaders are mainly urban-based; they keep aloof from rural problems and are naturally less concerned about the deteriorating rural economic and social conditions. The peasant fronts of leftist political parties are equally inactive. Leftist organizations, that are usually thought of to be more concerned with the problems of deprived people and are supposed to organize them for social change, do not exist in most of the areas I visited from February to April 2002. And in areas where they do exist, the left-wing leaders are less interested in organizing the peasants to protest state agricultural policies. Rather they are perceived as engaged in robbery, extortion, and threat of killings that create social anarchy.[22]

Group Conflicts and Differences

Group conflicts and differences play a critical role in discouraging the peasants from getting organized and defending their interests. Although ethnically and religiously the peasants are near homogeneous and ˉpeak one language—Bangla—still divergent opinions divide the peasantry and a lack of mutual trust characterizes their relations. Most of the peasants I interviewed are supporters of the two major political parties, the BNP and the AL, and in most cases the party preference has its obvious impact on local relations.

Peasants of Rudrakhar Village of Palang Upzilla in Shariatpur District, south-central Bangladesh, particularly referred to the possibility of group conflicts that might emerge and divide them whenever any attempts to float a peasant association or organization are to be made.[23] Such divides among peasants in other areas are also noticeable.

Threat of Punishment

Local protest movements or demonstrations, against pro-market policies in agriculture, also suffer the wrath of the beneficiaries of reforms. The traders or rich farmers usually get dealerships for distribution of agricultural inputs. The peasants complain that political connections do play a role in getting dealerships and in most cases party loyalty is considered as the criterion of dealership distribution. The economic positions and political connections set the dealers free to create artificial crises and raise inputs prices from time to time. Whenever there is any protest movement against price hikes, the dealers employ local *mastans* (armed hoodlums) to suppress the protestors. The organizers of protest movements are communicated the threat of severe punishment privately and are silenced completely.

The State as an Unfriendly Agent

The peasants, in general, lack confidence in local leaders as well as in the government. They view the state as an agent of the rich and wealthy class and find it unfriendly to the interests of the common man. A group of peasants, conscious of state policies towards agriculture, pointed out that the poor peasantry of Bangladesh has no future unless the state becomes more committed to protecting their interests. Indeed, except a brief period after Independence, the state of Bangladesh has pursued an urban-based industrial growth strategy to the detriment of agriculture, in general, and the peasantry, in particular. The development plans were exclusionary towards rural people as budgetary allocations for agricultural development continued to register a progressive decline. For example, government expenditures for all sectors during the period 1975–78 to 1987–89 increased more than 5.7 times in monetary terms. The expenditure on agriculture, however, declined from about 26 per cent in the period 1978–81 to about 14 per cent in the period 1987–89. The expenditure declined despite agriculture employing more people than the industrial sector and still remaining the largest contributor to the GDP.

The implementation of reform policies in agriculture substantially increased the sufferings of the poor peasantry. The various governments in Dhaka, however, were less concerned about these sufferings and more determined to proceed with reforms. The agricultural reforms have been carried out smoothly and without any hindrance since the farmers are disorganized and are also subjected to repression if opposition to reforms grows at all. The unfriendly attitude of the state towards rural Bangladesh makes the peasants passive and indifferent, but there is no denying the fact that they are opposed to reform policies and constitute a quiet sea of dormant resistance to globalization.

Conclusion

The discussion in this chapter has brought into focus that pro-market reforms enjoy the least social support in Bangladesh and that all social classes, except the business and industrial community, are opposed to reform policies. However, the implementation of reforms has not produced any broad-based anti-reforms social coalition to date. Albeit the majority of people are bearing the brunt of reforms. Strong resistance sprang out of the industrial sector where the labourers, faced with threats to their survival, had no choice other than resist the spectre of economic reforms. The labour unity to resist industrial reforms initially proved successful, but the emergence of a host of factors at the subsequent stage cut into labour unity and left the workers divided. Industrial resistance to pro-market reforms gradually became weak and fragmented. Unlike the industrial sector, peasants' resistance to liberalization policies in agriculture has never been close to taking any concrete shape. The principal weakness of the peasantry is their subjugation to both national as well as rural power structures that work against their interests. The peasants are affected by reforms, but, as disorganized and also demoralized groups, they are in no position to pool their strength together and forge a unity to push back the reform agenda. Rural resistance to pro-market reforms necessarily remains dormant, but—if organized—may explode into violent outbursts.

Notes

1. The author's formal and informal discussions with academics at the University of Dhaka, during February and March, 2002.
2. Personal interview with Abul Bashar, president, Jatiya Sramik Federation (National Workers' Federation) on 8 April 2002, in Dhaka, Bangladesh.
3. Personal interviews with Mujahidul Islam Salim, general secretary, Communist Party of Bangladesh, and Rashed Khan Menon, president, Bangladesh Workers' Party, on 9 April 2002, Dhaka.
4. Harun-ur Rashid Bhuiyan, vice-president, Bangladesh United Sramik (Workers) Federation, pointed out that Lutfar Rahman, the managing director of W. Rahman Jute Mills left the mills in early 1990s to become the local agent of Nestle Bangladesh Ltd., a Dutch multinational corporation. The interview was taken on 10 April 2002 in Dhaka.
5. *The Daily Star* (a Dhaka-based English daily), 14 January 2003.
6. See, ILO, *The Working Poor in Bangladesh: A Case Study on Employment Problems, Conditions*, 22.
7. See, ILO, *The Working Poor in Bangladesh: A Case Study on Employment Problems*, Conditions, 15.
8. US Department of Commerce (1999). Bangladesh: Foreign Labor Trends Report, 1993–94, 6–7 (downloaded from the web site: http://www.tradeport.org/ts/countries/bangladesh/flt.html). Accessed on 24 February 2003.
9. US Department of Commerce (1999). Bangladesh: Foreign Labor Trends Report.
10. Dr Abdul Hye Mondal, Senior Research Fellow, Bangladesh Institute of Development Studies (BIDS) and a member of the 1992 National Wage Commission. Personal interview on 3 April 2002, Dhaka.
11. Trade unions in India are structurally linked with political parties and influence party decision-making processes substantially. Many prominent politicians have special support for the working class. For example, India's first prime minister, Jawaharlal Nehru, was also the president of the All India Trade Union Congress for some time and many labour leaders were allocated central-level portfolios. One trade unionist, V.V. Giri, was appointed federal minister of labour and then rose to become the president of India. Such close connections between trade unions and political elites have always sought to protect the interests of the working class. When India embarked on pro-market reforms in the early 1990s, labour agitation against reforms was a regular phenomenon and the central government decided to hold tripartite negotiations to manage industrial restructuring by sectors. The prime minister's office is responsible for tripartite negotiations between labour, the industrial bourgeoisie, and the government.

12. Personal interview with Tipu Biswas, chief coordinator, Jatiya Gano Front, (National People's Front) in Dhaka on 9 April 2002.
13. The author obtained this information from Abul Bashar, president, Jatiya Sramik Federation (National Workers' Federation) and Nirmal Sen, president, Sramik Krishok Samajbadi Dal (Socialist Party of Workers and Peasants). The interviews were held in Dhaka on 8 April 2002 and 11 April 2002 respectively.
14. Personal interview with Abul Bashar, 8 April 2002.
15. Rashed Khan Menon, president, Bangladesh Workers Party, interview, Dhaka, 9 April 2002.
16. See, Left Democratic Front (1994).
17. Personal interview with Tipu Biswas, 9 April 2002.
18. Personal interview with Tipu Biswas, 9 April 2002.
19. See, Rehman (2002: 5).
20. Resistance is Fertile! Web site address: http://www.resistanceisfertile.com/english/articles/20020418-17.html. Accessed on 26 February 2003.
21. See, J. Arens and J. Van Beurden, *Jhagrapur: Poor Peasants and Women in a Village in Bangladesh* (New Delhi: Orient Longman, 1979); BRAC, *The Net: Power Structure in Ten Villages* (Dhaka: BRAC, 1980); E. Hartman and J. Boyce, *Quiet Violence: View From a Bangladesh Village* (London: Zed Books, 1983); Pk. Md. Matiur Rahman, 'Decomposition of Income Inequality in Rural Bangladesh' (a paper presented in a seminar organized by the National Association of Social Sciences, Bangladesh, held in Dhaka on December 10–11, 1988; M. Rashiduzzaman, *Politics and Administration in the Local Councils: A Study of Union and District Councils in East Pakistan* (Dhaka: Oxford University Press, 1968); G.D. Wood, 'Class Differentiation and Power in Bandakgram: The Minifundist Case', in Ameerul M. Huq (ed.), *Exploitation and the Rural Poor: A Working Paper on Rural Power Structure in Bangladesh* (Comilla: Bangladesh Academy for Rural Development, 1976).
22. Interview with a group of peasants at Mirpur Bazar, Mirpur Upazilla, Kushtia District, 28 March 2002.
23. The interview was taken on 16 March 2002.

References

Abdullah, Abu and Kazi Shahabuddin (1997). 'Critical Issues in Agriculture: Policy Response and Unfinished Agenda', in M.G. Kibria (ed.), *The Bangladesh Economy in Transition*, pp. 67–73. New Delhi: Oxford University Press.

Ahmed, Kamaruddin (1978). *Labor Movement in Bangladesh*. Dhaka: University Press.

Alavi, Hamza (1972). 'The State in Post-colonial Societies: Pakistan and Bangladesh', *New Left Review*, 74, July–August: 79–80.

Anderson, Kathryn H. and N. Hossain (1991). 'The Effects of Labor Laws and Labor Practices on Employment and Industrialization in Bangladesh', *Bangladesh Development Studies*, 19(1&2): 132–33.

Candland, Christopher (2003). 'New Social and New Political Unionism: Labor, Industry and the State in India and Pakistan', downloaded from the website: http://www. antenna.nl/waterman/candland.html. Accessed on 20 February 2003.

Doli, Shamsun Nahar Khan (2000). 'Peasant Women's Struggle for Land and Emancipation in Bangladesh', downloaded from the website: http://www. humanrights.de/doc_en/archiv/congress/2000/04/29/69. Accessed on 26 February 2003.

Dutt, Amitava Krishna (1997). 'Uncertain Success: The Political Economy of Indian Economic Reforms', *Journal of International Affairs*, 51(1): 326–28.

Farid, Shah M. (1993). 'Economic Reforms, Poverty and Social Safety Nets', ILO-ARTEP, Social Dimensions of Economic Reforms in Bangladesh, Proceedings of the National Tripartite Workshop, held in Dhaka, 18–20 May 1993: 190–91.

Haggard, Stephen and S.B. Webb (1994). *Voting for Reforms: Democracy, Political Liberalization and Economic Adjustment*. New York: Oxford University Press.

Hamphrey, Clare E. (1992). *Privatization in Bangladesh: Economic Transition in a Poor Country*. Dhaka: University Press.

ILO (1991a). *The Working Poor in Bangladesh: A Case Study on Employment problems, Conditions*, p. 15.

———— (1991b). *The Working Poor in Bangladesh: A Case Study on Employment problems, Conditions of Work and Legal Protections of Selected Categories of Disadvantaged Workers*. Dhaka: ILO Area Office.

———— (1991c). *The Working Poor in Bangladesh: A Case Study on Employment problems, Conditions*, p. 22

Islam, Mainul Md. (1983). 'Industrial Relations in Bangladesh', *Indian Journal of Industrial Relations*, 19(2): 166–67.

Islam, Nurul (1977). *Development Planning in Bangladesh: A Study in Political Economy*. London: C. Hurst & Company.

Jansen, Erik J. (1991). 'Process of Polarization and the Breaking-up of a patron-Client Relationship in Rural Bangladesh', in Safar A. Akanda (ed.), *Rural Poverty and Development Strategies in Bangladesh*. Rajshahi: Institute of Bangladesh Studies, University of Rajshahi.

Kashem, Abul Joarder (2000). 'Bangladesh' in Asian Productivity Organization (APO), *Privatization Experience of Asian Countries*, Tokyo: APO: 56.

Left Democratic Front (1994). *Manifesto: Declaration, Programs, Procedures and Rules*. Dhaka: Left Democratic Front Office.

Mathur, Ajeet N. (1993). 'The Experience of Consultation during Structural Adjustment in India (1990–92)', *International Labor Review*, 132(3).

Muhith, Abulmaal A. (1993). 'Privatization in Bangladesh', in V.V. Ramanadhan (ed.), *Constraints and Impacts of Privatization*, pp. 257–58. London and New York: Routledge.

Onis, Zia (1995). 'The Limits of Neoliberalism: Toward a Reformulation of Development Theory', *Journal of Economic Issues*, 29(1).

Pasha, Mustafa Kamal (1999). 'Liberalization, Globalization and Inequality in South Asia', in Francis Adam et al. (eds), *Globalization and the Dilemmas of the State in the South*, pp. 239–43. London and New York: Macmillan and St. Martin's Press.

Rahman, Atiur and Abu N.M. Wahid (1992). 'The Grameen Bank and Changing Patron–Client Relationship in Bangladesh', *Journal of Contemporary Asia*, 22(3): 303–21.

Rahman, Masihur (1994). *Structural Adjustment, Employment and Workers: Public Policies, Issues and Choices for Bangladesh*. Dhaka: University Press.

Rahman, Masihur and Zaid Bakht (1997). 'Constraints to Industrial Development: Recent Reforms and Future Directions', in M.G. Kibria (ed.), *The Bangladesh Economy in Transition*, p. 107. New Delhi: Oxford University Press.

Saha, Bimal Kumar (2001). 'Changing Pattern of Agrarian Structure in Bangladesh: 1984–96', in Abu Abdullah (ed.), *Bangladesh Economy 2000: Selected Issues*, pp. 74–75. Dhaka: Bangladesh Institute of Development Studies.

Siddiqui, Kamal (1990). *Social Formation in Dhaka City: A Study in Third World Urban Sociology*. Dhaka: University Press.

Sobhan, Rehman and Muzaffer Ahmad (1980). *Public Enterprise in an Intermediate Regime: A Study in the Political Economy of Bangladesh*, Dhaka: Bangladesh Institute of Development Studies: 67.

Sobhan, Rehman (2002). 'The Evolving Political Economy of Bangladesh in the Age of Globalization', BIDS public lecture on 'Millennium Celebration Program', 5 January 2002.

The Daily Star (a Dhaka-based English daily), 14 January 2003.

The World Bank (1994). *Bangladesh: Privatization and Adjustment*, World Bank Report No. 12318 BD. Washington DC.

——— (1999). *Bangladesh: From Counting the Poor to Making the Poor Count*. Washington, DC.: The World Bank.

US Department of Commerce (1999). Bangladesh: Foreign Labor Trends Report, 1993–94, 6–7, downloaded from the website: http://www.tradeport.org/ts/countries/bangladesh/flt.html. Accessed on 24 February 2003.

6

A Historical Perspective on Ethnicity, Tribalism, and the Politics of Frontier Policy in Pakistan

Lawrence Ziring

Pakistan is a creature of European imperialism, and those who sought self-determination for the Muslims in the Muslim-majority areas of the subcontinent were influenced more by the British experience than anything reflecting genius of the different regions. British rule in India had cast a long shadow over the vast region of southern Asia, obscuring from view the realities of disparate regions that were not figured to hang together as voluntary segments of a nation-state. The undoing of a unified subcontinent under British rule began with the Muslim demand for a separate self-governing homeland. Congress leaders who tried to prevent Partition understood the need to retain a semblance of geographic unity, but less than even-handed efforts only stoked passions unleashed by the Muslim League. The British also had their concerns in leaving an India divided and at odds with its severed parts. Moreover, the British had a more studied overview of the entire subcontinent, a view that was not replicated by the indigenous leaders of the Pakistan movement. More than anyone in the Muslim League hierarchy, the British were cognizant of the conditions that militated against the construction of a successful, integrated, and operative nation-state. Few among the colonial authority believed Pakistan was feasible, and virtually nothing was done to assist in the building of a national polity centred on bridging the many divides separating the people who in 1947 were to call themselves Pakistanis.

For the British, the notion 'Islam in Danger' meant only divisiveness. Similarly, the Muslim League emphasis on 'two nations' could not be acknowledged by the decision-makers in Whitehall. India was hardly the proverbial melting pot, and within its borders resided as diverse and polyglot a population as could be found in any other part of the world. The falsity of the 'two nations' was dramatized in the many nations inhabiting Asia's great geologic appendage. For the British, therefore, Pakistan's congeries of humanity could be administered, but it was foolhardy to believe the country, following the transfer of power, could be politically inspired to accept overarching, sophisticated political structures of self-government. The very demand of the Muslim League for a separate state demonstrated the validity of the British perception that Pakistan was at best an anachronism that simply could not succeed. It also explains why the British did what they could to prevent the Partition of their once vaunted colony. Indeed, it explains why Pakistan finally emerged in its truncated form, and why in the absence of the Muslim League's visionary leader, it was unable to realize the quest for a secular, progressive state.

Pakistan was a contradiction from the beginning. Cobbled together from the remnants of the empire, it included ruptured territories in its most vital sectors, namely, Bengal and Punjab. Pakistan also became the legatee to one of the newest but poorest provinces in Sind, as well as an ill-defined and turbulent tribal belt that stretched all along its Persian-Afghan frontier. No one in the Muslim League, in the period leading up to the transfer of power, had seriously pondered the nature, let alone the functioning, of the state. Pakistan was not just physically divided in two separate parts, a thousand miles distant from one another, it was hardly the expression of its distinctly different cultures. The leaders of the Pakistan movement were too consumed by their quest for a self-governing Muslim polity within the subcontinent to acknowledge the absence of elemental factors necessary to realize nationhood.

The British demonstrated that power could be transferred to indigenous hands, but those receiving the transfer could not, and, in many instances, would not share power with different ethnic and tribal groups that comprised the new nation. Nor could references to Islam and religious community satisfy those who, finally seeing the British retreat, now sought to obtain goals independent from those reflected in the behaviour of Muslim League leaders.

The Muslim League was not a welcome expression among the unrecorded majority of Pakistan's population whose loyalties lay elsewhere. Dissatisfaction with the central government was registered in all parts of the country, but no less so than among those inhabiting the frontier areas. It is the latter dilemma that is the focus of this chapter. The subject of ethnicity and politics in Pakistan, however, is too broad and too complex to be encompassed in a brief chapter and it is this author's intention to give expression to the least settled component of the Pakistan nation. The focus is on the Pashtuns, even more so on a portion of this Indo-European family that inhabits the tribal belt, a region almost twice the size of the North West Frontier Province and straddling the Pakistan/Afghanistan frontier from the Pamirs to the Takht-i-Sulaiman. The subject is too extensive to incorporate the broad sweep of Pashtun tribes here. The Yusufzais, Afridis, Mohmanda, Turis, and others are bypassed for a closer examination of the Wazirs, and especially those Wazir tribes inhabiting the region known as South Waziristan. South Waziristan is judged the key to Pakistan's integration efforts; it is also an area of principal concern in this first decade of the twenty-first century.

SOUTH WAZIRISTAN IN HISTORICAL PERSPECTIVE

The events of 11 September 2001, in the most dramatic fashion, spotlighted Pakistan's tribal people. In global terms, perhaps the most remote segment of humanity, the tribal Pashtuns were suddenly and without notice thrust upon the world stage. Moreover, special interest was given to South Waziristan, a mountainous and barren area bordering Afghanistan's Paktia Province, and Pakistan's North Waziristan as well as the more settled Zhob and Dera Ismail Khan districts. South Waziristan is a tangled mass of ravines and difficult hills of rugged inhospitable ridges. The area rises toward a watershed at 11,000 feet that divides the Indus from the Helmand river basins, some 300 miles apart. The rivers dominate the life source in Pakistan and Afghanistan, respectively. The main and dominating mountain range is the southern portion of the Sulaiman group, and the Pakistan/Afghanistan, boundary runs along the crests of the western slopes of the range from north to south.

In addition many smaller ranges branch off from the Sulaiman and also run in a north–south direction. The highest peaks in South Waziristan rise in excess of 10,000 feet, and of the 11 major peaks only one is below 7,000 feet. South Waziristan's climate moves from below freezing in winter to scorching heat in summer.

The British assumed a presence in South Waziristan after displacing the Sikhs on the northwest frontier in 1849. It is important to note, however, that neither the Moghuls (before the Sikh invasions) nor the Sikhs penetrated the tribal area of South Waziristan. Only the British set a course to dominate the tribal Pashtuns and in the British scheme South Waziristan was originally to be administered by the deputy commissioner of Dera Ismail Khan. A treaty with the Emir of Afghanistan in 1893 established a boundary (the Durand Line) between British India and Afghanistan. The Durand Line divided tribal families and Britain assumed responsibility for the tribes on their side of the divide while English political officers were assigned as advisers to the general officer commanding (GOC) in the tribal belt. The tribal people, however, refused to conform to the colonial diktat. Accustomed to independence, the tribal Pashtuns resisted the British incursion and mounted an aggressive defence of their freedom. In 1894, in South Waziristan, the Pashtuns attacked the Delimitation Commission escort at Wana, the principle town in the region. The British, however, were not dissuaded from their plans and they organized a large and determined military operation that lasted through 1895. Successful in that campaign, the British installed a Political Agent for South Waziristan in Wana. Still another agent was dispatched to the Tochi area with headquarters in Miranshah. In 1908 the colonial government created the post of Resident in Waziristan. South Waziristan, however, had developed into a military staging area, and unlike North Waziristan that fell under normal bureaucratic routine, South Waziristan was the scene of sustained military operations involving thousands of combatants on both sides. Given the persistence of the tribal problem, the commanding officer in the region was placed under the direct orders of the Government of India in New Delhi.

In a subsequent effort at pacification, the British withdrew the occupying Punjab Frontier Force and replaced it with irregulars of the North and South Waziristan Militia, but the tribal people remained combative and their guerrilla tactics took an increasing toll of local forces. The British countered by replacing this militia with still another new unit, identified as the South Waziristan Scouts. With its headquarters at Jandola, and unlike the former militia, the Scouts comprised only of Pashtuns and included Khattaks, Orakzais, Bangash, Mohmands, Afridis, and Yusufzais. Interestingly, however, the British decided against recruiting from among the major tribes of South Waziristan, namely, the Masud and Ahmadzai Wazirs. Indeed, it was these tribal elements that had proven the most intractable. The Masuds and Ahmadzai, judged to be the least flexible and to have committed the most outrages against colonial authority, neither yielded to military force or diplomacy. In fact, the British, in spite of major efforts, never subdued them.

It was not until the emergence of Pakistan that the Muslim League government, but more so the martial law government of Ayub Khan (1958–69), developed a more conciliatory policy towards the tribal people and a modicum of compliance with central government authority was achieved. Ayub ordered the expansion of the Frontier Scouts to include Masuds and Ahmadzai Wazirs. Commanded by officers of the regular Pakistan army, the Wazir tribes were equipped and trained in accordance with Pakistan military policy. The role of the Scouts prior to the formation of Pakistan was to maintain internal security of the agency under the direct control of the Political Agent. However, peace was limited and relative and only possible during periods of truce and recovery. After Pakistan's independence, a more concerted attempt to win the favour of the tribes enabled the reorganized Scouts to play an important role in bringing tranquillity to the region. But the Masud and the Ahmadzai never fully accepted the writ of the Pakistan government and the latter were just as willing to leave the tribal people to their own codes and precepts.

Pakistan and Afghanistan

Pakistan was predetermined, in the major part, by the British decision to fashion a 'legitimate' border between British colonial India and Afghanistan. A boundary demarcated in 1893, through the work of Sir Mortimer Durand, and consecrated in a treaty between Durand and Amir Abdur Rahman of Afghanistan and confirmed by subsequent Afghan rulers, established the border adopted by

Pakistan on its Independence in 1947. The Durand Line runs 1,200 miles, beginning in the north at the Pamirs and running southwest until it reaches Iran in the barren regions that extend out from the Helmand River. The area of South Waziristan lies to the south of Peshawar and Kabul and forms a region somewhat midway along the Pakistan–Afghanistan border. Afghanistan never fully accepted the Durand Line and at the time of the British withdrawal from the empire the Afghan government was determined to obliterate it. Initially supportive of the Indian National Congress, and strong in the belief that independent and united India would renegotiate the boundary, Kabul opposed the Muslim League and the Pakistan movement.

The inroads made by the Muslim League in the settled areas of the frontier province, however, foreclosed the notion that India could achieve dominance in the area. The Afghan government, therefore, was left with the choice of either making peace with the Pakistanis or pressing the older claim of the Khudai Khidmatgars, led by Abdul Ghaffar Khan, for an independent Pushtunistan, that is, an exclusive state for the Pashtun nation. Anticipating the Balkanization of Pakistan and hence its early demise, Kabul and New Delhi collaborated in a strategy that would allow the Pashtuns on the Pakistan side of the Durand Line to choose independence or join with Afghanistan. Pakistan, however, did not collapse and the Pashtuns, despite their many tribal divisions, were more inclined to reinforce the notion of Pakistan than to fall within the ambit of Kabul. Kabul, it may be noted, was heavily influenced by Persian culture and reinforced by Turcoman, Uzbek, Tadjik, and Hazara ethnic groups that together outnumbered the Pashtuns. The Pashtuns, therefore, promised a more independent role in the new Pakistan, generally turned away from their Afghan moorings, and identified themselves, ever so loosely, with the new South Asian Muslim state.

In its own way, South Waziristan was the key to Pakistan's defences against Afghan incursions. The Ahmadzai and Masud Wazirs held fast to their land and refused all entreaties to join the Pushtunistan movement. In a 1961 White Paper the Pakistan government insisted that the formation of Pushtunistan would lead to the disintegration of Afghanistan, not Pakistan. The Pakistan government cited the July 1947 referendum on the frontier in which the electorate opted for Pakistan and the tribal *maliks* expressed their allegiance to the new Muslim state. When Pakistan pressed Kabul to permit a plebiscite among the Pashtuns on their side of the Durand Line, the Afghan government called the demand a ploy and a diversion and dismissed it as being without merit. The Afghans had known little of self-rule, having been dominated by the Persians, Mughals, and Sikhs. The British had defeated the Sikhs in 1849 and in 1901 Lord Curzon, Viceroy of India, separated the frontier from the Punjab and created the North West Frontier Province (NWFP), leaving the tribal Pashtuns to their own leaders and practices, but responsive to British Political Agents on the marchlands of the empire. Pakistan inherited the established order of 1947, reaffirmed in the 1921 Anglo-Afghan Treaty that said nothing about Afghan rights on the British side of the Durand Line. Not reconciled, however, the Afghanistan government in September 1947 cast the only negative vote against Pakistan's inclusion in the United Nations (UN), citing it could not recognize the NWFP and tribal areas as part of Pakistan. In all its subsequent dealings with Pakistan, Kabul insisted that the tribal areas between the two countries must be constituted into a sovereign province, and that an Afghan corridor should be opened through Balochistan to the Arabian Sea. Pakistan rejected these Afghan demands and in July 1949 Kabul refused to recognize the 'imaginary' Durand Line as the official border. More than words, however, the Afghan government identified and recognized a Pushtunistan government at Tirah, headed by Haji Mirza Ali Khan, better known as the *Faqir of Ipi*.

Heretofore, the Afghan government had exploited tribal passions and especially their devotion to Islamic practices to counter British power and notably its infidel character. With the formation of Pakistan this policy ceased to have the same influence and Afghan raids on Pakistani border positions had the reverse effect of causing the Pashtuns to rally around Pakistani interests in preserving the established border. It was in these early years that Pakistan and Afghanistan were drawn into the Cold War. With the Soviet Union pressing alliance with Afghan Uzbeks and Tadjiks on the Afghan side of their Oxus River border, the Pashtuns had more reason to associate their independence with the freedom and stability of Pakistan. In 1953, Vice-President Richard Nixon visited both Kabul and Karachi and the Americans sought to find a medium between the two parties so that a solid line of resistance could be formed against perceived Soviet penetration of the region. The Americans called for a joint defence and hence a joint foreign policy, while in Pakistan there was considerable discussion about a federation of Muslim states that not only included Pakistan and Afghanistan, but Iran and Turkey as well. Kabul, however, rejected all overtures, especially after Pakistan entered into a military assistance agreement with the United States (US) and soon thereafter became a member of both the Southeast Asia Treaty Organization as well as the Baghdad Pact. Indeed, Afghanistan's reaction to the Pakistani-American alliance was to become more intimate with Moscow, and Soviet military assistance in addition to political influence became more a factor in the region.

Soviet support for Afghanistan's Pushtunistan policy also framed Pakistan's policy in the tribal belt. Moreover, by 1961, Field Marshal Ayub Khan, who had taken control of the Pakistan government in 1958, saw the heavy hand of New Delhi in the movement to declare the Pashtuns a sovereign people. Afghan raids in the Bajour area north of Peshawar forced Pakistan to close its consulates and trade agencies in Afghanistan and Ayub called for a complete break in diplomatic relations in September 1961. The forceful and successful defence of the border areas was in no small part due to the assistance provided by the Wazirs of South Waziristan. When the Afghan king, Zahir Shah, acknowledged the loss of Masud and Ahmadzai assistance (the very tribes that had defeated the Bacha-i-Saqao, and had helped in the restoration of the Afghan monarchy in 1933), he forced his cousin and prime minister, Mohammad Daud, to step aside for a more moderate leader. With the Shah of Iran offering his good offices, relations between Pakistan and Afghanistan were restored and Kabul departed from its close association with India to side with Pakistan during the 1965 Indo-Pakistani War. In 1968 King Zahir Shah visited Pakistan, but Abdul Ghaffar Khan remained an Afghan hero and was nonetheless welcomed in Afghanistan as the original and chief spokesman of the Pashtunistan movement.

The Forgotten Frontier

Major events, however, were to obscure developments in the tribal areas along the Pakistan–Afghanistan border. In 1973, Mohammad

Daud led the coup that toppled the Afghan monarchy. With King Zahir Shah out of the country and with political instability effectively preventing the reforms that were aimed at Afghanistan's modernization, the erstwhile prime minister enlisted the services of the military and political factions, determined to end the monarchy. A key issue was the famine that swept Afghanistan in 1972 that the government was unable to respond to. With assistance from the newly formed People's Democratic Party of Afghanistan (PDPA), Daud enlisted the services of the frustrated urban elite and high-ranked military officers. The latter were particularly opposed to the king because he did not want to take advantage of Pakistan during its 1971 civil war in East Pakistan, especially during the Indian intervention that dismembered the country. If ever an opportunity to create Pushtunistan existed, it was during this period. The king, however, had entered into an agreement with Pakistan in a London meeting in 1971 and he refused to take advantage of Pakistan's weakened position. Moreover, the Soviets had become sufficiently suspicious of Zahir Shah's actions, especially his efforts at greater intimacy with Britain, the US, and neighbouring Iran. Moscow had invested heavily in the construction of Afghan infrastructure, in the building of airfields and highways, as well as in the development of the northern natural gas fields. The Afghan king was invited to Moscow in 1972 where the Soviet premier, Aleksei Kosygin, called for a collective security arrangement with Afghanistan that would provide the Soviets with strategic access to Iran, Pakistan, as well as India. Zahir Shah politely refused the Soviet entreaty and Mohammad Daud became Moscow's choice to lead the coup that brought down the Afghan monarchy.

Daud's coup was a stealthy manoeuvre, taken in the middle of the night, with the arrest of the Afghan head of government and the quick neutralization of the royal garrison and police force. With the backing of the PDPA and the Soviet Union as well as the disaffected members of Afghan society, Daud proclaimed the end of the monarchy and what he referred to as Zahir's 'pseudo-democracy'. His objective, he said, was 'real democracy' and a republic founded on the 'genuine spirit of Islam'. After consolidating his position, Daud reversed Afghanistan's more conciliatory foreign policy with Islamabad and revived the call for Pushtunistan. His government's policy, he said, was the 'liberation' of the Pashtuns on the Pakistan side of the Durand Line. In a well-organized public demonstration in Kabul on 21 July 1973, Daud demanded the freedom of the Pashtuns from Pakistani rule. Pakistan's response was immediate. The then President, Zulfikar Ali Bhutto, declared he would defend Pakistan's territorial integrity at all costs. Several coup attempts to unseat Daud followed. All failed, but Daud laid the blame for these actions at the feet of the Pakistanis who it was said wanted to reverse events in Afghanistan. Daud's harsh measures in response to continuing unrest in short order alienated all but the communists of the PDPA and their Soviet allies. Indeed, Soviet military assistance poured into the country, along with hundreds of advisors and technicians. In June 1974, Daud visited Moscow and entered into an agreement wherein the Soviets promised to pay higher prices for the natural gas that now flowed into the Soviet Union from the fields at Mazar-i-Sharif. The Soviets also began construction of an oil refinery as well as fertilizer and chemical factories. They also improved Afghanistan's irrigation system and generally expanded assistance to agricultural projects. Each project, however, involved the housing of numerous Soviet citizens, officials, and military personnel in the different regions of the country.

Afghanistan's closer ties to the Soviet Union raised questions in Pakistan about Moscow and Kabul's role in energizing rebellion in Pakistan's Balochistan rovince.

Daud had publicly claimed Balochistan as well as Pakistan's NWFP as Afghan territories, insisting the regions had been taken by the British and that Pakistan had no right to them. Pakistan rejected the claim and Bhutto was encouraged to bring the matter of Afghan intrigue before the UN and UN Secretary-General, Kurt Waldheim, was called upon to explore Afghanistan's actions in inciting sabotage and assassinations in Pakistan. Bhutto also demanded that Kabul deny safe havens to Pashtun and Baloch terrorists. The UN, however, refused to become involved and Bhutto's pleas to Soviet leaders had a similar fate. The Kremlin was determined to maintain the pressure on Islamabad to make concessions, not only with regard to Afghanistan, but also with regard to India in Kashmir. Bhutto, therefore, had little option but to order his forces to quell the Balochi insurgents. The increased violence in Balochistan reverberated in the frontier province where the assassination of a Bhutto compatriot had caused the Islamabad government to elevate the fighting. Bhutto used the incident to lash out against the leaders of the National Awami Party in the NWFP, banning it and imprisoning many of its pro-Afghan leaders.

Daud's socialist leanings were in evidence with the nationalization of banks and land reforms that broke the back of Afghanistan's privileged landlord class. Agricultural cooperatives were established and government bureaucrats drawn from the ranks of the PDPA assumed leadership roles. Moscow increased its financial commitment to Kabul and in time the Afghan army and air force came under direct Soviet influence. Concern was registered in several quarters over this display of intimacy, especially from among Afghanistan's urban elite and tribal organizations. Daud, however, continued to press his reform policies. The promulgation of a new constitution describing Afghanistan as a secular republic only deepened the crisis atmosphere. The opposition became more brazen in its defiance of the regime and it was brutally suppressed by Daud's police.

With resistance mounting to Daud's policies, Pakistan seized the opportunity to ward off the Pushtunistan threat to its territorial integrity. The tribal population on both sides of the frontier for the first time looked to Islamabad to address their grievances. Moreover, the perception that Daud had sold out to the communists played into the hands of the Pakistanis who had contained the insurgency in Balochistan and now turned their attention to undermining the Daud government.

Sensing disaster, Daud abruptly changed course and accepted the good offices offered by the Shah of Iran to mediate the dispute with Pakistan. Daud met with Bhutto to begin the process of settling their differences, but the Pakistan army had other ideas about the content of the negotiations. Bhutto for a variety of reasons had alienated the army rank and file, and in the midst of the negotiations with Daud, the army high command forced Bhutto from office. The leader of the Pakistan coup, General Zia-ul-Haq, promised to continue the talks with Daud, but insisted on a different emphasis. The Pakistan army had been humiliated in its 1971 war with India and the loss of East Pakistan had refocused its attention on Kashmir. Less interested than Bhutto in a settlement with India, the army's Inter Services Intelligence (ISI) Directorate had been authorized to create a clandestine resistance movement in Kashmir. Inter Services Intelligence was also given responsibility for linking forces with the tribal Pashtuns on the Afghan frontier. Aware that Daud's PDPA supporters were still intent on winning the favour of the Pashtuns by pressing the Pushtunistan issue, the ISI was ordered to exploit Muslim sensitivities against the communists. With Bhutto gone, events soon overwhelmed Daud. It was too late to shift course away from the communists. Daud's peace overtures to General Zia were anathema to the PDPA, and his visit to Pakistan in March 1978 infuriated its leadership. The two major factions of the PDPA, the Khalq and the Parcham, found common cause in their opposition to Daud, and their combined efforts were directed toward terminating Daud's rule. In a futile effort to save his regime, Daud moved against the PDPA and jailed their leaders. On 27 April 1978, however, army units favourably disposed towards the PDPA struck violently against Daud, his family, and members of the government. All were murdered or seized and summarily executed and the PDPA took control of the government of Afghanistan.

The Soviet Invasion and its Consequences

Operating on two fronts, in Kashmir and along the Afghan frontier, the ISI reached out to the Pashtuns of the tribal areas. South Waziristan was deemed a critical region in drawing the different tribes together in defence of 'infidel' regimes. While operations moved forward in Kashmir, developments in Afghanistan where the communists had taken power appeared most pressing. The ISI appealed to the spiritual concerns of different tribes and their services as guerrilla forces were enlisted in an effort to ward off the threat to Pakistan's territorial integrity in the northwest. Moreover, because of the recent loss of East Pakistan, Islamabad was convinced that the Soviet Union, the communist government in Kabul, as well as New Delhi had allied to dismantle what remained of the Pakistan state. South Waziristan's location was critical in defence of the country and passivity was not considered a useful strategy. Pakistan was deemed to be in an undeclared war against powerful and multiple enemies, capable of moving in concert, or in some cases alone. An active defence was called for, and Afghanistan seemed to offer the best opportunity to deal with the mounting threat. Thus, the ISI assisted disaffected and alienated Pashtuns on the Afghan side of their mutual border, while reinforcing and providing linkages with tribal elements on their own side. Islamabad, in fact, adopted the Pushtunistan movement and reworked it to serve its own interests. The objective was to turn the cause of Pushtunistan against the communists and to establish a Pakistani presence on both sides of the border.

Exploiting differences between the Khalq and the Parcham members of the PDPA, the ISI saw in the Khalq, especially after the purge of its Taraki elements, the greater opportunity to slow down the Afghan government's communization programme. But when Hafizullah Amin eliminated his rival and sought an alliance between the Afghan Ghilzai and Pakistan's Wazir Pashtuns, the ISI could not remain idle. Amin had a reputation for ruthlessness, but he was also approachable, especially if his personal interests were threatened. The ISI therefore sought a working relationship with Amin. But before Amin could consolidate his power in the PDPA or develop more intimate ties with the Pakistanis, the Kremlin decided to act against him.

Soviet advisors, officials, and development officers were easy targets for Afghans of different persuasions and identity. A people long accustomed to independent ways found unity in opposition to the atheism of the communists. With Taraki dead and Soviet citizens at risk, the Kremlin pondered the decision to intervene more forcefully in Afghanistan. Moscow was driven by the urgency to thwart a mounting Islamic revolution in Pakistan under the guise of Zia's Islamization programme. But even more important to Moscow was the success of the Khomeini-led Islamic revolution in Iran. The secular forces represented by Zulfikar Ali Bhutto and the Shah of Iran had given way to the fundamentalist cry of 'Islam in Danger'. Moscow, therefore, believed it had no other option than to secure its position in Afghanistan. On 27 December 1979, Soviet forces poured across the Oxus River, sweeping away the Amin government and installing the Parcham leader, Babrak Karmal, in the capital. Thus began a long and protracted conflict, that tore apart Afghanistan's fragile social fabric and set the scene for a mujahidin resistance, comprising many factions and tribal organizations.

The different mujahidin factions established their headquarters in Pakistan as Afghan refugees in the millions fled their country for a safe haven on the opposite side of the border. The mass movement of people caused the intermingling of Afghan and Pakistan Pashtuns as never before, and the Pakistan ISI called upon the government to seek assistance in servicing the mass exodus as it went about the business of organizing a protracted resistance. With military aid provided by the US, the Pakistan army and the ISI identified those resistance organizations that ISI deemed better equipped to carry the fight to the enemy. In a contest between the Pashtuns and the Tajiks and Uzbeks, Islamabad clearly favoured the Pashtuns. Mindful of the need to strengthen its hold in the frontier area, and suspicious that the Soviet Union and India were prepared to work in tandem against Pakistan, the Pakistanis bolstered the Pashtun position and settled on the more fundamentalist leaders in the factions based in Peshawar. The more significant ties were with Gulbuddin Hekmatyar's Hizb-i-Islami, and a major portion of American military transfers were made available to this most radical of the Pashtun Islamists.

The ISI moved into a long and indefinite campaign, and in need of more abundant long-term commitments, Pakistan turned towards the Arab world, notably to Saudi Arabia, Egypt, and the Gulf states. Volunteers were not difficult to find. Nor was money and material resources a problem. The oil-rich Arab states were eager to assist with both funds and personnel, especially with an eye toward Khomeini-dominated Iran that spearheaded an Islamic revival. The Saudis were especially mindful of their role as protectors of orthodox Islam's holiest places, and the Saudi monarchy could not allow the Iranians to outshine them in their spiritual representations. Pakistan therefore was the recipient of assistance from the richest members of the Arab world as well as the US that had reason to tilt against Iran but was even more inclined to thwart perceived Soviet ambitions in the Persian Gulf, the Indian Ocean, and, more immediately, South Asia. That such major geopolitical manoeuvring should centre on the tribal Pashtuns of Pakistan's western frontier is ironic. But in an age when conventional warfare had lost most of its meaning, guerrilla actions were dominant, and what better location to mount a guerrilla movement than from the mountains bordering Pakistan and Afghanistan. The futility of fighting a conventional war was demonstrated in the bloody encounter between Iran and Iraq, but the fusion of religion and sophisticated weapons had made it possible for some of the world's more primitive people to refine their tactics and hence magnify their presence on the world scene.

Pakistan had long sought a solution to its ethnic/tribal dilemma along its western frontier. In strange ways the Soviet invasion of Afghanistan not only offered the opportunity for Islamabad to meld the Pashtun tribes into a firm union, it also gave Pakistan a chance to reclaim its dignity as a Muslim state. In the aftermath of its humiliating dismemberment by India, Pakistan could again be seen heroically waging Muslim battles. Zia ul-Haq's emphasis on Islamization was more than a ploy to secure his legitimacy. His rejection of Pakistani secularism had come at a time when Pakistan needed a rebirth, and Zia sensed, more than his detractors, that Pakistan's security lay in the direction of the Muslim Middle East and that the Afghan border region was the pivot for the realization of a historic quest. The ISI, therefore, was unleashed as a fundamentalist force to excite and enlist the service of the most convinced Islamists among the tribal people. The addition of other Muslims, especially Arab participants with Wahabi practices, to the mix of resistance fighters assured the zealous acceptance of a no-surrender struggle. The jihadis had found their purpose in the Afghan struggle against atheist Marxism and Pakistan went for broke in overseeing the course of the conflict.

Enter the Taliban

South Waziristan was admittedly the most secure region in the tribal belt and it was from that rugged location that the defence of the extended border areas was mounted against the Red Army. It also became the territory for the melding of distant fighters with the local population. The Ahmadzai and the Masud as well as the Utmanzai, Ghaljis, and the Darwesh Khel, were receptive to the influx of foreign recruits, notably those drawn from Pakistan and the Arab world, and it was in South Waziristan that schemes were conceived that went far beyond the defence of Afghanistan. Indeed, when the UN brokered the withdrawal of the Soviet forces in 1988, little thought was given to the peace that had eluded Afghanistan in the previous 20 years. The different parties that had engaged the Soviets had their individual agendas and their separate objectives did not foretell a more tranquil Afghan state. In the first instance, Pakistan was fixated on the strategic need to hold the Pashtun region from Kandahar to Ghazni and on to Kabul. The Soviet pullout that had left a communist regime in Kabul was not allowed to stand, and the ISI maintained its role as the Pashtun's major provider and sustained its pressure on the Kabul-based regime. The PDPA leaders, however, put up stiff resistance and only after the implosion of the Soviet behemoth in 1991 was their fate sealed. The defection of the Uzbek leader, Abdul Rashid Dostam, and the concerted efforts of the Tajik, Ahmad Shah Masood, spelled the demise of the communist government. Pakistan's ISI, operating from South Waziristan, and reinforced by significant numbers of Pakistanis as well as several thousand foreigners, were concerned that Dostum and Masood's forces could frame a situation that, in the aftermath of communist rule, could bring Afghanistan under their influence. The rivalries between these major actors had been a matter of record and Pakistan was determined to thwart their efforts and guarantee the Pashtuns a formidable, if not dominating role in post-war Afghanistan.

Thus, when Afghanistan attempted to put its house in order and formed a provisional coalition government, forces were already at work to assure its failure. The Peshawar Accord of 1992 provided a structure for the projected new Islamic state of Afghanistan with Sibgatullah Mojadiddi initially heading a 51-person *Shura-i-Intiqali* or advisory body drawn from the several mujahidin groups. Once stability had been assured, the accords called for Burhanuddin Rabbani to take up the office of President of the country and operate with the advice of a *Shura-i-Qiyadi* or leadership council. More critical, however, was the distribution of cabinet posts, with the prime minister's office offered to Hekmatyar and defence going to Masood, the would-be prime minister's archenemy. Hekmatyar therefore declined the opportunity to serve and instead launched a rocket attack on Kabul that reportedly killed no less than 1,000 people in its first onslaught. Dubbed a dangerous terrorist by Rabbani, Hekmatyar did not operate alone, and Masood, among others, saw the hand of Pakistan's ISI in the carnage. Although a *Shura Ahl-i Hal va Aqd* or form of legislative assembly was constituted affirming Rabbani's role as President, the government was unable to function. Hekmatyar's assault had ignited a new internecine war, and with casualties mounting, and fearing events were spinning out of control, Pakistan intervened and called a meeting between Rabbani and Hekmatyar in Islamabad in March 1993. An agreement was hammered out between the principals, but within a month it too had broken down when Hekmatyar demanded the removal and isolation of Masood. Unable to avoid the pressure of the Pakistanis, Rabbani agreed that the defence ministry should be placed in the hands of a commission. All this manoeuvring illustrated the absence of real institutions in the new Afghanistan. Everything had been shattered during the long years of resistance to the Soviet invasion. Afghanistan was without a national army to oversee the peace, and the different factions in the different regions moved to consolidate personal power over their respective domains. Warlordism, as such, was less a feature of Afghan culture, and more a response to the anarchy that consumed the country.

Pakistan was the only political actor in position to take advantage of the anarchic conditions. With financial assistance provided by Saudi Arabia, and to some extent the United Arab Emirates, plans were activated to create a force capable of eliminating the power-seekers and terminate the fighting. The intensification of the civil war had fallen heavily upon an exhausted and desperate people, eager to find a modicum of peace. Taking advantage of popular sentiment, Pakistan continued to play the religion card, and with assistance from the Saudis, it expanded the number of religious schools throughout the Pashtun region, most notably along the border in Pakistan. The religious schools attracted young people not only from Afghanistan and Pakistan but also from the Arab nations and extended Muslim world. These schools on the Pakistan frontier had multiplied during the Soviet incursion and had offered a semblance of normalcy to the refugee community that was comprised essentially of women and children. Sponsored in the major part by Saudi Arabia in the aftermath of the Soviet withdrawal, the madrassas set a future for the post-war generation. Most prominent in the NWFP was the *Dar al-Ulum Haqqaniyya*, supported by the ISI and directed by Sami ul-Haq, leader of Jamiat-i-Ulema-i-Islam, a Pakistani faction of a larger organization, and favoured by the Pakistan army. This particular Pashtun religious school was responsible for the recruitment and training of hundreds of young jihadis.

Thus was born the Taliban, the Pakistan–Saudi Arabian sponsored organization that would in short order lay claim to the role of saviour of Afghanistan. The Taliban was viewed by some in the

Muslim world as the modern version of the *Ghazi* force that had contested the power, and eventually defeated ancient Byzantium. Moreover, it was not long before the ISI linked the Harkat-ul-Ansar, a guerrilla organization in Kashmir, with the Taliban in Afghanistan. The rise to prominence of the Jayash-i-Mohammad and Lashkar-i-Tayyaba in Kashmir also could be credited to the success of the ISI-inspired Taliban connection. Indeed, the battlefield successes of the combined Taliban were dramatic and almost immediate. By 1996, given the fall of Kabul to an overwhelming and inspired force, plans for broader conflict were arranged in the Al-Badr training camp, created by Khalid ibn-i-Walid, a mentor of Osama bin Laden. Bin Laden returned to Afghanistan to bask in the glory of the Taliban forces in Kabul and assumed control of Al-Badr. He also called for the establishment of still another camp, Muawia, in the rugged mountain areas on the Afghan border in the vicinity of Pakistan's Waziristan. Bin Laden also took possession of the Mektab al-Khidmat from which Al-Qaeda was to emerge. In the meantime, the Taliban conquered the region of Nangarhar Province and Bin Laden and Mullah Mohammad Omar, the Pakistan-ordained emir of the Taliban, sealed their union in a pledge to destroy the infidels.

In 1998, from his Afghan base, Bin Laden publicized the formation of the International Islamic Front for Jihad. The Front was a hydra-headed organization. It not only included the Taliban and his own Al-Qaeda, but also Jamaat-al-Islamia and Islamic Jihad of Egypt, Hezbollah in Lebanon, Hamas in the Gaza Strip, Harkat-ul-Mujahiddin and Lashkar-i-Ansar in Pakistan, Abu Sayyaf in the Philippines, the Islamic Movement in Uzbekistan, the Islamic Salvation Front in Algeria, and numerous others. For Muslims, long imposed upon by alien and heathen forces, the appeal of the jihadi movement was impossible to overstate.

The Pakistan ISI and indeed high ranked members of the Pakistan army were hardly oblivious to what was happening in Afghanistan. Pakistan not only did not ignore these developments, it aided and abetted the thousands of Afghans and non-Afghans that flocked to join the Taliban and Al-Qaeda. Islamabad believed it had found the answer to its weakness demonstrated during the 1971 war with India. It also believed the answer to its ethnicity problem on the North-West Frontier lay in its support for Pashtun dominance in Afghanistan. The role played by the Pakistani army in pressing for Islamization, however, had its consequences. Most prominent was the sacrifice of Pakistan's secular state, the neutralizing of the Pakistani middle class, as well as the dramatization of the fundamentalist cause. The Islamists had not only been legitimated as a potent force in Pakistani political life, but also achieved the power to transform the Muslim nation into their vision of an Islamic state. Thus, succour was given to extremist Sunni organizations like the Pakistani Sipah-i-Sahaba and the Lashkar-i-Jangvi. These organizations not only increased hostilities in Kashmir, but also incited violence against Shia Muslims in Pakistan. Sectarianism, long a scourge in the country, assumed new intensity in the 1990s. Radical *Deobandi* madrassas, akin to Wahhabism in Saudi Arabia, multiplied and spread under the aegis of Pakistani army officers who themselves were swayed to identify with them. What had occurred in the frontier area therefore spread to the Punjab, Sindh, and Balochistan. Networks were envisioned that stretched from the ethnic slums of Karachi to Peshawar and Afghanistan, and ultimately impacted the new independent Muslims states of Central Asia.

The madrasas prepared thousands of militant recruits for duty in Afghanistan, Kashmir, and elsewhere. It can only be mentioned how underplayed this Islamist/jihadi movement was in the West, especially in the US. American officials initially accepted the Taliban as a pacifying force. Heavily influenced by Islamabad and Riyadh, Washington believed the Taliban was a useful instrument in containing the Shia/Khomeini revolution in Iran. Not only did Washington like the idea that the Taliban meant order would be substituted for chaos in Afghanistan, it also was led to believe a shift in Islamic doctrine had occurred from an anti to a pro-Western posture. Although the US did not rush to officially recognize the Taliban, the self-described students were nevertheless provided opportunity to open channels to the outside world. Masood, Dostum, and Afghan Shia leaders of Hazarajat were made to appear as little more than rapacious perpetrators of the continuing agony in Afghanistan. Indeed, American thinking with reference to Afghanistan did not change until the Al-Qaeda attacks on the US embassies in Kenya and Tanzania in 1998. It was only then that the realization dawned that a major challenge had been posed to the US's global hegemony and that the events that had transformed Afghanistan had global significance.

11 September and Pakistan

The attacks that destroyed the World Trade Centre in New York City and seriously damaged the Pentagon in the American capital on 11 September 2001 demonstrated in no uncertain terms how fragile the world had become in an age of globalization. More significant for this chapter, the tragedy dramatized how so remote a region as the Pakistan tribal belt, particularly, South Waziristan, and subsequently North Waziristan, could impact the most powerful nation in world history. If unnamed US officials are to be believed, a 'summit of terrorists' met in a 'pivotal planning session' in South Waziristan in 2000. It was at this meeting that the final plans for the attack on American cities were allegedly made. But whether or not such a 'summit' occurred, the fact remains that a relatively small number of people, dedicated to the destruction of the global nation-state system, had set in train a programme, no less threatening than that represented by the Nazis and the Bolsheviks of the 20th century. With the war against Soviet aggression in Afghanistan as the catalyst, contemporary terrorism, assisted by advances made in science and technology, had assumed a presence heretofore reserved for the most powerful states. 11 September revealed the almost meaninglessness of the elements of national power that classified the different state actors. Conventional military capabilities never appeared more feeble and economic and financial prowess never seemed more inconsequential as the jihadis of the Al-Qaeda and their sundry partners threw down the gauntlet and mocked the world to meet their challenge.

Confronted with the US's determination to strike at what was judged to be the source of the terrorist movement in Afghanistan, Islamabad, now under the control of still another man in uniform, was called to declare its position in what was described as a new form of total war. General Pervez Musharraf, Chief of Army Staff (COAS) of the Pakistan Army and the self-installed President of Pakistan following his 1999 coup, was trapped between a strategic policy that had gone critically awry and another policy that was intended to keep his country in the global milieu of nation-states. The two policies were no longer compatible. Although Musharraf hesitated in withdrawing support to the Taliban or feigned disbelief that the events of 11 September had any connection with the long sought 'liberation' of Kashmir, he had little time to shift course. Given Washington's eagerness to strike the Al-Qaeda and the Taliban, Musharraf backtracked from a course long in train. Pakistan offered the US operational support for military strikes against Afghanistan and reluctantly joined in the American-declared war on worldwide terrorism that supposedly emanated from the remote mountain ranges bordering Pakistan and Afghanistan.

Musharraf had been an instrument in the creation of a jihadist network he could no longer influence. Called to reverse years of planning and support for the more radical Pashtuns and their associates from distant lands, he began with the dismantling of the ISI, or at least its reformation and subordination to the dictates of an altered security policy. Repeating his support for Kashmir's right to self-determination, he nevertheless endeavoured to minimize the religious aspects of the quest as he deftly attempted to place the Pakistan nation back on the rails of secularism. Musharraf insisted on reciting his democratic objectives and his belief that Pakistan, despite its overriding Muslim character, was accommodative to all persuasions and capable of living in a world of diverse expressions and cultures. The extraordinary emphasis on religious training, therefore, had to be monitored and the many madrassas that had sprouted up on the frontier and throughout the nation had to be revisited and given new orientation. Moreover, the negative and angry reaction from the Islamists was not unexpected and whatever alliance had been forged in the past with the army high command was seemingly broken. According to the leaders of the religious parties, no less so the Jamaat-i-Islami, Musharraf had joined the camp of the infidels and only his removal could temper their opposition.

The centre for Pakistan's Islamist coalition that became the Muttahida Majlis-i-Amal (MMA) drew together all the organizations (not the least of which was the Jamaat) representing the demand for an Islamic state. The centre for the MMA movement was located in the Pashtun areas of the frontier. But the Islamabad government singled out the Jamaat for offering refuge and succour to Taliban and Al-Qaeda members in various areas of Pakistan. Musharraf's about turn, his retreat from the fundamentalist cause, however, left him with no other choice than to press ahead with democratization. Hence the General's decision to proceed with the

October 2002 elections, aimed at re-establishing Pakistan's parliamentary system. Musharraf's unsurprising success at the polls, however, brought an unexpected result. The MMA was permitted to contest the elections and the public responded by transforming it into a formidable opposition party. It was the MMA not Musharraf that enjoyed the allegiance of the frontier Pashtuns. Moreover, the American military campaign against the Taliban had routed the organization and scattered the forces of the Al-Qaeda, but it could not close the book on jihadi activity. Indeed, neither Mullah Omar nor Osama bin Laden was killed or captured in the fighting, and their reputation and popular appeal among the Pashtun population had significantly increased. Neither Afghanistan's nor Pakistan's frontier region had been truly pacified. Despite the installation of a symbolic Afghan government in Kabul, Afghanistan remained a scene of latent anarchy and regional leaders and militias raised questions about the unity of the country, let alone the sovereignty of the would be central government.

US forces were joined by NATO troops in helping to police the stabilization of Afghanistan. Even after NATO assumed overall command of coalition forces in July 2006, it was the Americans who assumed the major responsibility for tracking and destroying the scattered shock troops of the Afghan Taliban and Al-Qaeda. Numerous forays along the border with Pakistan were launched as Pakistan was encouraged and pressurized to destroy jihadist enclaves on their side of the frontier. Islamabad penetrated the tribal Pashtun region as never before and Musharraf mused about integrating the region with the NWFP in an effort to bring decorum as well as the fiat of the government to the region. The Pashtuns, however, no longer in league with the ISI and now seemingly opposed by the Pakistan Army, had no intention of yielding their historic autonomy. Nor were they prepared to withdraw their offer of hospitality to the Al-Qaeda or yield their support for the Taliban—both sentimentally and, from their point of view, strategically. Tied to the Taliban, the tribal areas continued to provide a safe haven for those fighting, what they judged was, an American-controlled Pakistan Army. Musharraf may have had his eye on Pakistan as a modern state, but the conditions prevailing on the frontier bore little resemblance to an experiment in advanced living. In point of fact, the view from the frontier was not forward but backward, indeed back to a time when tradition and tribal custom were the only accepted practices. Thus, the more Musharraf insisted on the tribal Pashtuns accepting responsibility as 'good' Pakistanis, the more they resented this latest intrusion in their long-guarded and semi-isolated domains.

The Taliban and Al-Qaeda by contrast to the Islamabad government represented everything that a Pashtun could desire. Religious zealotry, austerity, and discipline were key features of the Pashtuns. Hatred for the intruder-enemy struck a historic accord among people long accustomed to defending their land from forces near and afar. Nowhere was this more in evidence than in Waziristan, whose people had long prided themselves for shaping their own destiny. Having withstood the ages and more recently the Soviet Red Army, the Pashtuns of Waziristan were fiercely determined to deny Islamabad's writ. Moreover, it was Waziristan that drew the more determined members of the Taliban and Al-Qaeda. The region's remoteness, its complex terrain, and its resolute inhabitants offered primary refuge for those seeking to sustain the struggle in both Afghanistan and Pakistan. For the Americans and Pakistanis, therefore, South and North Waziristan became the key to long-term objectives; but for the Masud, Ahmadzai, and others among their brethren, including those they harboured, the region had to be defended at all cost. It came as no surprise, therefore, that the major offensive launched by the Pakistan Army in the early spring of 2004 was directed at South Waziristan and its dogged defenders.

As the battle was joined and more Pakistani troops were pressed into battle, rumour circulated that the Al-Qaeda's number two personality, Ayman al-Zawahri, and possibly Osama himself, were holed up in South Waziristan. The reported clash in March 2004 was intense, but when the Pakistanis pulled back anticipating the opening of a dialogue with the Wazir tribes, neither individual had been killed or captured. Nonetheless, much destruction and loss of life had resulted from the engagement and Islamabad had reason to question its intelligence or the application of such force against the people they sought so long to woo. Moreover, little prevented the alienated Pashtuns from filtering through the mountains into Pakistan's major cities and linking forces with the numerous and growing bands of Islamists that found Musharraf's government anathema. Suicide bombers were judged the principal threat to Musharraf, who in December 2003 had survived two assassination attempts. In the summer of 2004, the government spread a broad net seeking to intercept suicidal operatives planning to carry out a number of attacks that included the President, the parliament building, and the US embassy. A senior cleric and head of a madrasssa in Islamabad was arrested when his school was discovered stockpiling weapons of sophisticated design. Simultaneously with this raid, Pakistani troops backed by artillery and aircraft attacked suspected terrorist hideouts along the rugged Afghan border in South Waziristan. Striking near Shakai, the scene of several earlier counter-terrorism campaigns against the Al-Qaeda and Taliban forces, Pakistani fighter-bombers also unleashed an assault on suspected strongholds, but the tribal Wazirs stubbornly refused to yield the jihadis living among them.

Fighting was also fierce in and around Wana, South Waziristan's major settlement, and specially strong resistance had come from members of the Ahmadzai tribe. A truce between government forces and the Ahmadzai had been Islamabad's objective, but when several cease-fire agreements were ignored, economic sanctions were imposed on the tribe and the main bazaar was sealed and prevented from conducting business. The hardship such measures imposed on the tribal people was only one part of the dilemma. Roadside bombs took an increasing toll of Pakistani army patrols and when the troops returned fire, more often than not, the innocent were the victims. Operating in hostile territory, the Pakistan army contingents were unable to discern the enemy from passers-by and the pain inflicted on the general population only added to the bitterness directed at Islamabad. A tribal *jirga* from the Ahmadzai met with the governor of the NWFP and entered into still another agreement with Islamabad about the handing over of persons deemed to be 'foreigners' in South Waziristan. For this cooperation, the Pakistan government promised the lifting of sanctions and a resumption of development projects. Nevertheless, battles raged all along the Afghan border and spread from South to North Waziristan, through Datakhel, Bangi Dar, Hassankhel, and all the way to Miramshah.

In mid-August 2004, Musharraf spoke of the continuing conflict on Pakistan television. Asserting that although more than 500 Al-Qaeda operatives had been apprehended in different regions of Pakistan, many had, nevertheless, retreated to South Waziristan. The general argued against the Pashtun codes of asylum and promised a total effort to destroy the terrorists wherever they took refuge. Operations therefore commenced in earnest in Wana, Shakai, Santoi and Mantoi, although efforts were made to minimize collateral damage and casualties. But separating the tribesmen from the foreigners proved to be a daunting task. For example, one such foray in the region of Bangi Dar, according to the government, took the lives of three Uzbek militants. Indeed, Uzbek members of the Al-Qaeda were reportedly planning suicide attacks as far away as Karachi. Villagers in the region, however, insisted that the victims were their own innocent brethren and they demanded the return of the bodies. When the Pakistan Army refused the demand, the government reported that 500 armed Pashtuns and clerics from various religious schools in the area approached the Political Agent in Mirali with a 24-hour ultimatum to hand over the bodies or face the consequences. The villagers displayed national identity cards of the deceased, but the official indicated the matter was out of his hands and that the army had spirited the bodies to Rawalpindi for identification. It was such daily incidents that intensified the fighting, and indeed North Waziristan could not be insulated from the spreading struggle. Pakistan's Northern Areas Regiment suffered significant casualties. So too the South Waziristan Scouts Camp at Wana. In North Waziristan, the Shawal Rifles was targeted south of Miramshah, and a paramilitary convoy was destroyed near Shinbaba. A major battle also ensued with militants in the region of Razmak, close to the Afghan border. The government estimated upwards of one thousand foreign fighters were located there, particularly in the high altitude Shawal mountain region that demarcates South of North Waziristan. In the meantime a delegation of tribal elders and clergy from North Waziristan visited Rawalpindi and after several pleadings it finally gained retrieval of the bodies of the men that the government still claimed were foreigners.

Acknowledging the inability to produce a military victory in Waziristan, the Musharraf government in September 2004 offered amnesty to all foreigners in the region if they surrendered their weapons, pledged not to incite rebellion, and agreed to pursue peaceful objectives. A two-member team comprising the NWFP governor and interior minister were deputized to commence a dialogue with tribal elders that would prevent the arrest or transfer to foreign custody of anyone accepting the amnesty offer. The government team made it clear they respected the tribesmen's centuries-old traditions and that there could be no resolution to the frontier dilemma by 'dint of force.'

An Unending Struggle

Pakistan's ethnic problem has been compounded by the war on terror. Al-Qaeda chose well in establishing its base of operations in the remote areas of the Hindu Kush. The inhabitants of the region, the Pashtuns, have a celebrated history of defiance to any distant authority seeking to conquer or control them. The land of the Pashtuns is not unknown to history, but the followers of Osama bin Laden are the first to penetrate the area not as an invading force, but for the tribal folk, seemingly as a bulwark against encroachment from outsiders seeking superior standing. This is an important consideration and the debate in Pakistan's National Assembly in September 2004 reflected the difficulties encountered by government forces seeking to oust the Al-Qaeda operatives from the tribal areas. In the long term, perhaps even more significant, was the alienation of tribesmen throughout the extended Pashtun population. Although Islamabad officials repeated their intention to remove the yoke of terrorism from the region, there was no gainsaying the fact that the Pashtuns had been long intertwined with those targeted by the government, and separating the interlopers from the indigenous population had become more, not less, difficult. Highly significant, this meeting of the National Assembly was the first since the installation of Pakistan's prime minister, Shaukat Aziz. From the noisy scenes in the parliament and the angry words exchanged by the opposition and the government over the Waziristan operations it was obvious the new prime minister would have a hard time furthering his government's policies.

The MMA aligned themselves totally with the Pashtuns in condemning the government action on the frontier. 'Stop Wana Operation' was the chant adopted by the MMA for this occasion as they stormed from the assembly hall. The Pakistan Army was reported killing several dozen Chechens, Uzbeks, and Arabs in a 2004–2005 campaign in the region, and the government cited its regrets for the loss of innocent villagers in the fighting. 'Pakistan's soil is being used for training [of militants].... Wherever there are terrorists, we will act against them because we want to save Pakistan', noted a government official. Air force assaults on reported Al-Qaeda training areas indicated the intermingling of the local population with the terrorists and suggested that despite Islamabad's efforts the tribal people remained distant from Pakistan, and particularly the central government.

The ethnic questions plaguing Pakistan from the first day of Independence deepened in the years following the Soviet invasion of Afghanistan. Pakistan's role in Afghanistan, both during and following the Soviet withdrawal, was in large part a response to the country's ethnic dilemma. Moreover, Islamabad's decision to link the Kashmir conflict to the problems of the frontier and Afghanistan only caused more problems. The attention given to Islamization in the 1970s was to some extent understandable, but this emphasis on Islam was more a ploy than genuine. Indeed from hindsight it is evident Islamization did not prevent, but rather contributed to the loss of East Pakistan. Nor did the attempt to make religion the central policy in both combating the Soviets in Afghanistan and, subsequently, in resurrecting Afghanistan following the Soviet demise, achieve the desired results. The emphasis given to Islam, never in danger in the overwhelmingly Muslim areas, in fact had serious consequences for Pakistan's future. Pakistan's territorial integrity was more threatened by religious expression and religious practices than it was from its old nemesis, India. The descendents and disciples of those who rejected the Muslim League programme for the formation of Pakistan in 1947, since the 1970s have paradoxically become the driving political force to transform and dominate the country. The MMA, the self-styled guardians of Pakistan's religious tradition and the 21st century representation of the anti-Pakistan movement, shows little concern for Pakistan's ethnic problems. The MMA cares not a wit for the structural manifestation of Pakistan as a nation-state because, like those elsewhere who emulate its style, it calls for a different political experience.

A Struggle Without an End?

The attempt to identify and destroy the Al-Qaeda in Waziristan carried through 2005 and into 2006, but the resistance seemed to gain not lose strength. Framed by a resurgence of aggressive Taliban elements across the border in Afghanistan, and despite the capture or killing of numerous Al-Qaeda and Taliban operatives on both sides of the Durand Line, fighting in the Pakistan tribal belt became more intense. Moreover, Balochistan was in tribal revolt in 2005–06 and thousands of Pakistani troops and considerable air power could not prevent the guerrillas from disrupting the region's economy and general decorum. Virtually the entire Pakistan border area was in crisis. In January 2006, tribal passions were especially aroused when an American CIA Drone-aircraft attacked Damadola, supposedly targeting Al-Qaeda's number two personality, Ayman al-Zawahri. On close scrutiny, however, the only casualties were a score of innocent villagers. Following the attack, 8,000 tribesmen were reported taking to the streets to denounce the US and especially President Musharraf. In March, Pakistani helicopter gunships attacked a village in North Waziristan, allegedly killing 40 Al-Qaeda fighters. This action also prompted a violent response from the tribal inhabitants and most notably from the students of a nearby madrassa who ransacked government offices and attacked members of the Pakistan armed forces.

The intensity of the conflict impacted the larger towns in the region from Wana to Miramshah and the fighting led to the seizure of government installations in Miramshah by a renascent Taliban movement that in the end could not be dislodged without support from heavily armed Cobra helicopters. The road between Miramshah and Mirali was blocked during the military campaign and refugees trying to flee the fighting were cut off and many were caught in the crossfire. Indeed, the nature of the action was enough to swell the ranks of a rejuvenated Taliban. Moreover, the army's destruction of Maulvi Abdul Khaliq's Darul Uloom Faredia Gulshan-I-Ilum, housing an estimated 200 disciples, only added to the ranks of the jihadis and even a *jirga* of *ulema*, intent on restoring peace, was ineffective. With almost 200 reported killed in this operation, local human rights organizations condemned the central government for increasing the sufferings of the local population. In Waziristan it was noted there was 'no security, no food, no medical facility, and no electricity', only the unrelenting punishment of the innocent. Two weeks later, however, army troops cordoned off Madrassa Al-Khalifa Islami and blew it up because alleged terrorists had used the building, long abandoned, for attacks on government forces. The region's lawyer forum condemned the Musharraf government's behaviour and tactics and demanded an end to the military campaign and the immediate restoration of full tribal autonomy. Islamabad's response was hardly compliant and officials continued to cite the transit and stockpiling of illicit arms in the region. Musharraf insisted the government had no option but to cleanse the Federally Administered Tribal Areas (FATA) of all foreign fighters and their supporters.

A representative *jirga* of the North and South Waziristan agency assembled on 21 March to beseech the government to initiate a process of dialogue and to withdraw troops from the region. The leaders denied that foreign fighters had infiltrated their community but admitted that Afghan Taliban associated with the Al-Qaeda had occasionally crossed the border. But whatever the explanation, there was no abatement to the fighting. In April, Pakistan forces were attacked by jihadis using more sophisticated weapons. The army responded with heavy artillery killing more than two score of the militant force. To prove that foreigners continued to foment disorder in the region, security forces carried some of the dead from this encounter to Miramshah where their bodies were displayed in the open square. Clashes were subsequently reported in Tolkhel, Qutabkhel, Chashma, Shawal, and Datakhel. Three major tribes in the agency, the Ahmadzai Wazir, Dawar, and Utmanzai, however, complained that they had been erroneously targeted and that the government action had only steeled their resistance. Shortly thereafter, however, the Egyptian, Muhsin Musa Matwalli Atwah, alias Abdur Rehamn, alias Abu Muhajir, wanted by the US for the 1998 bombings of the American embassies in Kenya and Tanzania, was killed by government forces. The whereabouts of the Al-Qaeda operative was apparently obtained after the Shawal campaign and, indeed, the Egyptian had a $ 5 million bounty on his head.

Moved to comment on the killing of the prominent terrorist, President Musharraf said the incident confirmed that foreign terrorists remained active in Waziristan and that only the cooperation of the tribesmen could terminate the military intrusion in their region. Musharraf also announced FATA's development budget would be raised from Rs 5 billion to Rs 10 billion if peace could be restored to the area. But despite this carrot, June brought a heightened increase in fighting when Pakistani and US forces, the latter just across the border in Afghanistan, carried out an operation in tandem. Air strikes in both North and South Waziristan reportedly took a toll of Al-Qaeda and Taliban foot soldiers. But in the closing days of summer 2006, and in spite of an accord reached with the resistance in North Waziristan, there was little indication that the conflicted frontier region was ready for extended peace. Indeed, suicide and roadside bomb tactics, employed by the insurgents in Iraq, were now in full evidence in Afghanistan and Pakistan.

Concluding Note

It is impossible to see too far into the future, but it can be said that the passing of Musharraf and his generation may well usher in an era of structural and institutional reorganization not heretofore contemplated. Pakistan has from its beginning failed to develop the civic institutions, let alone the civil society that might offer a predictable and workable course of action. The repeated interventions of the army in the country's political life demonstrates like nothing else that Pakistanis have not been able to establish a form of governance acceptable to its polyglot population. Political failure, however, has not prevented the Pakistan army from going nuclear. Moreover, political failure, coupled with the failure of ethnic integration, has provided fertile ground for the intensification and spread of the country's most radical and obscurant religious doctrines. Burdened by the weight of history, Pakistan's future appears to rest on its capacity to reclaim the secular vision of its founder, but with the passage of time that message grows ever more dim and, to many, irrelevant.

Select Bibliography

Ahmed, Feroz (1975). *Focus on Baluchistan and Pushtoon Question*. Lahore, People's Publishing House.

Barton, Sir William (1939). *India's North-West Frontier*. London: John Murray.

Bhattacharya, Shanti Ranjan (1946). *The Demand of Pakhtoonistan*. Calcutta: Lala Jan Khan.

Caroe, Olaf (1958). *The Pathans*. London: Macmillan & Co.

Government of the NWFP (1954). *Yearbook of the North-West Frontier Province, 1954*. Peshawar: Information Department.

Government of Pakistan (1961). *Census Report of Tribal Agencies*. Islamabad: Office of the Census Commissioner, Ministry of Home and Kashmir Affairs.
Gupta, Amit Kumar (1976). *North West Frontier Province Legislature and Freedom Struggle, 1932–47*. New Delhi: Indian Council of Historical Research.
Maley, William (2002). *The Afghanistan Wars*. New York: Palgrave/Macmillan.
Musharraf, Pervez (2006). *In the Line of Fire, A Memoir*. New York: Free Press.
Nojumi, Naematollah (2002). *The Rise of the Taliban in Afghanistan*. New York: Palgrave.
Qaiyum, Abdul (1945). *Guns and Gold on the Pathan Frontier*. Bombay: Hind Kitab.
Razvi, Mujtaba (1971). *The Frontiers of Pakistan*. Karachi: National Publishing House.
Tendulkar, D.G. (1967). *Abdul Ghaffar Khan: Faith is a Battle*. Bombay: Popular Prakashan.
Ziring, Lawrence (2003). *Pakistan: At the Crosscurrent of History*. Oxford: Oneworld Publications.

7

Sri Lanka: To Federalize or Not to Federalize?

Veena Kukreja
Mahendra Prasad Singh

In South Asia, India and Sri Lanka (formerly Ceylon) are the two countries that have continued to adhere to a vigorous electoral democracy and a semblance of democratic politics and judicial review despite growing internal and external pressures and violence. Sri Lanka has an unbroken record of democracy, though the post-Independence parliamentary constitution has had to undergo the trauma of national emergencies and a transition to a semi-presidential-cum-parliamentary regime of cohabitation between a directly elected president and a prime minister and his cabinet put in place by a parliamentary majority.

Sri Lanka became an independent state nearly six months after India. Both gained freedom from British colonial rule, with one difference between the two. While the transfer of power in both the new nations was legal under Acts of the British Parliament, unlike India, Sri Lanka did not have any freedom struggle in which extra-constitutional methods of political agitation were used. The two are in the select group of very few Afro-Asian countries where the post-World War II constitutions have either survived (India) or democratically transited to a new constitution (Sri Lanka). In both these countries, the democratic agenda is not how to introduce but how to consolidate democracy. So far as the foundations of democracy are concerned, Sri Lanka is in many ways a pioneer in the establishment, maintenance, and consolidation of democracy in South Asia. Sri Lanka has the unique distinction of experimenting with adult franchise earliest in South Asia (as early as 1931) under the Dunoughmore Constitution of British colonial vintage.[1]

At Independence one saw, according to a keen observer:

> ...the seemingly successful transplanting of British democratic institutions and organizations of civil society in Sri Lanka under the UNP [United Nationalist Party], a smooth blending of the democratic experience under the 1931 Constitution, with post-colonial aspiration for the maintenance of the democratic form of government. Apart from a vocal Marxist minority advocating a radically different political system and social order, the vast majority of the educated elite, who had grown up under a national legislature based on universal suffrage, the State Council established in 1931, and in a political culture suffused by the tradition and conventions of British Parliamentary democracy, was attracted to this by a process of osmosis and treated it as the only one worth adopting (de Silva, 2000: 49).

Sri Lanka exemplifies:

> ...a typical case of the changing nature and role of nationalism in developing countries. Initially, it grew as a composite nationalism of both the major communities who had a common grouse against the imperialist power. But the process of modernization created differences and sharpened cleavages.... A cursory look at broad trends and political developments would suggest that the crisis of politico-national identity erupted particularly after 1956 'Sinhala only' Act. This has finally culminated into a fratricidal war between the Sinhalese and the Tamils. The Tamils have been fighting a relentless war for a separate Tamil state since 1983. They fear threat to their cultural identity and material interests in the Sinhalese dominated polity of Sri Lanka (Gopal, 1998: 81).

For the last two decades, Sri Lanka has been plagued by an acute and intractable ethnic problem that has threatened to destroy the territorial integrity of the country. The island's constitutional history has been dominated by the question of sharing political power between the majority Sinhalese and minority Tamils, and a fierce debate continues to rage over the appropriate model for devolution.[2]

Ethnic Conflict in Sri Lanka

Sri Lanka is a multi-ethnic, multi-religious, and multi-lingual country inhabited by Buddhists, Hindus, Muslims, and Christians. While Sri Lanka is a small, but ethnically divided island republic, the Sinhalese (about 74 per cent, 69 per cent among them Buddhist) and Hindus, Muslims, Tamils, besides Christians (all together 26 per cent) make up the major cultural divides in the population.[3] The Sinhalese are mainly concentrated in the south, west, and central parts of the country. The Sri Lankan Tamils with 12.6 per cent of the population form the next major ethnic group. Linguistic and religious cleavages are territorially reinforced with the bulk of the Tamil minorities concentrated in the northern and eastern part of the island.

The prime factor that triggered Sinhalese–Tamil conflict was discrimination against the Tamils through governmental policies in five main areas—land, language, education, employment, and power-sharing. Further developments in this regard '...sowed the seeds of what has become a protracted and violent conflict that was particularly exacerbated by anti-Tamil riots in 1958, 1977–78, and 1983' (Lewer and William, 2002: 483).

A case study of Sri Lanka's ethnic conflict exemplifies how ethnic grievances that remain unresolved soon become militarized. Once militarized, finding a solution becomes extremely difficult. The fratricidal civil war between the Sinhalese and the Tamils since 1983 poses a serious challenge to the multicultural nation-state and presents a scenario of disintegration and destabilization in the island (Jayawerdene, 1988: 6). While the Sinhalese are holding state power on the basis of the electoral process and majoritarian rule, the Tamils are alienated and seek redressal of their grievances through violent means. Their ultimate aim is a Tamil state. The challenge before the Sri Lankan state and the ongoing peace process is to bridge this fatal divide.

Compared to other British colonies in the region, Sri Lanka achieved Independence relatively easily on 4 February 1948, with a brief political activity. The Sri Lankan elite did not have to fight for Independence either through a non-violent mass movement or by armed struggle against British imperialism (Oberst, 1985: 760). It meant there were no birth pangs and the immediate post-Independence era up to 1956 was crisis free. There were hardly any pressures on the social and political structure. English language, western ethos and secularism were dominant features of the elite of all communities at that time (Singer, 1967: 37).

In the early phase of Independence, one of the major preoccupations of the government was to deepen the roots of Sri Lankan nationalism on territorial lines. The first government led by D.S. Senanayake was intent on subordinating ethnic differences to the common goal of composite nationalism. The government tried to establish a stable equilibrium of ethnic forces in Sri Lanka's multi-ethnic polity (Zeylanicus, 1970: 224). In those days, aggressive and narrow nationalism did not emerge on the island. In fact, the Sri Lankan Tamils had some significant representation in the United National Party (UNP) cabinet, headed by D.S. Senanayake. The Sri Lankan Tamils were more or less satisfied with the arrangement.

There was one exception to the arrangement, however. Sri Lankan Tamils never felt strongly about that. The government led by D.S. Senanayake passed the Citizenship Act in 1948 which disenfranchized about 975,000 Indian Tamils, who were brought to Sri Lanka as estate workers by the British. These workers, lagging far behind their Sri Lankan counterparts, in substantial proportion were aligned with the leftist-forces in seven parliamentary constituencies in the central provinces. Thus, their concentration in parliamentary constituencies was to adversely affect the electoral prospects of the UNP and thereby its strength in the parliament, particularly when it was not yet feeling secure (Arasaratham, 1986: 13). Such a step as disenfranchizement was apparently not considered as sectional or discriminatory by the ruling elite of both communities. At this juncture, the leaders of the Tamil Congress (TC) which was a partner in the government argued that this disenfranchizement was not against the Sri Lankan Tamils. However, in 1956, when Sir John Kotelawala's government decided to have 'Sinhala only' as the official language, differences began to emerge between the UNP and the TC. Whatever cooperation appeared, during the colonial days and after, was simply a cooperation among the English-speaking elite of southern communities. The cracks surfaced when power slipped into the hands of a broad-based middle class after 1956.

Sri Lanka achieved Independence in 1948, and at that time appeared to be one of the most developed and constitutionally minded of former British colonies. However, there were great potential rivalries between the Sinhalese majority and the Tamil minority, and also between the constitutionally conservative ministers drawn from the English-speaking elite led by Dudley Senanayake and groups of revolutionary students. The rise of violent opposition and terrorism within the Sinhalese community itself was first seen in the revolt of students and intellectuals inspired by the doctrines of Guevara and others. The Janatha Vimukhti Peramuna (JVP) revolt in the early 1970s was an ideologically based movement; although primarily restricted to the Sinhalese, it was a left-wing revolutionary manifestation. The revolt was decisively repressed, but the JVP has re-emerged in recent years as a violent pressure group, which regards any concessions to the Tamils as a betrayal of the country (Dent, 2004: 71–72).

However, within a decade of the attainment of Independence, the legatees of the British institutional rule were confronted with a systematic attack by populist nationalists

> Who... challenged two of the fundamentals of the post-colonial system, the emphasis on softening the dominance of the Sinhalese through a recognition and encouragement of pluralism, and the maintenance of a clear distinction between state power and religion but which nevertheless recognized the need to afford some protection and assistance to Buddhism (de Silva, 2000: 50).

The political campaign of the populist nationalists reached its zenith in the mid-1950s and triumphed in 1956. Prime Minister S.W.R.D. Bandaranaike, who was known for his liberal policies and who once championed the cause of federalism and supported the rights of the minorities, came into power on a Sinhala-Buddhist-Nationalist (Chauvinist) platform. The Sri Lanka Freedom Party's (SLFP) victory over the UNP with the slogan of 'Sinhala only' also marked the first phase of Sri Lanka's ethnic conflict in the post-Independence era, in the re-assertion of indigenous values emphasizing an ethnic identity, based on religion and language. The influence of Buddhist ideas grew considerably from 1956 onwards (de Silva, 1988: 135). This was the beginning of the prolonged ethnic strife.

Sri Lanka represents a paradox. On the one hand, it manifests one of the longest democratic traditions in Asia with reasonably fair and free elections, high voter turnout, and regular change of government. This seems to indicate a high degree of legitimacy of the political system. On the other hand, Sri Lanka faces serious problems with regard to its ethnic conflicts and political stability. In Sri Lanka where the transfer of power was marked by continuity, not upheaval, democratization processes were not affected by the competing of ethnic and religious diversity and politicization of ethnicity till the failure in state-building became apparent after the early 1970s. The periods of rapid political and social change since 1970 placed enormous pressure on the country's democratic traditions, its legislatures, administrative and judicial institutions, and its economy alike. Since 1983, Sri Lanka is embroiled in an ethnic civil war (de Silva, 1993), which has resulted in the loss of some 65,000 lives and displacement of 1.6 million persons. The country is frequently governed by emergency regulations, which curtail liberties. It seems to have become a 'guided democracy'. The interval has caused a sharp increase in political violence and human rights violation, and questioned the legitimacy of the political system as a whole (Wagner, 1997: 194–206).

Genesis of the Conflict

The genesis of the Tamil–Sinhala conflict in Sri Lanka could be traced back to the colonial times. It has three broad dimensions: remote historical, perceptual, and recent. The historical dimension was the upshot of the post-Independence governments' policies (de Silva, 1998). Historically, Sinhalese and Tamils are two distinct communities with different languages, religions, traditions, cultures, values, etc. While the Sinhalese have Indo-Aryan origins and claim to be the original inhabitants of the island country, the Tamils are ethnic Dravidians settled in Ceylon following the Tamil incursion from south India. They are divided into two groups, the Ceylon Tamils (who claim to be the 'sons of the soil') and the estate Tamils, brought into the country by the British colonial rulers in the 19th and 20th centuries as indentured labourers. Both Tamil groups, however, consider themselves the original settlers of the country on the basis of their contribution to the nation in the past (Effendi, 2003–2004: 90).

Besides this burden of history, both Sinhalese and Tamils share an antagonistic perception of each other. Sinhalese perception maintains that the Tamils are the ethnic brothers of the Tamils inhabiting the Tamil Nadu state of India and enjoy strong racial, cultural, and religious affinities with them. Besides, the Sinhalese suspect that this socio-cultural affinity of Sri Lankan Tamils with Indian Tamils across the Palk Strait poses a great danger to Sri Lanka's integrity as both of them joining together seek to set up a separate state of Tamil Eelam.

> Associated with this belief are subsidiary beliefs such as the one that the Tamils as a community would never be contended with whatever is given, and that they are a people that will continue to ask for more and more, until the whole island is taken over by them. Even in the closing decade of the twentieth century, the average Sinhalese is ridden with these archaic misconceptions which led to apprehension and ethnic tension (Gunaratna, 1993: 55).

Causes of Sinhalese and Tamil Conflict

The major causes of conflict between the Sinhalese and the Tamils have been multidimensional, including ethnic, religious, and linguistic differences. These differences have been sharpened in the post-Independence period due to increasing conflict of political and economic interests. In this context, one analyst aptly remarks that:

> The cleavage between the Sinhalese and Tamils deepened as a result of the conflicting perceptions of the two groups about the distribution of benefits and opportunities in at least five fields: language, education, employment, distribution of land and land settlement, and devolution of power (Vaidik, 1980: 68).

Besides, the Sinhala bias in the governmental policies has immensely contributed to alienating the Tamils from the national mainstream. The Sinhalese, by legislative and administrative acts, have put forward the new philosophy of Sinhalese–Buddhist-centric state. This created a fear complex and a sense of deprivation among the Tamils. The Sinhalese majority has ruled the island country in the name of democracy since Independence. The net effect of all these decisions of the government has been to ensure various benefits to the Sinhalese majority at the cost of the Tamil minority (Kathiravelupillai, 1979: 9). As a result, the educated but frustrated middle-class Tamil youth, many of whom had not been able to get admission to the universities and hence had fewer opportunities in public services, were driven towards secessionism taking recourse to violent means to fight back the domination and oppression (Ram, 1989: 47).

After it gained Independence in 1948, Sri Lanka, till the present era of ethnic conflict, according to one observer:

> '...has been in the double-edged process of the ethnicization of politics and the politicization of ethnicity. The state effectively came into being managing and serving not only the common affairs of the elite but also the common affairs of the majority community. This was done in a manner that the state turned into an instrument of legitimizing the tyranny of the majority; it also turned into a coercive agency. The state in its desire to satisfy the demands and aspirations of the majority community used both coercion—repressive state apparatus such as the military, and the police—and the consent of the people through the voting system. Hegemonic groups gave their consent. The modern state that came into being in Sri Lanka, which inherited certain legacies of the colonial state, also inherited from other agencies certain other ideologies, such as caste groups, ethnic groups and religion groups, which have claimed exclusivity and have a constructed image of 'other' with regard to other communities (Thiruchandran, 2004: 66).

These processes are reflected in a very strange manner when the subjects who have now become citizens start to play their roles politically. Power came to be vested in the state through a process of ethnic majority collaboration. The majority ethnic and religious community was very smoothly elected into power through the party system. The political parties have carried ethnic name boards and policies, and plans to carry out a biased/particular agenda. The state was, in fact, trapped into action. Conversely,

> the state is also seen as very powerful with powers to pass laws, regulate the lives of the people, form and create a willing and consenting citizen. When one single party did not get an absolute majority, coalition governments were formed with other parties who could be ideological partners in the state formation (Thiruchandran, 2004).

The fact that religion is tied to ethnicity among the Sri Lankans, has its implications for an overall lack of an ideology of pluralization. The manifestation of this implication is very well captured in the phrase: 'Sinhala Buddhist Nationalism'.[4]

This phraseology, as one analyst maintains:

> ...has an in-built sense of exclusivity in a multi-ethnic society, especially when the state is the chief protagonist in the promulgation and an adherent of the ideology through legislation. The principle of democratic secularism has been eroded. The Sri Lankan state made Buddhism the state religion and introduced clauses in the Constitution which provided, amongst others, the clauses that Buddhism should be protected by the state, thereby giving a privileged position to Buddhism, the religion of the majority Sinhalese (Thiruchandran, 2003: 63).

As far back as 1939, a future prime minister of independent Ceylon was to make a speech with the following words: 'we [the Sinhalese] are one blood and one nation; we are a chosen people' (Jayawardene, 2003). The Sinhalese, it is believed, are a chosen people because of the religion they practice, that is, Buddhism, which according to a myth in a chronicle was specially bestowed by the Buddha. This kind of political rhetoric further contributed to the idea of the tyranny of the majority to which the state was socially and politically held responsible (Thiruchandran, 2003: 63).

In 1956, a language bill was passed that replaced English with Sinhala as the official language of the country. The Language Act did, as one scholar aptly remarks,

> in practical terms, impose restrictions on the recruitment and promotion of Tamils in the civil services and, hence, did also have a direct bearing on the economic existence and social aspirations of the Tamil middle and professional classes, as well as aspirations of to that stratum (Loganathan, 1996: 11).

Many high school graduates became unemployed in the wake of the new law.

Similarly, a 'Standardization Formula' was introduced in 1970. According to it, for admission to the science faculty at universities, Tamils were required to have maximum marks to meet admission criterion whereas minimum marks were required to secure admission to the arts faculty. Due to the 'standardization' policy, Tamils viewed themselves as an aggrieved minority denied any opening to careers in engineering and medicine. Given their past privileged and sometimes pampered status in the fields of education, government services, and private sector under the British colonial rule they see the national cake of benefits and opportunities rapidly shrinking for them (Institute of Regional Studies, 1986: 10). For example, in 1946, Tamils constituted 26.7 per cent in the civil services while in 1978, the percentage came down to 5 per cent only (de Silva, 1997: 245; Rahman, 1986: 238). All such measures and policies contributed to turning the Jaffna Tamil into an alienated segment of Lankan society.

The extension of the ethnic differentiation of the state has manifested in the way the racial riots of 1958 and 1977 were handled by the state repressive state apparatus, the police and the army looked on passively as terror was inflicted on the common men and women and the property of the minority ethnic group destroyed. In 1958, 1977, and 1983 (the last was the worst and is referred to as the 'pogrom'), the riots against the minority Tamils were engineered, planned, and activated by close collaboration of the state, which purposefully delayed the declaration of emergency and the imposition of curfew.

Rather provocatively, the state passed the 6th Amendment to the Constitution, which effectively outlawed the advocacy of secession, which meant that the Tamil political parties were denied representation in the legislature. This was a move to placate Sinhala chauvinism. With this move from 1983–88, the north-east of Sri Lanka was denied any political representation (Edrisinha and Pankiasothy, 1993).

The nation-building experiment of Sri Lanka suggests that it failed to secure the political, economic, and cultural claims of minorities in a multi-ethnic state. Unlike India, which preferred to declare the country as a secular state guaranteeing equal rights and opportunities to all citizens independent of their ethnic or religious affinities, Sri Lanka, at the same time, was regarded as the holy island of Buddhism (Phadnis, 1976). The strategy of regarding the Sinhalese as the 'chosen' people was not compatible with the basic character of a multi-ethnic society and resulted in ideological prejudices. In this context, Singer succinctly remarks that '...the Sinhalese have surely never understood the concept of "federalism"' (Singer, 1992: 713). 'Therefore, decentralization became politicized and the term federalism became synonymous with the issue of separatism' (de Silva 1993: 102).

The landmark victory of the SLFP[5] in 1956 caused considerable change in the economic and political system. Nationalist Buddhist propaganda argued that the Sinhalese people were discriminated against in favour of Tamil employment in the public sector. These claims could be supported by statistics and they opened the door for a policy of 'Sinhalization'. The idea of personal educational merit with regard to the entrance to certain courses was replaced by the idea that ethnic quotas were the right instrument to overcome the perceived disadvantages of the Sinhalese. Thus, Sinhalization became closely connected with the language, education, and employment policy, with land settlement, and with the question of regional autonomy.

After the passage of the Sinhala Only Act, S.J.V. Chelvanayakam, the leader of the then Federal Party and then acknowledged leader of the Tamil people, vigorously campaigned for a federal system of government. He was branded a racist wanting to divide the Sri Lankan nation. Quite contrarily, Chelvanayakam's approach to the question of federalism was centripetal. He did not envisage the division of the Sri Lankan nation. He believed in all communities comprising one nation but with constituent states with a government at the centre, thus preserving the sovereignty of Sri Lanka and also its political integrity (Jayahanthan, 2004: 50).

The difficulty of a negotiated peace has been compounded by the inability of the political elite representing the country's distinct ethnic communities to agree on a power-sharing formula over the past nearly six decades. In Sri Lanka the democratic principle of one-person-one-vote has led to the domination of the numerically much larger Sinhalese. But while the Sinhalese are a majority in the country taken as a whole, the Tamils are in majority in the northern and eastern parts of the country. If Sri Lanka had been provided with a federal constitution at the time of Independence from the British, the Sinhalese and Tamil leaders might have been able to politically bargain with each other from their power bases at the centre and region, respectively. Instead, Sri Lanka was provided with a unitary form of government that vested all power at the centre and, therefore, in the hands of the Sinhalese.

Origin of the Recent Crisis

1970 was a fateful year for the Tamils. Having been elected with a resounding majority as prime minister, in coalition with the major Marxist parties, the Lanka Sama Samaja Party (LSSP) and the Communist Party (CP), the leader of the Sri Lanka Freedom Party, Sirimavo Bandaranaike, did not require Tamil support to remain in power: Tamil parliamentary representation entered an era of sterile politics, never to be reversed.

Emboldened by her success in quelling the youth insurgency, led by the JVP, during the second year of her rule by the massacre of thousands of Sinhalese youth in the south with ruthless brutality, she was in no mood to negotiate with the Tamil leaders to settle the national question. In the constitution of 1972, with claims to create a socialist state, for the first time 'Sinhala entry' was realized which had remained, hitherto, only as an Act of Parliament. Buddhism, too, became the religion of state. Even the few safeguards provided for the protection of the minorities in the Soulbury Constitution were removed.

The remaining hopes of the Tamils:

> ...who at time stood for equal status for the Tamils, Sirimavo Bandaranaike would recognize their due rights in the making of the constitution, were shattered. Bandaranaike now sought to rule the Tamils of the north and east with a new breed of persons called 'SLFP Organisers', drawn from sycophants, political turncoats and megalomaniacs. The introduction of 'standardization' for entry to universities and the choosing of two leading public schools to be converted to university campuses were some of the factors that undermined the educational base. It is in this atmosphere that the militant youth who had secretly vowed to create a separate state for the Tamils began to act (Jayahanthan, 2004).

Thus, began a national liberation movement.

The Rise of the LTTE

The frustrations and repeated failure of the democratic and mainstream Tamil political parties to redress Tamil grievances led, in the 1970s, to a demand for a separate Tamil state, articulated by the Tamil political parties themselves. This was followed by armed resistance and ultimately civil war. In 1972, the Tamil political parties joined to form the Tamil United Front and threatened to take 'non-violent direct action against the government in order to win the rights of the Tamil nation of the basis of the right to self-determination' if the government failed to amend the constitution to take their aspirations into account. The first political assassination took place in 1975 with the assassination of the mayor of Jaffna, Alfred Duraiappah, a government supporter. The leaders of the Tamil political parties refrained from explicitly condemning the use of violence. As a result they permitted the steady erosion of the norms of democracy, and intolerance of any deviation from the nationalist line. The rise of militant Tamil nationalism can be traced back to this period.

In 1976, the Tamil United Front was renamed the Tamil United Liberation Front. At its first national convention held in Vaddukoddai, it resolved that

> the restoration and reconstitution of the free and sovereign secular socialist state of Tamil Eelam based on the right of self-determination inherent to every nation has become inevitable in order to safeguard the very existence of the Tamil nation in this country (Gunatilleke, 2001: 51).

Thus, the uncompromising stand for an independent and sovereign state of Tamil Eelam has its democratic antecedents. The hard-line Liberation Tiger of Tamil Eelam (LTTE) emerged as the main armed movement among the Tamils and gradually established its control over most of the Jaffna Peninsula.

The Constitution of 1978 under the UNP government of J.R. Jayawardene aggravated the problems between the ethnic groups. Buddhism was given state protection and promotion to the detriment of minorities. It is ironic that the demand of the Buddhist nationalists to preserve the unity of Sri Lanka as a Buddhist heritage paved the way for a civil war which promoted the further fragmentation of the island.

The Open Warfare

In 1983, the conflict entered a new critical phase turning a political conflict into open warfare between the Sri Lankan army and the LTTE after riots against Tamils in Colombo. The Sinhalese parties like SLFP and Buddhist groups still refused any form of decentralization. One part of the Tamils, the LTTE, after ousting Tamil United Liberation Front (TULF) and other separatist groups by killing their political and military leaders, stuck to the goal of Tamil Eelam, although it had a mixed population of Tamils, Sinhalese, and Muslims. An analysis of the Tamil response to different governmental policies suggests that during 1948 to 1956 the Tamils provided responsible cooperation. It was with the introduction of the 'Sinhala Only' Act, that Tamils started demanding a federal state and started resorting to peaceful satyagraha; the demand escalated for a separate state in 1977, but campaigning was through peaceful means. Gradually, militancy began to creep into Tamil politics. The state-sponsored violence against the Tamils further swelled the ranks of the Tamil militants. From a miniscule number in the early 1980s, the number of Tamil militants began to increase significantly after 1983. Many groups came into existence after 1983, but gradually the LTTE, under the leadership of V. Prabhakaran, emerged as the only viable, well-knit and organized militant group among the Sri Lankan Tamils.[6] They became extremely popular and powerful in the northern parts of Sri Lanka.

Since 1983, the civil war was internationalized and the Indian government became more and more involved (de Silva, 1998). Tamil refugees sought shelter in refugee camps in south India and the LTTE enjoyed considerable military, political, and financial support in Tamil Nadu. At first, the Indian government acted only as a mediator in peace talks, but India's involvement increased when the UNP government sought assistance of Israeli and Pakistani military advisors to train the security forces and asked for military support from the United States (US). This move was seen as a threat to India's regional strategic doctrine (Nagerty, 1993) and it caused the Indian government to directly intervene in the conflict.[7]

The political experience of Sri Lanka suggests that neither ethnic predominance nor a strong executive government is an open sesame to democratic success. If anything, these two in heady combination may exacerbate ethnic tensions and political conflicts to such a high pitch that even the early political achievements of an exceptional order may eventually be bogged down in the mirage of the politics of majority-ism. Parliamentary government may in some conditions be faced with the problem of instability. Yet the accommodation and consensus that it forces on the political class is good for national integration in multicultural societies. Within less than half a decade after adopting the Constitution providing for executive presidency, Sri Lanka was deep in the throes of ethnic conflicts between Sinhalese and Tamil linguistic communities in the main, but not without the complicating fault lines of religious divides involving Buddhists, Hindus, Muslims, and Christians. The civil war that flared up in the early 1980s has continued since then, with uneasy spells of ceasefires used by both parties for treacherous violations and bloodier encounters. Suicide human bombs have resulted in countless deaths among the public and of mostly moderate leaders on both sides of the political and social divide. Its fallout in the Indian state of Tamil Nadu also claimed in 1991, the life of Prime Minister Rajiv Gandhi, who sent the Indian Peace Keeping Force (IPKF) to Sri Lanka in 1987 on the invitation of President J.R. Jayawardene. International diplomatic mediation by Norway and academic advocacy of the federal option by the Forum of Federations, a Canadian non-governmental organization, have facilitated dialogues, but have not yet met with any breakthrough. Sri Lankan governments have themselves gone on record expressing a desire to go back to the parliamentary system, this time with some kind of devolution of powers. But any concrete move in this direction has been a will-o'-the-wisp so far. Since 1983 Sri Lanka has been, almost continuously, under a constitutional emergency with relaxations for brief periods and limited areas. To complicate things, hardened ethnic extremism on both sides is also compounded by left-wing extremism.

In the year 2000, the extremist LTTE temporarily routed the Sri Lankan security forces from the strategic isthmus called the Elephant Pass connecting the upper part of the Tamil-majority northern province of Jaffna with the main island. The LTTE practically ruled the roost in the northern and eastern coastal areas predominantly peopled by Tamil Hindus and Tamil Muslims respectively.

Human rights bodies associated with the United Nation (UN) and Amnesty International have reported abuses on both sides. Judicial strictures on violation of fundamental rights and pleas for relaxation of censorship and press freedoms by the European Union have also not been missing.

Peace Process

The history of the Sri Lankan peace process can be traced back five decades to the 1950s. With growing discontent among the Tamils, several peace efforts were made by different governments, but remained ineffective. Several serious efforts made by government leaders to work out a solution with the Tamil political leadership failed due to the inability of the government leadership to obtain the backing of their own party, let alone the opposition. The most noteworthy instance was the agreement reached in 1957 between the prime minister at that time, S.W.R.D. Bandaranaike, and the leaders of the largest Tamil party, Chelvanayakam. The prime minister unilaterally abrogated the agreement when it proved generally unpopular in the country. Buddhists even demonstrated in numbers against the agreement which gave autonomy to the Tamil areas. Since then the Tamils were not offered anything even closer to it. Perhaps J.R. Jayawardene, who from the opposition led the protest marches to Kandy, demanding the abrogation of the Bardaranaike–Chelvanayakam Agreement, in hindsight, regretted this when he subsequently became the president. If the Sinhalese could have gotten away with this version of devolution, perhaps the national question could have been resolved forever (Jayahanthan, 2004: 50).

The pacts of 1957 and 1965 were signed to address the issues of Tamil language, devolution of power, and land settlement. Both, the Bandaranaike–Chelvanayakam Pact and the Senanayake–Chelvanayakam Pact were never implemented. Similarly, in 1985, talks took place in the Bhutanese capital of Thimpu with Indian sponsorship, but failed to lead anywhere. Likewise, in 1987 the Indo-Sri Lanka Agreement was signed but left a disastrous impact due to the induction of the IPKF on the island (Effendi, 2003–04: 88–90).

The 1990s witnessed several rounds of talks. In 1994, Chandrika Kumaratunga came into power with a peace plank pledging to redress the grievances of the Tamils (Keerawella and Samarajiva, 1995: 156). She held direct negotiation with the LTTE in 1994–95. But the talks failed as the two sides could not find common ground to resolve their differences.

The peace process in Sri Lanka since 1994 has taken many twists and turns. The initial phase of the peace process, 1994–95, consisted of three rounds of talks between the government and the LTTE that finally collapsed (Schaffer, 1996: 217). President Chandrika's peace proposals, including the devolution package, did not succeed in satisfying the Tamils.

First, the negotiation of 1994–95 and the devolution package became a victim of military differences between the Sri Lankan armed forces and the LTTE. Chandrika Kumaratunga did not receive cooperation from the armed forces to implement government promises such as lifting the economic embargoes in the north-east.

Second, the devolution package did not get a positive response from the LTTE because Kumaratunga launched her two-pronged policy (of war for peace and devolution package) without any prior negotiation with the LTTE. The LTTE considered the peace plan as an imposition from the government. In this context, an analyst remarks that

> President Chandrika neglected one basic principle of conflict resolution, which is that both parties to conflict should contribute towards the final solution. If only one side develops a solution the other side feels no peace efforts failed because they did not accommodate both parties to the conflict but rather saw one party seeking to unilaterally impose its own decided solution (Effendi, 2003–04: 118).

Third, Kumaratunga had to face domestic outcry and criticism from the racist ideologies particularly from the Sinhalese–Buddhist chauvinists. The Sinhalese clergy largely opposed her peace plan, especially the devolution package, as in their view it challenged the unity and sovereignty of the island country. Her '...peace proposals lacked national consensus and conviction. Chauvinist ideologies were entrenched in both the Sinhalese and Tamil communal groups. These extremists needed to be controlled through building a national consensus' (Effendi, 2003–04).

The profound mistrust between the Tamil and Sinhalese extremists towards Chandrika Kumaratunga's peace overtures created a paranoid environment. Both were captives of mutual mistrust and scepticism. Moreover, President Chandrika lost her minority's support when she launched her 'war for peace' against the LTTE (Effendi, 2003–04).

Confrontation to Accommodation: Ceasefire Agreement of 2002

A major breakthrough in the peace process occurred when President Chandrika Kumaratunga invited the Government of Norway in February, 2000, to act as a third party intermediary with the LTTE. The appearance of Norway on the scene as facilitator to help resolve the 25-year old Sri Lankan ethnic conflict would count as the most significant event bearing upon a negotiated settlement over a decade.[8]

Soon after the Norwegian facilitators entered the picture, they set the broad parameters within which a political settlement would have to be negotiated. The Norwegians stated that their facilitation was contingent on the two parties accepting a common framework of a united Sri Lanka in which Tamil aspiration would be substantially met.

In February 2002, the Sri Lankan government and the LTTE signed a ceasefire agreement under Norwegian government auspices that appeared to offer the real prospect of a final end to violence as a means of conflict resolution. International financial assistance from key donor states, LTTE's willingness to have a negotiated settlement under a federal framework, keen interest of the world powers in the issue, and, above all, the favourable attitude of both the parties towards the peace process were the positive developments that took place in 2002.

Despite the progress in the peace process, there remained concerns about the sustainability of the peace process. Sections of the opposition, especially the JVP (People's Liberation Front), a Marxist-oriented group vigorously opposed the ceasefire agreement on various grounds, as being unconstitutional, a 'sellout' and as paving the ground for a renewed LTTE military campaign for separation.

The measures adopted by the government at the outset of the ceasefire were taken with only a minimum of consultation with the other political parties, general population or with civil society (Perera, 2004: 104).

After nearly two decades of violence and a near-civil-war-like situation, Sri Lanka saw some real peace. The barricades, which had become a normal part of Colombo life, disappeared and tourists began trickling back. There was hope in the air, even though most Sri Lankans were aware of the imponderables: an unpredictable LTTE, which could back off from the peace talks at any time and the breakdown of the delicate arrangement between President Kumaratunga and Prime Minister Wickremasinghe given the long history of bickering between the two leaders (Bhatia, 2003: 6). The first happened in April 2003 when the LTTE while declaring its intention to stick to the ceasefire and which was held for nearly two years, withdrew from further talks. The second, which in some ways was even more worrisome, took place on 4 November 2003, when the president suspended three cabinet ministers and declared a state of Emergency.

Challenges Before the Peace Process

Ms Kumaratunga's 'constitutional coup' was staged at a time when Prime Minister Ranil Wickremasinghe was away on a state visit to the US, ironically to solicit support for the peace process, charging the latter with compromising the 'national interest' in the peace process. In an address to the nation, Kumaratunga maintained that she was compelled to take this action because of the Wickremasinghe government's compromises with the LTTE that could gravely damage the territorial unity of Sri Lanka and would subvert Sri Lanka's Constitution and endanger vital aspects of national security. The president declared that she was 'willing to discuss with the LTTE a just and balanced solution within the parameters of unity, territorial integrity and sovereignty of Sri Lanka' (*Asian News Digest*, 2003: 3262).

Though Kumaratunga has been critical of the way Wickremasinghe's government has been negotiating with the LTTE as well as of Norwegian interlocutors showing a bias towards the LTTE, her drastic steps have clearly been prompted by the proposals for an Interim Self-Governing Authority (ISGA) submitted by the Tigers. Covering all the eight districts in Sri Lanka's north-east region, including Sinhala- and Muslim-dominated areas, it will have all the power the Sri Lanka government now enjoys in the area, including those pertaining to rehabilitation, reconstruction, resettlement, development, revenue collection, maintenance of law and order, and the management of land, water, and other natural resources. Not only that, it will have a separate judicial system with 'sole and exclusive jurisdiction to resolve all disputes' except in the area of human rights and certain provisions pertaining to the ISGA's functioning and constitution (Dixit, 2003: 14). The ISGA, which will also have the powers to conduct the region's external financial and trade relations, will be controlled by the LTTE, which will enjoy an absolute majority within it, with nominees of the Sri Lankan government and Muslims accounting for the rest.

Needless to say, the LTTE proposal for an ISGA allows the Sri Lankan government no role whatsoever in the running of the north-east, nor does it refer even once to the principle of federalism. Kumaratunga's Sri Lanka Freedom Party, therefore, maintains that the proposal seeks to lay the 'legal foundation for a future, separate, sovereign state' (*Pioneer*, 2003). In this sense, the proposal for the ISGA, if accepted, will only truncate Sri Lanka (de Silva, 2003: 8).

In effect, the LTTE' s proposals aims at controlling and ruling two-thirds of the land area of Sri Lanka (northern and eastern provinces), and four-fifths of the sea coast of Sri Lanka, including control over and access to all the urban centres and ports of the region (Mahanama, 2003: 9). Prime Minister Wickremasinghe of the UNP reacted, stating that these proposals go far beyond a reasonable arrangement for provincial autonomy and self-government for the Tamil areas.

In this context, it is worth noting that Kumaratunga and Wickremasinghe have been political rivals for two decades. Wickremasinghe had lost the presidential election to Kumaratunga in 1999. The reason Kumaratunga went for the kill was the uncomfortable cohabitation between the two since Wickremasinghe's UNP won the 2001 parliamentary polls. The rivalry manifested itself in the tussle for power between the two high offices, the directly elected president and the prime minister as the leader of parliament through the past two years. Clearly, a major reason for the showdown lies in Sri Lanka's system of political dyarchy—an institutional arrangement, cutting across many South Asian states, which allows for more than one centre of legitimate constitutional authority, invariably giving rise to an unstable environment (Shankar, 2003: 7).

It is noteworthy that after decades of operation as a monolithic force, the LTTE split between the northern wing under the erstwhile supremo V. Prabhakaran and the eastern wing under V. Muraleetharan alias 'Karuna'. This happened about a month prior to the date of the parliamentary elections of 2004. The LTTE as usual boycotted the polls, but backed the four-party Ilankai Tamil Arasu Katchi (ITAK) or Tamil National Alliance (TNA).

At the same time, the current peace process carried negative developments; for example, resumption of suspicious activities by the LTTE such as arms smuggling, recruiting child soldiers, and the non-participation of the LTTE in the Japanese-sponsored talks held on 10 and 11 June 2003, broke the smooth communication between the Sri Lankan government and the Tamil Tigers.

Elections 2004 Results: Implications for the Peace Process

The final electoral outcome expectedly resulted in a hung parliament. Wickremasinghe's UNP lost the majority it commanded in the dissolved parliament. The 2004 elections in Sri Lanka have resulted in a sharp polarization of the electorate (*Frontline*, 2004: 130–32*)*, where the hardline parties, on both sides of the political spectrum, have gained at the expense of the moderate, mainstream parties. It is significant to note that monks (Subramanian, 2004: 18), marxists and Tamil rebels made unprecedented gains turning the new parliament into one of the most polarized and sharply divided along ethnic and religious lines as well (Sambandan, 2004: 18). At the same time the election results have drastically changed the ground situation in Sri Lanka and increased the strain on the ongoing peace process between the Sri Lankan government and LTTE.

The most formidable challenge the new government confronted was translating its electoral victory into effective governance. However, the United Peoples Freedom Alliance (UPFA) has its own factions. While the SLFP favoured devolution of powers and a move away from Sri Lanka's unitary system, the JVP, a one-time champion of violent, chauvinistic Sinhala sentiments, opposed devolution and is an ardent advocate of the unitary structure, which it considers synonymous with the island nation's unity.

Besides, the position adopted by nine Buddhist monks of the Jathika Hela Urumaya (JHU), to save the island from domination by the minorities, is a natural inhibitor to the path charted since 1994, when Chandrika Kumaratunga first proposed devolution as a solution to the ethnic conflict.

So far as the response of the new government towards the peace process was concerned, although Kumaratunga stressed throughout her campaign that she would abide by the Norway-brokered ceasefire in force, few expected her to tread the same path her predecessor Wickremasinghe took in negotiating with rebels. Her main election plank was that Wickremasinghe conceded too much to the Tigers. She has repeatedly accused the LTTE of continuing to smuggle in arms despite the truce and to recruit children as fighters. While Kumaratunga showed willingness to grant some degree of devolution, it will be far short of the autonomous body the LTTE wanted in the country's north and east, the ISGA, before a final political solution is forged. The rebels are already in control of the area where they collect taxes, run the police force and courts of law. The LTTE, now honouring a bilateral truce, lost little time in threatening to resume their struggle for independence. In the LTTE's post-split scenario, the peace negotiations seemed to be further complicated.

Although Karuna's revolt against the LTTE chief Prabhakaran proved short-lived, it effectively undermined his authority. When Karuna, LTTE's eastern commander, split from the LTTE, claiming discrimination against the eastern region, he had a sizeable section of the LTTE's eastern ranks with him. The rebellion showed chinks in Prabhakaran's claim of support, but his greater firepower forced Karuna to pull back. It exposed the cracks in the LTTE's solidarity and challenged its legitimacy of being the sole representative of the Tamils. It also took the lid off the question of merging the north and the east. Moreover, after Karuna's election and the fight between the north and east, the LTTE will never be the same again. In sum, re-crafting the peace process with a shell-shocked LTTE is going to be tough (Mehta, 2004: 6).

Problems in Sri Lanka have been compounded by external powers like Norway and Japan that give far too much consideration to the views of the LTTE and constantly equate the LTTE with the democratically elected government of Sri Lanka. In June 2003, the Tokyo Donors' Conference pledged US$ 4.5 billion as aid to Sri Lanka. But the Japanese have made disbursement of such aid conditional on the progress of talks between the Sri Lanka government and the LTTE—a terrorist outfit with an avowedly separatist agenda. Further, unlike the US, the British government appears to be far too relaxed in its links with pro-LTTE outfits and NGOs in Sri Lanka (Parthasarathy, 2004: 6).

The Deadlocked Peace Process

Since the peace process seems to be deadlocked, the Norwegian facilitators, especially Eric Solheim, have been working overtime to revive the talks. The new government proposal carried by Solheim was given to the chief LTTE negotiator, Anton Balasingham, in London in November 2005. It sought to extract a formal commitment from the Tigers that they would honour Sri Lanka's sovereignty and integrity and not work towards a separate Tamil state. What the government wanted was for the LTTE to accept the idea of a federal solution. The LTTE, on the other hand, wanted discussion on its proposal of ISGA and not an interim authority suggested by the government. Therefore the proposal was rejected (Mehta, 2004: 8).

In a belligerent annual Hero's Day speech, Prabhakaran warned the Lankan government that the Tigers would be 'compelled to launch a freedom struggle' unless there was unconditional resumption of talks. He revived the issue of the 1980 Thimpu Principles: homeland, nationality, and self-determination. Prabhakaran had told the Norwegians that he wanted an assurance from Kumaratunga that her proposals had the backing of a 'southern consensus' to include the JVP. The latter is seen by the LTTE as the main stumbling block to resumption of talks.

As far as the peace process is concerned, it has moved into a protracted stalemate threatening the Ceasefire Agreement. Mixed signals have been coming from the LTTE about war and peace, especially after Prabhakaran's 27 November Hero's Day speech and rejection of the governments' latest proposal to start talks (Mehta, 2004).

More recently, Foreign Minister Lakshman Kadirgamar's assassination (on 12 August 2005), in the midst of a functional ceasefire (which, for all its flaws and breaches, was still holding), is a setback to the peace process. Kadirgamar, who entered politics in 1994 after a successful legal career, was instrumental in getting the LTTE banned internationally. Since then he had been high on the LTTE's hit list.[9] The international community condemned the assassination of Kadigamar. The Kadirgamar killing can also be interpreted as a sign of the growing frustration of the Tigers about the 'no war, no peace' situation. The LTTE has been at the receiving end of a series of spectacular attacks on its political activists and a few military cadre, provoking the rebel group to accuse the army of backing the 'renegade' Karuna faction, which came into existence in March 2004, and other 'paramilitary' groups. Evidence on the ground does suggest the security forces support the renegades (Venkataraman, 2005: 2).

On the political side, the LTTE has been angry that the move to create a joint mechanism for distributing Tsunami aid in the north-east, through the Post-Tsunami Operational Management Structure (P-TOMS), had been stymied by a court order in response to a legal challenge by Sinhala nationalists. Tamils see in the governments' failure to operationalize P-TOMS yet another story of 'deception' by the Sinhala establishment against their interests (Venkataraman, 2005).

The Sri Lankan government on 15 August called for a review of certain policies and procedures in the current peace process, in the aftermath of the assassination of its foreign minister Kadirgamar. Scandinavian truce monitors had warned that the assassination of Kadirgamar was a major setback for the truce and could jeopardize the entire peace process.

Prospects for the Peace Process

The challenge to contemporary Sri Lanka today is to find a suitable structure of governance in which two or more groups of people can coexist, cooperate, and be partners within a single state without the members of one group being able to unilaterally impose their wishes on the members of the other groups.

The present situation in Sri Lanka is critical. The current chaos creates uncertainty and, therefore, it is difficult to outline the future moves of the LTTE or the Sri Lankan government. But despite such problems, prospects for peace should remain hopeful.

Mahinda Rajapakse has won the recent Sri Lankan presidential election with extremely weak support among the country's minorities and the LTTE hopes to exploit this too. The first task before President Rajapakse must be to reach out to the Tamil and Muslim minorities, and to Wickremasinghe's voters, and assure them that he intends to work towards a just solution that will meet their aspirations within a united Sri Lanka. In his manifesto, he promised to adopt a 'fresh approach' to the stalemated peace process with the LTTE, based on the premises of 'undivided country, a national consensus, and an honourable peace' (*The Hindu*, 2005: 10). Given the nature of his mandate, the margin of his victory, and the complexity of the national question, the road from here on will not be easy.

The best course open to the government is to create the widest possible consensus between the government and opposition, and resume the peace process with a mind to give the federal option a chance. Mere devolution may not be enough to craft a lasting solution to the separatist problem. Neither LTTE's proposal for an ISGA of October 2003 (which the government thought was a way to an independent Tamil state out of Sri Lanka), nor the government-opposition agreement on constitutional reforms of July 2000 (which stops short of the federal option) can be the basis of the resumed dialogue in the changed context.

The peace strategy based on extending the greatest possible political autonomy to the Tigers within the framework of a united Sri Lanka remains the only reasonable basis for a negotiated settlement to the Tamil question. While the problem of secessionist movements cannot be resolved through the creation of yet more states, staying with the old statist paradigm of majoritarian will, absolute sovereignty and extreme cartographic anxiety is even less helpful. What is required is a new political imagination which goes beyond the antiquated logic of the nation-state to forge reasonable regional and global economic and federal political integration. In one word, no 'independence' but unlimited 'devolution'. And that's as true of the Tamil question in Sri Lanka as it is of the separatist movements anywhere in the world.

In this context, Rupak Chattopadhyay, a programme officer with the Forum of Federations, Ottawa, has aptly observed: 'Some form of asymmetric (federal?) devolution now seems a foregone conclusion as part of the peace settlement. Asymmetric devolution implies that the constituent units of a new Sri Lankan government structure would not have identical powers and responsibilities, but would assume roles appropriate to their situations. The concept also implies that there could be a system of cultural minority rights alongside the basic constitutional and political structure—a system that might, for instance, guarantee certain cultural rights to Tamils living in Sinhalese dominated areas or Sinhalese living in Tamil Areas'(*Federations*, 2002).

Notes

1. On the introduction of universal suffrage to Sri Lanka, refer to K.M. de Silva (1981).

2. For an in-depth study of Federalism and Devolution in Sri Lanka, consult Partha S. Ghosh (2003).
3. According to the last census the proportion of different ethnic groups is as follows: Sinhalese 74.0 per cent, Sri Lankan 12.6 per cent, Moors 7.1 per cent, Indian Tamils 5.5 per cent, others 0.8 per cent. See Central Bank of Sri Lanka (1992: 9).
4. For the rise of Sinhala Buddhist nationalism refer to Richard Gombrich and Gananath Obeyesekere (1988) and Elizabeth Nissan (1989).
5. In 1951, S.W.R.D. Bandaranaike split from the UNP and founded the SLFP which offered a home to those who rejected the concepts of poly-ethnic policies, of Sri Lankan nationalism, and of a secular state. Refer to K.M de Silva (1988: 135).
6. For structural aspects of the LTTE, consult Sahadevan (2002).
7. After secret consultations, the Indo-Sri Lanka Peace Accord was signed in 1987. The Indian Peace Keeping Force (IPKF) was deployed in the north and east to disarm the LTTE. The policy to disarm the LTTE failed and the IPKF became involved in heavy fighting with the LTTE. The fighting in the north and east between the IPKF and the LTTE and violence in the south between the security forces and the JVP forced the UNP government to reconsider its policy. President Premadasa renegotiated the accord with India and achieved a withdrawal of the IPKF in 1990.
8. In his new book *War and Peace: Armed Struggle and Peace Efforts of the Liberation Tigers*, Balasingham has acknowledged that CFA of February 2002 is of 'paramount importance to peace in Sri Lanka' and 'a substantial achievement of the entire peace process.' He has noted that the set back to the talks was due to a dual power structure and the conflict between the executive president and the elected prime minister.
9. *Asian News Digest*, 6(36) (28 August–3 September 2005) pp. 734. For the LTTE Kadirgamar was a 'traitor'. He was a Jaffna-born Tamil but did not set much store by his ethnic identity, choosing to be known simply as a Sri Lankan. The LTTE had a long charge sheet against him! For details refer to K. Venkataramanan (2005).

References

Arasaratham, Sinnappah (1986). *Sri Lanka after Independence: Nationalism, Communalism and Nation Building*. Madras: University of Madras.

Asian News Digest (2003). 4(48), 24–30 November 2003: 3262.

Asian Survey (1992). 32(8), August 1992: 713.

Bhatia, Sidharth (2003). 'The Colombo Crossing', *The Pioneer* (New Delhi), 11 November, 2003, p. 6.

Central Bank of Sri Lanka (1992). *Economic and Social Statistics of Sri Lanka 1991*. Colombo: Central Bank of Sri Lanka.

de Silva (1993). 'Regionalism and Decentralization of Power', in K.M. de Silva, *Sri Lanka: Problem of Governance*, New Delhi: Konark, p. 102.

de Silva, Jayanatha (2003). 'Whither Sri Lanka?', *The Island* (Colombo), 19 November 2003, p. 8.

de Silva, K.M. (1981). 'The Introduction of Universal Suffrage', in K.M. de Silva (ed.), *Universal Suffrage, 1931–1981: The Sri Lankan Experiment*, pp. 48–62. Colombo.

———— (1988). 'Buddhist Revivalism, Nationalism, and Politics in Modem Sri Lanka', in J.W. Bjkoman (ed.), *Fundamentalism, Revivalists and Violence in South Asia*. New Delhi: Manohar Publications, pp. 107–58.

———— (ed.) (1993). *Sri Lanka: Problems of Governance*. New Delhi: Konark.

———— (1997). 'Affirmative Action Policies: The Sri Lankan Experience', *Ethnic Studies Report*, 15(2) (July 1997): 245.

———— (1998). *Reaping the Whirlwind—Ethnic Conflict, 'Ethnic Politics in Sri Lanka*. New Delhi: Penguin.

———— (2000). 'The Working of democracy in South Asia' in V.A. Pai Panandikar (ed.), *Problems of Governance in South Asia*. New Delhi: Konark.

Dent, Martin J. (2004). *Identity Politic: Filling the Gap Between Federalism and Independence*. Hampshire: Ashgate.

Dixit, J.N. (2003). 'Gloves come off in Lanka', *Sunday Hindustan Times*, New Delhi, 16 November 2003, p. 14.

Edrisinha, Rohan and Saravanamuttu Pankiasothy (1993). 'The Case for a Federal Sri Lanka', in Uyangoda Edrisinha (ed.), *Essays on Constitutional Reforms*. Colombo: Centre for Policy Research Analysis and University of Colombo.

Effendi, Maria Saifuddin (2003–04). 'Sri Lanka Peace Process—With and Without Mediation (1994 to Date)', *Regional Studies* 22(1), (Winter 2003–04): 88–90.

Federations (2002). Ottawa, 2, November 5: 8.

Frontline (2004). 21(8), April 2004: 130–32.

Ghosh, Partha S. (2003). *Ethnicity Versus Nationalism: The Devolution Discourse in Sri Lanka*. New Delhi: Sage.

Gombrich, Richard and Gananath Obeyesekere (1988). *Buddhism Transformed: Religious Change in Sri Lanka*. Princeton: Princeton University Press.

Gopal, Krishna (1998). 'Ethnicity and Conflictual Nationalism in Sri Lanka: Ramification and Emergent Scenario', in Gopal Singh (ed.), *South Asia: Democracy, Discontent and Societal Conflicts*. New Delhi: Anamika.

Gunaratna, Rohan (1993). *Indian Intervention in Sri Lanka*. Colombo: Gunaratne Offset.

Gunatilleke, Godfrey (2001). 'Negotiations for the Resolution of the Ethnic Conflict', *Marga*: Monograph Series on Ethnic Reconciliation No. 1: 51.

Institute of Regional Studies (1986). 'Indo-Sri Lankan Relations: Retrospect Problems and Prospects', *Spotlight on Regional Affairs*, Islamabad: April 1986, p. 10.

Jayahanthan (2004). 'The Tamil Question', *South Asian Journal* (January–March): 50.

Jayawardene, J.R. (1988). 'The Democratic Option: The Solution to the Ethnic Conflict in Sri Lanka', *The Parliamentarians*, LXXIV, (January 1988): 6.

Kathiravelupillai, S. (1979). 'Co-existence, Not Confrontation', *Lanka Guardian*, Colombo, 2(l), May 1979: 9.

Keerawella, Gamini and Rohan Samarajiva (1995). 'Sri Lanka in 1994: A Mandate for Peace', *Asian Survey*, 35(2) (February 1995): 156.

Kumari, Jayawardena (1985). *Ethnic and Class Conflict in Sri Lanka*. Colombo: Sangiva Books.

Lewer, Nick and Joe William (2002). 'Sri Lanka: Finding a Negotiated End to Twenty-Five years of violence, in Monique Mekenkamp, Paul Van Tongeren and Hans Van de Veen (eds), *Searching for Peace in Central and South Asia: An Overview of Conflict Prevention and Peace Building Activities*. Boulder: Lynne Rienner Publishers.

Loganathan, Ketheshwaran (1996). *Sri Lanka: Lost Opportunities—Past Attempts at Resolving Ethnic Conflict*. Colombo: Centre for Policy Research and Analysis, 11.

Mahanama, Prematilaka (2003). 'LTTE's ISGA Proposals go far beyond those Agreed on', *Daily Mirror*, Colombo, 19 November 2003, p. 9.

Mehta, Ashok K. (2004a). 'Karuna, Elections and Peace', *The Pioneer*, New Delhi: 21 April 2004, p. 6.

——— (2004b). 'War and Peace in Sri Lanka', *The Pioneer*, 29 December 2004, p. 8.

Nagerty, D.T. (1993). 'India's Regional Security Doctrine', *Asian Survey*, 31, (April): 351–63.

Nissan, Elizabeth (1989). 'History in the Making: Anuradhapura and the Sinhala Buddhist Nation', *Social Analysis*, 25(1), (1989): 64–77.

Oberst, Robert (1985). 'Democracy and the Persistence of Westernized Elite Dominance in Sri Lanka', *Asian Survey*, 25(7), (July 1985): 760.

Parthasarathy, G. (2004). 'Need for Proactive Diplomacy', *The Pioneer*, New Delhi, 22 April 2004 p. 6.

Perera, Jehan (2004). 'Sri Lanka: Confrontation to Accommodation', *South Asian Journal*, (January–March 2004): 104.

Phadnis, U. (1976). *Religion and Politics in Sri Lanka*. New Delhi: Manohar.

Rahman, Mahbubur (1986). 'Ethnic Conflict in Sri Lanka: Future Dimensions', *Bliss Journal*, 7(2) (1986): 238.

Ram, Mohan (1989). *Sri Lanka: The Fractured Island*. New Delhi: Penguin.

Sahadevan, P. (2002). 'LTTE and the Peace Process', *AGNI*, 6(3) (September–December 2002): 22–56.

Sambandan, V.S. (2004). 'New Equations in Sri Lanka', *The Hindu*, New Delhi, 11 April 2004, p. 18.

Schaffer, Howard B. (1996). 'Sri Lanka in 1995: A Difficult and Disappointing Year', *Asian Survey*, 34(2) (February 1996): 217.

Shankar, Kalyani (2003). 'Kumaratunga Conquest', *The Pioneer*, 7 November 2003, p. 7.

Singer, M.R. (1992). 'Sri Lanka's Tamil–Sinhalese Ethnic Conflict: Alternative Solutions', *Asia Survey*, 32(8) (August 1992): 713–25.

Singer, Marshal R. (1967). *The Emerging Elite: A Study of Political Leadership in Ceylon*. Massachusetts: MIT.

Subramanian, Nirupama (2004). 'The Bikhu Effect', *The Hindu*, New Delhi, 11 April 2004, p. 18.

Tambiah, S.J. (1992). *Buddhism Betrayed? Religion, Politics, and Violence in Sri Lanka*. Chicago: University of Chicago Press.

The Hindu (2005). New Delhi, 19 November 2005, p. 10.

The Pioneer (2003). 5 November 2003, p. 10.

Thiruchandran, Selvy (2003). 'Sinhala Buddhist Nationalism', *South Asian Journal*, October–December 2003: 63.

———— (2004). 'Sinhala Buddhist Nationalism', *South Asian Journal* (January–March 2004): 66.

Uyangoda, Jayadeva (2004). 'Sri Lanka after Elections', *The Hindu*, New Delhi, 12 April 2004, p. 10.

Vaidik, V.P. (1980). *Ethnic Crisis in Sri Lanka: India's Options*. New Delhi: National Publishing House.

Venkataraman, K. (2005). 'Kadirgamar Assassinated', *Sunday Pioneer*, 21 August 2005, p. 2.

Wagner, Christian (1997). 'Sri Lanka—Crisis in Legitimacy', in Subrata K. Mitra and Dietmar Rothermund (eds), *Legitimacy and Conflict in South Asia*, pp. 194–206. New Delhi: Manohar.

Zeylanicus (1970). *Ceylon between Orient and Occident*. London: Elek Books.

8

Domestic Turbulence in Nepal: Origin, Dimensions, and India's Policy Options

Nalini Kant Jha

Events in Nepal moved so rapidly in the year 2006 that King Gyanendra's April proclamation restoring parliament seems to belong to another political universe. Like the Long Parliament in Britain, which Charles I was compelled to summon in 1640, the reconvened House of Representative in Nepal moved swiftly to assert the sovereign will of the people against monarchy. It stripped the king of his powers, renamed the government and army in accordance with popular democratic aspirations, and released political prisoners. But unlike England, which descended into civil war as the Crown and Westminster struggled for supremacy, the assertion of popular will against the monarchy, offers the best chance for an end to a decade-old Maoist insurgency in the Himalayan state. But before we examine the challenges and prospects of recent and rapid political transformations in Nepal, it is relevant to discuss the origin, evolution, objectives, strategies, magnitude, and support base of Maoist insurgency in Nepal and the way in which the Nepalese government and the international community have responded to this menace.

The Backdrop

Though the origin of Maoist insurgency in Nepal can be traced back to the 1960s when the radical section of Nepalese Communists demanded an end to the autocratic panchayat system imposed by King Mahendra and the formation of an elected constituent assembly to draw up a new constitution for Nepal,[1] the serious preparation for beginning of the Maoist movement was made only with the formation of the Communist Party of Nepal-Maoist (CPN-M) in 1994. The party, led by Pushpakamal Dahal (popularly known as Prachand), decided to boycott the mid-term polls in Nepal and opted for armed struggle. It adopted a resolution to overthrow the existing constitutional system through an armed revolution and establish a republic, based on a Marxist-Leninist and Maoist prototype (Khanal, 2003: 28). The CPN-M got a boost in 1996, when the Samyukta Jana Morcha or United People's Front of Nepal (UPFN), led by Baburam Bhattarai, a Ph.D. from Jawaharlal Nehru University of India, who had captured nine seats in the 1991 General Elections, left mainstream politics and joined hands with the CPN-M to start a 'people's war' (Thapliyal, 2001).

The Maoists predominance in Nepali politics has been facilitated by the inability of successive governments to address the basic economic problems of the people, discriminatory social order, and a fractured, inefficient and instable polity. For instance, economic factors like poverty, unemployment, under-employment, lopsided development, and concentration of wealth in few hands had alienated the vast majority of poor Nepalese from the state apparatus. Since Nepal is predominantly an agricultural country with 80 per cent of population still dependent on agricultural land for their livelihood, the agriculture sector has become critical to economic development (Thapa, 2001: 30). While respective political establishments made certain efforts towards accommodating various ethnic groups and tribes, and thereby building the Nepalese nation, the political elites bungled in prioritizing basic requirements and in not having a proactive agenda for containing the genesis of Marxist insurgency. In contrast to India, where accommodative measures were at play, and had been experimented with in empowering local autonomous councils at the institutional level, similar measures such as granting even limited autonomy were not even conceived of by the Nepalese government.

Besides, the successive governments failed to make any significant headway in land reform measures as well as in creating avenues to generate employment in other sectors, and divert people from the agricultural sector to other sectors for gainful employment.

Not surprisingly, 71 per cent of the wealth, even in the relatively well developed capital, is in the hands of the top 12 per cent of the households, and only 3.7 per cent of the national income reaches the poorest 20 per cent of the country's families. The per capita income in Kathmandu averages Rs 20,939, while it is as low as Rs 5,000 in the poorest district in the north-west region.[2] It is estimated that with an average economic growth, approximately 4 per cent per year for the past five years, it is insufficient to absorb the estimated 500,000 young people who join the labour force each year (Tewari, 2001).

The political class's pre-occupation with political squabbling and survival of regimes deepened the crisis of governance. In particular, the virtual absence of governance in rural Nepal, an indifferent monarchy, widespread corruption, and lingering political instability contributed to the general dissatisfaction. Within a few years of multiparty democracy, the administrative shortcomings became so apparent that the expectations of the people for better governance slowly diminished. If the principal Communist Party government led by Man Mohan Adhikari failed to deliver on the land reforms front, the political instability syndrome manifested in the coming and going of eleven prime ministers in Nepal within 12 years, eroded any hope of implementation of any long-term policy for the amelioration of the weaker sections of the society.[3] Lack of confidence and trust among the political leaders, the king, and the military, thus, helped to make the situation only worse, and the Maoists to grow.

Finally, the marginalization of the ethno-linguistic minorities leading to their alienation also played an important role in the rise of the Maoists. The cohesive structure of Nepali society was shaken in 1990 when the new constitution declared Nepal a Hindu state and Nepali, the only official language. Minority groups like the Tibeto-Burman community questioned the propriety of declaring Nepal a Hindu state, as they do not consider themselves Hindus. Though predomination of the dominant groups and castes in education, employment, etc., was prevalent during the panchayat regime as well, the commencement of democracy and the new constitution brought the problem to the fore by guaranteeing freedom of expression, and thereby giving voice to the people who were earlier silent spectators. This enabled ethnic groups in Nepal to organize themselves against socio-economic and political discrimination, including the imposition of Sanskrit as a compulsory subject in schools, or Nepali as the country's official language.

Maoist Strategies

These problems of governance enabled the Maoists to hijack the basic agenda of economic development. They assured the people that they would remove the monarchy and the servile government and replace it with a communist state, which would end the exploitation of poverty-stricken farmers and labourers in remote Nepal. This appealed those people, who were mostly from the poor and socially marginalized class.[4] They further proclaimed that they would establish a 'people's government' through a 'people's war' in line with the ideology of Peru's Shining Path group. To form a 'people's government,' the CPN-M, which bases its ideals, aspirations, and course of action on Mao's style of dictatorship of the proletariat, adopted the 'strategy of surrounding the city from the countryside'(Khanal, 2003: 20).

In the initial stages, they made symbolic attacks against some police posts and such installation as the Small Farmers Development Project, which provided loans for small farmers giving the impression that they had liberated them from the loans. But their main targets were the grassroot workers of the Nepali Congress (NC) and teachers who were supporters of the NC. The Maoists were, therefore, able to neutralize possible resistance from the cadres of other political parties. Consequently, political parties could not develop an approach compatible with this problem. Even the NC, which was in power most of the time, was divided on handling this challenge. It helped the rebels tremendously in unabatedly growing both in organization and actions. By acts such as threats of kidnapping, torture, killing, and so on, they first weakened the organizational base of the NC.

Crippling the NC apart, the insurgents targeted local informers of the intelligence units. Most of the victims of Maoist violence were these local informers. Needless to add, this helped them to sabotage and destroy the intelligence network of the police.

Besides, the Maoists began to use the ethnic cleavage to their advantage by promising self-rule and autonomy to ethnic minorities in areas where they were in majority. They also vowed to recognize the culture and language of the ethnic minorities. In a pamphlet distributed on 13 February 1996, they declared: 'To maintain the hegemony of one religion [Hinduism], language [Nepali], and nationality [Khas] the State has for centuries exercised discrimination, exploitation, and oppression against other religions, languages and nationalities' and has conspired to 'fragment the forces of national unity that is vital for proper development and security' (Thapa, 2001). The Maoists, therefore, appealed to these indigenous ethnic groups to join the people's war, which got a favourable response from groups like the Khamuan Mukti Morcha.

In order to achieve their objectives, the Maoists declared on February 1996, the inevitability of a bloody war. In the same month, they submitted a 40-point memorandum to the government, then led by Prime Minister Sher Bahadur Deuba, demanding the abolition of royal privileges, promulgation of a Republican Constitution, and abolition of the Mahakali Treaty with India, etc. When the government failed to pay heed to their demands, they carried out simultaneous attacks on different parts of Nepal on 13 February 1996. Since then, the guerrillas have attacked government installations, indulged in loot and arson, and killed local bureaucrats, village headmen, and influential people especially in the western, central hill areas, and the western terai. The army, left untouched in the initial stages of what the Maoists call 'peoples war', became a target later on. They adopted methods like blowing conch shells to gather their supporters. In Nepal, this has been the traditional means of communication across the mountains and valleys for centuries.

Growing Strength of the Maoists

As discussed earlier, the near collapse of development work and civil governance in violence-affected areas, break down of the rule of law, and lack of democratization at the grass-roots level have, understandably, enabled the Maoists to not only to set up parallel structures of governance in many parts of the country, including their own visa and taxation system, but also to exert considerable influence in the urban centres. This was vividly demonstrated during their weeklong blockade of the Kathmandu Valley in

August 2004. The capital city, which depends on land routes for most of its supplies, was cut off, since the CPN-M called the blockade demanding the release of its arrested cadres. The ease with which the Maoists could manage to ensure compliance of their order was not surprising, considering that the armed insurgency had grown rapidly since its launch in 1996.

Thus, by the time the Maoists began to make major attacks on police posts, killing a large number of police personnel and seizing their weapons, they had grown beyond the control and capacity of the police. Beginning with six western districts—Rukum, Rolpa, Jajarkot, Salyan, and Gorkha—and Sindhuli in the east in 1996, their influence has now spread to 73 of Nepal's 75 districts, particularly in the poverty-stricken, economically backward western parts of the country, where Maoists leaders are treated with reverence. According to the government's own admission, there were 32 districts where guerrillas roamed freely and organized open mass meetings.[5] By the late 1990s, in many of the hill and mountain districts of western and mid-western Nepal, they virtually rendered the state apparatus ineffective and assumed control over the rural areas with their own system of governance.

Socially, championing the cause of minorities and weaker sections has enabled the Maoists to gradually extend their traditional social support base from the Brahmins, Kshthris, and Newars combine, to new groups such as Rais, Limbus, Burungs, Magars, Tamangs, etc. (Thapliyal, 2001). This forced the former Nepalese prime minister, Deuba, to acknowledge that the 'Maoists are successful in attracting frustrated people' (*The Kathmandu Post*, 5 December 2001).

The number of Maoist guerrilla fighters was estimated to be around 2,500, backed by 10, 000 or more militia at the end of the year 2001. Their strength is rapidly growing since the intra-palace regicide that took place in 2001. According to Royal Nepal Army sources, the Maoists had more than 6,000 trained fighters by the end of 2004, with several times more active cadre which could be mobilized as a crude fighting force at short notice. They are largely recruited from the rural poor, though many criminals have also joined the Maoists on the promise that they will be protected from the Nepali police. Interestingly enough, one-third of the guerrilla squads are women. Every village has a revolutionary women's organization. There are usually two women in each unit of 35–40 men, and they are used to gather intelligence and act as couriers (Gunaratne, 2001).

The main sources of funding of Maoists have been through bank robberies, voluntary donation, extortion from rich businessman, and tax collection in areas under their control. According to reports, the Maoists have looted more than Rs 250 million from banks and other institutions. They collected around Rs 5 billion in the form of 'donations' and 'taxes'. Thus, despite their declared ideology, the Maoists have not desisted from crime to fill their coffers, before resorting to more lucrative option of 'asking' businessmen, contractors, civil servants, and professionals to pay token sums as contribution every month. On 10 September 2004, the Maoists were able to explode two bombs at the highly guarded American Information Resource Centre in Kathmandu (Jha, 2004: 455; Thapa, 2001).

The growing strength of the Maoists raises the question about the sources of their arms, ammunitions, and training. Maoists are said to have procured arms from three sources, namely, raids on police stations, purchases from the illegal arms market, and locally made improvised explosive devices. The possibility of Nepalese Maoists getting arms and ammunitions from their fraternal comrades in India such as Maoist Coordination Centre (MCC) and People's War Group (PWG), who are operating in Indian provinces like Bihar, Andhra Pradesh, etc., cannot be ruled out. Coming to the source of training, the Nepalese government sources suspect that the well-trained Gorkha soldiers, who have retired from the British and Indian Army and are residing in the Maoist infected areas, as well as retirees and deserters from the Nepalese Army are involved in providing training and combat manpower to the Maoist guerrillas (Tewari, 2001).

Counter-insurgency Measures

While the origin of the Maoist rebellion lies in socio-economic and political factors, the main thrust of the counter-insurgency operations launched by the Nepalese government has been excessive use of force. Accordingly, the government worked on a policy of strengthening the Royal Nepal Army (RNA) with sophisticated weapons from India, the US, the UK, Belgium, and other countries.

It is estimated that the 25 per cent of the total national budget is now allocated to security. The considerable augmentation of the RNA notwithstanding, the ground reality remains alarming. Though the security forces achieved some successes in counter-insurgency operations, the task became difficult due to lack of adequate state presence in the violence-affected areas.

As a result, the government was not able to supplement the success of counter-insurgency in one area with strengthening or restoration of civil governance, institutions of law enforcement and democratic processes. The experience of the counter-insurgency operations, therefore, necessitated an assessment of the broad direction of government policy and implications of continuous strengthening of the RNA. This was all the more important because governmental operations alienated a large segment of the rural population and thereby gave a new lease of life to the insurgents. On the other hand, the governmental efforts to initiate talks with the Maoists failed to make any headway due to several preconditions set by them, including release of all party activists from jails and withdrawal of police from the insurgency affected areas.[6] That the Maoists were in a stronger position became evident when they refused to talk to the Deuba government, which was reinstalled (after its dismissal by the king in October 2002) in June 2004. They instead favoured direct negotiation with the king and reiterated their demand for an election of a new Constituent Assembly under UN auspices.

The King's Follies

Unfortunately, however, while the Maoists were successful in gradually pushing their agenda through violence and intimidation, the lust of power of King Gyanendra and the disarray among the political leadership aggravated the domestic turmoil in Nepal. Instead of showing prudence and statesmanship in dealing with the Maoists rebels, the king showed more interest in exploiting the situation in his favour. First, he dissolved Nepal's parliament on 22 May 2002, and then dismissed the Sher Bhadur Deuba government in October that year accusing Deuba of being incompetent in running the government beset by an increasingly deadly Maoist insurgency.

He nominated Lokendra Bahadur Chand as prime minister. When, however, the street rallies organized by the main opposition parties for restoration of democracy forced him to resign, the king handpicked Surya Bahadur Thapa as Nepal's prime minister in June 2003. Though political parties relaunched their agitation and street protests against this undemocratic practice of the king, they too let down the country by not coming out with a consensus candidate for the post of prime minster. Under the circumstance, the king once again nominated Deuba as prime minister of the country in June 2004. But the refusal of the country's biggest political party, the Nepali Congress led by B.P. Koirala to join the new government deprived it from getting legitimacy even though the Deuba government consisted of four political parties including the Communist Party of Nepal-United Marxist-Leninist (UML) (*Hindustan Times* [Patna], 4 June 2004).

Not surprisingly, the Deuba government could not come out with a consensual, clear, and coherent approach to deal with the Maoist menace. If it could not effectively prevent the military blockade of Kathmandu, which demonstrated the capability of the Maoists to move insurgency where it could hit the country hardest, the government also prevaricated over the rebels' offer of a ceasefire during the Hindu festival of Dussehra in 2004 (*Hindustan Times*, [Bhopal], 18 October 2004). The government's delay in positively responding to the Maoist call for ceasefire is, of course, understandable in view of the fact that twice before—from July–November 2001 and from January–September 2003—the government's declaration of ceasefire and conducting of six rounds of direct talks could not bridge the divide between the two sides.[7] But as stated earlier, when the Deuba government expressed willingness to talk to the Maoists, they refused to conduct any negotiations with the government and instead favoured direct negotiation with the king and reiterated their demand for an election of a new Constituent Assembly under UN auspices.

This strengthened the king, who used the inability of the Deuba government to tame the Maoists to once again dismiss his government and impose emergency in February 2005. The king also suspended fundamental rights and assumed all executive powers in the name of 'bringing back peace and effective democracy'. But in reality he hurtled his kingdom into the abyss of absolute monarchy. Though the king announced the lifting of emergency in Nepal on 29 April 2005, that is, soon after his meeting with the Indian prime minister, Manmohan Singh, in Jakarta, he did not withdraw the draconian executive orders suspending fundamental rights. The king began to govern the country directly and incarcerated political leaders continued to languish in jails.

Dangers for India

Needless to add, India that shares a 15,000 km long border, which is even more open and porous than that between the US and Canada, as well as close social ties with Nepal, cannot remain unaffected by domestic turbulence in Nepal. This is especially true in the context of Nepal's Maoist rebels, who have an anti-India bias. The document adopted at the third plenum of the CPN-M central committee in March 1995 declared that the armed struggle was specifically against 'Indian imperialism'. It also voiced opposition to the recruitment of Gurkha soldiers in the Indian Army. It is alleged that the Maoists were being trained by the ex-Gurkhas of the Indian Army. Further, the Maoists demanded the abrogation of India-Nepal Treaty of 1950 and the Mahakali Treaty.

Moreover, the Maoists, masquerading under various names such the PWG and the MCC, are very active in some Indian states like Andhra Pradesh, Bihar, West Bengal, Sikkim, and Assam. The timing of the attacks by the PWG in Andhra Pradesh after the breakdown of Maoists ceasefires in Nepal (November 2001 and August 2003) are noteworthy. The PWG, for instance, attacked the Andhra Pradesh chief minister, Chandra Babu Naidu, in October 2003, that is, after the breakdown of talks between the Maoists and the Nepalese government. It is said that the Maoists got electronic detonators and explosives from the PWG, while pistols, ammunition, and high-quality detonators were provided by the MCC.

Of late, they have established their foothold in West Bengal and Bangladesh also. As the Nepali consul-general in Kolkata pointed out to the West Bengal chief minister, Maoists from not just India and Nepal but also from Bangladesh have been holding conclaves in places like Silliguri in the narrow 'neck' of Indian territory that separates Bangladesh from Nepal. Besides, there are reports to indicate that Maoists are providing bases to insurgent groups such as the United Liberation Front for Assam (ULFA) in India's north-east and getting arms and tactical training in return. The other side of the coin is that the Nepali Maoists, as and when under pressure from the army, try to escape to adjacent Indian territories and seek sanctuary in the hideouts of their soul mates.[8] The arrest of top Maoists leaders in Silliguri and Patna in 2004 clearly indicated their links with Indian militants. As the director general of police of Sikkim, T.N. Tensing, observed that they are aware of the likelihood of a spillover of Maoists from Nepal into border states like Sikkim and West Bengal. This forced these states to sound an alert to check infiltration of these rebels into Indian territory.[9]

Not surprisingly, Nepal is emerging as the conduit for illegal arms brought from India, which are smuggled back again to India. By establishing its linkages within India, the Maoist in combination with the PWG and MCC are in a position to pose a security threat to at least four Indian mainland states. They are in no way embarrassed by their cynical exploitation of the anti-Indian sentiment in the Himalayan kingdom that assumes outlandish proportions some times. The hijacking of Indian Airlines flight IC-814 from Kathmandu in December 1999, anti-India demonstration in that country over an unproved and repeatedly refuted statement of an Indian film star, and the assassination of the royal Nepalese family in the summer of 2001 clearly brought to the fore a realignment of political forces, which pose a serious challenge to India (Jha, 2003c: 31–32).

The Maoist insurgents in Nepal have also forced some Indian companies to move out of Nepal. A host of top Indian firms led by Dabur and ITC temporarily shut down operations in Nepal after Maoist rebels bombed a luxury hotel in August 2004, raising fears about the safety of conducting business in the Himalayan kingdom. The attack came on the eve of a deadline set by the rebels to shut down 10 companies including Nepal's oldest Indian luxury hotel, accusing them of adopting unfair labour practices, which these companies denied (*Times of India*, 2004).

The socio-political turmoil in Nepal has, thus, a spillover effect in India. The anti-India sentiments of the Maoist rebels, their unbridled use of the India–Nepal border for shelter, training, supplies, and arms smuggling, and their deepening linkages with the Indian left-wing and north-east extremist groups poses a serious security threat to India. Further, there is an apprehension that

Pakistan's Inter Services Intelligence (ISI), active in border areas, could forge links with the Maoists to destabilize the region.

The Indian Response

Not surprisingly, India had been among the forerunners in extending both moral and material support to the Nepalese authorities in their fight against the Maoist menace. With political turbulence rocking Nepal and political parties decaying, India, under the National Democratic Alliance (NDA) rule, saw a clear interest in preserving the institution of monarchy as stabilizing a force in the restive Himalayan state. India's then minister for external affairs and defence, Jaswant Singh, therefore, visited Nepal in August 2001 to establish personal rapport with the new king, King Gyanendra. Besides, India extended diplomatic support to declaration of emergency in Nepal in November 2001 and condemned violence by the Maoists (Jha, 2003c). More importantly, both the countries reinvigorated the traditional system of joint management of the border. When the chief of staff of the Nepal Army visited New Delhi in November 2001 and met his Indian counterpart, he went back with a message of India's fullest sympathy and support of what ever the Nepalese government required and asked for from India.

Soon after the collapse of the ceasefire in Nepal in November 2001, Prime Minister Atal Behari Vajpayee talked over the telephone with his Nepalese counterpart, Deuba, on 8 December. He assured India's full support and cooperation to Nepal at all levels in meeting the challenges posed by the Maoists. New Delhi declared all Moaist groups, including the Indian Maoist groups, as terrorists and increased action against them. India supplied helicopters that the Nepali security forces required immediately in meeting the challenges. The border areas were kept on 'high alert' to check the movements of the Maoists. Their possible hideouts in the border districts and towns were searched, and some of the Maoist activists, who were undergoing treatment, were handed over to the Nepali police.

When the then Nepalese prime minister, Sher Bahadur Deuba, visited India in March 2002, New Delhi offered him help to face the ongoing insurgency in Nepal. But at the same time it clearly expressed its desire to see him address its concerns about the misuse of Nepalese territory and hospitality by some forces inimical to India's national interest. The Nepalese leader reportedly showed his sensitivity to India's concerns about the Himalayan kingdom's vulnerability to penetration by some anti-India forces. Both the countries decided to intensify their efforts and cooperation to combat terrorism and cross-border crimes including sharing intelligence and information regarding terrorists' movements (*The Hindu*, 2002).

Besides, India's fear of the Nepalese Maoists and Indian left-wing extremists carving a corridor linking their movements all the way from the Dankaranya to the Himalayas has led it to supply its INSAS rifles at a heavy discount of nearly 70 per cent and trained officers and soldiers in various army-run counter-insurgency schools. The then Indian deputy prime minister, L.K. Advani, warned that the Government of India had an integrated programme to get rid of the trouble once and for all (Navlakha, 2003: 1033). In response to Kathmandu's request, India rounded up Nepali citizens who had allegedly been in cahoots with the terrorists and sent them back home (Padgonkar, 2002). The NDA government in India, thus, showed no hesitation in endorsing the steps taken by the Nepalese government to contain the Maoists.

The United Progressive Alliance (UPA) government, which came into power in India in May 2004, continued with the policy of the previous government. The joint statement issued at the end of the visit of the Nepalese prime minister, Sher Bhadur Deuba, to India in September 2004, for instance, reiterated the determination of both the countries in combating terrorism and further intensifying cooperation in curbing the activities of the extremists and terrorists. Prime Minster Deuba thanked the Government of India for the timely and substantive support provided by India in Nepal's efforts to deal with the Maoist insurgents. In response to India's expression of concern over the increasing anti-India activities of Pakistan's ISI and the Dawood Ibrahim gang in Nepal, Deuba assured India of Nepal's determination to not allow any anti-India activities in Nepal. This promoted New Delhi to agree on 9 September to upgrade its security assistance to Nepal, including a fresh consignment of military hardware, training to the RNA and intelligence sharing between the two countries (Singh, 2004: 7). This made the Nepalese Maoists launch a scathing attack against India. In a press statement posted on their party website (www.cpnm.org), the CPN-M chairman, Prachand, said that Indian 'expansionism' backed by US imperialism was directly impinging on the 'people's war' launched by the Maoists in Nepal.

This Nepalese government faced a dilemma when the Nepalese king imposed emergency in Nepal in February this year. Since this step invited the ire of the Maoists as well as all democratic political parties in Nepal, the present regime in New Delhi rightly suspended military aid to Nepal. This was in consonance with India's long cherished tradition of opposing autocratic rule in India's neighbourhood. At the same time, this policy enabled India not only to align with democratic parties and intelligentsia in Nepal, but also to avoid needlessly alienating the Maoists. As the UPA government rightly realized that Maoists could not be tamed by military action alone, it did not hesitate to abandon its half-century old policy of bilateralism in its dealing with Nepal and built a common front with the US, UK, and the European Union to bring additional pressure to bear on the king to restore democracy and allow the political leaders to resume negations with the Maoists (Jha, 2005: 40).

Within three months of this bold move to use its leverage in Nepal to make the king see reason, the UPA government, however, made a U-turn in its Nepal policy. Not only did Prime Minster Manmohan Singh meet King Gyanendra in Jakarta in April 2005, he even promised to expedite the delivery of arms suspended at the time of the royal coup. But what did India get in return? As stated earlier, though the king announced the lifting of emergency, he did not annul the draconian executive orders suspending fundamental rights. Worse, the two countries learned about the U-turn in India's policy only from the king, who chose to make public Manmohan Singh's assurances to him during their Jakarta meeting. It took the Government of India 17 days to confirm something that the Nepalese monarch had already announced. While constraints of time and space prohibit us from going in to reasons for this volte face in India's Nepal policy,[10] it should suffice to point out here that this dangerous flip flop is a betrayal of the Nepalese political parties struggling for the restoration of democracy.

India's ill-advised decision to resume the supply of arms to Nepal provided a shot in the arm for the king. Spurred on by New Delhi's benediction, the Nepalese security forces are likely to go all out to find a bloody 'military solution' to the Maoists question, and intimidate democratic opponents and critics in the bargain. India's decision to go back to playing ball with King Gyanendra could increase disarray in the democratic camp. This is why the king was so eager to go public about the Indian U-turn immediately after his Jakarta meeting with Prime Minister Manmohan Singh. The arms matter less to him than the legitimacy. India has bestowed on him and his not-so-secret project to turn the clock back to the bad old days of the panchayat system (Jha, 2006: 29–49; Jha and Kumar, 2003: 113–24).

It is, however, heartening to note, as stated at the outset, that finally the king had to bow down to the demands of the people in Nepal. In bowing to the force of popular pressure, announcing the revival of parliament, and paving the way for the Seven-Party Alliance (SPA) to form a government, King Gyanendra only accepted the inevitable. When he found that not only his repressive measures, but also his earlier offer of 22 April—inviting the parties to form an interim government with the promise of executive power—was too little too late to quell the swelling tide of the pro-democracy movement, he had no choice but to climb down further. It is, therefore, a historic victory for the country's pro-democracy movement and a true measure of what a genuine people-based movement can achieve in the face of repression. The quick nomination of Girija Prasad Koirala as the consensus choice for the post of prime minister—without the unseemly bickering that had characterized similar exercises in the past—demonstrated the maturity gained by the political parties during the anti-king struggle since imposition of emergency by him in February last year. The SPA also reiterated, and rightly so, its commitment to the agreement, which it has concluded with Maoists in November 2005 and March 2006 for the formation of a Constituent Assembly that has gained widespread popular support as evident during an 18-day agitation.

As far New Delhi is concerned, it must extend all assistance to a legal government in Kathmandu to meet the challenges that it will confront in restoring democracy, peace, and order in Nepal. While extending assistance to the democratic government in moving Nepal towards peace and prosperity, New Delhi and the international community must also remind the political parties that the last thing they can afford now is to get lulled into complacency by their triumph.

As regards the fate of the king and the institution of monarchy, which he personifies, his belated realization of the democratic urge of the people, probably prompted by a desperate urge to salvage whatever he could of a besieged monarchy, earned him no kudos. On the contrary, this only reinforced the distrust he has earned for his brutal disregard of people's democratic aspirations. This means that the SPA, parliament, the government, and the people have to continue to remain watchful that the king does not contrive to obstruct the SPA plan to restore democracy and peace. Unfortunately, the institution of monarchy, which was earlier accepted by the people as the great unifier and a symbol of the state, has now come into question. The question now is, whether the people will persuade themselves to regard the monarchy in the same light. Only the coming weeks and months will reveal the fate of the king as well as the crown.

While realigning its stance in Nepal, Indian foreign policy establishment should/must undertake initiatives to win the confidence of the Nepalese people directly. This can include low-cost options such as opening of primary schools, healthcare centres or other institutions for providing humanitarian relief, preferably with the help of non-governmental organizations. This will help India in earning the good will of the Nepalese people, which alone can provide a sound footing to India–Nepal friendship.

Notes

1. Khalid Mahmud (2002–03: 5) See also, Nalini Kant Jha (2003a, 2003b, 2006), Khanal (2003: 25–37), and Pattanaik (2002: 119–20).
2. Study report of a Kathmandu based think-tank, the Nepal South Asia Centre, as cited in Bertil Lintner (1999: 43).
3. In a bizarre game of musical chairs, G.P. Koirala has held the post of prime minister three times, while K.P. Bhattarai and Deuba have had two tenures each.
4. Khanal (2003: n. 1, p. 20). Also see, editorial, 'Time to Quell', *Pioneer* (New Delhi), 27 November 2001.
5. See Nirupama Subramanian's report from Kathmandu, 'Nepal's Expanding Insurgency', *The Hindu*, 26 July 2004. Also, Tewari (2001).
6. See, for details, Jha (2003b: 197–209).
7. See Rita Manchanda's dispatch from Kathmandu (Manchanda, 2002), and John Kifner (2003). Also, see Mahmud (2002–03: 13).
8. See Malhotra (2002). Also, see Farzand Ahmed's dispatch from Kathmandu (2002: 14). According to Rohan Gunaratne, the Indian organizations with whom the Maoists have links include: the ULFA, Northern Bihar Liberation Front, Bhartiya Communist Youth League, Bharat Ekta Samaj, All Nepal Youth Association (Chennai Committee) of India, etc. See Gunaratne (2001: 33).

9. Marcus Dam's dispatch from Kolkata (2004a, 2004b).
10. For details concerning causes of volte face in its Nepal policy by the UPA government, see Chandra (2005), Varadrajan (2005), and Sudarshan (2005).

References

Ahmed, Farzand (2002). 'Palace Coup', *India Today* (New Delhi), 27(42): 15–21 October 2002: 41.

Chandra, Satish (2005). 'India's Nepal Policy: Dangerous Flip Flop', *The Hindu*, 10 May 2005.

Dam, Marcus (2004a). 'India, Nepal Begin Operations against Maoist Rebels', *The Hindu*, 21 August 2004.

———— (2004b). 'Nepal to Seek Help of Indian States', *The Hindu*, 24 August 2004.

Gunaratne, Rohan (2001). 'Nepal's Insurgents Balance Politics and Violence', *Jane's Intelligence Review*, October 2001.

Jha, Nalini Kant (2003a). 'Domestic Turmoil in Nepal: Implications for Nepalese and Indian Security', *Journal of Peace Studies*, 10(2), April–June 2003: 2–18.

———— (2003b). 'Domestic Conflict in Nepal: Origin, Challenges and Prospects', *Asia Annual*, 2003: 197–209.

———— (2003c). 'India's Security Concerns in a Turbulent World', in Nalini Kant Jha and V.T. Patil (eds), *India in a Turbulent World: Perspectives on Foreign and Security Policies*. New Delhi: South Asian Publishers.

———— (2006). 'Implications for India of an Unstable Nepal', *Nepali Journal of Contemporary Studies* (Kathmandu), 6(1), March 2006.

Jha, Nalini Kant and Pramod Kumar (2003). 'India and Nepal: Imperatives of a Good Neighbourliness', in Nalini Kant Jha (ed.), *South Asia in 21st Century: India, Her Neighbours, and Great Powers*, pp. 113–24. New Delhi: South Asian Publishers.

Jha, Prem Shankar (2005). 'Follies of the Kingdom', *Outlook* (New Delhi), 45(9), 7 March 2005: 40.

Jha, Sanjay K. (2004). 'Nepal: Quest for Elusive Peace', *Strategic Analysis* (New Delhi), 28(3), July–September 2004: 455.

Khanal, Krishna P. (2001). 'Time to Quell', *Pioneer* (New Delhi), 27 November 2001.

———— (2003). 'Post-11 September Developments in Nepal: Implications for Curbing the Maoist Insurgency', in Dipankar Banerjee and Gert W. Kueck (eds), *South Asia and the War on Terrorism*, pp. 25–37. New Delhi: India Research Centre.

Kifner, John (2003). 'The Power Play in Nepal', *New York Times*, 5 August 2003.

Lintner, Bertil (1999). 'Nepal Struggles to Cope Diehard Maoist Violence', *Jane's Intelligence Review*, June 1999: 43.

Mahmud, Khalid (2002–03). 'Maoist Insurgency in Nepal', *Regional Studies* (Islamabad), 21(1), Winter 2002–03: 5.

Malhotra, Inder (2002). 'Focus Shifts to Nepal', *The Hindu*, 28 November 2002.

Manchanda, Rita (2002). 'Emergency and the Crisis', *Frontline*, 2 March 2002.

Navlakha, Gautam (2003). 'From Battle of Arms to Battle of Ideas', *Economic and Political Weekly*, 38(11), 15–21 March 2003: 1033.

Padgonkar, Dilip (2002). 'Nepal Adrift: Constitutional Crisis Looms Large', *Times of India* (Lucknow), 18 July 2002.

Pattanaik, Smruti S. (2002). 'Maoist Insurgency in Nepal: Examining Socio-Economic Grievances and Political Implications', *Strategic Analysis*, 26(1), January–March 2002: 119–20.

Singh, Anil Kumar (2004). 'Indo-Nepalese Relations and India's Security', *South Asia Politics* (New Delhi), 3(7), November 2004: 7.

Sudarshan, V. (2005). 'When it Reigns, It Pours', *Outlook*, 45(18), 15 May 2005.

Tewari, Chitra K. (2001). 'Nepal: Maoist Insurgency', *South Asia Monitor*, 31, 1 March 2001, available at www.csis.org/saprog.

Thapa, Deepak (2001). 'Day of the Maoist', *Himal South Asia* (Kathmandu), 14(5), May 2001.

Thapa, Prem Jung (2001). 'The Cost-Benefit of Land Reforms', *Himal*, 14(10), October 2001: 30.

Thapliyal, Sangeeta (2001). 'Maoists in Nepal', *The Hindu* (Madras), 18 December 2001.

The Hindu (2002). 'Cross Border Bonhomie with Nepal', *The Hindu*, 20 March 2002.

Times of India (Lucknow) (2004). 'Top Indian Firms Move out of Nepal', 19 August 2004.

Varadrajan, Siddharth (2005). 'A Policy in Search of a Rationale', *The Hindu*, 14 May 2005.

9

Ethnic Engagement in Bhutan and Its Regional Consequences*

Awadhesh Coomar Sinha

A state is a civil community having its own government and law. As per convention, it is attributed to have a definite territory, a population of citizens, a functioning government, and its sovereignty of governance. It is entirely another matter that these ideal and typical conditions are rarely met even in the case of the most appropriate example of the state. The Indian Union as a state is similarly no exception to this generalization. What it legally claims as her territory is disputed by some of her neighbours. There are non-citizens residing illegally within her boundary. Its government does not govern in a similar way all her regions and citizens. And in the matter of sovereignty, its helplessness gets occasionally exposed when terrorists mount attacks with impunity. Northeast India provides an example to the utter negation of all the attributes of an ideal Indian state. But one cannot be happy with the status quo. A rational solution to the problem demands a realistic appraisal of territorial limits or boundaries of the neighbouring countries by their consensus. One such country is Bhutan, which is more exclusive, different, distant and dissimilar to India, yet the Bhutanese scenario has far-reaching implications for northeast India in particular and South Asia in general.

We assume that the claimed state system of Bhutan is sacrosanct. Similarly, the territorial limits, legal citizens, and her functionaries provide us with a given parameter. Bhutan's location is

* Reprinted with permission from *Dialogue*, Volume V, No. 3 (January–March 2004), 149–60.

in the eastern Himalayan ranges on the north-eastern boundary of India. It has been painted as having an ideal system of its own. Its monks, forts, snow, and the royalty were all described as otherworldly. It was a blissful Shangri-La away from the din and the bustle of the crowded metropolises. It had a few people and plenty of space; dense forests with roaming wild creatures; perennial snow-fed rivers and monasteries, with monks and nuns, perched on the hanging snowy slopes. This idea and otherworldly image of the Druk kingdom is totally shattered today, because of the ongoing ethnic strife. The country is undergoing a phase of low intensity conflict (LIC),[1] a new phenomenon for her, but with a serious potential for a regional conflagration. This chapter is an attempt to trace the background of the ethnic conflict and its consequences to India in particular, and the South Asian Association of Regional Cooperation (SAARC) countries, in general.

Ethnic Background

The Drukpa state of Bhutan is the creation of Tibetan immigrants. Shabdrung Ngawang Namgyal (1594–1651), one among them, laid the foundation of this unique polity in the first half of the 17th century. Some significant aspects of this polity may be identified with the theocratic legitimacy based on incarnation, ubiquitous oligarchic conflict, duality of authority, and extremely fragile and limited economic base (Sinha, 1998). The mode of theocratic government continued up to 17 December 1907, when Ugyen Wangchuk (1861–1926) founded the present ruling dynasty. He was crowned as the Maharaja of the Bhutanese princely state under the tutelage of the British. Ugyen Wangchuk's rise in 1880s also coincided with the arrival of another ethnic group, the Nepalese (who were later designed as the Lhotshampas) on the southern Bhutanese Duars as lumbermen, herdsmen, and farmers.

Ugyen Wangchuk and John Claude White, the British political officer at Gangtok, struck a good working relationship. So much so, that the latter was invited, after his retirement in England, to introduce tea plantation and timber farming in the southern Bhutaneese foothills. Much earlier in life, White had been impressed by the industrious Nepalese, and it was he who was instrumental in introducing them to develop southern Sikkim and Darjeeling from where the bulk of the Lhotshampas moved to Bhutan. He was in close contact with the Bhutanese agent, Ugyen Dorji, who was appointed in 1898 as the chief of the Haa region (the entire Bhutan Duar), with a right to settle the Lhotshampas. For the next six-and-half decades, the cash-starved Bhutan *durbar* (court) was provided with their cash requirements by the Bhutan agent, which he extracted from the new settlers. It was a case of classical exploitation. The settlers had no tenancy rights. Their settlements were haphazard and huddled bamboo huts built after clearing the dense tropical forests.

There were no means of communication and transportation. They had neither education nor any facilities for health. They had no civil rights and they were exposed to the exploitation and brutalities of the *durbar* functionaries. Dissent was suppressed with a heavy hand so that the settlers did not deny any demands made on them. There were instances when an alleged difficult tenant could be sewn alive in a raw leather sack and thrown away in the turbulent river to meet his watery grave (Dhakal, 1994). In this atmosphere of stark suppression, there was no way that a resistance could be organized against the *durbar* brutalities. The settlers had a limited choice; either to comply with all sorts of demands made on them or leave Bhutan for good. But all the available alternative destinations to the Nepalese in the first half of 20th century had almost the same features. Thus, the bulk of them stayed put on the slippery Bhutanese Duars.

Bhutan could not remain untouched by the fast changing political scenario all around the neighbouring countries. China had invaded Tibet in the north. The British had withdrawn from India, leaving behind two successor states—the Indian Union and Pakistan. The two Himalayan kingdoms on the western border of Bhutan, Sikkim and Nepal, were under the spell of anti-feudal agitation and for the installation of popular governments. Needless to add that the Sikkim State Congress and the Nepali Congress—both spearheading the populist movements in Sikkim and Nepal respectively—were predominantly Nepali. In the very first year of the third Druk Gyalpo's regime (1952–72), one finds the ripples of the Lhotshampas', agitation in the form of the Bhutan State Congress. The agitation programme on the part of the Bhutan State Congress was ill timed because of the fact that in a universally illiterate, isolated, and an extremely despotic regime, a popular agitation for civil and political rights, abolition of landed estates, and a responsible government, was premature. No doubt, the movement was suppressed with an iron hand and all types of political agitations were banned on the soil of Bhutan for the time to come. Naturally, the leaders of the Bhutan State Congress kept away from Bhutan and lived in exile till royal pardon was granted to them in the 1960s.

Events forced the third Wangchuk ruler to review the Bhutanese approach to the Lhotshampas from a cold tolerance to reluctant acceptance in the Drukpa state structure. For the first time the Bhutan Citizenship Act, 1958 was enacted, which provided a status to the Lhostshampas. Their language was recognized and it soon began to be taught in the primary schools. They were permitted to build their shrines and teach Sanskrit, the language of their scriptures. Moreover, the state adopted a conscious ethnic policy of assimilating the Lhotshampas in the Drukpa fold by encouraging inter-ethnic marriages by granting first Rs 5,000 then increasing it to Rs 10,000 as incentives. Further, the Lhotshampas were encouraged to participate in the proceedings of the Tsongdu (national legislative body), they were sent abroad on scholarship for higher studies, were appointed as bureaucrats, were accorded membership to the Royal Advisory Council, the council of ministers, when such dispensations were introduced in the 1970s.

The Lhotshampas provided a much-needed labour force when Bhutan decided to undertake planned development through the five-year plan in 1962. J.B. Pradhan, the commissioner of southern Bhutan, was entrusted by the *durbar* to provide manual labourers and ration required for their consumption on construction sites. Transport, buildings for schools, rural dispensaries, administrative and public offices, hydro projects, electric installations, and a host of developmental activities were undertaken in a big way.

Erstwhile insignificant sleepy border settlements such as Samchi, Penden, Phuntshilling, Geylegphu, Samdrung Jongkhar, and the like turned into border townships with thriving commercial activities. These settlements also housed the infant industrial establishments such as fruit preservation, liquor, cement, woodcraft, and the like. It is needless to add that it was the Lhotshampas, who were the only local labour available to handle these demanding accomplishments. It also goes without saying that the Bhutan *durbar* went out of its way to make the Lhotshampas' life as comfortable as possible. Bhutan was plunged into political turmoil in 1964, when the first and only prime minister of the country was shot dead at Phuntshilling. The Lhotshampas kept away from the ensuing royal factional conflict. In fact, the two decades from 1962 to 1982 or say 1985 were the heydays of the Lhotshampas in Bhutan. Reluctantly, in the beginning, but slowly and steadily, they developed a sense of assertion and by the late 1970s, the Lhotshampas found their feet planted on the ground and began to voice their opinions. To the utter surprise of the Bhutanese ruler, the democratic fever caught up in Sikkim and the 334 years old Namgyal rule came to an end in 1975. This was the movement almost entirely organized by Nepalese with support from Indian democratic forces. Sikkim joined the Indian Union that year.

Land Tenure and Feudal Social Structure

The Bhutanese commoners could be divided into two, the farmers and the serfs, of which the latter were further divided into a number of local variations. Further, various districts had different land tenure practices. For example, Tashigang Dzokhang paid taxes to the king. There were regions, which paid taxes to the queen mother, queen, king's sisters, royal uncles, crown prince, and other relatives. There were aristocratic families with free land grants, dependent peasants, and hundreds of serfs. The important monasteries had estates for their maintenance. Then, there were tracts of land, which paid taxes directly to the state treasury. Southern Bhutan was in the charge of the Dorji family, who depended on the Nepali *thickedar*s for revenue collection. Further, the incarnate *lamas* with estates were a special charge of the king. For example, Tullku Gangtey, a constant companion to the second Druk Gyalpo, died in 1931. His estate in Bumthang Valley lapsed to the royal household because of the delayed discovery of his incarnation.

All the households in a village were subjected to an obligatory labour tax (*chunidon* or *woola*) to the state, which could be allotted for a number of assignments decided by local-level functionaries. There could be three types of households in a Drukpa village: *trepla* (liable to pay taxes), *zurpa* (splinter household not yet liable to pay taxes) and *suma* (the households paying taxes to the nobility, for example, the royal family). There were two types of grain taxes:

wangyon (levy for blessings) and *thojab* (grain tax on land output). There were numerous other taxes to be paid such as textile tax, butter tax, etc. A typical taxpayer would pay annually the following items to the state functionaries: 462 kg of paddy, 28 kg of butter, 120 pairs of wooden shingles, besides textiles baskets, paddy straw, mustard, dry chillies, dry sliced pumpkins, bark for paper and ash for the field. They had to till the land for the monasteries and local officials in varying man-days without payment. On an average, a Bhutanese farmer spent half of his time working for the state without any express benefit to himself.

There were royal, aristocratic, even monastic herdsmen, and slaves grazing cattle. These herdsmen had to provide butter, calf, wool, hide and meat, and yak tails in taxes. Though there were regional variations, but, in effect, there were two types of slaves: *drabas*—who worked for their masters in lieu of land granted to them for their up-keep—and *zabas*—who worked only for sake of food and cloth. The *sumas* were privileged serfs, who paid taxes in kind to the aristocracy and ran errands for them. There were other types of slaves as well. It was an extremely violent, unequal, and exploitative system in which commoners had a difficult time. No wonder, many of them turned to the monasteries for the life of the clergy.

In such a situation, one may surmise the welcome waiting for the members of the mission (Bangchen) sent to levy fines/penalty to the defaulting peasants. There existed a number of officials at the district level, who consumed the bulk of revenue paid in kind. For example, there existed till the 1960s in every *dzong* (fort) the post of a fodder master, a chief of stable, a cattle master, a meat master, a gate collector, a senior store master, a chamberlain, a chief attendant, a guest master, a fort governor, and so on. Needless to add, all these functionaries had an impressive array of staff under them to help perform their official duties. Evidently, any tax reform intended to alleviate the sufferings of the peasantry equally demanded an administrative reform.

The Lhotshampas were subjected to a classical tenancy pattern. As the southern foothill were assigned to the Dorji family since the 1890s to develop the region through the migrant Nepalese labour, these newly settled tenants did not pay taxes in kind. However, they were also not free from labour tax. The Dorjis collected taxes from the heads of the families through their contractual officials in cash, on the basis of cultivated land, number of cattle, fruit, and other considerations. Even the Dorjis did not transmit the collected taxes regularly to the king. However, they were supposed to provide for the cash requirements of the ruler and his establishment as and when required.

Stimuli for the Ethnic Conflict and Strategy to Tackle it

We have enumerated elsewhere the steps initiated by the Durkpa establishment to contain the alleged demographic invasion of the Lhotshampas (Sinha, 2002). These may be recounted as (*a*) the Bhutan Citizenship Act, 1985, (*b*) the Green Belt Policy, and (*c*) the Population Census 1988. These steps created so much upheaval among the Lhotshampas that they failed to comprehend the situation initially in the absence of a tradition of acknowledged dissent. By June 1990, students, teachers, bureaucrats, village headmen, and even *chimes* (the members of the Tshongdu), all felt so suffocated that they began to attack state property, schools, offices, factories, workshops, electric installations, and even loyal state functionaries. They spontaneously organized the common people, agitators, students, teachers, and all the sundry elements under the banner of the Bhutan Peoples Party in June 1990. The police and army of the Royal Government of Bhutan were equally determined to suppress the dissension. As their homes and settlements were no longer safe shelters against organized state terror, the dissident Lhotshampas fled from Bhutan first to India and then to Nepal. The refugee exodus significantly picked up after the demonstration at Samchi in September 1990. And within two years, their number swelled to about a hundred thousand: 70,000 in the United Nation High Commission for Refugees (UNHCR) run refugee camps in Nepal and the rest scattered in India.

The Royal Government of Bhutan decided to reverse its ethnic policy of assimilating the Lhotshampas within the Drukpa fold. The earlier efforts to find commonality between the Drukpas and the Lhotshampas were discarded. Teaching of Nepali and Sanskrit was stopped. Monetary award to couples engaged in inter-ethnic marriages was discontinued. State holidays on significant Nepali festivals were given up altogether or were reduced to the bare minimum.

For example, the *Dasai* holiday, which used to be five days in a year, has been reduced to one day. The three-day long *Diwali* holiday has been done away with and so has the festival of *Holi*.

Rounds of talks between the delegates of the Royal Government of Bhutan (RGB) and the Royal Government of Nepal (RGN), were held alternately in the two royal capitals at Kathmandu and Thimphu, respectively, for as long as about 10 years. After the initial bickering and impasse, the two sides agreed to verify the identities of the refugee family lineage and the individuals, as demanded by the RGB. By December 2001, the Joint Verification Team had checked the papers of 12,374 refugees from 1,960 families at Damak and eastern Nepal and found that almost all of them wanted to go back to their respective lands in Bhutan from where they were allegedly evicted. However, the RGB is silently and stealthily resettling the shifting cultivators and alleged landless Drukpas from the 'north' on the land left behind by the Lhotshampas refugees. This development was first mildly disclaimed and then grudgingly accepted on the plea that even the RGB had limited land for its landless farmers from the north who needed to be settled in the 'south'.

The RGB adopted a four-pronged strategy to tackle the international outcry in favour of the suppressed Lhotshampas: (*a*) expanding and consolidating their hold on the nation, (*b*) façade of talks and verifications of the refugees in the UNHCR camps, (*c*) building pressure on the left-over Lhotshampas in Bhutan, and (*d*) using the presence of the ULFA/National Democratic Front of Bodoland (NDFB) insurgents in Bhutan to stall the refugee and resettlement (Sinha, 2003a). The RGB continued to negotiate with the ULFA/NDFB insurgents to leave Bhutan peacefully and willingly. The Indian rebels, flushed out of Bangladesh and India found sanctuary in thinly populated and poorly defended eastern Bhutanese districts. At one time, they had as many as 32 camps in Bhutan. When the RGB threatened to use force to expel the unwelcome guests, the ULFA even threatened to blast away the Thimphu palace of His Majesty, the King. There are unconfirmed reports that some of the state functionaries were even provided with inducements by the ULFA. The rebels used a two-pronged strategy vis-à-vis the RGB: they used threat and inducement. They paid a very handsome price to the villagers for the commodities they procured from them so that they did not turn hostile to the rebels. Ultimately, the RGB had to use force to flush them out.

It is said that an agreement was reached between the rebels and the RGB to the effect that the former would disband four of the nine rebel camps by December 2001. In case the agreement was not honoured, the RGB might use armed forces to evict the unwanted guests. The Government of India had been pressing the RGB to jointly flush the rebels out of Bhutan. The RGB has been avoiding confronting the rebels as well as seeking armed support from India in this context. It goes without saying that the insurgents were located in the districts that are predominantly settled by the Lhotshampas. Anticipating a potential linkage between the two, the RGB advised the Lhotshampas to vacate their settlements and shift to a safer region preferably in the 'north'. The Lhotshampas saw it differently. They felt that the RGB was using the opportunity to displace them from the fertile and well developed agricultural fields to the barren north.

This kind of a situation was reported from thickly populated Bhanthar sub-division of Samdruk Jongkhar District, the south-eastern most part of Bhutan. The Lhotshampas of Bhantar were advised to shift to safe places in the north. Or, they could remain in site at their own risk, as the RGB was not in a position to provide them with security against the imagined onslaught of the rebels. The residents saw through the game played by the establishment. They reasoned among themselves and realized that the land-hungry Drukpa functionaries were behind the eviction conspiracy. They felt that once they left their land, they would have no control on the affairs, and the only alternative left to them would be to join their brethren in the refugee camps as all the promises of alternative land would vanish in the thin air. Incidentally, the settlers' dilemma was resolved by the rebels, who advised the harassed farmers to say put and promised to see to it that the former did not suffer because of the presence of the latter.

The Triangle-ULFA/NDFB: NGALOP and the Druk Establishment

The RGB frequently alleges that the Lhotshampas refugees from their camps in Nepal terrorize the Drukpa subjects inside south-west Bhutan and even the Drukpas travelling in northern

West Bengal (Kuensel, Vol. XVII, nos 6.5). On the eastern side, it was reported that the Indian rebels holed up in Bhutan got a much-frequented hi-Fi guest house located at the district town of Samdruk Jongkhar bombed. The RGB has also been raising an issue of the Lhotshampas involvement in the movement for Greater Nepal in the eastern Himalayan region (Dixit, 2002). Apparently, the bogey of Nepali design on the eastern Himalayan foothills was raised as a propaganda and, thus, nobody took it seriously. However, a vague warning was issued on the part of Lhotshampa refugees (Dhakal and Strawn 1994) way back in 1994.

The future of the Greater Nepal scenario is uncertain, but several factors could shape existing tensions into a violent reality. The Nepali Bhutanese really have not developed their external links, not even with Darjeeling and Sikkim. Outside the region, there are other terrorist groups and, of course, China, which the Nepalis could approach for links. Needless to say, this would create a virtual war, and Nepal would probably resettle the refugees in Nepal rather than risk an all out war with India. If all the conditions are there, if the violence seems the only option for the refugees, Nepal and Darjeeling in India could face a frighteningly serious terrorist movement, a disturbance of a Himalayan scale. This plan might have its supporters, and there are plenty of people. Possibly militants in Assam and Darjeeling, people who fought for themselves and achieved little, would support this kind of action for their own gain—this is probably something that New Delhi cannot and should not take lightly.

The presence of Indian rebels in Bhutan was simply intriguing, to say the least. It appears that a segment of the RGB was hand in glove with the ULFA/NDFB as a counter-foil against the Lhotshampa refugees (Gopalakrishna and Saikia, 2001). The presence of the Indian rebels on Bhutanese soil would provide a counterbalance against the possible support to the Lhotshampas from the Indian and the Nepalese democratic forces. But the story is taking a sinister turn now in case the so-called *Ngalop* (the anti-national in Dzongkha, the Bhutanese national language).

The 10th Ministerial Joint Committee (MJC) in 2000 had established the joint verification team of the Bhutanese and the Nepalese officials to categorize into four the refugees claims of being bonafide Lhotshampas. The respective positions of the two sides were harmonized is 2003 and 3,158 families from the first camp of

Khundanbari were divided into four agreed categories (Kuensel, 2003: Vol. XVIII, no. 10). Among them, 74 families were identified as bona fide Bhutanese, 2,182 families were termed as the Bhutanese, who claimed to have emigrated forcefully, as much as 817 families were found to be non-Bhutanese, and only 85 families belonged to the Bhutanese, who had committed criminal acts in Bhutan. As both the governments have agreed to these stipulations, the refugees have had little options left to them and continue to wait for its implementation.

The Tshongdu, the national assembly, debated the issue threadbare on the floor of the house and Lynop Jigme Thinely, the foreign minister, explained the implications of the four-point categorization of the refugee, 'the bona fide 74 Bhutanese families consisting of 293 persons would be repatriated to Bhutan from September onwards this year. On their arrival in Bhutan they would be given full citizen's status and all the right and privileges enjoyed by a Bhutanese citizen' (Kuensel, 2003: Vol. XVIII, no. 10). Thinely explained that some of the people placed in this category were those who had proved that they were served with written eviction notices. Further, the minister informed the House that, in early 1990, some officials and *gups* (headmen) had gone beyond the call of duty and had issued eviction notices to the Lhotshampas.

Second, the Bhutanese who emigrated to Nepal willingly will be permitted to apply for Nepalese citizenship in accordance with the law of the land. Those of the emigrants, who were forcefully evicted from Bhutan and were willing to return will be permitted to re-apply for citizenship. It is the most numerous category in which 2,182 families and 8,595 persons are affected. Re-application for Bhutanese citizenship is permitted under provisions of the Citizenship Act of Bhutan. Article NGAI of the Citizenship Act, 1977, stipulates that if a Bhutanese citizen, having left the country, returns and applies for citizenship, his application will be kept pending on probation for a period of at least two years. Citizenship will be granted to him provided he has not been responsible for any activities against the government during the probation. It is possible that some of these people may apply for Bhutanese citizenship. They shall be dealt with under the provisions of the law of the land.

Third, 817 families of non-Bhutanese extraction must return to their respective countries. Fourth, 85 families falling in the fourth category had criminal records behind them such as: (*a*) terrorist activities, (*b*) destruction of schools, bridges, and other service facilities, (*c*) violent demonstration, (*d*) kidnapping, extortion, and blackmail, (*e*) loan default, embezzlement of public funds, and (*f*) attempts to undermine Bhutan's good relations with neighbouring and donor countries. On their arrival in Bhutan, they will be handed over to the police for custody. They shall be charged for their crimes in the high court and will be given an opportunity to prove their innocence. If they are innocent, they shall be treated as if they fall under the second category. And those who are found guilty by the court will serve their full sentences.

When Lhotshampas refugees and the ULFA/NDFB coordinate their anti-state actions, one wonders why the RGB has bargained for such an eventuality? One may take even an indulgent view that India, with her five-decade old experience of counter-insurgency, may face the situation some way or another, but how will the poorly manned, ill-equipped, and inexperienced RGB forces fare in the confrontation? It goes without saying that Bhutan, by its own admission, is undergoing a phase of low intensity conflict. It is maintaining its armed presence in southern Bhutan, right from Samchi in the west to Bhanthar in the east. Its limited human and material resources are overstretched and, in spite of all the bravado, it is finding it hard to maintain a semblance of presence within the region.

Jaideep Saikia (2001) reported on a possible ULFA-RGB coalition in terms of a temporary gain in logistics and manoeuvring. The Indian Press reported that ULFA was desperately trying to gain the status in the Unrepresented Nations Peoples' Organization (UNPO). So much so, that it claimed to invite two European human rights activists on 7 April 2002, on its raising day at their clandestine camp at Marshala in Bhutan (*The Telegraph*, 7 April 2002). Needless to add, the Marshala ULFA camp is one of the leftover camps ideally located on the most strategic vantage point and shortest route between their Bhutanese haven and their Bangladesh sanctuary. Its location on the riverine and marshy *char* land of the Manas and Brahmputra rivers and the Manas Wild Forest Sanctuary suits human trafficking across the three countries.

This scenario invites our attention to a shared destiny of the SAARC countries. Is it not ironic that professed anti-national elements have clandestinely been defying national barriers for their anti-national activities and the 'states', which are recognized representatives of the people, are helpless to do any thing positive? National priorities, ideologies, ethos, ego, and vanity—all are all right to the extent that they contribute to the well being of citizens. It looks like every thing for which SAARC was envisioned, such as the Bhutanese ethnic conflict, is taking place but its charter and noble objectives remain largely unattended. It is a fact that some of the founding leaders could see the limits of the SAARC agenda. But should the future generation be a captive of past helplessness? In a recent academic conclave on the comprehensive security of South Asia, a noted Nepalese scholar, M.P. Lohani, rightly identified the urgent agenda for regional security: 'The common threats [for the region], include ethnic crisis, national and trans-national terrorism, religious fundamentalism, atmospheric pollution, poverty, trans-border migration and re-definition of state sovereignty in accordance with the burgeoning trend of supranationalism' (Lohani, 2001: 105).

French diplomat, Thierry Mathou, has identified three circles of Bhutanese foreign policies since 1961: the Indian circle, the regional circle, and the multilateral circle (Mathou, 1994). He also found its diplomatic policy steady, cautious, and remarkably stable. The Bhutanese elite realized the existential reality of South Asia much earlier than most of her partners among the SAARC countries. According to a former foreign minister: India, by virtue of its size and technological achievements, has a pre-eminent role in the region. The smaller South Asian countries have to live with this reality. However, it is not clear how deep the Indian factor is in the on going conflict in Bhutan. As per the past practice there must have been consultation between the two. But the view that Indian advice would prevail in all cases is to expect too much. However, one must hasten to add that there is an impression that Indian silence on ethnic conflict in Bhutan is too eloquent to be ignored. Is India alienating Nepal at the cost of Bhutan?

Unfortunately, this is the impression among a section of the Indian intelligentsia. It is a fact that the entire Himalayan region, from Kashmir in the west to the northeast Indian states in the east has turned into a zone of conflict. Besides India, the two Himalayan kingdoms are embroiled in the worst type of conflicts ever experienced by them. In such a situation, the Indian experience to handle inter-state issues should have come handy to the smaller neighbours. But it appears that India turned out to be a prisoner of her own priorities. In the words of the former Indian foreign secretary, J.N. Dixit,

> India seems to be imprisoned in a jacket of assertiveness and excessively narrow Indo-centric considerations. The argument that India should be generous with its smaller neighbours put forward by some analysts is not a relevant point. Generosity smacks of a certain incipient big brotherly hegemonic attitude. A co-operative and accommodating approach towards Nepal is of a most vital interest to India in political, geostrategic and economic terms. Good Indo-Nepalese relations have ramifications for our relations with other neighbours in the South Asian Association for Regional Co-operation as well as China. This is the empirical reality to which our Nepal policy should respond (Dixit, 2002).

Roughly, for the last two decades the Druk-Gyalpo had been talking about gross national happiness (GHP) instead of gross national product (GNP) as the cardinal concern of the Bhutanese strategy of development planning. By this he means that for the Bhutanese development planners, (*a*) economic growth and development, (*b*) preservation and promotion of cultural heritage, (*c*) preservation and sustainable use of environment, and (*d*) good governance, are the nodal points of the philosophy of national planning. This strategy of planning specially views development as a continuous process of balancing between the material and intangible needs of individual and society. It is pleaded that this should be seen against the universal concern for measuring the achievements of development in a country through statistics invariably forgetting the 'individual'. The Bhutanese effort should also be seen in its uniquely indigenous Buddhist tradition of concern for all forms of life. But critics of the royal approach see it as a camouflage for its poor showing as a developing country. No doubt, Bhutan is counted among the least developed countries (LDCs) of the world. Even in the ancient Greek city states such as Athens, there were citizens and slaves, and all the civic rules were meant for the citizens and life of the slaves could border on the animals. Perhaps drawing a leaf from the ancient Greece, Bhutan seeks all the elements of Gross National Happiness (GNH) for the Drukpas and they maintain a different yardstick for the left over Lhotshampas. And thus, one could look at the plight of the Lhotshampas in Bhutan, who continue to remain on the margin of existence, beyond the scope of the GHP. However, some steps have been taken by the Druk-Gyalpo during the last couple of years that may have serious consequences for the kingdom in the years to come.

Two Steps Forward and Three Steps Backward on the Lhotshampa Refugees

The RGB refuses to recognize the Lhotshampa refugees as a party to discuss their possible return to Bhutan, as a strategy to assert its mono-ethnic identity. In view of that, the RGN, the host of about a hundred thousand refugees languishing in the eastern Nepalese districts, was constrained to take up the issue with the RGB. The two governments held 15 rounds of talks alternately in two capitals to resolve the refugee problems. The 10th Ministerial Joint Committee (MJC) established in 2000 a joint verification team (JVT) consisting of five representatives each from both the governments for classifying the refugees into the four agreed categories. The positions of two governments were harmonized in 2003 with reference to 3,158 families of the first camp of Chidambaram, Jape District in eastern Nepal. Among them, 74 families were (*a*) bona fide Bhutanese, (*b*) 2,182 were termed as Bhutanese who claimed that they were forced to emigrated, (*c*) 817 families were found to be non-Bhutanese, and (*d*) only 85 families were identified as Bhutanese who had committed criminal acts in Bhutan (whether the criminals were individuals or the families). As both the governments had agreed to these stipulations, the refugees had little option, but to wait for its implementation (Kuensel, 2004: Vol. 28, no. 4). However, 575 people from 36 families registered in this camp could not be interviewed, as they were away from the camp in the hospital or engaged in some chores.

If one believes the foreign minister, there are bound to be many returnees from the refugee camps, who would be legally Bhutanese, and in spite of reservations on the part of Bhutan, they would have to be welcomed back to Bhutan. But the RGB is silently and stealthily settling the 'shifting cultivators' from the 'north' to the southern Duar on land left behind by the Lhotshampas refugees. Social scientist, Minar Rimple and human rights expert, Seema Mishra, prepared a special report on behalf of 'Habitat Coalition' on Lhotshampa refugees based on interviews conducted in September–October 2001. They found that the RGB had amended its citizenship laws retrospectively with a view to deny citizenship rights of the Lhotshampa refugees. The authors also found that the RGB was resettling the southern Nepalese fields with the landless

Drukpas from the 'north' (Sinha, 2003b). Ram Sharan Mahat, the then minister of finance, the RGN, and the leader of the Nepalese team to the JVT, reacted on behalf of the refugees: 'This is unfortunate. This will not be helpful in resolving the refugee issue. Forced resettlement of the "northerners" into southern Bhutan has always been the aim of the Druk regime. But we have been protesting the plan for a long time. Our position was and is that the Bhutanese refugees should be allowed to return to their original homes in a dignified manner. They had indicated that they would provide adequate land somewhere in the country. We are against this and want the refugees to be provided with their original homes'. However, Bhutan has informally informed Nepal that they too face the problem of landless settlers, particularly in the 'north,' and desired to settle them in the 'south' ignoring the fact that the southern Duars are the most thickly inhabited part of the country.

The announcement of the results of the verification team on 18 June 2003, led to a serious stir among the refugees residing in the various camps. Refugee demonstrators, numbering thousands, marched along the camp roads carrying placards and chanting slogans denouncing the results. Students abandoned their classes and joined the protest marches. Protest rallies were organized in Birtamod and in front of the office of the JVT at Damak. However, the refugees were encouraged to make their appeals against these decisions and submit their appeals within 15 days of the deadline. At long last, 94 per cent of the refugees falling in categories two, three and four from the Khudanabari camp filed their applications against the decision. The 15th JMLC met in Thimphu on 20–23 October 2003 and agreed to repatriate all the refugees from the Khudanabari camp from categories 1, 2, and 4 by 15 February 2004. The RGB also committed full coverage of the expenses that it would incur in the repatriation process.

In the words of one of the refugee activists:

> On 22 December [2003], three weeks after their arrival in Damak, the Bhutanese and [the] Nepalese representatives of the JVT scheduled a week long information campaign for the refugees in the Khudanabari camp to inform them about the conditions under which they are expected to return to Bhutan. The conditions revealed were extremely harsh, falling short of basic international standards of return. The assembled crowd became agitated with a heightened sense of anxiety and anger and there was no possibility for questions

> in a coherent manner, as many individuals were speaking together and [some] others began shouting. The situation resulted in a scuffle between the refugees and the Bhutanese JVT members and as a consequence the Bhutanese JVT members left for Bhutan the very next day, cancelling the rest of their planned stay in Nepal. This incident derailed the whole bilateral process, and efforts are still being made by the RGN to put the process back on track. No repatriation movement started as planned in February 2004 (Adhikari, 2004).

Will these stipulations be applicable to the individuals or the families? All these stipulations are being debated and argued by others and also the most concerned people. The Lhotshampa refugees are deliberately being kept out from the entire process by the Bhutanese establishment. It is patently absurd that those, whose future is being debated, are not heard. And the result is frustration. This was exhibited last December as mentioned earlier, when the JVT visited the refugee camps in Nepal. For the last couple of years Nepal has been in turmoil. First, there was the massacre of the royal family by the crown prince, leading to the crowning of a new king. Then, the king dismissed the duly elected prime minister and disbanded parliament. The political parties are in the street agitating for restoration of their democratic rights. The king goes on experimenting with the office of the prime minister by appointing long-discredited politicians of the 'panchayati era'. Meanwhile, the country is faced with one of the most violent phases of its history in the form of the Maoist movement, in which armed forces and the royal establishment are the main targets. In fact, in the current chaotic situation of Nepal, everybody is against somebody. In this chaos, the Lhotshampa issue has been relegated to the margin of Nepalese concern. In fact, the Bhutanese policy-makers are enjoying the discomfort on the part of the Lhotshampa spokesmen. They happily announced that they were ready to take steps to resolve the issue, but the delegates of the RGN did not turn up due to the confused national political scenario in the country. In the process, the agony of the Lhotshampa refugees has been further prolonged.

But how long will this uncertain situation be permitted to continue? In the words of a perceptive scholar, though

> the Bhutanese strategy had not been conceived in a geopolitical vacuum: forces beyond the kingdom's control swirled and buffeted it.... Yet to accept that the Lhotshampas, who remained in Bhutan would have to live, as one informant put it, "with heads hung low",

> would be implicitly to assent to the preposition that the extent to which a nation affords human and cultural rights to its members is in some way related to its size and location; that the mono-ethnic states are viable, while multi-cultural states are not. It would also be to surrender to the hegemony of the idea, which constructs Bhutan, as "essentially", and "exotically particular kind of place"—a typological stereotype (Hutt, 2003: 281–82).

Perhaps, chaotic political conditions in Nepal made RGB bold enough to ignore the Lhotshampas pathetic plight in the past. In the now changed political equations in Nepal, it appears that difficult days are ahead for the managers of the ethnic policy of Bhutan.

Flushing out the Indian Insurgents Sheltered in South-eastern Bhutan

It is not surprising that the Indian rebels began to descend on the Bhutanese hills and forests during the period of exodus of the Lhotshampa refugees to Nepal. It is alleged that Bhutan

> wanted to utilize the militant infiltrators as a bargaining chip to discourage India from supporting any pro-democracy movement in Bhutan; to maintain a neutral stand on Bhutanese refugees and to pressure India to extradite United Front for Democracy (UFD) leader Rongthong Kuenley Dorji (Lama, 2004: 18).

Even RGB representatives accepted that the rebels were helped in a number of ways in Bhutan, including overt and covert support, by state functionaries. But the unwelcome guests continued to stay ignoring even mild protests from the RGB. They increased their presence in number and association, and in course of time there were as many as 32 known camps operating in the country. The government of Bhutan was forced to open negotiation with the rebel to withdraw from their country voluntarily within a time frame. But it was not to be. The ULFA leadership even threatened to blow up the royal palace in the event of a crack-down on them. There were long debates, on the presence of rebels in Bhutan, on the floor of the Bhutanese National Assembly.

So much indulgence was involved that a number of well-placed functionaries were reportedly provided a variety of support to the unwelcome guests (Saikia, 2003). *Kuensel*, Bhutan's National

Newspaper, reports that 111 collaborators were sentenced after the operation flush out. It is entirely a different matter that as much as 60 per cent of the convicts were Lhotshampas, which may be interpreted in more than one way. We had earlier hinted a possible coalition between the Lhotshampa dissenters and the Indian insurgents (Sinha, 2003b). There is another possibility. Given the situation, the Royal Government might have used the ploy to further harass the beleaguered Lhotshampas. The RGB will use any cudgel to beat them and show them in bad light. In this context, the Green Belt Policy, adopted by the Tshongdu on 19–20 March 1990, and subsequently abandoned, may be mentioned. It was obvious that this policy was meant for harassing and evicting the Lhotshampas from their patrimony.

At long last, a number of developments occurred, which forced the RGB to order its armed forces to flush the rebels out of Bhutan. First, the Government of India was consistently demanding that the Indian rebels be expelled from Bhutan. The Bhutanese response was that the Assamese, Boros, and Kochs had been its traditional neighbours and Bhutan had to think seriously of its future relations with them in case it took action against the rebels. This reasoning never sounded logical to the Indians, as if India does not consist of these three ethnic groups. State leaders from Assam and West Bengal, military functionaries on state visits to Bhutan, diplomatic representatives and even the prime minister's principal secretary on security affairs suggested that the time was running out for Bhutan to take action against the rebels. Considering the sensitivity of the Bhutanese, regarding its territorial sanctity, the Indian armed forces scrupulously maintained a distance from Bhutanese territorial limits. At long last, while His Majesty was in India on a state visit in October 2003, the Druk-Gyalpo was 'very firmly' told by the Indian leadership about the action expected. The very next month, the newly appointed home and former prime minister and the 'Bhutanese Man of Crisis', Lyonpo Jigme Thinley, went to the rebels in view of the Tshongdu's resolution to finally negotiate a withdrawal from Bhutan.

Second, there have been demands on the floor of the Tshongdu to take action against the rebels. The rebels had been harassing Bhutanese subjects. Bus routes from the eastern part of Bhutan across the Indian highways was disrupted, passengers were killed when buses were ambushed, even members of the armed forces were not spared, and a senior army officer was killed. The Chimis were particularly upset with the rebels because they did not honour their words given to the RGB to close certain camps by 31 December 2001. So much so, that the rebels were operating from 304 villages affecting 66,464 individuals, and from 10 out of 20 districts in the country, that is, almost half of the country. A member of the house sounded the warning and told the RGB: 'We cannot wait until they reach the capital'.

Third, we had indicted the possible link and association between the rebels and the Lhotshampa refugees (Sinha, 2003c). We had also described the Banthar episode in which the Indian rebels (read ULFA) frustrated the efforts on the part of the RGB to dispossess the Lhotshampas of their fertile land on the plea that the government could not insure their security against rebels. Many of the disgruntled and frustrated young boys and girls were vulnerable to the Robin Hood style of the rebels. And the emergence of Bhutanese Communist Party (Marxist-Leninist-Maoist) (BCP [MLM]) was possibly the last straw. The Maoists (*Maobadis*) in Nepal were literally killing armed forces and policemen in Nepal almost every day. In case of a possible link between BCP-Lhotshampas, *Maobadis* and ULFA-NDFB-KLO, it would have been a nightmare for the Himalayan Shangri-La of Bhutan.

The RGB and the rebels held four rounds of talks between 1998 and 2001 to find a way so that the rebel camps could be dismantled. The talks led to no concrete steps in these regards. They turned out to be defiant and arrogant: 'If they met petrol of the Royal Army, they would refuse to give way... they were arrogant. It was unbearable. They were tremendously confident vis-à-vis their military prowess as far as Bhutan and India was concerned', informed the home minister of Bhutan with anguish to a journalist (Hazarika, 2004). As a last-ditch effort, the rebels were summoned to a meeting in October 2003, to get them to see reason and honour their commitment to leave the country peacefully. Then the RGB gave them a 48-hours ultimatum to leave Bhutan peacefully otherwise the Bhutanese armed forces would evict them forcefully. The rebels advanced a specious logic that as they were fighting for freedom from India and it was their right, for their survival, to be in Bhutan as long as their fight continued.

The RGB gave a 48-hour ultimatum to the rebels on 13 December and the Royal Bhutan Army was ordered to flush them out. The

16,000 strong Bhutanese army has largely been a ceremonial one, which had not seen any real action in the battlefield. It is an army, which is trained by the Indian Military (Indian Military Training Unit: IMTUNIT) and its top brass had been at the Indian Military Academy at Pune and Dehra Dun. The operation was swift and effective. It was reported that the king and one of the princes moved to the area of operation and guided the troops in actual operation. Within two days of its start on 15 December, all 32 rebel camps were dismantled; about 100 rebels were killed; about 500 of them were either captured or they surrendered; 27 children and 37 women were handed over to the Indian Military. The operation continued even after two weeks from its start, as the topography was mountainous and forested. The ULFA saw the operation as Bhutan's betrayal of its cause, and charged that it was largely an Indian Army operation. The Indian Army claimed that they did evacuate the wounded to the hospitals for urgent treatment and they did seal the Indo-Bhutanese borders so that no fugitive could take shelter in the south. Bhutan continues to be vigilant on its security threats for its future. Buses to its eastern parts are still not plying; necessary travel to the east is made in convoys, and trade and administration continue to be paralyzed. However, it appears that the ULFA menace is back in Bhutan. *The Statesman* reported from Calcutta on 14 August 2006 that ULFA insurgents had re-opened three camps in the south-eastern district of Samdruk Jongkhar.

Constitution Construction by the Courtiers

It appears that Ugyen Wangchuk deliberately chose the British colonial model of administration for his domain. He saw to it that no aristocracy emerged in the land as a potential challenge to the Wangchuk authority. In course of time, the British found Wangchuk's relative and associates, Ugyen and Sonam Dorji, more pliable and convenient to deal with. For the next six decades, the Wangchuks and Dorjis almost jointly ruled Bhutan. The writer of these lines remembers the apt remark made by a shrewd and educated Lhotshampa functionary in the late 1960s that the common people of Bhutan did not maintain a distinction between the two families and considered them as the 'joint rulers' of the country.

Things began to change fast after the assassination of Prime Minister Jigme Dorji in 1964. By then the first generation of educated Bhutanese from among the commoners had begun to appear on the scene, and by the mid-1970s they had begun to challenge the old order in a subtle way. Within a decade or so, this new category of the Bhutanese elite found the Drukpa polity crowded, and with a view to find enough space for themselves, they initiated with a nod from 'above' an ethnic conflict between the Drukpas and the Lhotshampas. And within a few years, Bhutan exploded with an unprecedented ethnic conflict, which is yet to be sorted out.

The Lhotshampa dissenters had been demanding that Bhutan must have a responsible government, a written constitution, and universal adult franchise. The Druk-Gyalpo is of the view that the Bhutanese system cannot afford all the tenets of democracy right now. In view of the prevailing circumstances, the democratic norms are being introduced slowly. The king had surrendered his role as the head of the administration in 1998 to an annually and indirectly elected council of ministers. However, he did not designate a prime minister and made a provision that the cabinet would have a chairman on the basis of annual rotation from among the six members initially selected by the Tshongdu, the Bhutanese national assembly. The candidates for the cabinet must have at least experience of being the deputy secretary or the above in the government. Thus, it will always be a body of select loyal government servants. It is pertinent to note that ever since the new experiment in cabinet making has started, not a single Lhotshampa has adorned the Drukpa cabinet unlike in the past.

In September 2001, the king took another significant step to appoint a Constituent Assembly to draft the Constitution for the country. Lyonpo Sonam Tobgyel heads the Constituent Assembly. Besides, there are the chief justice of the High Court and other 38 members. Apart from the chairman, other members of the body are: the Speaker of the Tshongdu, one representative each from the 20 district development councils (DYTs), the chairman and the members of the royal advisory council (ten), five representatives of the royal government and two lawyers from the High Court of Bhutan. Their mandate was 'to ensure the sovereignty and security of the nation and the well being of the Bhutanese people for all time to come. Bhutan must move with the time, ensure that the nation not only over comes all the internal and external threats, but also continue to prosper in an atmosphere of peace and stability'. Once more, it is the king, who desired the new constitutional dispensation for the people. Serious observers have not missed the point that in this new dispensation, there is no specific representation of the Lhotshampas, who were the first to voice such a demand in the kingdom.

By the end of 2002, a draft Constitution was ready for discussion and it was placed before the Tshongdu for its views. The Druk-Gyalpo commanded that the draft Constitution be debated all over the country and public opinion be sought on it. For that it was decided that every district development council would discuss the draft. It is intended that every proposed stipulation would be explained to the subjects in simple language. Once they understand them and accord their consent to them, only then these provisions will be placed before the Tshongdu for its consideration and possible approval. It is also intended that the Constitution should incorporate the time-tested traditional laws of the land propounded by the Shabdrung along with the modern tenets of democracy. Rules should be simple enough so that the common Bhutanese can understand them, remember them, and put them into practice.

The king and the crown prince have moved from district to district explaining the nuances of the 34-article constitution and educating the subjects about its nuances in a paternalistic style.

Article 2 of the Draft Constitution declares the king to be 'the head of the State and the symbol of the unity of the kingdom and people of Bhutan' who will retire at the age of 65. Article 4 requires the state to 'preserve, protect and promote' the linguistic heritage of the country. This could amount to the promotion of Dzongkha, the state language, and denial of rights of the Lhotshampas' language. The clause on spiritual heritage guarantees the continuation of religious variety under the traditional Lamaist rubric. Article 6 maintains the provisions of the Citizenship Act of 1985, which was extremely discriminatory towards the Lhotshampas leading to unrest, and their expulsion from the Shangri-la. Article 7 stipulates that those citizens will be deprived of their property by acquisition or requisition, and they are forbidden to sell their land to non-citizens. In a clever way, a legal framework has been woven to exclude the Lhotshampas' from a formal role in the body politic of Bhutan. It is ironic that it was the Lhotshampa dissenters who demanded constitutional monarchy and a written constitution, and once such provisions are in place, they will be the ones deliberately debarred from being a part of the polity.

Wangchuk rule in Bhutan completes a hundred years on 17 December 2007 and naturally a big celebration is on the way. Jigme Singye Wangchuk, born in 1955, succeeded the third Druk-Gyalpo, Jigme Wangchuk, his father, after his demise in 1972. He is the fourth and the longest ruling monarch of the dynasty. He has announced his abdication after the centenary celebration and enforcement of the new Constitution. He has already begun grooming the crown prince, Jigme Khesar Namgyel Wangchuk, to take over the task from him. With the new Constitution in place, a newly elected democratic government installed, secured financial assets in terms of revenue from hydropower sold to energy-starved India, and the Lhotshampas ethnic dissenters castrated, the ruler has really placed his successor on a sound footing, free from any immediate worries for a prosperous rule.

To conclude the discourse till the 1980s was that Bhutan was a model state in the South Asian region with a favourable 'land to man' ratio. Its king had an image of being a benevolent ruler, who encouraged integration of the Lhotshampas in its body politic. So much so, that its capital, Thimpu, was considered an ideal locale for holding 'peace talks', between the Government of Sri Lanka and the Liberation Tigers of Tamil Eelam (LTTE) in 1985. Since then much water has flown in the Torsha and Raidak rivers. Bhutan has joined the sister nations of the South Asia with its own form of ethnic conflict. We have tried to acquaint the readers with the ethnic scenario and the feudal social structure of Bhutan, which bred ethnic hostility. Second, we have traced out the stimuli for the conflict and the strategy adopted by the Drukpa state to cope with the ethnic flare up. Third, we have tried to caution the concerned citizens of the SAARC nations about the pitfall of the Bhutanese situation, in which there is a possibility of a linkage between the Lhotshampa refugees and the Indian rebels holed up in south-eastern Bhutan. God forbid, if this were to happen, considering the limited experience in handling violent ethnic conflicts and also resources in terms of manpower and materials available to it, the RGB is simply not capable of managing the emergent scenario. It is already aggravated with the existing explosive ethnic situation. As a concerned student of the northeastern Indian ethnic scenario, we apprehend an ominous development, fraught with serious consequences for the region.

We have tried to review the most significant events in Bhutan during the last couple of years in the direction of resolution of the ethnic conflict. Among them, we came across three significant issues confronted by the Drukpa regime on which certain steps were taken to give them a direction. It is not that all three of them have been solved, but decisive measures have been initiated for their resolution. First among them was the issue of the Lhotshampa refugees in the Nepal. This issue between the two royal governments is partly stalled because of the political uncertainty in the body politic of Nepal and excessive touchiness of the Bhutanese members of the JVT. However, to us it appears unfair to ignore the refugee representatives in this regard. Unless they are associated with moves to find a solution to their uncertain future in the camps, there is no hope for an acceptable solution to the problem and an end to the refugees' misery. But a very serious and disturbing development is under way in Bhutan. And that is the efforts made by the Bhutanese regime to reorient its polity from its limited pluralistic form to a mono-cultural base, in which the Lhotshampas will have no role to play. Second, the Bhutanese actions against the Indian rebels holed up in its eastern parts exposes the delicate leverage the Drukpa regime has in the inter-ethnic conflicts in the region. It also uncovers the limits of the claimed mono-cultural context of the Bhutanese nation-state. Bhutan is still apprehensive of the aftermath of its actions. And lastly, one expects that the Constitution making exercise in Bhutan may not be reduced to another farce in the name of the country's uniqueness. After all, the process of democratization is being accomplished on the express demand of the time and it has to incorporate the concern of democratic opinion expressed universally for meaningful representation. A Constitution may draw inspiration from past tradition of the land, but it is certainly a document controlling the lives and times of the living generations and their progeny, who are yet to be born. It has to be the pole star for the future, which guides them in the darkness. Once these initiatives are taken to their logical completion, a hope may emerge on the Bhutanese horizon (Sinha, 2004).

NOTE

1. Essentially low intensity conflict (LIC), is armed conflict for political purposes, short of a direct combat between the regular armed forces. Such

conflicts are ambiguous, and conventional, and very often develop into war of attrition. LIC poses a serious and long-term threat to nation-building exercises and regional peace and security. LIC subsumes guerrilla wars, insurgency, separatist movements, insurrections, communal violence, terrorism etc. There is little evidence of LIC declining. On the contrary, LIC is on the rise because it is more cost-effective, especially in the short term, than conventional war and because it carries less risk of escalation. Cold war had a restraining influence on the eruption and spread of LIC. Its subsidence has realistic and cost-effective solution to many groups pursuing different political, ideological and territorial goals, heightened aspirations of the people, improved means of communication, and easy availability of light weight sophisticated weapons have ensured that various ethnic, racial and religious issues turn into uncompromising demands for self-determination and political independence. All these factors make LIC both desirable and possible. Refer Mishra (2001).

References

Adhikari, Khem, K. (2004). 'Bhutanese Refuges in Nepal' at the UNHCR Round Table, Solution for Refugees: A Place to Call Home, IIC New Delhi, 18 June.

Dhakal, D.N.S. and Christopher Strawn (1994). *Bhutan: A Movement in Exile*. Jaipur: Nirala Publication.

Dixit, J.N. (2002). 'Borderline Friendship', *The Telegraph* (Kolkata and Guwahati), 5 April.

Gopalakrishna, R. and J. Saikia (2001). *Development Challenge in India, Assam in 21st Century*. New Delhi: Omson Publication.

Hazarika, S. (2004) 'Bhutan: Strength sans Showmanship', *The Statesman*, 9 June.

Hutt, M. (2003). *Unbecoming Citizens: Culture, Nationhood and Flight of Refugees from Bhutan*. New Delhi: Oxford University Press.

Kuensel, *News Bulletin*, Vol. XVII, Nos 6 & 5, The Royal Government of Bhutan, Thimphu.

——— (2002). *News Bulletin*, Vol. XVII, Nos 5 & 6, The Royal Government of Bhutan, Thimphu.

——— (2003). *News Bulletin*, Vol. XVIII, No. 10, The Royal Government of Bhutan, Thimphu.

Lama, Mahendra P. (2004). 'Experiments with Democracy', *Frontline*, vol. XXI, No. 1, 3–16 January, pp. 17–21.

Lohani, M.P. (2001). 'Nepal', in *Contemporary Security for South Asia*, edited by Delhi Policy Group. New Delhi: India Habitat Centre, p. 105.

Mathou, T. (1994). 'The Growth of Diplomacy in Bhutan, 1961–1991: Opportunities and Challenge', in M. Aris and M. Hutt (eds), *Bhutan: Aspects of Culture and Development* (London, Kiscadale Asia Research series, No. 5), pp. 51–85.

Mishra, O.P. (2001). 'Intensity Conflict and the Challenge of Forced Displacement in Northeast India', Draft paper in the Low Intensity Conflict in Eastern India, Department of International Relations, Jadavpur University, Kolkata.

Saikia, Jaideep (2001). *Contour*. Guwahati: Sagittarius.

———— (2003). 'Terrorism Sans Frontiers: ULFA Digs Deeper in Bhutan', in O.P. Mishra and Sucheta Ghosh (eds), *Terrorism and Low Intensity Conflict in South Asian Region*, pp. 447–79. New Delhi: Manak Publications.

Sinha, A.C. (1998). *Bhutan: Ethnic Identity and National Dilemma*. New Delhi: Reliance.

———— (2002). 'Dialogue Between Deaf and Dumb: The Lhotshampa Refugees and Their President', in C.J. Thomas (ed.), *Dimensions of Displaced People in North-East India*. New Delhi: Regency Publication.

———— (2003a). 'Terrorism and Low Intensity Conflict in Bhutan', Seminar on 'Terrorism and Low Intensity Conflict in Eastern India', Department of International Relations, Jadavpur University, Kolkata.

———— (2003b). 'Terrorism in and Low Intensity Conflict in Bhutan', in O.P. Mishra and Suchita Ghosh (eds), *Terrorism and Low Intensity Conflict in South Asian Region*. New Delhi: Manak Publications.

———— (2003c). 'The Indians of Nepali Origin and Security of Northeast India', in A.C. Sinha and T.B. Subba (eds), *The Nepalis in Northeast India: A Community in Search of Indian Identity*. New Delhi: Indus Publishing Company.

———— (2004). *Himalayan Kingdom Bhutan: Tradition, Transition and Transformation*. New Delhi: Indus Publishing Company.

10

India–Pakistan Conflict over Kashmir: Peace through Development Cooperation*

Rajen Harshe

The course of the bilateral relationship between India and Pakistan, ever since the inception of these two states in 1947, has never been smooth. Differences over a wide range of issues, such as the lack of a mutually acceptable international border, the sharing of resources, including water resources, the role and status of religious minorities in the respective countries, and to top it all the unresolved question of the status of Kashmir, have perennially placed India and Pakistan in an adversarial mould. The two countries have already fought three major and two minor wars since their Independence. Moreover, the arms race between the two countries has reached a point where the two adversaries, by exploding nuclear devices in 1998, have transformed the South Asian region into a plausible theatre of nuclear conflict.

The ongoing peace efforts through détente between the two countries, initiated since the Lahore (1999) and Agra (2001) summits, have started showing positive results, as manifested in the resumption of the Delhi–Lahore bus service and also the growing interaction between the two countries in the domains of culture, sports, economy, and trade. Since the beginning of 2004, the two countries have formally set in motion the process of composite bilateral

* Reprinted with permission from the *South Asian Survey*, 12(1), 2005: 47–60.

dialogue to promote cooperation and resolve all their outstanding differences, including those over the status of Kashmir, in a time-bound framework. Irrespective of these developments, the resolution of conflict over the Kashmir issue still appears distant. Over the past five decades, people in the Indian as well as Pakistani part of Kashmir have consistently been forced to live in the shadow of insecurity with Kashmir becoming the site of an acute contest between the two adversaries. In fact, the conflict has inevitably led to the loss of lives and property and a continuous flow of refugees from Kashmir into different parts of India and Pakistan.

This chapter essentially argues that the causes for the Kashmir conflict are rooted in the processes of state formation and nation-building in India and Pakistan since Partition. As resolution of the Kashmir question depends on favourable India–Pakistan ties, this chapter offers constructive alternatives to prevent conflicts and improve India–Pakistan relations, on the basis of prevailing realities, in two ways. First, it reflects briefly on the possible measures to reconstruct the conflict-ravaged state of Kashmir. Second, it underscores the significance of peace-related projects built through trade and development cooperation—projects that have so far been neglected. Since this exercise is going to revolve around the notions of state formation, nation-building, and regional cooperation, it is important to situate a few key terms within this discourse.

Situating Key Terms

The keys terms that constitute conventional concepts in any social scientific inquiry such as state, identity, nation, and ethnicity form a crucial part of this analysis. In fact, continued encounters with complex social realities in South Asia have enriched the explanatory potentials of these intrinsically dynamic terms. In view of this, let me place them in the South Asian setting. In substance, as a juridical entity, the state performs coercive as well as extractive functions. It represents an association with a virtual monopoly of organized physical force at its command. The organization of such a force could be legitimate or even illegitimate; the military dictatorships that have ruled Pakistan at various times since the 1950s hardly enjoyed any legitimacy comparable to popularly elected democratic regimes. Perceived with a little more imagination, the state could be construed as a complex historical formation that continuously interacts with larger social identities like classes as well as linguistic, racial, religious, tribal, and ethnic communities. The identities of the larger social groups are built and internalized around a sameness by exacerbating the distinction between 'self' and the 'other'. And the ongoing and vibrant interactions between the state structures and identities have built-in potentials to create or recreate new state structures.

Unlike the state, the nation is a psycho-cultural concept. Elements of both ethnic-cultural and civic-territorial realities are fused into building the construct of a nation (Einagel, 1997: 232–52). While ethno-cultural realities help in constructing biographical narratives of a nation, civic territorial realities endow any nation with notions of citizenship. The notion of citizenship, in its turn, is operative within the defined geographical border of a nation through the state. Furthermore, the geographical basis of any nation is socially constructed with the help of the boundaries of the territorial state. Finally, in spite of the significant role of ethnicity in nation and state formation, it is difficult to define the term ethnicity with some precision. Suffice it to mention that ethnic identities manifest themselves through the formation of regions as well as through religious, racial, tribal, caste, and language communities in the overall South Asian context. It also needs to be noted that larger social identities do not function as watertight compartments. In most socially plural and heterogeneous societies, identities tend to be fluid, multiple, and hence overlapping. Keeping the contextual significance of these key terms in mind, I shall proceed to reflect on the state-formation and nation-building processes in India and Pakistan.

State and Nation-Building in India and Pakistan

The processes of state-formation and nation-building in India and Pakistan were shaped by an act of surgical Partition of the Indian subcontinent. Looking back at the post-Second World War years, it becomes evident that the process of Partition assumed two predominant forms. The first form was related to the outcome of the

Second World War as also the Cold War—that eventually led to the Partition of Germany, Korea, and Vietnam. The second type of Partition was related to decolonization. The Partition of the Indian subcontinent fell into the latter category. With Partition, India and Pakistan had to socially reconstruct and imagine their respective and distinct notions of national identities over the territorial states legitimized by the post-Partition map.

After Partition, there have been two dominant versions of imagining India. Out of these, the first version that upheld the notion of secular India was dominant for almost four decades after Independence. It must be recognized that the term 'secular' appears rather vague in the Indian context. It can imply either a religion-neutral state or equal respect to all religions. In essence, secularism would imply disallowing religious or communal considerations from having an impact on any vital public decision. In fact, leaders like Nehru worked tirelessly to translate their notion of secular India at the level of praxis. For instance, through memorable writings like *The Discovery of India,* Nehru emphasized the socially plural, inclusive, composite, and tolerant character of the people and civilizations that flourished in India (Nehru, 2002). Sanjay Chaturvedi argues that through such writings, Nehru consistently reconstructed the map of India so that over 3,000–4,000 communities would be able to visualize the geopolitical space of India under the comprehensive umbrella of secular nationalism. Under the Nehru regime (1947–64), the immediate post-Partition bitterness between the Muslim and the Hindu communities was overcome rather smoothly and the country plunged into the project of nation-building and modernization. As a part of social and political engineering, Nehru endeavoured to deploy the resources and manpower in India to promote gigantic developmental activities including the building of large dams like the Bhakra Nangal and steel plants like the one built at Bhilai. Simultaneously, a plethora of scientific research institutions such as the Indian Institutes of Technology (IITs) and universities were built to provide trained manpower for developmental projects.

With the demise of Nehru in 1964 and the end of the one-party dominant system (run by the Indian National Congress) in 1967, the notion of secular nationalism began to face increasing challenges. The Congress regimes led by Indira Gandhi (1967–77 and 1980–84) and Rajiv Gandhi (1984–89) that succeeded the Nehru regime, did support secular nationalism, but not as convincingly as the Nehru regime. The covert support of Mrs Gandhi to fanatic religious leaders like Bhindranwale in Punjab, for short-term tactical purposes, and the susceptibility of the Rajiv Gandhi regime to the pressures of fundamentalist Muslim groups in the case of Shah Bano, a Muslim divorcee fighting for the right to receive alimony under the secular law of the land, are examples of this trend. In the process, the Congress regimes could neither evoke sympathy from the Hindu majority nor retain the support of the Muslim and Sikh minorities. Consequently, they could neither contain the massive tide of Hindu nationalism nor arrest the growth of Sikh and Kashmiri separatism, built on explicitly religious bases, by the late 1980s. This paved the way for the rise of Hindu nationalism.

In fact, Hindu nationalism constitutes the second important version of imagining India. The high priests of this version, such as Savarkar and Golwalkar, and their followers stood for making India a Hindu *rashtra* (nation). They wanted to give Hinduism a privileged position over any other religion and integrate India from the Indus to the seas on the basis of the dominant Hindu ethos (Golwalkar, 1939, 1966; Savarkar, 1989). This group had little following till the early 1990s. However, capitalizing on the deficiencies of the secular nationalist forces led by the Congress, the Bharatiya Janata Party (BJP) and its allied parties—the *Sangh Parivar*—began to grow after the mid-1980s to contest and unmask the pseudo-secularism of the secular nationalists. Events like the demolition of the Babri Masjid (1992), the rise of the BJP as the single largest party in the ruling coalition in the central governments (1998–2004), the growing strength of the *Sangh Parivar* and the forces of Hindu nationalism, have by now transformed the complexion of the political process in India. Moreover, as a consequence of the clash between the secular and fundamentalist forces, especially after the demolition of the Babri Masjid, the meanings as well as modes of executing secular policies have become an intensely contested area among the major political parties (Varshney, 1993: 227–61). Likewise, separatism in Punjab in the 1980s and ongoing separatist movements in Kashmir have once more brought home the role of religion and ethnicity in constructing modern nation-states. In a word, since secularism has become a contested concept within India, diverse political forces are imagining India as an entity in different ways. Perhaps the only silver lining is that India's vibrant liberal democracy has provided a space for diverse political forces to work out the meaning and status of secularism in the changing political context. The defeat of the BJP-led coalition in the 2004 General Elections, in a way, can be viewed as unwillingness on the part of the people to subscribe to the narrow agenda of Hindutva as propounded by the BJP. Hence they voted for the forces that were closer to 'secular' nationalism.

In contrast to India, the so-called two-nation theory has consistently haunted Pakistan's political evolution. In more ways than one, the birth of Pakistan was remarkable in the history of the formation of the nation-states. Like Israel, Pakistan was constituted fundamentally on the basis of religion (Ali, 1970). Obviously, the diverse linguistic communities were brought under the umbrella of Islam while constructing the notion of the nation-state in Pakistan. Moreover, the areas which had a predominantly Muslim population sprang up as natural candidates to form Pakistan. Initially the founding fathers of Pakistan conceived of it by separating the western, eastern, and southern parts of the subcontinent. The plans to carve out the southern wing of Pakistan through the state of Hyderabad were buried when the Government of India under Sardar Patel's stewardship integrated the State of Hyderabad, ruled by the Nizam, with the Indian Union.

Pakistan, unlike most contemporary nation-states, came up as a geographically non-contiguous state. Its western and eastern parts were separated by around 1,400 km, and these had little in common other than religion. Owing to the obvious linguistic and cultural differences between these two parts, it was difficult to bring about the national integration of Pakistan. The lack of internal cohesion virtually pushed the ruling elite in Pakistan to unite its population against an external enemy, India. The so-called inimical state of India was constructed in Pakistan through active propagation of the myth of aggressive designs of the Hindu majority in India over Pakistan. Thus, anti-Indianism became one of the important planks to keep Pakistan together. By constructing the notion of Hindu India, it was also easier to invoke the bond of Islamic affinity to unify Muslims of the two wings of Pakistan. However, Pakistan's failure to keep the two wings together eventually led to the birth of Bangladesh in 1971. Owing to its bifurcation, anti-Indian sentiments became more acute in Pakistan. Furthermore, unlike India, Pakistan alternated between civilian and military rule.

The instability of political regimes in Pakistan further induced insecure rulers in Pakistan to invoke anti-Indian stances to deflect the attention of the people from their poor performance.

It would be useful to analyse the status of disputed territories between India and Pakistan against the backdrop of state formation and nation-building processes in the two states. The Nawab of Junagarh had acceded to Pakistan by violating the principle of geographical continuity as well as people's aspirations. India took over the State of Junagarh in November 1947. The people approved this action of the Indian government in a plebiscite held in Junagarh early in 1948. The Nizam of Hyderabad was not keen to join India. The majority of the population of Hyderabad was being terrorized by a Muslim communal organization called the Razakars. Eventually, the Government of India opted for police action and the Nizam's forces were defeated. Ultimately, the Nizam agreed to the integration of Hyderabad with the Indian Union. In the process of constituting itself as a state, Pakistan could eventually reconcile itself to the integration of Junagarh and Hyderabad with India with some protest. But Pakistan fiercely opposed a similar integration of Kashmir. Unlike Hyderabad, the population of Kashmir was predominantly Muslim. The project of integrating a geographically contiguous Muslim state like Kashmir into Pakistan was a logical extension of the very notion of Pakistan and the two-nation theory that had brought the country into being. Since the Kashmir question has had a profound impact on peace and stability in South Asia, it would be worthwhile to analyse the strategic significance of Kashmir along with the legitimacy of the claims of contending power such as Pakistan and India over the territory of Kashmir.

Kashmir's Changing Strategic Significance

Being the source of the vital Indus River water system constituting the five rivers of Punjab—Jhelum, Chenab, Ravi, Beas, and Sutlej—Kashmir's significance for the predominantly agrarian economies of South Asia can hardly be underestimated. The Kashmir Valley has also been strategically important because of the communication links that it provides to Ladakh and Siachen. In fact, Kashmir began to enjoy enhanced strategic significance in the context of Cold

War dynamics. Kashmir shared common frontiers with India, Pakistan, Afghanistan, China, and the former Soviet Union. Even after the end of the Cold War, thanks to its location, Kashmir has become a gateway to South, South-west and Central Asia. Kashmir, therefore, has inevitably been affected by major developments in these regions. They include the flow of arms and drugs, the growth of cross-border terrorism and the rise of a host of fundamentalist movements that are promoting militant versions of Islam. Due to these movements, religion-based terrorism has become an important feature in the political landscape of several Central, West and South-west Asian states.

Kashmir is a keenly contested area between Pakistan and India because it is an integral part of the state-formation and nation-building processes in both the countries. Pakistan continues to perceive itself as an incomplete state devoid of strategic depth without the accession of Kashmir, a state with a predominantly Muslim population, within its territorial limits. In contrast, India fears that its project of building a secular nation would receive an irretrievable setback if India were to lose Kashmir. In addition to Pakistan and India, China has also become an involved actor in Kashmir after acquiring territory ceded by Pakistan following the Sino-Indian war of 1962. Thus, three nuclear powers, namely, India, Pakistan, and China have developed important stakes in Kashmir. Let me then proceed to analyse the claims of Pakistan and India over Kashmir.

Pakistan's Stance on Kashmir

From Pakistan's standpoint, India's occupation of Kashmir has been illegal because India has held on to Kashmir without going through the United Nations-supervised plebiscite. Paradoxically, it was the Nehru regime in India which ventured to introduce the Kashmir question in the UN in 1948. To garner support for its position on Kashmir, Pakistan initially turned to the Muslim world and later obtained military assistance from the United States (US) (Gupta, 1982). In 1953, the US entered into the politics of the subcontinent by providing weapons worth US$ 1.5 billion for 10 years to Pakistan. In the context of the Cold War, the US cultivated Pakistan along with Iran, Iraq, and Turkey as a part of its northern tier strategy, aimed at encircling the Soviet Union with US allies. What is more, Pakistan continued to be a significant US ally to counter the Soviet Union when the latter invaded Afghanistan in 1979. To counter the Soviet invasion of Afghanistan, the US offered US$ 2.36 billion worth of armaments to Pakistan between 1979 and 1988 (Harrison, 1997). In addition to US support, Pakistan took advantage of the growing Sino-Indian rivalry after the 1962 war between the two countries and sought Chinese support on Kashmir. China also provided assistance to Pakistan in its missile programme (Mattoo, 1997: 41–57). The growing Sino-Pak friendship only underscored the importance of Kashmir to India. By holding on to Kashmir, India could continue to press its claims over the Aksai Chin region of Ladakh, occupied by China, and ward off any threats to Punjab. Conversely, as Ramesh Thakur has put it, the loss of all of Kashmir would deprive Pakistan of the land link with its most important Asian ally and threaten its presence in strategically vital regions on the borders of Afghanistan and China (Thakur, 1994).

Apart from gathering support from major world powers like the US and China, Pakistan constantly exploited discontent among the people of the Kashmir Valley vis-à-vis successive central governments in India. During the 1980s, Pakistan went so far as to prop up diverse terrorist outfits in Kashmir in the hope of stage-managing the eventual secession of Kashmir from the Indian Union (Ganguly, 1996: 145–50, 1997: 414–18). Such efforts were crowned with success in the late 1980s when the people of Kashmir experienced an acute sense of alienation from the central government in New Delhi. What is more, the people in the Valley rendered clandestine support to secessionist organizations like the Jammu and Kashmir Liberation Front (JKLF).

The JKLF was built on Kashmiri sub-nationalism and had an ethno-cultural basis. However, after the Iranian revolution of 1979, the political process in Kashmir began to witness a new breed of nationalism that fused Islam and Kashmiri nationalism. Gradually the rise of organizations such as the Students Islamic Federation or Jamaat-e-Islami not only sharpened the religious component within Kashmiri nationalism, but also reinforced the links between Kashmir and Muslim countries such as Afghanistan that were swept by the tide of Islamic fundamentalism. After 1992, some of the prominent Muslim groupings like Hizbul Mujahidin began to openly characterize the Kashmiri struggle for self-determination as jihad.

Further, Maulana Saifullah Akhtar, president of the Harkat-e-Jihad-i-Islami, an Afghanistan-based organization spread over 19 countries with an active branch in Kashmir, announced its decision to participate in jihad in Kashmir in 1992 (Punjabi, 2000: 60–61).

Besides, the political process in Kashmir was affected by developments in Pakistan and Afghanistan after the Soviet intervention in Afghanistan in 1979. Pakistan became a frontline state in the US strategy designed to ensure the retreat of Soviet forces from Afghanistan. Subsequently, the acquisition of US weapons by Pakistan, which in turn armed the mujahidin groups fighting against the Soviet forces, unsettled the security contours in South and South-west Asia, especially after the retreat of the Soviet Union from Afghanistan in 1988. Indeed, Pakistan went as far as propping up the Taliban regime in Afghanistan (1994–2001). Owing to its deep involvement in Afghanistan, Pakistan had to handle the question of Afghan refugees on its own soil as well as problems related to the drugs and arms trade. Irrespective of this, Pakistan seldom fought shy of supporting secessionist and terrorist activities in Kashmir. For instance, in the political process of Kashmir, Pakistan openly supported the All Party Hurriyat Conference (APHC), which represented an ensemble of pro-Pakistani secessionist groups. In addition, Pakistan also retained and bolstered its links with the militants in Kashmir by glorifying them as freedom fighters. Recurrent dastardly acts performed by terrorist outfits sponsored by the Inter Services Intelligence (ISI) in the Kashmir Valley, in particular, and other parts of India—the hijacking of flight IC 814 from Kathmandu to Kandahar in December 1999 and the abortive attempt to bomb the Indian Parliament on 13 December 2001—offer ample evidence of Pakistan's activities and intentions. Not surprisingly, Pakistan-sponsored cross-border terrorism became a major roadblock in the India–Pakistan peace process (Harshe, 2003b: 3621–25).

India's Attempts to Integrate Kashmir

Throughout the five-and-a-half decades since Independence, India has constantly ventured to swing the people of Kashmir on its side. By introducing Article 370 in the Indian Constitution, the ruling classes in India agreed to give more autonomy to Kashmir than to other Indian states. Under Article 370, the Indian Parliament cannot legislate on items listed on either the Union or the Concurrent list of powers without the approval of Kashmir Legislative Assembly. Similarly, India constitutionally incorporated its portion of Jammu and Kashmir as a separate Indian state in 1957. Over the years, Kashmir was made a part of India as it went through periodic elections held under the Indian Constitution. To counter the US and later the Chinese support to Pakistan, India banked on Soviet support at the UN Security Council. The Soviet veto at the Security Council continued to block any moves towards a plebiscite on the Kashmir issue. India also obtained Soviet military assistance through various military cooperation agreements. Eventually India signed a 20-year treaty of peace, friendship, and cooperation with the Soviet Union in 1971 and ensured Soviet support for its policies on a durable basis. With the disintegration of Pakistan in 1971, India began to enjoy a commanding position in the subcontinent. The India–Pakistan agreement of Simla, signed in 1972, particularly its clause (ii), tried to restrict the scope of the Kashmir issue to the bilateral ties between the two countries (Simla Agreement, 1972).

After the mid-1980s, India began to lose its upper hand in Kashmir as successive regimes in India failed to control Kashmir from New Delhi in a centralized manner (Widmalm, 2002). The dismissal of the Farooq Abdullah government in 1984 by the Congress (I) government at the centre was a watershed in this process. Furthermore, the Kashmiri people, by and large, opposed the alliance formed between the Congress (I) and the National Conference led by Farooq Abdullah in 1987. They perceived it as one more attempt to control Kashmir through the centre. Owing to the dominance of the centre as well as continued neglect of local aspirations, the people of Kashmir became increasingly restive. As a result, a new generation of politically conscious and assertive Kashmiris was rapidly getting mobilized against injustice, institutional decay, and increasing alienation of the people from the rulers in New Delhi. Under these circumstances, some of the disgruntled sections of the people in the Kashmir Valley went so far as to demand outright political independence from India. Emotional bonds between the people of Kashmir and the rest of India were severed. Nevertheless, after the early 1990s, India was able to steadily retrieve its hold over Kashmir by firmly handling the terrorists, on the one hand, and by holding elections in Kashmir, on the other. Voter participation during the elections held in Kashmir in September 2002, in spite of the threat from terrorist groups, offered evidence of the fact that the people of Kashmir desire peace and that they have faith in the democratic mode of governance. With the unfolding of the electoral process, the elite in Kashmir have gradually been co-opted in the management of the government at the state level. Activation of the electoral process has also blunted the sharp edges of the activities of the terrorist outfits, by once again making Kashmir a part of India's democratic experiment.

India has always regarded Kashmir as its indissoluble part. Just as Pakistan aimed at integrating Kashmir due to its predominantly Muslim population, India aimed at absorbing Kashmir to strengthen its secular foundations and image. For India, the strategic importance of Kashmir increased with the passage of time. Naturally, losing control over Kashmir has always been out of the question as far as India is concerned. Indeed, if the right of self-determination is conceded to the people of Kashmir, it might inspire several other states, especially those in the northeast, to demand the same right. Also, the very social fabric of India might be destroyed if Kashmir becomes independent, owing to the spiral of communal tensions such a development is likely to generate (Cheema, 1991: 281–92).

Since India cannot conceive of losing Kashmir, it is obliged to review several complexities that have kept the Kashmir problem alive. To start with, there is a growing demand from human rights groups to protect the civil rights of the people of Kashmir who are victims of state terrorism. In this context, maximum transparency on the part of the Indian government may bolster the Kashmiri people's confidence in the Government of India. Moreover, allegiance to India is certainly not synonymous with allegiance to the existing government at the centre. Hence, the people of Kashmir must be made to feel free to air their views, like other citizens, on Indian politics. Second, governments in New Delhi will have to be more receptive to the ethnic and cultural identities of Muslim and Hindu communities in Kashmir, for religious sentiments alone can hardly give full expression to their urges. For instance, Muslims as well as Hindus constitute the Dogras of Jammu. The Paharis too have people from both the religions while the Ladakhis include

Buddhists as well as Muslims. Only the Gujjars are entirely Muslims. It would be difficult for India to rule over Kashmir democratically without being sensitive to its plurality of identities. Without grasping such pluralities it is almost impossible to get even a rough idea of Kashmiri identity (Puri, 1998: 2830–32). In addition to managing the day-to-day problems of governance, India has also had to encounter the threats posed by several terrorist outfits tacitly backed by Pakistan's ISI Directorate. Moreover, the alleged presence of Taliban mercenaries from Afghanistan in Kashmir has caused grave concern to India's security community. The potential of terrorist outfits to generate the flow of arms and drugs across India could also prove subversive from the standpoint of the Indian Union. Irrespective of these threats to India's security, sensitivity to the plight of the people in Kashmir as also the project to reconstruct Kashmir is the dire need of the hour.

Reconstructing Kashmir for the Kashmiris

The India–Pakistani confrontation over Kashmir has had a traumatic impact on the lives of the people of Kashmir. In the midst of the death of thousands of people, over 50,000 widows, more than 100,000 orphaned children, and millions of displaced people awaiting resettlement have virtually forgotten the normalcy of life (Waslekar and Futehally, 2002). Owing to the fear psychosis generated by the activities of the terrorists as well as the state, thousands of them have virtually taken refuge either in the so-called Azad Kashmir, controlled by Pakistan, or in other states in India. The Government of Pakistan has dealt with the refugees from Kashmir by giving them 12 seats in the assembly of Azad Kashmir and by settling them in other Pakistani cities. Similarly, over 26,000 families, or about 200,000 Kashmiri Pandits, have fled Kashmir and settled in parts of Jammu and Delhi. For their sustenance, the Government of India has been paying them a meagre maintenance allowance (Country Report, 2004).

The inauguration of the process of rehabilitation of the displaced people of Kashmir as well as reconstruction of the war-ravaged state of Kashmir is feasible only if India and Pakistan are able to establish durable peace between them. Even under the best of circumstances, it may not be easy to resolve the Kashmir question in a mutually satisfactory manner because its resolution is linked to the national identities of both the states. Nevertheless, as far as Kashmir is concerned, a few immediate steps are warranted before the project of peace gets under way.

To begin with, the President of Pakistan, during the 12th summit of the South Asian Association of Regional Cooperation (SAARC) held at Islamabad in January 2004, reiterated his assurance that Pakistan will not allow its territory to be used by any terrorist outfits for the purposes of promoting their activities within or across the border of Pakistan. This ought to be treated as a positive development because peace can be restored in the state of Kashmir if terrorist activities are kept under control. Conversely, any ruling coalition in India has to recognize that without promoting secularism and respecting the intrinsic diversity of the heterogeneous communities that reside within India, it would be difficult to promote internal social harmony in India as also the India–Pakistan peace project. The communal violence that rocked the state of Gujarat in February–March 2002 has already driven home this point with stark clarity.

Second, the communication network by road between the two parts of Kashmir has to be re-established. For instance, a road link between Srinagar and Muzaffarabad can bring the Kashmiris from both sides of the frontiers closer together. Third, holding a plebiscite in Kashmir is an unviable solution at this juncture (Kishwar, 2003: 3773–77). However, the current line of control could be conceived of as an international border between the two countries by offering greater autonomy to the people of Kashmir in their governance. Finally, the peace process between India and Pakistan has to include representative groups from Kashmir to make it more authentic and representative. In addition, non-governmental organizations (NGOs), like the Pakistan–India People's Forum for Peace and Democracy (PIPFPD), which are promoting people-to-people contacts at the inter-societal level, also need to be constantly encouraged to bring the people from the two countries closer.

The most viable strategy to resolve some of the outstanding issues between India and Pakistan, including Kashmir, is sustained composite dialogue on the interrelated issues that promote cooperation between the two countries in diverse spheres of inter-state and inter-societal activities (Harshe, 2003a: 45–63). Such sustained dialogue, which has already been initiated at different levels since 2004, is likely to take cognizance of most of the central issues related to military-strategic, politico-diplomatic, and developmental spheres. More often the questions related to geo-strategic issues, including drawing of borders and other politico-diplomatic matters, acquire the central place in bilateral negotiations. However, international relations are currently conditioned by the trend towards globalization that subsumes a greater degree of regional economic cooperation mediated by the establishment and promotion of regional trading arrangements. Under globalization, it is indeed pertinent and also plausible to draw a road map to peace between India and Pakistan in the areas of trade and development cooperation. In this context, the hitherto neglected but significant economic dimension of building peace and security-related projects certainly merits serious consideration.

Peace through Development Cooperation

Politics and strained relations for over five decades have often overshadowed the economic dimension of the relationship between India and Pakistan. However, the strained relationship did not necessarily affect trade ties between the two countries. For instance, India–Pakistan trade received an impetus when Pakistan was under General Zia's military dictatorship. Further, under the military regime in 1987, the permitted traded goods from India were increased from 42 to 249 by Pakistan. In 1998, when the two countries carried out their nuclear tests, trade between the countries peaked to US$ 354 million. In 2001, when Pakistan was under the Musharraf regime, Indian exports to Pakistan were the highest ever at US$ 219 million (Taneja, 2004). Besides, there is also informal trade between the two countries, placed at US$ 2 billion that takes place through third countries. Half of it is through Dubai, the Commonwealth of Independent States (CIS), or Afghanistan, and the other half constitutes cross-border informal trade (Taneja, 2004: 326–27).

The trade potential between the two countries has not yet been fully explored. Several factors, such as mutual apprehensions, and at times misinformation, have acted as impediments in the course of building smooth trade ties. Moreover, India has accorded the most favoured nation (MFN) status to Pakistan, as a trading partner, while Pakistan has not extended the same facility to India. India can export several kinds of items to Pakistan, such as iron ore, steel, transport equipment like scooters, motorcycles, and passenger cars, plastics, textiles, drugs and pharmaceuticals, and a number of agricultural products. Pakistan, in turn, can export fruits, nuts, spices, pulses, and scrap metal to India. India's economy has been doing better than its Pakistani counterpart.

Since the Indian economy is the larger of the two, Pakistan is apprehensive that Indian goods will flood the Pakistani market. To counter such apprehensions, India, being the more powerful country, could apply the Gujral Doctrine of non-reciprocity in its trade relations with Pakistan, as it does with other South Asian states. The Gujral Doctrine—named after I.K. Gujral, India's foreign minister and later prime minister from 1997 to 1999—is a device to bring about harmony among the South Asian states. India, as the most powerful state, voluntarily forgoes the principle of reciprocity in bilateral ties. The Gujral Doctrine was applied by India in its trade ties with Sri Lanka and Bangladesh, significantly favouring the smaller countries (Harshe, 1999: 1100–1105).

Irrespective of the asymmetry of economic power between the two countries, Pakistan also enjoys a privileged position in relation to India if its trade and economic ties are seen from a long-term point of view. For instance, there is enormous potential to promote cooperation in the energy sector. Pakistan can meet an ever-increasing demand of the Indian economy by becoming India's energy supplier. Moreover, Pakistan is also part of a transit route from the energy heartland of Iran to India. Similarly, the prospective gas pipeline from Turkmenistan can only reach India via Afghanistan and Pakistan. Thus, Pakistan can collect hefty transit fees of roughly US$ 600–800 million annually if these routes materialize. In the process it can look after its own energy requirements as well. As for India, if there are diversified sources of pipeline gas, it will be able to reduce its dependence on more expensive liquid natural gas. When oil pipelines are eventually laid through terrorist-prone regions like Baluchistan, there will be the additional need to ensure security of the gas routes. Also, India and Pakistan need to work towards opening up two-ways transit routes through negotiations. For instance, if Pakistan allows India to trade with Afghanistan and the Central Asian countries via its territory, India's peninsular position, in turn, can be used by Pakistan to gain access to the markets of Bangladesh, Myanmar, Bhutan, and Nepal in the northeast (Mohan, 2004). Actually, trade can facilitate closer interaction between the two countries through the border regions and states of India and Pakistan, such as Sindh, Punjab, Rajasthan, and Gujarat.

Trade as well as other forms of interaction between India and Pakistan have to be facilitated through the improvement of the entire transport-related infrastructure. Building the connecting network of roads, rail lines, and air links forms a part of this process. Besides, introducing a Mumbai–Karachi ferry service and a coastal facility for cargo can further improve trade ties. In addition, India can share the gains of information communication technology (ICT) with Pakistan by opening up training centres in Pakistan to enhance capacity building of Pakistan in the ICT sector.

At the broader level, the agendas of development involving the fight against illiteracy, unemployment, poverty, environmental degradation, practices of child labour, trade in drugs and arms as well as cross-border terrorism, AIDS, and diverse forms of social discrimination need to be brought to the foreground in South Asia. After all, the two powerful nuclear states have to function as major partners in promoting regional trading and other cooperative ventures in the context of SAARC. In substance, the relatively unexplored area of trade and development cooperation has immense potential to open up fresh avenues towards inter-state and inter-societal ties of cordiality, built around mutual benefit, between the two countries.

Conclusion

The status of Kashmir has always been at the centre of India–Pakistan conflict over the past five decades. Since the Kashmir question is linked to the processes of state-formation and nation-building in both the countries, its resolution has been replete with hurdles. Both India and Pakistan perceive that the process of Partition would be incomplete without integrating a strategically significant territory like Kashmir within their respective borders. However, both these states have to seriously consider the plight of the people of Kashmir—the victims of this prolonged rivalry—before resolving the issue. Rehabilitation and reconstruction of Kashmir has to commence with India–Pakistan cooperation that grants autonomy to Kashmir and gives due respect to the aspirations of the people of Kashmir on either side of the current line of control. Since the Kashmir question is likely to belie easy solution, it would be desirable for both the countries to actively develop people-to-people contacts through inter-societal rapport and engage in the projects of development cooperation in crucial sectors like power and by consolidating trade and investment-related ties. In this context, the peace process initiated after February 2004 would hopefully replace the erstwhile confrontationist postures of India and Pakistan with constructive agendas of development cooperation. The outstanding controversial issues, including the Kashmir question, could as well get solved, in the long run, if the two countries promote development cooperation on a durable basis.

References

Ali, Tariq (1970). *Pakistan: Military Rule or People's Power?* London: The Trinity Press.

Cheema, Pervaiz Iqbal (1991). 'Security in South Asia: An Approach', *South Asia Journal*, 4(3): 281–92.

Country Report. (2004). 'Country Report of the Refugee Situation in India', 16 February 2004. Accessed from www.hri.ca./sahrdc/refugrr/fulltext.shtml-27k.

Dhaka Declaration (1985). Paragraph 4 of Dhaka Declaration of the Heads of State or Governments of the Member Countries of South Asian Cooperation, issued at 1st SAARC Summit, 8 December, Dhaka, Bangladesh.

Einagel, Victoria Ingrid (1997). 'Lasting Peace in Bosnia? Politics of Territory and Identity', in Ola Tunander, Pavel Baev, and Victoria Ingrid Einagel (eds), *Geopolitics in Post-Wall Europe: Security Territory and Identity*, pp. 235–52. London: Sage.

Ganguly, Sumit (1996). 'Uncertain India', *Current History*, 95(600), October: 145–50.

———— (1997). 'An Opportunity for Peace in Kashmir', *Current History*, 96(614), December: 414–18.

Golwalkar, M.S. (1939). *We, or, Our Nationhood Defined*. Nagpur: Bharat Publications (reprinted in 1996 as *Bunch of Thoughts*. Bangalore: Vikrama Prakashan).

Gupta, Sisir (1982). 'Islam as a Factor in Pakistani Foreign Relations', in M.S. Rajan and Shivaji Ganguly (eds), *India and International System: Selections from the Major Writings of Sisir Gupta*. New Delhi: Vikas.

Harrison, Selig S. (1997). 'The United States and South Asia: Trapped by the Past?', *Current History*, 96(614), December: 401–06.

Harshe, Rajen (1999). 'South Asian Regional Co-operation: Problems and Prospects', *Economic and Political Weekly*, 44(19): 1100–05.

———— (2003a). 'Indo-Pakistan Ties and Nuclear Confidence Building in Southern Asia', in B.R. Chari, Sonika Gupta, and Arpit Rajain (eds), *Nuclear Stability in Southern Asia*, pp. 45–63. New Delhi Manohar.

———— (2003b). 'Cross-Border Terrorism', *Economic and Political Weekly*, 37(35): 3621–25.

Kishwar, Madhu (2003). 'Why Fear People's Choice? Calling Pakistan's Bluff on Plebiscite in J&K', *Economic and Political Weekly*, 38(36): 3773–77.

Matoo, Amitabh (1996). 'India's Nuclear Status Quo', *Survival*, 38(3): 41–57.

Mohan, C. Raja (2004). 'Trade-off on Transit', *The Hindu*, 12 August 2004.

Nehru, Jawaharlal (2002). *The Discovery of India*. New Delhi: Oxford University Press.

Punjabi, Riaz (2000). 'Kashmir: Reading the Dream of an Islamic Caliphate', *World Affairs*, 4(2), April–June 2000: 60–61.

Puri, Balraj (1998). 'A Post-Pokhran Policy for Kashmir', *Economic and Political Weekly*, 38(45): 2830–32.

Savarkar, V.D. (1989). *Hindutva*. Bombay: Vir Savarkar Prakashan.

Simla Agreement (1972). 'Text of the Simla Agreement of 2 July 1972', *Peace Initiatives*, 6(4), July–December: 225–27.

Taneja, Nisha (2004). 'India Pakistan: Trade Relations: Opportunities for Growth', *Economic and Political Weekly*, 39(4): 326–27.

Thakur, Ramesh (1994). *The Politics and Economics of India Foreign Policy*. New Delhi: Oxford University Press.

Varshney, Ashutosh (1993). 'Contested Meanings: India's National Identity, Hindu Nationalism and the Politics of Anxiety', *Daedalus*, 122(3), Summer: 227–61.

Waslekar, Sundeep and Illmas Futehally (2002). 'Reshaping the Agenda in Kashmir: A Special Report', *The Kashmir Telegraph*, May 2002.

Widmalm, Sten (2002). *Kashmir in Comparative Perspective: Democracy and Violent Separatism in India*. London: Routledge Curzon.

About the Editors and Contributors

Editors

Veena Kukreja is Associate Professor at the Department of Political Science, University of Delhi. Recipient of Gold Medal for securing first position in B.A. (Hons.), Delhi University, Kukreja received her M.A., M.Phil. (both first class) and Ph.D. from Delhi University. She specializes in International Relations, South Asia and Pakistan Studies. Her published works include: *Military Intervention in Politics: A Case Study of Pakistan* (New Delhi: NBO Publishers, 1985), *Civil-Military Relations in South Asia: Pakistan, Bangladesh and India* (New Delhi: Sage Publications, 1991), *Contemporary Pakistan: Political Processes, Conflicts and Crises* (New Delhi: Sage Publications, 2003) and co-edited *Pakistan: Democracy, Development and Security Issues* (New Delhi: Sage Publications, 2005). She has published numerous research papers and articles in scholarly journals.

Mahendra Prasad Singh is Professor in the Department of Political Science at the University of Delhi, India. He has authored/edited/co-edited about a dozen books in Indian politics and contributed papers to scholarly journals in India and abroad. His publications include *India at the Polls: Parliamentary Elections in the Federal Phase* (New Delhi: Orient Longman, 2003 (co-authored), *Indian Federalism in the New Millennium* (co-edited) (New Delhi: Manohar, 2003), and *Coaliltion Politics in India: Problems and Prospects* (New Delhi: Manohar, 2003), *Indian Judiciary and Politics: The Changing Landscape* (co-edited) (New Delhi: Manohar, 2007) and *Indian Politics: Contemporary Issues and Concerns* (co-authored) (New Delhi: Prentice-Hall of India, 2008), among others. He has also been an active seminarist, attending national and international conferences on

India, Canada and the USA. He is on the editorial board of *Punjab Journal of Politics*.

CONTRIBUTORS

Rajen Harshe is Vice Chancellor of Allahabad University. He is an eminent social scientist and a leading scholar of international relations studies in India. He is the author of *Pervasive Entente France and Ivory Coast in African Affairs* (New Delhi, Arnold-Heinemann 1984 and New Jersey, Humanities Press, 1984), *Twentieth Century Imperialism Shifting Contours and Changing Conceptions* (New Delhi, London and Thousand Oaks, SAGE Publications, 1997). He has also edited books such as, *Interpreting Globalisation: Perspectives in International Relations* (New Delhi and Jaipur, ICSSR and Rawat Publishers, 2004) and *Engaging With The World: Critical Reflections on India's Foreign Policy* (New Delhi, Orient Longman, 2005). Besides, he has published over seventy five papers in major national and international journals and prestigious anthologies.

Nalini Kant Jha, is currently a Rajiv Gandhi Chair Professor at Allahabad Central University. A twice Fulbrighter at University of California, Berkeley (1992–93) and at Centre for South Asian Studies, School of Advanced International Studies of Johns Hopkins University, Washington DC (2006), Jha earlier acted as a Dean, School of International Studies, Head of the Department of Political Science and Director of South Asian Studies program at Pondicherry Central University. Having obtained his M.Phil. and Ph.D. degrees from the School of International Studies of Jawaharlal Nehru University, New Delhi, Jha taught as a Reader at L.N. Mithila University, Darbhanga (Bihar). He has been a Visiting Faculty at several universities such as Department of International Relations at University of Dhaka (2005), and University of Dalhousi, Halifax (Canada), etc. His major works include: *South Asia in 21st Century: India, Her Neighbours and Great Powers* (New Delhi, 2003); *Domestic Imperatives in India's Foreign* Policy (New Delhi: 2002); *India's Foreign Policy in a Changing World* (New Delhi, 2000); *Peace and Co-operative Security in South* Asia (New Delhi, 1999), etc. He has contributed more than 60 research papers in leading national and international journals.

Niraj Kumar was a UGC Senior Research Fellow successfully obtaining his Ph.D. degree from the University of Delhi and is presently a Lecturer in the Department of Political Science, Maharaja Agarsen College, University of Delhi. He has contributed a paper to *Ideologies and Institutions in Indian Politics* (ed. by M.P. Singh and Rekha Saxena) (New Delhi: Deep and Deep, 1998).

Mohammed Nuruzzaman completed his Ph.D. from the Department of Political Science, University of Alberta in 2003. Currently, he teaches international relations and comparative politics at Okanagan College, British Columbia, Canada. Dr. Nuruzzaman's principal areas of research interests are International Relations theory, global political economy, and the Third World in global politics. He has already published in leading international journals, including *International Studies Perspectives, Cooperation and Conflict, Journal of Contemporary Asia, International Studies, Journal of Asian and African Studies* etc.

Saleem Qureshi started with the University of Alberta in 1963. He has served in many capacities over the years, including Associate Dean of Arts, Chair of East Asian Languages and Literature, and Chair of Department of Political Science. He is presently teaching as a professor emeritus in the Department of Political Science, all the while performing teaching duties as a Professor. Professor Qureshi teaches courses in Islamic Politics, Politics of Middle East and South Asia, and Political Development. He has many publications in South Asian Politics including *The Politics of Jinnah*, and in Middle Eastern and Islamic Politics.

Awadhesh Coomar Sinha, an M.A. in anthropology (Ranchi) and Ph.D. in sociology (Indian Institute of Technology, Kanpur) has taught at Gujarat Vidyapeeth (Ahmedabad), IIT, Delhi and North Eastern Hill University, Shillong in India and was a Smuts Scholar in Cambridge University and a Senior Fulbright Professor in the California University, Santa Cruz, USA. He held position of visiting faculty in a number of Indian Universities such as Karnataka University, Dharward, University of Allahabad, Dibrugarh University, Dibrugarh, and Punjab University, Chandigarh. He researched on the elite in Sikkim, nation-building in Bhutan, small state syndrome in North East India, Urbanization in North East India, Christianity in Nagaland, ethnography of the Himalayas, forest history of North East India and Nepalis in India. His publications include *Politics of Sikkim* (1975), *Bhutan: Ethnic Identity and National Dilemma* (1991 and 1998), *Sociological History of the Eastern Himalayan Forests* (1993), *Urbanization in Eastern Himalayas* (1993), *Himalayan Kingdom Bhutan: Tradition, Transition and Transformation* (2003 and 2005) and *Nepalis of North East India* (2003 and 2007). Two of his manuscripts *Politics of Sikkim: Direction and Destiny* and *Ethnic Identity and Nationality of the Nepalis in India* are in press. After holding a series of academic positions in North Eastern Hill University for about three decades, Professor Sinha now resides in Delhi.

Lawrence Ziring is Arnold F. Schneider Professor of Political Science at Western Michigan University. Author/editor of more than twenty books, his latest release is *Pakistan: At the Crosscurrent of History*, Oneworld Publications, 2003. He also is the author of *Pakistan in the Twentieth Century* (Oxford University Press); *Pakistan: The Enigma of Political Development* (Westview); and *The Ayub Khan Era* (Syracuse University Press). A long time observers of the Pakistan scene, he served as an adviser to the Pakistan Administrative Staff College and taught at Dacca University. A graduate of Columbia University where he received his bachelor's, master's, and doctoral degrees, he also has been a member of the Faculty at Lafayette College and Syracuse University.

Index